Pioneers in Arts, Humanities, Science, Engineering, Practice

Volume 20

Series Editor

Hans Günter Brauch, Peace Research and European Security Studies
(AFES-PRESS), Mosbach, Germany

More information about this series at http://www.springer.com/series/15230
http://www.afes-press-books.de/html/PAHSEP.htm
http://afes-press-books.de/html/PAHSEP_Reardon.htm

Dale T. Snauwaert
Editor

Exploring Betty A. Reardon's Perspective on Peace Education

Looking Back, Looking Forward

 Springer

Editor
Dale T. Snauwaert
Department of Educational Foundations
and Leadership, Center for Nonviolence
and Democratic Education
The University of Toledo
Toledo, OH, USA

Acknowledgement: The cover photograph was provided by Berra Rearsdon who granted granted permission to use this photo as the cover photo for this book. Most other photos except one in this volume were taken from the personal photo collection of Betty A. Reardon who granted permission for publication in this volume. A book website with additional information on Karl W. Deutsch and his major book covers is at: http://afes-press-books.de/html/PAHSEP_Reardon.htm.

ISSN 2509-5579   ISSN 2509-5587   (electronic)
Pioneers in Arts, Humanities, Science, Engineering, Practice
ISBN 978-3-030-18386-8   ISBN 978-3-030-18387-5   (eBook)
https://doi.org/10.1007/978-3-030-18387-5

Copyediting: PD Dr. Hans Günter Brauch, AFES-PRESS e.V., Mosbach, Germany

This Springer imprint is published by the registered company Springer Nature Switzerland AG
The registered company address is: Gewerbestrasse 11, 6330 Cham, Switzerland

To Betty on the occasion of her 90th Birthday

Foreword

Betty A. Reardon at 90: A Nonviolent Feminist Peace Educator Who Linked Feminism and Peace Education

Betty Reardon was born into a family where her father was a military officer. During World War II, when she was 10 years old, she thought that war was a stupidity. There must be other ways to organize the world and to overcome the brutal violence and mass killing of innocent people, especially of women and children. She was also convinced that women must play an active role in peace-building; furthermore, she was attracted to future studies. She believed that only an authentic global approach may overcome violence, militarism, arms races, wars and promote a different world based on cooperation, equality, sustainability, and solidarity.

Betty understood that the formation of gender identity entails a process of consciousness raising. She insisted that gender security is normally taken for granted and that social relations are linked to one's gender status, as well as other social identities such as children, indigenous people, poor, minority, women, and all vulnerable groups who lack power.

Equity and identity are values at risk. The source of threat comes in the first instance from a patriarchal hierarchical and violent social order, characterized by exclusive and authoritarian institutions such as non-democratic governments, churches, and élites, that launch war, violence, discrimination, and exclusion to reinforce their personal aspirations for power. The distribution of power was established over thousands of years in generic forms, where men exercised a hierarchical and vertical power of domination and superiority. Women were excluded for different social, political, ideological, and cultural reasons. Without any doubt, patriarchal systems were regionally adapted and expressed different cultural behaviors and values, while the dominant traits of violence, exploitation, submission, and exclusion can be found globally.

Betty understood that women were systematically excluded for different social, political, ideological, and cultural reasons, and in this hierarchical exclusive and violent approach, she understood the role of violence, war, and destruction exercised by dominant men. Therefore, only education from the earliest stage of childhood could change these deeply rooted patriarchal beliefs and habits in the global society, where the distribution of power was established in generic forms over thousands of years. In her view, men exercise a hierarchical and vertical power of domination and superiority in their androgenic mindset.

Education was a great passion of Betty throughout her whole life. As a professional teacher who was deeply involved with the Peace Education Commission at IPRA, she influenced worldwide peace education, peacebuilding, and conflict resolution from a gender perspective (Reardon/Snauwaert 2015a, b). In education for a culture or cultures of peace with a gender perspective, she developed a "Manual on the Rights to Freedom of Religion and Beliefs". She was interested in different beliefs and peace experiences from various cultures. She also understood that the dominant androgenic control of international organisations, such as the United Nations and UNESCO, would never allow a deep critical questioning of the root causes of violence and exploitation. Therefore, she was convinced that only from an analytical perspective and though peace education and actions was it feasible to challenge the present world order and to promote an alternative world.

During the 1970s, she analyzed different guerrilla movements and later she understood that both from the right and the left the same androgenic system prevented a structural transformation of the present capitalist system. When she saw the execution of one of the female top leaders by the guerrilla in El Salvador, she understood that this was not the way to achieve greater equality and justice, but that it was an alternative way from the left to maintain the dominant structures of male power, as were practiced by the so-called progressive groups. The recent history of Central America indicates that the suffering of poor people during decades of civil war did not improve their living conditions. The massive migrations of entire communities, due to the present conditions of violence, unemployment, disasters, and destruction of livelihood, are cruel testimonies to the continuation of dominant power structures.

Betty also emphasized the point that gender security is normally taken for granted by the whole society, due to social relations being linked to gender status (caring, being for others), including other disempowered social groups, such as indigenous peoples, poor, minorities, and persons with disabilities. Equity and identity are the values at risk, and the mechanisms of domination constitute a systematic submission through undervaluation of their labor (unpaid, less paid, housewife, or slavery). The sources of threat emerge from the patriarchal, hierarchical, and violent global order, that is characterized by exclusive and authoritarian institutions, such as financial and corporate élites, non-democratic governments, and churches, which cause active or ideological war, violence, and/or discrimination. These global institutions are responsible for the present exclusion of four billion of people and maintain the *status quo* of poverty and misery of these social groups globally. Therefore, as a peace researcher, Betty Reardon studied systematically emerging theories of feminist thinking and action. Her dual goal of understanding and analysis, in addition to transforming the present androgenic world, led her to different currents of feminism. We mention here four dominant currents: empirical, situated, standpoint, and postmodern feminism.

Empirical Feminism in the Thinking of Betty Reardon

From the perspective of empirical feminism, Betty participated in United Nation actions against gender violence. The United Nations is responsible for global data collection, confirming that violence toward women and girls is very frequent and has increased globally. At least a third of woman in the world are beaten, a fifth is raped, and almost all suffer from psychological and often economic aggression and discrimination. Normally, this violent behavior happens at home without any visibility, but also in factories and public jobs. However, men who were responsible for these crimes and exploitation have often claimed that men from other cultural backgrounds, regions, religions, and social classes are the one's guilty of feminicides, rape, and sexual harassments. Further, this violence occurs mostly within the household, and such offenses are normally not denounced by the affected women. This prominent invisible intra-family violence cannot be addressed by the traditional system of domestic or military security. The use of physical punishment of women is normalized in order to maintain the status quo.

As a teacher and peace researcher, Betty Reardon understood that gender and, more general, patriarchal violence and competition have affected the well-being of families and the development of their countries. The World Bank (1998) stated that in North Africa, each year of education for girls would improve the gross domestic product (GDP) by one percent. Therefore, the education of girls is crucial for the future economic development of countries (UNFPA 2016), but also for their empowerment to achieve greater equality. McKinsey (2015) observed that globally women receive only 59 per cent of a man's salary for the same job. Only 23 per cent of women held political positions, generally at lower level usually in the Ministries of Education, Health and Social Welfare.

Today, a very limited number of countries have female presidents, prime ministers, governors, defense ministers, or chairs of parties. But even in Scandinavian countries with a greater degree of gender equality, women still spend 272 minutes on unpaid housework, while men devote only 138 minutes. Women still spend twice as much time on the household and on caring services as men, and in the Global South, the situation is even worse (WEF 2018). A greater justice and better distribution of unpaid work within the household between men and women would increase the global GDP by 11 per cent by 2025, and with a total equality, GDP could rise even by 26 per cent. Therefore, gender equality is not only an ethical, but it has also become an economic necessity.

Betty Reardon as a Situated Feminist

As a female teacher, Reardon understood that this system of violence, authoritarianism, inequality, and destruction has affected human beings, but also the Earth as a whole, pushing the physical–chemical processes of the planet toward irreversible tipping points. The values at risk due to the lack of gender equity and security, based on discriminative social representations, are survival, sustainability, and equality. Serrano (2009) argued that social identity exists in a world where processes of unification and diversification are spreading rapidly, faster than ever in history, and humans have basic necessities to simplify all stimuli of the complexity of social interactions through social comparison. These comparisons in a patriarchal system are generally helping to improve the self-esteem of men, but primarily at the costs of other social groups and especially women.

The analytical capacity of Betty Reardon allowed her to raise new scientific questions as women situated in an androgenic world, where her key approach was the war system based on patriarchy. Thus, women have played a crucial role in the transformation of scientific theories and concepts, when they questioned the dominant neoliberal and violent paradigm of elites, supported by religions and governments.

Betty Reardon's Focus on Patriarchy from a Standpoint Feminism

As a woman, trained in science and education, she used her epistemic privilege to ask who is benefitting from the dominant violent worldview and who is the subject of domination, exploitation, and submission? Female social roles, their subjectivity, and their identity have socialized them since childhood to care about others. This role of caring made Betty motivated to understand the dominant paradigm in peace research. Her perspective from within the system of gender inequality and her frequent discussions with women from the Global South, and with discriminated

Afro-American women, enabled her to overcome the dominant theories of peace developed by men such as negative, positive and structural peace (Galtung 2007), which did not include half of the world population in their analysis. In interaction with Elise Boulding (2000) she worked on peace culture or cultures, where she understood that structural violence and violence against women are crucial issues that have impeded a holistic peace education (Reardon/Jenkins 2007). Peacebuilding with a gender perspective must be trained from kindergarten through high school. Only a new masculinity and femininity, based on equal rights, respect for others and rigorous justice will allow new social relations and the transformation of the dominant power relations.

Betty Reardon Reviewing Postmodern Feminism

Judith Butler (1993) affirmed that no truth is eternal and the meanings and social representations are constantly subverted by new actions and additional knowledge. Thus, Betty also questioned the universality and objectivity of the positivist understanding of science in the field of peace research and peace education. Understanding the tensions among her conflicting identities as a woman, teacher, activist, peace researcher, and friend, she proposed disruptive discursive systems, which were built individually and collectively in the peace community. Therefore, after her activities at the Teacher's College, she built an international peace education network, demilitarization, and women's movement for human rights and peace, as well as the International Institute on Peace (IIPE), established in 1982 at Teacher College, Columbia University. She received the UNESCO Price for Peace Education in 2001 in recognition of her international achievements and contributions, and she was nominated by the International Peace Bureau in Geneva for the Nobel Peace Prize in 2013.

An Integrated Dual Vision of Thinking and Actions in Peace Research and Education

Without any doubt, from childhood on Betty Reardon, as a girl and later as a woman, professional and teacher, she understood well the differences between negative peace as the absence of war, achieved by the prevention and/or the general reduction and eventual elimination of armed conflicts (Blue Helmets of UN), and a real peace from a gender perspective. She concluded that an authentic peace was the abolition of the war system based on patriarchy and the establishment of global justice and a global civic community with equality as a way to achieve justice and equity. For her, the ethical imperative of peace is a fundamental right, with duties to *avoid depriving* another right, to *protect* the other from deprivation of any right, and to *aid* the deprived to overcome unjust inequality. This general approach included women, children, ethnic, race, sexual minorities, and any other vulnerable groups that are dominated and exploited by the global neoliberal system.

Thus, Betty Reardon is an ecofeminist (Reardon/Nordland 1994), a pioneer on global cooperation, an advocate for a healthy planet and a society with solidarity and equality. The ways to achieve this transition are through education and the transformation of the dominant androgenic behavior in all societies at global level. Her teachings, publications, and actions have a future that is worth hoping for and that is the sole possibility that humankind may survive under the present conditions of human-made global environmental and climate change, where humankind and nature are exploited.

Cuernavaca, Morelos, Mexico   Úrsula Oswald Spring
March 2019   Center for Regional Multidisciplinary
                                                       Research (CRIM), National Autonomous
                                                          University of Mexico (UNAM)

References

Boulding, E. (2000). *Cultures of peace: The hidden side of history*, New York, Syracuse University Press.

Butler, J. (1993). *Bodies that matter: On the discursive limits of "sex"*, New York, Routledge.

Galtung, J. (2007). Peace studies: A ten points primer. In Úrsula Oswald Spring (Ed.), *International security, peace, development, and environment*, Encyclopaedia on life support systems, 39(3), Oxford, UNESCO-EOLSS.

McKinsey Global Institute (2015). *The power of parity: How advancing women's equality can add $12 trillion to global growth*, New York, McKinsey Global Institute.

Reardon B. A. (1996). *Sexism and the war system*, New York, Syracuse University Press.

Reardon, B. A. (1980). Moving to the future, *Network*, 8(1), 14–21.

Reardon, B. & Jenkins, T. (2007). Gender and peace: toward a gender inclusive, holistic perspective. In C. Webel & J. Galtung (Eds.), *Handbook of peace and conflict studies*, New York, Routledge, 209–231.

Reardon, B. & Nordland, E. (1994). *Learning peace: The promise of ecological and cooperative education*, Albany, State University of New York Press.

Reardon, B. & Snauwaert, D. T. (2015a). *Betty A. Reardon: Key texts in gender and peace*, Cham, Springer International Publishing.

Reardon, B. & Snauwaert, D. T. (2015b). *Betty A. Reardon: A pioneer in education for peace and human rights*, Cham, Springer International Publishing.

Serrano Oswald, Eréndira S. (2009). The impossibility of securitizing gender vis á vis engendering security, in Hans Günter Brauch et al. (Eds.), *Facing global environmental change. Environmental, human, energy, food, health and water security concepts*, Berlin-Heidelberg, Springer, 1151–1164.

UNFPA [United Nations Population Fund] (2016). News on World Population Trends. http://www.unfpa.org/world-population-trends.

WB [World Bank] (1998). *World development report*, Washington, D.C., World Bank.

WEF [World Economic Forum] (2018). *World gender gap report*, Davos, WEF.

Acknowledgements

This book was made possible by the editor of the *Pioneers in Arts, Humanities, Science, Engineering, Practice* (PAHSEP) Book Series published by Springer, Dr. Hans Günter Brauch. I thank him for his vision and generosity. I would also like to thank the contributors to this volume for their valuable contributions, patience, and cooperation. I am truly grateful to Betty for her encouragement and support regarding the publication of this volume, but most importantly for her steadfast friendship. I am very happy that this book will be a part of her 90th Birthday. Finally, I would like to acknowledge and thank Mary Darbes for all of her love and support, in particular, her dedication to and adroit, tireless editorial assistance. I cannot put into words how grateful I am.

Toledo, OH, USA   Dale T. Snauwaert
March 2019

Introduction: The Peace Paradigm

This volume brings together a unique collection of commentaries, reflections, and elaborations regarding Betty Reardon's peace education theory, pedagogy, and intellectual legacy by a distinguished international group of peace education scholars and practitioners. Building on Reardon's foundational work each chapter in this collection explores original, visionary lines of inquiry which advance the theory and potentially the practice of peace education with a number of different contexts and domains. While deeply grounded in her legacy, this book examines the question: How does her foundational work point us toward the cutting edges of the field of peace studies and peace education?

Betty A. Reardon is a world-renown pioneer in the development of peace education and human rights. Her groundbreaking work has laid the foundation for a cross-disciplinary field that integrates peace and human rights education from within a gender-conscious, holistic perspective. In recognition of her many contributions, achievements, and awards as a teacher, activist, researcher, author, and consultant, including the founding of the International Institute on Peace Education, she was nominated by the International Peace Bureau for the Nobel Peace Prize in 2013. My association with Betty Reardon has spanned close to three decades. Our mutual interest and dedication to the formulation of global peace and international human rights education have given rise to meaningful collaboration over the years; in important ways, this volume constitutes a culmination of that collaboration.

This introduction seeks to outline an interpretation of the overarching goal of Reardon's body of work: the articulation and justification of a fundamental paradigm shift in worldview—a shift from a paradigm of war toward a paradigm of peace as the primary means of transforming society, including local, national, international, and global social structures (Reardon 1989, 1994b; Reardon/Snauwaert 2015a, b). Her conception and practice of peace education can best be understood within the framework of this paradigm shift. She writes:

> ... the general purpose of peace education, as I understand it, is to promote the development of an authentic planetary consciousness that will enable us to function as global citizens and to transform the present human condition by changing the social structures and the patterns of thought that have created it. This transformational imperative must, in my view, be at the

center of peace education. It is important to emphasize that *transformation*, in this context, means a profound global cultural change that affects ways of thinking, world views, values, behaviors, relationships, and the structures that make up our public order. It implies a change in the human consciousness and in human society of a dimension far greater than any other that has taken place since the emergence of the nation-state system, and perhaps since the emergence of human settlements (Reardon 1988, p. x).

At the core of this, paradigm shift is the transformation of a militaristic, patriarchal worldview, to one grounded in social justice, human rights, and gender equality; a worldview that honors the equal dignity of all persons and is morally, socially, and politically inclusive. The goal is to make violence unacceptable on all levels of human interaction. The changes sought are behavioral and institutional but primarily emphasize changes in thinking and in the formation of values and principles. The transformation of both the structures of society *and* the structures of consciousness comprise the central aim of the paradigm shift.

The War Paradigm

In Reardon's view, patriarchy in symbiotic relation with militarism (the war system) constitutes the essence of the war paradigm and the basic structure of an unjust society. She writes: "I continue to insist [that] … the oppression of women and the legitimation of coercive force which perpetuates war, the two major pillars of patriarchy, are mutually dependent conditions… (Reardon 1996, p. 98)." She maintains that "… militarism and militarization [are] the bastions and bulwark of patriarchy… (Reardon 1994a, p. 6)." Patriarchy and militarism are interrelated and interdependent ideological systems. As ideological systems, they work to justify domination and oppression (Reardon 1996), and thus violence and social injustice (Reardon/Jenkins 2007).

Patriarchy is a belief system which assigns value to different groups of human beings based upon innate characteristics; it assigns differential value to ascriptive characteristics that are portrayed as natural attributes. This "fixed order" thinking is common to belief systems based upon the inequality of human beings (e.g., racism) (Reardon 1981). Thus, unequal and exclusionary gender differentiation constitutes the structural element of the patriarchal social system as well as providing its ideological justification.

Implicit in these systems is the presupposition that a perpetual threat of coercive force is necessary to maintain power. The credibility of this threat requires monopoly control of the means of lethal, and thus military, force. As Reardon suggests:

> Militarism is a belief system, emerging from a world view, founded on the basic assumption that human beings are by nature violent, aggressive and competitive, and from the corollary assumption that social order must be maintained by force. Authority, according to this world view, derives from the capacity to muster and apply force to maintain social control and to determine human behavior. Social worth can be achieved by

a willingness to be an instrument of existing authority in the application of force to maintain order and security and/or in risking harm from the force of a rival authority (Reardon 1981, p. 8).

A political system conceived and justified in terms of militarism will understand political sovereignty in terms of this coercive power and will tend to be organized on the principles of hierarchical command (Reardon 1981, p. 8–10). Such a political system tends toward domination—the morally arbitrary rule of a few over the many. Domination in turn often leads to various forms of oppression. Both constitute violence. Reardon defines violence in terms of dehumanization, the violation of human dignity:

All violence degrades and/or denies human dignity. This is why I assert that the substance of the field should comprise an inquiry into violence as a phenomenon and a system, its multiple and pervasive forms, the interrelationships among the various forms, its sources and purposes, how it functions and potential alternatives for achieving the legally sanctioned, socially accepted, or politically tolerated purposes commonly pursued through violence (Reardon 2011, p. 55).

These violations of human dignity are instantiated in social systems of domination and oppression ideologically justified (not morally justified) and normalized by the war paradigm.

The Peace Paradigm

As conceived by Reardon, the peace paradigm is the transformative response to the war paradigm. The peace paradigm is comprised of an interdependent web of values and understandings that foster the universal actualization of human dignity, including: holism; human rights; feminist values; human security; and the self-aware reflective capacity of citizens. This integral web is seen by Reardon to be foundational in evolving a worldview that is necessary for the transformation of a social system prone to violence and injustice, to one that cultivates full realization of human dignity, and a just peace.

Holism

Reardon maintains that "Holism and critical reflection are essential and necessary to the transformation of thinking (and transformational thinking) conducive to the political processes requisite to the realization of human rights as the basis of a peaceful world order ... (Reardon 1994b, p. 46)." Holism generates an understanding of life that is interrelated and interdependent: Life is understood as an interdependent web of relationships within which respect and care for the inherent dignity of life is imperative. This view is a perspective of deep equality. She writes for example: "Clearly, peace studies must begin to pursue wholism as the framework, process as the primary method, and peace in its widest sense as the goal, if it is to energize the intellectual transformation necessary to a paradigm of peace (Reardon 1989, p. 25)." This holistic ontology in turn leads to the inclusion of all life in the moral community, thereby bringing the moral consideration of the natural world and ecological balance under the umbrella of just peace (authentic form of peace that is defined by the presence of justice—a just society on all levels).

Human Rights

The language of rights can be understood as foundational to the principles of an ethic of human dignity. As Reardon maintains: "Human rights study provides us with tools of definition and diagnosis of what comprises violence, experientially as well as conceptually … (Reardon 2009, p. 55)." She maintains that: "Human rights standards are the specific indicators and particular measures of progress toward and the realization of peace. Human rights put flesh on the bones of the abstraction of peace and provide the details of how to bring the flesh to life (Reardon 2009, p. 47)." In turn, Reardon conceives peace in terms of the realization of human rights and duties: "A sustainable world peace can only be assured through the universal actualization of human dignity (Reardon 2009, p. 46)." Reardon writes:

> As a political framework for the actualization of human dignity, human rights are the ethical core of peace education; not a complement, or a particular component, and certainly not an alternative or an educationally equivalent substitute for peace education. Human rights are integral to peace education, that is, without human rights peace education lacks a primary component of its core and essential substance. Human rights are the essence and the arbiter of peace, the antithesis of violence, touching on multiple and complex aspects of the human experience, illuminating the necessity of holism to the field. The potential of human rights as the means to cultivate transformational thinking lies in viewing all human rights norms and standards as a whole, an integrated ethical system (Reardon 2009, p. 47).

A society, both national and global, that secures the human dignity of all citizens through the realization of their rights is the standard for a just peace.

Feminist Values

While acknowledging there is no monolithic conception of feminism, the common core of the various conceptions of feminism is the normative assertion of the equal human value of all persons, male and female, and maintaining that patriarchal society is founded upon gender (and other types of) inequality (Reardon 1990).

The general adoption of this perspective is necessary for the transformation of the patriarchal worldview (Reardon 2010).

The peace paradigm entails a profound shift in values toward positive feminine values. As Reardon maintains:

> Feminists assert that current societal problems require the application of the following societal values: love, genuine caring for others; equity, fairly sharing all that is available to the group; and empowerment, helping group members to achieve fulfillment, cooperation *and maturity—making* together for mutual fulfillment. Feminism is profoundly transformational, for it calls for fundamental changes in personal values and human relationships as well as in structures and systems ... This position is particularly feminist because it calls for the extension into the public sphere of the values of caring, cooperation and mutuality that have been traditionally confined to the private sphere. Such an extension would be transformational because the equal application of feminist criteria to public policy would result *in more concern for* human needs and less concern for the maintenance of military power— the ultimate result of the distorted weight given masculine values (Reardon 1980, p. 14).

The widespread inclusion of feminine values in public life is a necessary condition for the realization of human rights, which protects and cares for the equal dignity of all persons (Reardon/Jenkins 2007, p. 228). This value shift inspires, in turn, a transformation of our conception of security.

Human Security

In opposition to common militarized notions of national security, the idea of human security pertains to the "wellbeing made possible through the elimination of all forms of violence, assured by institutions designed specifically to achieve and maintain wellbeing ... (Reardon 2010, p. 33)." It presents an alternative conception of security to the conception of state security, one that is consistent with the ethical and moral imperatives of feminism and human rights. Reardon maintains that:

> human security never can be achieved within the present highly militarized, war-prone, patriarchal nation-state system. Neither, as I have argued for more than two decades, is it achievable within patriarchy, which is the foundation of the war system (Reardon 1985).... Two propositions lie at the center of [my] assertions and arguments: first, if human security is to be achieved, patriarchy must be replaced with gender equality, and second, war as an institution must be abolished in favor of nonviolent structures and processes for resolving conflicts and achieving national policy goal ... (Reardon 2010, p. 7).

From this perspective, the aim is to "protect life and to enhance its quality." Questions of security would be transformed into: "What are the fundamental threats to human life? And, how can we overcome these threats in a life enhancing manner" (Reardon 1990, pp. 139–140)? Thus, security should concern human well-being.

Self-Aware, Reflective Citizens

Within a paradigm of peace, the internal psychological dynamics of fear and projection as underlying elements of patriarchy and the war system would be replaced
by a widespread increase in reflective capacity and self-awareness. Reardon articulates three forms of reflective capacity that would be widespread in the population
of citizens: critical/analytic; ethical/moral; and contemplative/ruminative reflective
capacity.

   Critical/analytic reflection pertains to the discernment of power, an understanding and critique of social institutions, analysis of the structural dimensions of
social life, and a critical consciousness of the political-economic origins of violence. Ethical/moral reflection addresses questions of justice guided by the principles of a human rights framework. This capacity of reflection is necessary for
ethical and moral justification of political decisions and basic matters of justice as
well as the critique of invalid justifications. Contemplative/ruminative reflective
capacity is conceived as commitment to self-examination of internal moral motivation and internal psychological dynamics. It further involves reflection on what is
meaningful and valuable, and involves the exercise of imagination to envision
alternative realities necessary for transformative action (Reardon/Snauwaert 2011).
These modes of reflection are the vehicles used to traverse the transformational
pathways identified above.

   In summary, these features of a paradigm of peace constitute a worldview that
Reardon emphasizes is necessary for the transformation of a patriarchal and militaristic society, as well as providing a framework for conceiving a just and peaceful
world.

A Pedagogy of Reflective Inquiry

The transformative process required for this paradigm shift entails pedagogical
processes of learning and development. Reardon defines the educational task in
holistic and transformational terms; people undergo a learning process that is
reflective and dialogical. This transformational approach transcends but includes the
two other prominent traditions in peace education: the reform and reconstruction
traditions (Reardon 2000). The reform approach is devoted to the prevention of war,
including the control and balance of arms. The reconstructive approach seeks to
reconstruct international systems, to abolish war, and to achieve total disarmament.
Its primary objective is structural and institutional change and the establishment of
global conflict resolution, peacekeeping, and peacebuilding institutions. Reardon's
transformational approach aims at the rejection of all forms of violence: direct;
structural; and cultural. The goal of this approach is a shift to a paradigm of peace,
including the development of the human capacities to sustain this vision and
realization.

The transformational approach employs a pedagogy that elicits learning. Reardon describes this approach as follows:

> [transformational] peace educators ... describe their goal as eliciting (not imposing or inculcating) positive responses, recognizing that education is not so much a process of imparting knowledge as it is "drawing out" the capacity to learn ... In eliciting awareness, the intent is to strengthen capacity to care, to develop a sincere concern for those who suffer because of the problems and a commitment to resolving them through action. Awareness infused by caring becomes concern that can lead to such commitment when one action is followed by other actions, and when action for peace becomes a sustained behavioral pattern, part of the learner's way of life. The objective is to elicit an ongoing and active response to the problems of peace and a commitment to their resolution ... this cycle of care, concern, and commitment is the core of the peace learning process (Reardon 1988, pp. 21–22).

Reardon maintains that a transformational peace education should draw out "a new mode of thinking that is life-affirming, oriented toward the fulfillment of the human potential, and directed to the achievement of maturation as the ultimate goal of ... positive peace (Reardon 1988, p. 53)." More specifically, peace education should be fundamentally concerned with the development of the *political efficacy* of future citizens—the capacity to engage in transformative political action (Reardon/Snauwaert 2011).

Reardon's transformational pedagogy addresses the core problematic of how to promote authentic planetary consciousness in the movement from domination to empowerment. She argues that this pedagogy, and its reflective, dialogical inquiry, must be critical, ethical, and contemplative, which will cultivate the human capacities necessary for the political empowerment and efficacy of citizens foundational to the called for paradigm shift.

The pursuit of this societal paradigm shift from war to peace remains urgent as we face both the rise of authoritarianism and fascism as well as an eminent environmental catastrophe. Reardon's work provides us with a framework for understanding and transforming the ideological structures and forms of thought that undergird and justify violent systems. Looking forward, this framework can be widened and deepened by all of us who follow in her path. The remaining chapters of this book are an attempt to do just that.

The Outline of the Book

As noted above, the chapters in this volume explore ways in which we, as an international group of peace education scholars and practitioners can build Reardon's foundational work to advance the theory and practice of peace education. This unique collection of authors all examine the question: How does Reardon's groundbreaking work point us toward the cutting edges of the field of peace studies and peace education? Contributors explore three general areas of inquiry: (1) Theoretical Foundations of Peace and Human Rights Education; (2) Feminism and the Gender Perspective as Pathways of Transformation Toward Peace and Justice; and (3) Peace Education Pedagogy and Applied Practice. The book concludes with a reflective commentary by Betty Reardon.

Part I: Theoretical Foundations of Peace and Human Rights Education

Chapter 1: *Realization of a Just Peace and the First Question of Power*—Dale T. Snauwaert

Reardon argues that the achievement of peace and justice cannot be realized without a fundamental change "in the distribution and locus of power in the world order and the global economic system," and that a "democratic redistribution of power" is a necessary condition for its realization (Reardon 2018). The purpose of this chapter is to elaborate upon Reardon's discourse on power; she identifies power as the first question of justice, and asks, what constitutes a morally justifiable distribution of power, and what is the valid source of political legitimacy in a democracy? These questions are explored from within the perspective of what the political philosopher Rainer Forst (2012) refers to as the basic right to justification. This human right entitles one to demand both justifiable reasons for actions that affect one, as well as critical scrutiny of ideological power arrangements and actions (i.e., policies, laws, practices, institutions, etc.) that affect citizens in various ways that are unequal and unjust. In this essay, Reardon's call for a democratic redistribution of power is conceptualized and explored within current thinking and developments in moral and political philosophy.

Chapter 2: *"Peace Education for Global Citizenship" The Genuine Global Dimension of Betty Reardon's Concept of Peace Education*—Werner Wintersteiner

Werner Wintersteiner explores the relationship between peace education and global citizenship. He maintains that the two are interconnected fields. He analyzes the "global" in Betty Reardon's concept of peace education and argues that peace education has a genuine Global Citizenship Education dimension, or in other words, peace education should be understood as a necessary element of Global Citizenship Education. He argues that Betty Reardon's elaboration of this interconnection is the clearest such treatment in the literature. Moreover, he maintains that her treatment offers an excellent foundation for a "productive conversation" between critical peace education and postcolonial and decolonial approaches (Zembylas 2018, p. 18).

Chapter 3: *Peacebuilding Education in Posttruth Times: Lessons from the Work of Betty A. Reardon*—Kevin Kester, Toshiyasu Tsuruhara, and Tim Archer

Kevin Kester, Toshiyasu Tsuruhara, and Tim Archer examine several of Reardon's seminal works in order to uncover how she intellectually approached the Cold War. From within Reardon's perspective, the authors offer insight into how current peace scholars can respond to the many challenges and contradictions of educating for peace in the posttruth era. They argue for three conclusions regarding crucial elements of peace education under the conditions of posttruth: (1) Engagement of the rational and affective capacities is essential for a holistic and inclusive approach to peace learning; (2) The mitigation of posttruth tensions requires engagement in a critique of the systems of militarism and patriarchy, as well as their interrelationship with gender and racial inequities; and (3) A democratic, informed dialogic, and critical pedagogy remains the most promising pedagogic response to posttruth alternative facts and "epistemological gerrymandering."

Chapter 4: *Peace Education Confronting Reality*—Magnus Haavelsrud

Magnus Haavelsrud conceives peace education as part of the "process of *becoming* and *being* politically aware," which can be identified as *politicization* (Hellesnes 1994, p. 136). He understands *politicization* as being closely related to Freire's (1972) concepts of *conscientization* and *praxis*. The process of becoming and being politically aware entails that the core contents and forms of peace education to confront the "problems, conflicts, issues, themes, topics, events, and contradictions" of social reality. He suggests that this process of politicization is not a high priority of current educational policy makers, and this neglect constitutes a "paradox in a world faced with unprecedented social, cultural, and political challenges." He argues that it is imperative that *politicization* be a priority in order to meet these challenges. To this end, he revisits Reardon's call for peace education to confront reality. He concludes that the purpose of peace education entails the development of the "capacity to engage in transformative political action and to contribute to the socialization of future citizens' political efficacy."

Chapter 5: *Reardon's Conception of Human Rights and Human Rights Learning*—Fuad Al-Daraweesh

The purpose of Al-Daraweesh's chapter is to explore and discuss Reardon's conception of human rights and human rights learning. To this end, Al-Daraweesh explores the relationship between human rights and human dignity, as well as the relationship between human rights and peace, as articulated in Reardon's writings. He identifies Reardon's conception of human rights learning as a unique and original contribution. The main focus of the chapter is an account of the main characteristics of Reardon's concept of human rights learning. These characteristics include: (1) social transformation through Freirean pedagogy; (2) the pedagogy of human rights learning is grounded in ethical reflection actualized through the politics of learning; (3) human rights learning entails a holistic approach that addresses not only human rights but also issues related to vulnerability and violence; (4) a gender perspective is essential for human rights learning; (5) human rights learning is a significant advancement of the theory and practice of human rights education; and (6) at its core, human rights learning takes into consideration cultural pluralism. Al-Daraweesh concludes that a "critical transformative pedagogy is of cardinal importance to change the current paradigms of injustice and violence that are aimed at the vulnerable."

Chapter 6: *"Learning and Living Human Rights" Betty Reardon's Transformative Pedagogies and Politics of Peace Legacy*—Anaida Pascual-Morán

Anaida Pascual-Morán explores Reardon's contention that an engagement with *"learning and living human rights"* is essential for both peace education and solidarity action. Furthermore, she argues that social transformation requires these fundamental reciprocal processes. They also require an "enlightened problem-posing pedagogy," which includes envisioning "projects of possibility" grounded in "investigative and creative transformative actions." To this end, Pascual-Morán argues that peace educators should be committed to human rights learning and, following Reardon, the generation of "a critical, creative, and courageous citizenry". Pascual-Morán situates her exploration in the context of the challenges, injustices, and solidarity actions of post-hurricane Maria Puerto Rico.

Part II: Feminism and the Gender Perspective as Pathways of Transformation Toward Peace and Justice

Chapter 7: *Exploring Betty A. Reardon's Perspective on Peace*—Ingeborg Breines

Ingeborg Breines explores Reardon's work with UNESCO, notably on the culture of peace. In this context, Breines explores what Reardon wrote, participated in, contributed, inspired, in particular, the development of the UNESCO concept of a culture of peace, including women's contributions to the idea of a culture of peace and the conceptualization and practice of an education for a culture of peace. The chapter also explores her work on and for disarmament, including disarmament education—related to UNESCO, the UN, as well as the International Peace Bureau (IPB). Finally, the importance of role models is explored: the importance of believing in a person in order to want to learn or make improvements in your own life/teaching/behavior; the ways in which Betty is an exceptionally inspiring person, not only through her writing and teaching, but also through her personality, her sharing of values, her capacity for friendship and care, as well as, how she bridges the personal and the political, the analytic and the practical—how she manages "to be the change you would like to see."

Chapter 8: *Peace Education and Gender in Africa: Reflections on the Work of Dr. Betty Reardon*—Colins Imoh

Colins Imoh explores the transformation of patriarchal hegemony in the African context and the role of Reardon's theory and practice of peace education in that transformation as a urgent matter of human rights and justice. He asks: What role can peace education play? What role does Reardon's work play in encouraging practitioners and advocating for breaking the patriarchy system and enthroning a more progressive society in Africa? The chapter provides a reflection on the application of Reardon's gender perspective and peace education in Africa. Imoh concludes that an education for empowerment through both the process and content of education is needed. Furthermore, the required transformation of patriarchy requires not only a change in social structures but also a change in human relations.

Chapter 9: *The Letters: An Exchange on Patriarchy, Militarization and Feminist Peace Activism*—Swarna Rajagopalan and Asha Hans

Swarna Rajagopalan and Asha Hans offer an innovative approach to their reflection on Betty Reardon's pioneering work on the connection between patriarchy and militarism. They engage in dialogue with each other as activist scholars through an exchange of ideas and experiences in letters; in engaging in this dialogue, they identify and reflect on the ideas and activist themes in Reardon's life's work. The focus of their dialogical exchange in the form of letters to each other is the interconnected ideas and themes of patriarchy, militarization, and feminist peace activism central to the paradigm shift from war to peace and justice. These ideas and themes have resonance for their own work, and they share them in this unique form in the hope of resonating with others.

Chapter 10: *Dehumanization and Trauma in Palestine: Representations of the Occupation and the Great March of Return in the Patriarchal War System*—Tina Ottman

Tina Ottman examines the nature of how, in the overarching context of the patriarchal war system, violence occurs as a result of dehumanization. She situates this inquiry in a case study of the ongoing Great March of Return in Gaza, a protest along the borders of the heavily blockaded Hamas-controlled Gaza Strip. Building on Reardon's formulation of core components of human security, she concludes that the possibility of a "peaceful solution to the Israel-Palestine conflict lie[s] strongly with such an 'actualization of human dignity,' as part and parcel of with the restoration of human security, of which health is one of the critical barometers … ." Echoing Reardon's analysis, she concludes that the hope for a good life for Palestinians is contingent upon the recognition of structural and political conditions, conditions whose transformation is an urgent matter of justice.

Chapter 11: *Some Questions from Popoki to Betty Reardon About Human Security, Gender and Teaching/Learning/Creating Peace*—Ronni Alexander

Ronni Alexander employs the creative device of "Popoki the Cat" who like Betty Reardon and other peace educators understands that inquiry, critical thinking, and reflection are essential capacities and practices for the pursuit of peace and justice. Popoki understands that the "creation and maintenance of peace are a process which begins from our bodies and encompasses our total capacity for thinking, feeling, and being." This understanding aligns with Reardon's holistic perspective. Furthermore, Popoki understands that to establish and maintain peace, we need to analyze and understand what Reardon calls "militarized patriarchy," including the "system of institutionalized misogyny," and to envision a peaceful world and how it might be different from what we have learned about how peace from our feelings. Popoki tries to "envision the smells, tastes, textures, sounds, and appearance of that world. He dreams of a feminist world free of violence to the environment, others, and ourselves." Using examples and stories primarily from work in Guam and Northeastern Japan, Ronni Alexander, in the voice of Popoki, questions Betty Reardon about how to envision and create a secure future.

Chapter 12: *Media, Sexism and the Patriarchal War System: Why Media Literacy Matters to Peace Education*—Sally McLaren

Based upon a reading of Betty Reardon's groundbreaking book, *Sexism and the war system*, Sally McLaren provides a deep analysis of sexism and the media. She reflects on Reardon's analysis of the interrelationship between sexism, patriarchy, militarism, and the war system, with application to the current media landscape. She also offers an appeal to peace educators to include media literacy with a gender perspective in their scholarship and teaching in order to increase the understanding of the mediated nature of the patriarchal war system. Furthermore, she discusses the practical applications of Reardon's work, in particular, how media literacy can contribute to and compliment the work of peace education. In the end, McLaren illuminates the nature of the "global patriarchal media system" through the lens of Reardon's insight into the relationship between sexism and militarization. Given the emergence of a media-saturated social environment and the unprecedented power of media organizations to "shape our world views, influence our behavior and provoke extreme reactions," her perspective and analysis have urgent importance.

Chapter 13: *Language, Gender and Power: Possibilities for Transformation of Political Discourse*—Michele W. Milner

From within the perspective of applied linguistics, specifically critical discourse analysis, Michele Miner employs linguistic analysis and an understanding of the dialectic relationship between language and power in order to "increase awareness of the ways language maintains key aspects of patriarchal ideology, such as stereotypical gender differences and inequitable power relationships." Building upon Reardon's understanding of the core problematic for peace and human security and her holistic feminine perspective, Milner asserts the importance of language as a necessary component of understanding how and in what ways "gender identities and relations are constructed and maintained through social interaction." She argues that the analysis of language is necessary in order to "recognize the transformative possibilities of conceptual reframing as part of Reardon's alternative paradigm for a positive global future."

Part III: Peace Education Pedagogy and Applied Peacebuilding Practices

Chapter 14: *Toward a Just Society: An Account*—Janet Gerson

Janet Gerson lays a theoretical foundation for a pedagogy of reflective inquiry. This foundation is grounded in a comparative analysis of Reardon's vision of a just society and the pedagogical path to it and the moral and political philosophy of Rainer Forst. The analysis demonstrates how political processes can be both philosophically grounded *and* practical, in ways that are "democratic in a dynamic sense, beyond the reified institutional form." In this way, Gerson maintains that discursive critical practices, such as the affirmation of a basic human right to justification, coupled with democratic processes of reflective inquiry are needed as counters to the "proliferation of invalid justifications, unjust social orders, unjust narratives, and anti-reasonable political argumentation." Gerson concludes that this perspective forms the "scaffolding for the theory and practice of an *intersubjective relational paradigm* of justice."

Chapter 15: *Reardon's Edu-learner Praxis: Educating for Political Efficacy and Social Transformation*—Tony Jenkins

Building on Betty Reardon's identification of the development of the political efficacy of citizens as the fundamental social purpose of peace education, Tony Jenkins explores the questions: "What does this look like in practice? How might we actually go about educating for political efficacy without falling prey to pedagogies of indoctrination?" Mirroring these questions is the issue of developing the educational–political efficacy of the teacher: "how do we facilitate transformative modes of learning that support the development of those inner capacities that are the basis for external action? How do we help learners step over the lines of knowing, to doing, to being?" Jenkins argues that no singular or combined pedagogical approach can assure these outcomes. He argues that political engagement is an active disposition, requiring ongoing ethical reflection on action. He concludes that political efficacy and transformative pedagogical practice are therefore linked to reflective praxis. Jenkins demonstrates how and in what ways this reflective praxis are manifested in Reardon's vision of teacher as "edu-learner," a practitioner/theorist who while helping others to learn is engaged herself in the process of learning. Jenkins's reflections on teaching as the practice of reflective praxis embodied in the teacher as an edu-learner illuminates the basic conception of Reardon's approach to peace education as a process of reflective inquiry devoted to the development of the transformative political efficacy of citizens, current and future.

Chapter 16: *Practicing Peace Education: Learning Peace and Teaching Peace with Betty Reardon*—Ian Gibson

Ian Gibson begins his chapter with a discussion of his experience of Betty Reardon's classes at Teachers College in Tokyo. He reports that the class modules incorporated human security, gender perspectives, non-violence, the Culture of Peace, and training in teaching peace education. He also reports that Reardon was an exemplary facilitator by encouraging group work, stressing critical inquiry, and facilitating further discussion and inquiry. In Reardon's pedagogy, the principles of peace education were practiced through one's own teaching, leading to the internalization of those principles. Gibson suggests that the adoption of Reardon's pedagogy has profoundly shaped his own practice of teaching leading to a dynamic learning experience for students. Gibson's pedagogical reflections offered in this chapter illuminate Reardon's approach to peace pedagogy and offer a valuable case study of her work as a teacher.

Chapter 17: *Shared Reflections and Learnings from Betty Reardon—Action Planning Models: National and International Partnerships in Asia*—Kathy R. Matsui

Kathy Matsui discusses peace education activities as well as peacebuilding aspirations conducted in Asia. She argues that there is a need for "strategic ways of educating for a culture of peace." She maintains that peace education is a "personal teleology, a personal lifework." She examines the possibility of how a "peacebuilding program can transform the negative feelings and mindsets of the people of Northeast Asia toward the Japanese people and government." Furthermore, Matsui identifies peace education as a peaceful method for establishing a foundation for reconciliation and diplomatic relations. She discusses in what ways the Northeast Peacebuilding Institute (NARPI) is devoted to the pursuit of educating "peace leaders to build a culture of peace and to transform the potential sources of conflict in Northeast Asia into a resourceful region of collaboration and peace." The chapter provides us with a case study of the application of Reardon's conception of peace education as adapted to the Asian context.

Chapter 18: *Health Promotion for Peace Promotion: Applying Reardon's Holistic Model to Health*—Albie Sharpe

Albie Sharpe explores the relationship between health and peace through the lens of Reardon's holistic perspective. He demonstrates that there are "multiple shared and reciprocal links and processes between the broader concept of health and Reardon's vision of a feminist human security." He calls for collaboration between health workers, social workers, peace workers, and educators, understanding them as natural allies who share a common purpose. He concludes that "health promotion is peace promotion," demonstrating the significant interconnection between health and peace education.

Chapter 19: *"Walking the Talk" on Peace Education with Betty Reardon: Reflection and Action Towards a Transformative Pedagogy*—Anita Yudkin

Anita Yudkin reflects upon Betty Reardon's contributions to peace education through an examination of her written works in relation to her practice as a peace scholar and activist. In particular, she focuses on: *Learning to Abolish War: Teaching Toward a Culture of Peace* (Reardon and Cabezudo 2002) and *Human Rights Learning: Pedagogies and Politics of Peace* (Reardon 2010); these works explore key themes concerning her understanding of peace, education, and pedagogy. Yudkin also reflects upon Reardon's pedagogy and agency as experienced at the International Institute on Peace Education (IIPE). She discusses two other events that showcase the connection between knowledge and action toward peace in Reardon's work, the *Vieques Okinawan Women Solidarity Encounter*, and the symposium *Calling the Phoenix: Learning Toward Transcending Political and Natural Disasters*. Yudkin concludes that Reardon's perspective provides "an ethical and practical framework for action to claim human dignity," exemplifying the transformative power of education. She argues that Reardon affirms a Freirean perspective concerning learning as an "act of political engagement toward an active global citizenship." She also examines the nuanced nature of Reardon's pedagogy of ethical and critical inquiry as a form of transformative learning. She concludes: "Certainly, Reardon has walked the way toward peace by means of her ideas and actions, leading us to continue this walk equipped with pedagogical knowledge, clarity, hope, and courage"—a fitting conclusion to the book.

Overall, this collection of commentaries, reflections, and elaborations constitutes a rich and profound exploration of Betty Reardon's legacy and the future of peace education. It is our hope that you the reader will find much value and insight into these reflections in ways that enhance your understanding of the theory and practice of peace education and its advancement in the world. Looking forward, Reardon's transformational pedagogy cultivates human potential and political efficacy within a holistic peace-learning process; the promotion of authentic planetary consciousness is essential in the movement from domination to empowerment and the creation of a just peace for all.

Prof. Dr. Dale T. Snauwaert
Professor of Philosophy of Education
and Peace Studies, University of Toledo, Ohio, USA
dale.snauwaert@utoledo.edu

References

Forst, R. (2012). *The right to justification* (J. Flynn, Trans.). New York: Columbia University Press.

Haavelsrud, M. (2015). The academy, development and modernity's "other". *International Journal of Development Education and Global Learning, 7*(2), 46–60.

Hoppers, C. O. (2018, May 27, 2018). [Global Institute of Applied Governance of Science, Knowledge Systems and Innovations].

Reardon, B. A. (1980). Moving to the Future. *Network, 8*(1), 14–21.

Reardon, B. A. (1981). Militarism and Sexism: Influences On Education For War. *UME Connexion, 9*(3), 1–29.

Reardon, B. A. (1988). *Comprehensive peace education: educating for global responsibility.* New York: Teachers College Press.

Reardon, B. A. (1989). Toward a paradigm of peace. In L. R. Farcey (Ed.), *Peace: meanings, politics, strategies.* New York: Praeger.

Reardon, B. A. (1990). Feminist concepts of peace and security. In P. Smoker, R. Davies, & B. Munske (Eds.), *A reader in peace studies.* New York: Pergamon Press.

Reardon, B. A. (1994a). *A feminist critique of "an agenda for peace".* Retrieved from.

Reardon, B. A. (1994b). Learning our way to a human future. In B. A. Reardon & E. Nordland (Eds.), *Learning peace: The promise of ecological and cooperative education.* Albany, NY: State University of New York Press.

Reardon, B. A. (1996). *Sexism and the war system* (1st Syracuse University Press ed.). Syracuse, N.Y.: Syracuse University Press.

Reardon, B. A. (2000). Peace education: a review and projection. In R. Moon, M. Ben-Peretz, & S. Brown (Eds.), *Routledge international companion to education.* London: Routledge.

Reardon, B. A. (2009). *Human Rights Learning: Pedagogies and politics of peace.* Paper presented at the UNESCO Chair for Peace Education Master Conference, University of Puerto Rico.

Reardon, B. A. (2010). Women and human security: A feminist framework and critique of the prevailing patriarchal security system. In B. A. Reardon & A. Hans (Eds.), *The gender imperative: Human security vs. state security.* New Delhi, India: Routledge.

Reardon, B. A. (2011). Concerns, cautions and possibilities for peace education for political efficacy. In B. W. a. P. Trifonas (Ed.), *Critical peace education: difficult dialogue.* Cham: Springer Press.

Reardon, B. A., & Jenkins, A. (2007). Gender and peace: towards a gender inclusive, holistic perspective. In J. Galtung & C. Webel (Eds.), *Handbook of peace and conflict studies.* New York: Routledge, 209–231.

Reardon, B. A., & Snauwaert, D. T. (2011). Reflective pedagogy, cosmopolitanism, and critical peace education for political efficacy: A Discussion of Betty A. Reardon's assessment of the field. In Factis Pax: *Journal of Peace Education and Social Justice, 5*(1), 1–14.

Reardon, B. A., & Snauwaert, D. T. (Eds.). (2015a). *Betty A. Reardon: A pioneer in education for peace and human rights.* Heidelberg: Springer.

Reardon, B. A., & Snauwaert, D. T. (Eds.). (2015b). *Betty A. Reardon: Key texts in gender and peace.* Heidelberg: Springer.

Zembylas, M. (2018.) "Con-/divergences between postcolonial and critical peace education: towards pedagogies of decolonization in peace education". *Journal of Peace Education, 15* (1): 1–23.

Contents

Abbreviations

AAAH	Australian Association for Adolescent Health
ACRI	Association for Civil Rights in Israel
AFSPA	Armed Forces Special Powers Act
CDA	Critical discourse analysis
CEDAW	Convention on the Elimination of all Forms of Discrimination Against Women
CESCR	Committee on Economic, Social and Cultural Rights
CICI	International Committee of Intellectual Co-operation
COMEST	Commission on Ethics of Science and Technology
DAW	United Nations Division for the Advancement of Women
FeDem	Feminist Scholars and Activists Working for Demilitarization
GCED	Global Citizenship Education
GCPE	Global Campaign for Peace Education
GDP	Gross Domestic Product
HR	Human Rights
HRL	Human rights learning
IBE	International Bureau of Education
ICC	International Criminal Court
ICSU	International Council of Scientists
IDF	Israel Defense Force
IIPE	International Institute on Peace Education
IPB	International Peace Bureau
IPRA	International Peace Research Association
IWO	Institute for World Order
LGBT	Lesbian Gay Bisexual Transgender
MSF	Medècins Sans Frontiéres
NARPI	Northeast Asia Regional Peacebuilding Institute
NGO	Nongovernmental Organization
OECD	Organization for Economic Cooperation and Development
ORT	Oral rehydration therapy

PCHR	Palestinian Centre for Human Rights
PHC	Primary health care
PHM	People's Health Movement
PISA	Programme for International Student Assessment
PNA	Palestine National Authority
SDGs	Sustainable Development Goals
SIPRI	Stockholm Peace Research Institute
UDHR	Universal Declaration of Human Rights
UN	United Nations
UNDP	United Nations Development Programme
UNESCO	United Nations Educational, Scientific and Cultural Organization
UNHCR	United Nations High Commissioner for Refugees
UNICEF	United Nations Children's Fund
UNSC	United Nations Security Council
WHO	World Health Organization
WILPF	Women's International League for Peace and Freedom
WINGHS	Women's International Network for Gender and Human Security
WPS	Women, Peace, and Security

Part I
Theoretical Foundations of Peace and Human Rights Education

Chapter 1
Realization of a Just Peace and the First Question of Power

Dale T. Snauwaert

Reardon argues that the achievement of peace and justice cannot be realized without a fundamental change "in the distribution and locus of power in the world order and the global economic system", and that a "democratic redistribution of power," is a necessary condition for its realization (Reardon 2018).

The purpose of this chapter is to elaborate upon Reardon's discourse on power; she identifies power as the first question of justice, and asks, what constitutes a morally justifiable distribution of power, and what is the valid source of political legitimacy in a democracy? These questions will be explored from within the perspective of what is called the basic human right to justification. This human right entitles one to demand both justifiable reasons for, and critical scrutiny of ideological power arrangements and actions (i.e., policies, laws, practices, institutions, etc.) that affect citizens in various ways that are unequal and unjust. In this essay, Reardon's call for a democratic redistribution of power is conceptualized and explored within current thinking and developments in moral and political philosophy.

Reardon's discourse on power is central to the pursuit of a just peace. In commenting on the UN's Sustainable Development Goals (SDGs) she writes:

> Only transformative changes in global power structures are likely to achieve them. Poverty results from lack of power, and any serious attempt to eliminate poverty should recognize this uncomfortable reality. The concept of transformation invoked here is a deep-rooted change in the core values of the societies and institutions confronting the problem and undertaking the intentional institutional reconstruction of power arrangements ... that I would describe as a democratic redistribution of power. A review and assessment of the core values is made possible by framing the goals within the problematic of the war system which cannot be transformed without deep rooted, sustainable change in social and political values. Transformative processes arise from values changes which in turn result from changes in world view. They also derive from choices, intentional political choices, not available to the poor ... Without such structural change the *elimination* of poverty is not possible (Reardon 2018).

Prof. Dr. Dale T. Snauwaert, Department of Educational Foundations and Leadership, University of Toledo, Ohio, USA; Email: dale.snauwaert@utoledo.edu.

© Springer Nature Switzerland AG 2019
D. T. Snauwaert (ed.), *Exploring Betty A. Reardon's Perspective on Peace Education*, Pioneers in Arts, Humanities, Science, Engineering, Practice 20, https://doi.org/10.1007/978-3-030-18387-5_1

Reardon asserts that the major obstacle to the realization of a just peace is a profoundly unequal and unjust 'global power arrangement' linked to the war system legitimized by patriarchy. Reardon offers here a strong and insightful argument that the core obstacle to this redistributive transformation of power is the interrelated structure of patriarchy and the war system (Reardon 1981, 1996; Reardon and Snauwaert 2015b). Both are grounded in a hierarchical structure of power. She writes: "The global patriarchal order, a power hierarchy that places all human beings on various levels of a hierarchy of human value and political power, is the essential problematic that must be addressed in assessment of and prescription for solutions to development and other world problems (Reardon 2018)." In order to elucidate and to provide further support to the validity of Reardon's identification of power as the first question of justice, we turn to an examination of current moral and political philosophy.

1.1 Power

Just as a game is defined by the basic rules that constitute it, the basic political and social structure of a society is constituted by its rules. These rules must be understood and complied with by citizens in order for a political order to exist. Being rule-based, the political order is normative in the sense that its rules define what should be. As the political philosopher Rainer Forst observes, being a normative order, it is in turn an "order of justification (Forst 2017, p. 44)." In other words, "there are certain justification narratives on which such an order or system is founded (Forst 2017, p. 44)." The exercise of power is being able to determine, occupy, distort, undermine, or seal off the space of reasons within which the justification and legitimacy of the rules that constitute and organize the political order is determined. The essential power is to define the values, norms, and rules of the political order. Power is the capacity to "determine the space of reasons within which social or political relations are being framed—relations which form a structured, durable, and stable social order of action and justification (Forst 2017, p. 49)." The legitimacy of power is contingent upon the validity of the justifications it rests upon.

It is generally recognized that the first question of politics is: "What confers authority on government (Grayling 2018, p. 50)?" In other words, what constitutes legitimate political power? Government is based upon the possession of coercive power, in that government enacts laws *and* claims monopoly control over the means of force in order to enforce its laws. Given this fundamental coercive dimension of government, it is often suggested that power involves solely a command-obedience relationship. This assumption is grounded in the traditional view of power as a coercive relation. The command conception understands the essence of power as the capacity to command, by the threat or actual deployment of physical force, the obedience of others. The command theory equates political power with the organization of violence. From this perspective political power is contingent upon one's capacity to project physical force, for in open conflict an opposing power can only be controlled or destroyed by overwhelming physical force. Militarism is a manifestation of a command conception of power; the continual organization of the means of force is the very foundation of political power. If political power is conceived in terms of command-obedience, then militarism, the creation and maintenance of a war system, logically follows.

How can the exercise of coercive power be legitimate in a democracy composed of free and equal citizens? It is clear that the command theory of power suffers from moral arbitrariness. It fails to offer a valid basis of justification in the sense that the conception neglects the basic democratic principle that political legitimacy should be based upon the free consent of equal citizens. If citizens are conceived as free and equal, then the exercise of coercive power must be based in the consent of citizens. Consent means that the people freely endorse the founding values and principles of the government and its laws and policies in light of those values and principles (Rawls 1971, 1993, 1997; Rawls/Kelly 2001). Such consent renders the coercive power of government justifiable and legitimate. Democracy is, therefore, grounded in a consensual theory of power.

The consensual theory of power understands power as a collective act grounded in consensual agreement (Arendt 1970; Sharp 1973). As Hannah Arendt suggests: "Power is indeed the essence of all government but violence is not. Violence is by nature instrumental ... power ... is an end in itself (Arendt 1970, p. 51)." Power requires legitimacy, derived from consent, and, therefore, power can never grow out of coercive force. Power is the ability to act in concert, and such action is grounded in consensual agreement. Therefore, "[p]ower is never the property of an individual; it belongs to a group and remains in existence only so long as the group keeps together (Arendt 1970, p. 44)." The consensual nature of power is revealed "[w]here commands are no longer obeyed, the means of violence are of no use; and the question of this obedience is not decided by the command-obedience relation but by opinion, and of course, by the number with those who share it. Everything depends on the power behind the violence ... (Arendt 1970, p. 49)." Consensual power is the opposite of command; it is created by free, non-coercive consent, not by the threat of force.

The principle of government by consent is at the core of democracy. As John Dewey put it: "Democracy.... means a way of living together in which mutual and free consultation rule instead of force ... (Cited in Tozer 1993)." Political consent refers to mutually recognized agreements that are justifiable and therefore politically legitimate. John Rawls refers to as the *liberal principle of legitimacy*. This principle asserts that the exercise of coercive power by the state should be exercised only in ways that all citizens may reasonably be expected to endorse or have no reason to reject (Rawls/Kelly 2001). As Rawls suggests:

> A legitimate regime is such that its political and social institutions are justifiable to all
> citizens – to each and every one – by addressing their reason, theoretical and practical.
> Again: a justification of the institutions of the social world must be, in principle, available
> to everyone, and so justifiable to all who live under them. The legitimacy of a liberal regime
> depends on such a justification (Rawls/Freeman 2007, p. 13).

In other words, *valid justification, rather than coercive force, is the source of political legitimacy in a democracy.*

1.2 The Right to Justification

From a moral perspective, when power is exercised without the consent of those subjected to it, thereby being imposed, it is morally *arbitrary*. The basic moral constraint on power, upon which its legitimacy is dependent, is whether it is justifiable to all those affected by it. Justice therefore is based upon a basic right of justification: the idea that the equal, intrinsic, human dignity of each person provides the foundation of a basic human right to receive justification, and a correlate duty to offer justification to others, as a fundamental matter of respect (Forst 2012, 2014a, b). As free and equal, citizens have a basic right to ask for reasons of justification and to question those reasons—a right not be subjected to norms and practices that reasonably persons would have grounds to reject (Forst 2012; Rawls 1971; Scanlon 2000).

The right and duty of justification is grounded in respect for persons. Other persons are not means, but are ends in themselves; all possess equal inherent value and dignity that obligates one to treat each person with respect. This respect further structures a duty to offer all people justification for the basic moral norms that will govern their relationship as citizens (Forst 2012). As Rawls maintains: "Citizens are equal in that they regard one another as having an equal right to determine, and to assess upon due reflection, the first principles of justice by which the basic structure of their society is to be governed (Rawls 1997, p. 309)." Respect for persons demands that each person has a *basic right to justification*, a right to be offered, and a correlative duty to offer, valid justification for the social and political rules and institutions to which they are subjected. This right provides a moral ground for consensual power, which in turn provides a rational basis for the legitimacy of a democratic structure and distribution of power (Forst 2012).

From this perspective, it can be argued that respect for persons is the condition of non-domination; the condition of persons not being forced to comply to demands and practices that are unjustifiable, and having reason therefore to reject them. In positive terms, respect manifests as deserving and receiving valid justifications. In turn, if you deserve valid justifications for the norms and practices you are subject to, justifications that are based upon sharable reasons, then so does everyone. To be subjected to norms and practices that do not have valid justification is to suffer domination, and domination in turn lays the ground for various types of oppression.

From this perspective, justice is the practice of justification, and persons should be active agents, and not mere recipients of justice (Forst 2012).

1.3 Invalid Justification

Those who seek power often traffic in invalid, ideological justifications that distort the space of justification. Unjust social structures and practices are sustained by invalid justifications and patterns of thought that constitute "cultural violence ... the symbolic sphere of our existence ... that can be used to justify or legitimize direct or structural violence ... and thus rendered acceptable in society (Galtung 1990, pp. 291–292)." The validity of these justifications fail to survive when brought under the light of critical scrutiny, and often involve attacks on truth, expertise, language, and education. The delegitimization of truth, expressed as hostility to verifiable reality and even the very idea of truth itself, is a prominent feature of attempts to distort and undermine the space of justifications. It is often executed by repeated dishonesty and the advocacy of conspiracy theories. Furthermore, accompanying efforts to delegitimize institutions that promote and sustain independent thought, in particular, universities and the free press, are continually pursued, which in turn undermines the value of expertise as a source of truth. This attack on truth and its institutions leads to the delegitimization of valid moral and legal norms. This normative delegitimization seals off the space of justificatory reasons, which degrades and debases public deliberation, turning it into mere sloganeering and appeals to fear and anger, rather than reasoned argument (Frum 2018; Snyder 2017, 2018; Stanley 2018).

Reardon identifies patriarchy as perhaps the most fundamental system of invalid, ideological justification for the perpetuation of political and social injustice. *Patriarchy* is an ideological system structured in terms of a hierarchy of human relationships and value that is based in socially constructed gender differentiation. A naturalistic understanding of gender (that gender differentiation and inequality is a natural phenomenon) is the defining element of patriarchy; in truth, however, it is a social construct. As such, socially constructed gender differentiation justifies unequal power to males who exhibit a particular set of 'masculine' values and traits, excluding and oppressing those who do not, whether biologically male or female. As Reardon suggests,

> "Gender", as the concept is generally used in works that deal with the differences and inequalities between men and women, is a socially derived concept, a culturally varied construct that assigns to men and women a set of cultural roles and social functions, only minimally determined by their respective reproductive and sexual characteristics (Reardon 2010, p. 13).

Unequal, hierarchical, and exclusionary gender differentiation serves as both the defining structural element of the patriarchal social system and as the basis of its ideological justification. As Reardon maintains:

> Through the tenacity of patriarchal thinking, hierarchal arrangements of society based on race, class and gender, buttressed by inequitable access to the benefits of production based on what has become global, corporate, free market capitalism, psychologically reinforced by the fear of others engendered by fundamentalist religious precepts and ultranationalist xenophobia, patriarchy as the basic paradigm of human institutions continues to prevail (Reardon 2010, p. 14).

Patriarchy thereby functions as an ideological system of justification for social injustice, that is, upon critical scrutiny, normatively invalid.

1.4 Democratic Counter Point: A Critically Informed Citizenry

As Reardon suggests, the capacity of citizens to engage in critically informed participation in public deliberation and justification is necessary for the pursuit of peace and justice. This capacity is referred to by Reardon as political efficacy. Political efficacy is not necessarily a matter *per se* of *what* to think; it is more fundamentally about *how* to think. At the core of this capacity for thinking is *critical reflection, which* pertains to the analysis and critique of invalid, possibly hegemonic, justifications which serve as ideological, culturally violent justifications for structures of domination and oppression. As discussed above, patriarchy and militarism are primary examples of arbitrary power structures resting upon unfair, and thus, invalid justification. Critical reflection further involves an understanding and critique of the functioning and impact of power within social institutions, knowledge and analysis of the structural dimensions of social life, and the nature of ethical and moral justification. It requires that everyone submit their values, principles, and claims to critical scrutiny as a test of their validity through the processes of ethical and moral justification. Furthermore, in addition to the capacity to critical reflect on and critically analyze invalid justifications, there are two types of justification that justify the validity of normative claims: ethical and moral. As Forst suggests: "Ethical values and universally binding norms represent *different answers* to *different practical questions* that correspond to *different validity criteria* (Forst 2002, p. 28)."

1.5 Ethical Justification

Ethical justification refers to justification based upon the coherence between our political norms, rules, and actions *and* the values (goods) that define our individual conception of the good life, in relation to particular others (e.g., family), and the collective self-understanding and identity of the social group (cultural, national, international, global). When we employ ethical justification, we ask: Will the choice of political norms, rules, and actions realize our values, our self-understanding of who we are and want to be (Habermas 1996)? From the perspective of ethical justification, political legitimacy is a collective's "ethical self-clarification" (Habermas 1988b, p. 245).

Ethical reflection suggests the possibility of a common political identity grounded in generally shared political values; the generally shared affirmation of moral political principles and norms that have achieved moral justification (to be discussed below) and thus are recognized as higher-order political values. Here there is a valid distinction between ethical and political identity. The basis of a unified political community can be found in agreement and acceptance of shared moral and constitutional principles (Forst 2002, p. 101). The noted American historian Arthur Schlesinger expresses this idea: "Yet what has held the American people together in the absence of a common ethnic origin has been precisely a common adherence to ideals of democracy and human rights … (Schlesinger 1992, p. 123)." We can affirm and value general moral political principles and thereby form an ethical political identity that is common across the plurality of differences. These ethical values, however, must be generally accepted as valid, and that validity is contingent upon general moral justification. This point suggests that, while publicly shared ethical values can serve as valid justificatory reasons, moral justification is primary in the context of general political values and principles. Political justification, legitimacy, and consent require valid moral reasons (Rawls 1993).

1.6   Moral Justification

The hallmark of human reason of all kinds, theoretical, practical, and instrumental, is that its validity is grounded in intersubjective mutual understanding and agreement (Habermas 1984, 1995, 1996, 2011). The validity of moral justification rests upon intersubjective mutual understanding and agreement concerning moral principles *under fair conditions*. This constitutes the "moral point of view"; moral norms and principles are to be justified in terms of fairness. A moral principle is reasonable and hence valid if it can be mutually agreed to under fair conditions. Valid moral norms must pass the test of fairness, resting on valid, sharable reasons. The process of justification of moral norms goes through a procedure of deliberation that is structured and defined in terms of *fairness*, such that the fair conditions of agreement between the parties "represent what citizens would adopt in a situation that is fair between them (Rawls/Freeman 1999, p. 310)." The moral justifiability of the values and principles agreed to as a result of deliberation between those affected is derived from the normative validity of the criteria of fairness that regulate the deliberation. In other words, "[t]he fairness of the circumstances under which agreement is reached, transfers to the principles of justice agreed to … What is just is defined by the outcome of the procedure itself (Rawls/Freeman 1999, pp. 310–311)." This constitutes a methodological approach to moral justification known as *constructivism*, an approach to moral justification that determines the validity of moral norms from within the criteria of fairness, understood as presuppositions that constitute the nature of moral judgment (Rawls/Freeman 1999).

There are at least three *criteria of fairness*: *generality (reciprocity of mutual agreement), impartiality, and equality*. These criteria are the presuppositions of fairness in the sense that they constitute the meaning of what fairness is, as the basic rules of a game define the game.

First, moral justification is a demand for reasons that can be *accepted* by one's social group (whatever that group may be, as defined by who is affected), and they must be *generally acceptable* (Forst 2012); Forst refers to this criterion of fairness as the criterion of *generality*: "… the objections of any person who is affected … cannot be disregarded, and the reasons adduced in support of the legitimacy of a norm must be capable of being shared by all (Forst 2012, p. 49)." *Generality* is conceptualized by Rawls as *reciprocity of mutual agreement*, which requires that the terms that regulate the moral and political relationship between citizens must be acceptable to all affected (Forst 2002, 2012, 2014a; Rawls 1993; Rawls/Freeman 1999; Rawls/Kelly 2001; Scanlon 2002). Generality or reciprocity of agreement therefore requires that we "… arrange our common political life on terms that others cannot reasonably reject (Rawls 1993, p. 124)." As Thomas Scanlon suggests: "thinking about right and wrong is, at the most basic level, thinking about what could be justified to others on grounds that they, if appropriately motivated, could not reasonably reject (cited in Sen, p. 197)." This principle establishes the ground of justification—"categorically binding norms against whose validity no good reasons can speak (Forst 2012, p. 21)."

In turn, to achieve legitimate general acceptance the moral claim or moral norm must be impartial. "Bare-faced appeal to self-interest will not do (Singer 2011, p. 93)." Fairness entails impartiality (Rawls 1971; Rawls/Kelly 2001): "A man whose moral judgments always coincided with his interests could be suspect of having no morality at all (Rawls/Freeman 1999, p. 54)." At a basic level of understanding, to be fair is to be unbiased; fairness demands that we impartially justify our claims *as well as* consider the claims and interests of others.

What Forst conceives as the "principle of reciprocal justification" is an expression of impartiality in two different ways: First, the idea of the reciprocity of contents: "… one cannot raise any specific claims while rejecting like claims of others (Forst 2012, p. 49)." To claim the validity of a norm for oneself and not for others is to violate impartiality as a kind of reciprocity, for in this case one is biased in favor of one's interests. Impartiality also entails the idea of the "reciprocity of reasons": "one cannot simply assume that others share one's perspective, evaluations, convictions, interests, or needs … (Forst 2012, p. 49)." The terms of the agreement must also be impartial in the sense that to project the specific meaning of one's terms onto others, is to bias the agreement in one's favor.

Both the criteria of generality and impartiality in turn, rest upon equality. Fairness requires that the parties to the agreement pertaining to shared moral norms have equal standing in the sense that they are symmetrically situated as equals in the deliberation. Equal standing in turn ensures the equal consideration of their interests in the deliberation. A valid moral norm must give equal weight to the interests of all affected. Equality expresses the point that "our own interests are no more important than the interests of others (Singer 2011, p. 111)." From a constructivist perspective, moral justification is grounded in the criteria of fairness-impartiality, equality, and generality-reciprocity. The first question of justice is: what constitutes legitimate political power? Politically legitimate power is in principle limited by particular general ethical-political values and moral norms which constitute the rational basis of its legitimacy. The exercise of power is arbitrary when it does not adhere to particular ethical and moral constraints that define the boundaries of its justifiability and hence legitimate exercise.

1.7 Conclusion

Reardon's call for a democratic redistribution of power grounded in a critical analysis of patriarchy and militarism as ideological justifications of a global hierarchy of unequal power, points toward the discursive nature of power and thus the central role of ethical and moral justification and the critique of invalid justifications. The establishment and enactment of democratic institutions wherein citizens can participate in processes of public justification, including the critique of invalid justifications such as patriarchy and militarism, is a necessary condition for the democratic distribution of power. The institutionalization of a basic structure of justification is necessary but not sufficient. Citizens need to possess the capacity to participate in the practice of public justification. In order for citizens to be democratic agents of consensual power, they must be capable of *and* committed to reasoned justificatory argument. Reardon captures this democratic necessity: "Militarism and sexism require that service and sacrifice be performed without reflection. Freedom and equality, to the contrary, require the full development of the reflective and analytic capacities of all citizens (Reardon 1981, p. 12)." When Reardon asserts that the primary purpose of peace education is the development of the political efficacy of future citizens, it is this capacity as agents of justice that she invokes. The empowerment of future citizens through development of their political efficacy builds a formidable bulwark against arbitrary power and constitute both the necessary conditions and the means for realization of a just peace.

References

Arendt, H. (1970). *On violence*. New York: Harcourt Brace & Company.
Forst, R. (2002). *Contexts of justice: Political philosophy beyond liberalism and communitarianism*. Berkeley: University of California Press.

Forst, R. (2012). *The Right to justification* (J. Flynn, Trans.). New York: Columbia University Press.

Forst, R. (2014a). *Justification and critique: Towards a critical theory of politics* (C. Cronin, Trans.). Cambridge, UK: Polity Press.

Forst, R. (Ed.). (2014b). *Justice, democracy and the right to justification: Rainer Forst in dialogue*. New York: Bloomsbury.

Frum, D. (2018). *Trumpocracy: The corruption of the American Republic*. New York: HarperCollins.

Galtung, J. (1990). Cultural violence. *Journal of Peace Research, 27*(3), 291–305.

Grayling, A. C. (2018). *Democracy and its crisis*. London: OneWorld Publications.

Habermas, J. (1984). *The theory of communicative action*. Boston: Beacon Press.

Habermas, J. (1995). Reconciliation through the public use of reason: Remarks on John Rawls's political liberalism. *Journal of Philosophy, XCII* (3 March), 109–131.

Habermas, J. (1996). *Between facts and norms: Contributions to a discourse theory of law and democracy*. Cambridge, Mass.: MIT Press.

Habermas, J. (2011). 'Reasonableness' versus 'true,' or the morality of worldviews. In J. G. Finlayson & F. Freyenhagen (Eds.), *Habermas and Rawls: Disputing the political* (pp. 92–113). New York: Routledge.

Rawls, J. (1971). *A theory of justice*. Cambridge: Belknap Press of Harvard University Press.

Rawls, J. (1993). *Political liberalism*. New York: Columbia University Press.

Rawls, J. (1997). The idea of public reason revisited. *The University of Chicago Law Review, 64* (3), 765–807.

Rawls, J., & Freeman, S. (Eds.). (1999). *John Rawls: Collected papers*. Cambridge: Harvard University Press.

Rawls, J., & Freeman, S. R. (2007). *Lectures on the history of political philosophy*. Cambridge, Mass.: Belknap Press of Harvard University Press.

Rawls, J., & Kelly, E. (2001). *Justice as fairness: A restatement*. Cambridge, Mass.: Harvard University Press.

Reardon, B. A. (1981). Militarism and sexism: Influences on education for war. *UME Connexion, 9*(3), 1–29.

Reardon, B. A. (1996). *Sexism and the war system* (1st Syracuse University Press ed.). Syracuse, N.Y.: Syracuse University Press.

Reardon, B. A. (2010). Women and human security: A feminist framework and critique of the prevailing patriarchal security system. In B. A. Reardon & A. Hans (Eds.), *The gender imperative: Human security vs. state security*. New Delhi, India: Routledge.

Reardon, B. A. (2018). On Frameworks and purposes: A response to Dale Snauwaert's Review of Jeffrey Sachs' *The Age of Sustainable Development*: Patriarchy is the problem. *Global Campaign for Peace Education*. Retrieved from http://www.peace-ed-campaign.org/patriarchy-is-the-problem/.

Reardon, B. A., & Snauwaert, D. T. (2011). Reflective pedagogy, cosmopolitanism, and critical peace education for political efficacy: A discussion of Betty A. Reardon's assessment of the field. *In Factis Pax: Journal of Peace Education and Social Justice, 5*(1), 1–14.

Reardon, B. A., & Snauwaert, D. T. (Eds.). (2015a). *Betty A. Reardon: A pioneer in education for peace and human rights*. Heidelberg: Springer.

Reardon, B. A., & Snauwaert, D. T. (Eds.). (2015b). *Betty A. Reardon: Key texts in gender and peace*. Heidelberg: Springer.

Scanlon, T. (2002). Rawls on justification. In S. R. Freeman (Ed.), *The Cambridge companion to Rawls* (pp. 139–167). Cambridge: Cambridge University Press.

Scanlon, T. M. (2000). *What we owe to each other*. Cambridge, MA: Belknap Press.

Schlesinger, A. J. (1992). *The disuniting of America: Reflections on a multicultural society*. New York: Norton.

Sharp, G. (1973). *The politics of nonviolent action*. Boston: Porter Sargent.

Singer, P. (2011). *The expanding circle: Ethics, evolution, and moral progress*. Princeton, NJ: Princeton University Press.

Snyder, T. (2017). *On tyranny: Twenty lessons from the twentieth century* (1st ed.). New York: Tim Duggan Books.

Snyder, T. (2018). *The road to unfreedom: Russia, Europe, America*. New York: Tim Duggan Books.

Stanley, J. (2018). *How fascism works: The politics of us and them* (1st ed.). New York: Random House.

Tozer, S., et al. (1993). *School and society: Educational practice as social expression*. New York: McGraw Hill.

Chapter 2
"Peace Education for Global Citizenship" The Genuine Global Dimension of Betty Reardon's Concept of Peace Education

Werner Wintersteiner

> *A strategy of change, designed for the achievement of peace and the pursuit of human fulfillment, in short, the antithesis of the present world order.*
>
> Betty Reardon 1978

Peace education and Global Citizenship Education are not only related but also interconnected fields. In this paper, I analyze the 'global' in Betty Reardon's concept of peace education. I argue that peace education has a genuine Global Citizenship Education dimension, or (to put it the other way around) peace education is a necessary element of Global Citizenship Education. I state that this connection is nowhere elaborated as clearly as in Betty Reardon's work. Moreover, her concepts offer an excellent starting point for what Michalinos Zembylas calls a "productive conversation" between critical peace education and postcolonial and decolonial approaches (Zembylas 2018, 18).

2.1 The Challenge of Global Citizenship Education

In the last years, Global Citizenship Education (GCED) has become a very popular pedagogical concept (which does not necessarily mean that it is likewise implemented in educational practice, especially in Europe). Namely the appeal of then UN Secretary General Ban Ki-Moon, "we must foster global citizenship" (Ki-Moon 2012) and the fact that UNESCO has adopted GCED as one of its key strategies (since 2013) has essentially contributed to disseminate this educational approach. Furthermore, GCED is integrated as one of the key issues into the educational program of the Sustainable Development Goals (SDGs). Target 4.7 reads (UN 2015):

Prof. Dr. Werner Wintersteiner, German Didactics, Klagenfurt University, Austria; Email: Werner.Wintersteiner@aau.at.

© Springer Nature Switzerland AG 2019
D. T. Snauwaert (ed.), *Exploring Betty A. Reardon's Perspective on Peace Education*, Pioneers in Arts, Humanities, Science, Engineering, Practice 20, https://doi.org/10.1007/978-3-030-18387-5_2

By 2030, ensure that all learners acquire the knowledge and skills needed to promote sustainable development, including, among others, through education for sustainable development and sustainable lifestyles, human rights, gender equality, promotion of a culture of peace and non-violence, *global citizenship* and appreciation of cultural diversity and of culture's contribution to sustainable development. (My emphasis)

It may be by chance that "education for global citizenship" here is mentioned immediately after "promotion of a culture of peace", but it definitely reflects an inherent logic that both are mentioned in one breath. For global citizenship (education) loses much of its meaning and its transformational energy if it is not closely linked to the concept of a culture of peace, which implies the need for a profound change of our basic assumptions, ways of life, habits and cultural practices.

However, the growing popularity of GCED is also problematic. While it is natural that there are different GCED discourses and multiple practices, Vanessa Andreotti has very clearly shown the difference between a 'humanitarian' and a critical approach. She criticizes a GCED "based on a moral obligation to a common humanity, rather than on a political responsibility for the causes of poverty." She argues that a politics and education on this moral basis "end up reproducing unequal (paternalistic) power relations and increasing the vulnerability of the recipient" (Andreotti 2006, p. 42). What she describes as humanitarian approach or "soft global citizenship education" is, in my view, indeed a soft variant of a neoliberal global worldview, expressed in Francis Fukuyama's claim of the "End of History" as the ultimate triumph of Western liberal democracy. His liberal cosmopolitanism supposes that other systems, all of them inferior to the West, are slowly disappearing, giving way to the liberal capitalist system.

The criticism of this Eurocentric and Western-centric worldview is justified, but we have to keep in mind that there is an even more aggressive variant, defending openly and recklessly the interests of the Western elite, supposedly threatened by the rise of other ideologies and worldviews, in this moment mainly so-called "political Islam", which is defined as "the enemy" par excellence.[1] Ironically, this nationalist and reactionary political current, gaining more and more influence all over the world, develops as well a "global worldview", considers the global as its political arena, and thus is functionalizing GCED for its own interests. Under the umbrella of 'internationalization' or 'globalization' of education, GCED is used to strengthen the trend of commodification of the educational system. Within this logic, students are trained to function as "citizens who are mobile, competitive, and entrepreneurial" (Shultz 2011, p. 17), perfectly adapted to the globalized economic structures. This is not a 'soft' GCED (in Andreotti's terminology), but a 'harder',

---

[1]This is in line with Stefan Weidner's distinction between the two currents within the Western thinking, the 'cosmopolitan' liberal variant, represented ideal-typically by Fukuyama whose universalism blurs all existing differences, and the culturalistic variant, formulated by Huntington with the unavoidable "clash of civilizations" who overemphasizes the differences (Weidner 2018). (For an English review of this German book see: https://en.qantara.de/content/non-fiction-stefan-weidner-on-the-future-of-the-west-next-level-cosmopolitanism).

openly egoistic variant. Admittedly, this harder version is seldom openly defended in academic publications, but it can be reconstructed from educational policies.

Recently, the OECD has started, within its *Programme for International Student Assessment* (PISA), assessing the "global competences" of the learners. This periodic testing program on student performance (15 year-olds) across countries has proved a very influential factor on educational policies in all OECD member states.[2] This leads one to expect that testing so called global competences will soon have an impact on the curricula in the respective countries. The PISA approach seems to be an attempt to reconcile the 'hard' and a 'soft' GCED. The OECD defines global competence as "the capacity to examine local, global and intercultural issues, to understand and appreciate the perspectives and world views of others, to engage in open, appropriate and effective interactions with people from different cultures, and to act for collective well-being and sustainable development" (PISA 2018). Whereas the overall aim of "collective well-being" and the understanding and appreciation of "world views of others" is postulated, there is no mention of any injustice in the world order, nor allusion to the colonial past that has led to this order and that still forms the background of global relationships, or to racism as the ideology to justify these inequalities.

Thus, we can roughly distinguish three uses of Global Citizenship Education – a neo-imperialistic (or 'hard'), a liberal humanistic (paternalistic or 'soft'), and a critical (postcolonial) use. Admittedly, in practice we find mixed approaches. One more reason to highlight the political and emancipatory potential of GCED which does not only help learners to act as truly global citizens but which, in so doing, contributes to create a global public sphere, and thus, the necessary precondition for global citizenship. In line with Andreotti, Karen Pashby defines GCED as "a project of decolonization", encouraging "students to adopt a critical understanding of globalization, to reflect on how they and their nations are implicated in local and global problems and to engage in intercultural perspectives" (Pashby 2012, p. 9).

In the following table, I contrast an emancipatory use not only with the soft use identified by Andreotti (2006), but in particular with the 'hard' mainstream use. For I realize that the more business globalization leads to marketization of education and knowledge, the more the neoliberal approach to GCED is common. There is a risk that it will be considered in the long run as the normal and proper approach. All three approaches are 'Western' from their background but the critical approach connects with postcolonial concepts of citizenship from the 'South'.

This Table 2.1 may help to criticize existing and upcoming dangerous trends in education. But first and foremost, it shows the emancipatory potential of critical Global Citizenship Education and its close affinity to peace education in general:

– GCED deepens and concretizes the rather abstract or metaphoric notions of global education and global citizenship, it takes the formula at its word

---

[2]For an overall view of PISA see: http://www.oecd.org/pisa/.

Table 2.1 Neo-imperialistic, liberal and critical Global Citizenship Education

Dimension	Hard (Neo-Imperialistic) Global (Citizenship) Education	Soft (Liberal) Global Citizenship Education	Critical (De-colonial) Global Citizenship Education
Pedagogy			
Main target groups	Global elites (in the North and the South)	People in Western countries	All, with a special focus on the underprivileged groups
Concept of education	*Global competences* Skilling learners for the global economy, and insofar for global issues, supports (silently) the project of global coloniality	*Global awareness* Skilling learners for greater awareness of some global problems and injustices	*(Self) awareness within the global* Skilling learners as (global) responsible citizens, challenges overtly the project of global coloniality
Educational virtue	*Competitiveness* "Cosmopolitanism of the fittest"[a]	*Solidarity* Moral obligation of the privileged	*Solidarity* "Planetary conviviality"[a]
(Educational) interest in globalization	*Opportunities* Focus on the own individual opportunities	*Development* A chance for the 'development' of the poorer nations	*Democracy* A new arena for the struggle for global justice: globalization from below
Global worldview			
Paradigm	*Globalism (business globalization)* Western-centric universalism, as the imperial form of "methodological nationalism"	*Cosmopolitanism (globalism with a "good face")* A 'sentimental' universalism, helping the poorer to 'develop' = to adapt to the Western model	*"Cosmopolitan localism"[1]* A pluriversal world without any domination
Self-image	*The entrepreneur* Confirms and defends the own position, a mostly unspoken feeling of superiority	*The savior* A mostly unspoken (and often unconscious) feeling of superiority, behind an humanitarian engagement	*The fellow* Problematizes the own standpoint, self-criticism of Eurocentrism and metro-centrism
"Homeland Earth"	*Common interests of humankind* (which are hardly anything but the own interests), but even more concerned with the 'threat' for the own interests by other players	*Common interests of humankind* Believes that this is a way to reduce inequalities	*Differences in positions and interests* Emphasizes global power structures and thus divergent interests while striving for the survival and a good life for all human and other beings

(continued)

Table 2.1 (continued)

Dimension	Hard (Neo-Imperialistic) Global (Citizenship) Education	Soft (Liberal) Global Citizenship Education	Critical (De-colonial) Global Citizenship Education
Global inequalities	Laments the global inequalities without any ambition for radical change, considers the own country (mostly without evidence) as a victim of globalization	Tackles some of the global inequalities	Deals with the root causes of global inequalities, including (but not exclusively) the "war system"
Knowledge	Takes the dominant Western knowledge produced about the international order for granted as "the knowledge"	Takes the dominant Western knowledge produced about the international order in general for granted as "the knowledge"	Criticizes the epistemic violence of our knowledge production, works on a critical assessment of any knowledge
Overall picture			
Keyword	*Interconnectedness* (obscuring the differences in political power, wealth, and epistemic power)	*Interconnectedness* (mostly obscuring the differences in political power, wealth, and epistemic power)	*Inequity and interconnectedness* (as an argument for changing the unjust world order)
Overall approach	Accepts the world as it is	Wants the world to change but does not tackle the power structures as such	Strives for fundamental structural and cultural transformations

Source The author; colon 2 is inspired by Andreotti (2006)
[a]Formulations taken from Mignolo (2011)

- GCED defines as its overall goal to contribute to overcome the unjust world order, the war system, and a way of production and relations of production that destroy the natural bases of human life
- In so doing, GCED reflects the own standpoint of (Western) teachers and learners, and their privileged role as part of the unjust world system
- GCED combines both the cosmopolitan view of the unity of humankind and the postcolonial critique of universalism as Western dominance: planetary consciousness *and* local needs and views from the own standpoint; there is not one, but many GCEDs
- GCED takes the epistemic violence of the world order into account.

Like peace education, GCED is not simply concerned about the competences of the individual learners, but it sees also the structures of the educational systems at stake. This parallel shows one more time the strong connection to peace education: the global approach, the political approach and social purpose of global justice are the common features. For GCED has its origins not only in development education, global education or anti-racist education, but to a large extent also in peace education. Global Citizenship Education, in my view, is the broader concept, while peace education focuses more concretely on violence as a main obstacle to a just world order. Critical GCED needs its peace education dimension in order to differ from its soft and neo-imperialistic variants, while peace education needs the concept of global citizenship in order to elaborate on its political dimension.

2.2 Peace, Cosmopolitism and Education in the Post WW II Era

Peace education (in its Western tradition) is a child of the democratic and revolutionary movements of the 19th century, and as such imbued by both bourgeois cosmopolitanism as well as by proletarian internationalism – two opposed currents, but ultimately both within the Western epistemic framework. In some sense, the peace (education) movements were a product of the first wave of globalization which is described by Marx and Engels in their *Communist Manifesto* stating that the bourgeoisie "through its exploitation of the world market [has] given a cosmopolitan character to production and consumption in every country" and "universal inter-dependence of nations […] as in material, so also in intellectual production." (Marx/Engels 2010, p. 16).

Thus, from the outset, peace education has been an international endeavor, and peace education, understood as civic education, was education for global citizenship *avant la lettre*. International cooperation among peace educators (in Europe) was already common before 1914. They tried – alas in vain – to overcome enmity and hatred between nations by creating common summer camps with French and German youth, on the eve of World War I. After the Great War, these efforts resulted in the foundation of the *International Bureau of Education* IBE (founded in 1925, today integral part of UNESCO), the *International Committee of Intellectual Co-operation* (CICI, founded in 1922) and its executing agency, the International Institute of Intellectual Co-operation (IICI). Especially the *League of Nations* dealt with peace education on a global scale.

After World War II, the foundation of UNICEF (1946), and of UNESCO, in 1945/1946, marked another important step in extending the scope and the international impact of peace education. International understanding, underpinned by an appropriate education, was the guiding idea, set out in some landmark documents, like the UNESCO declaration *Education for international understanding, co-operation and peace* (1974). In the first phase after World War II, the focus was on overcoming nationalist thinking, rivalry and hatred – a very hard and contested task. In such a situation, it was understandable to refer to an abstract (and idealized) world society. This reference was, as it seems, still without a full recognition of the global inequalities and the history of these inequalities – slavery, imperialism, colonialism. However, these early attempts for a genuine global (peace) education were surely influenced (even if this influence was not always recognized) by what we call now the first wave of postcolonial thinking, inspired by authors like Aimé Césaire, Frantz Fanon, but also Paulo Freire and Ivan Illich.

Among the most important steps towards a global peace education I count – beside Betty Reardon's work – Hermann Röhrs' appeal to teach for world citizenship instead of a "German education" (1953, see Röhrs 2000); Herbert Kelman's essay on the cognitive and psycho-social obstacles to cosmopolitan loyalties and how education could overcome them (1968); Elise Boulding's groundbreaking book *Building a global civic culture* (1988); and Martha Nussbaum's plea for an education that prioritizes world citizenship before national citizenship (1996). They all come from different backgrounds: Herbert C. Kelman (USA, born in Austria), a pioneer of peace research, worked as social psychologist with some educational ambitions; peace educator Hermann Röhrs (Germany) came from the *New Education Fellowship* movement, which already in the 1920s formed the *World Alliance for Renewal of Education* – one of the oldest educational organizations with a global aspiration; Elise Boulding (USA, from Norwegian origins) was an influential peace researcher and peace educator, whereas the American philosopher Martha Nussbaum, specialized in ethics, developed the bases for global justice. While their starting points and their results may vary, they all converge in a search for ways to educate for peace from a cosmopolitan perspective. And all of them, as it seems, by struggling against the epistemic dominance of what we call today "methodological nationalism", are overemphasizing the unity of humankind on the whole planet, neglecting or downplaying the contradictions within the world system. In so doing, they remained in the Westernized framework of universalism, now challenged by postcolonial thinkers.

It was in this cosmopolitan context that also Betty Reardon developed her pedagogy, combining education for world citizenship and education for peace. However, it was also the time of the Cold War, when, especially in the U.S., the growing global awareness of a mainstream audience did not necessarily constitute a concern for global justice, but, more often than not, support for U.S. foreign policy (see Reardon/Snauwaert 2015, p. 8).

2.3 Betty Reardon: From World Order Studies to Education for Global Responsibility

In 1963, Betty Reardon, then a classroom teacher, moved to the *Institute for World Order* (IWO, originally called *World Law Fund*) to develop its schools program. For today's postcolonially trained ears, "world order" sounds suspicious, like a (neo-)imperialistic attempt to organize the world according their own (Western) ideals. Indeed, the concept of "world order" emerged from the international peace movement at the eve of World War I. "Organize the world" was in these times for instance the motto of the Austrian peace movement, and this was symbolized in their logo with three interacting gear-wheels. The idea behind was that international regulations (as later partially realized with the creation of the League of Nations) could overcome the international anarchy and thus lead to peace. Economic and structural reasons for war were not fully addressed. World Order Studies after World War II were definitely making one step forward, including an analysis of structural, political and economic reasons of violence and war. However, the protagonists did not yet fully confront themselves with their own position within the global war system, and they believed there could be universal action plans to surmount global injustice, what Walter Mignolo criticizes as "a master plan concocted and executed from above" (Mignolo 2011, p. 293).

As for Betty Reardon, in any case, she worked to shape the "world order approach" of the institute to clearly distinguish it from neocolonial and imperialistic tendencies. In an article from 1975, she opposes World Order Studies to International Relations (as taught at that time). It is interesting, and terrifying at once, that this opposition is to some extent identical with the table in this chapter that opposes neoliberal and critical GCED. It seems that the same struggles remain.

In conformity with the (Western) spirit of these times, issues of the nuclear threat and of the survival of humankind were central concerns of world order studies (Reardon 1973, 1975, 2015a, b). In her work for IWO, Betty Reardon defined world peace as the basic issue and world order as "political education for world citizenship" (Reardon 2015a, b, p. 54). She put multilinguism as a necessary precondition for a democratic world order on the agenda: "Mutual respect and human dignity for all can only exist in a polyglot global society" and advocated the decolonization of education (Reardon 2015a, b, p. 59). Step by step, she developed her distinct peace education concept which she only accomplished after leaving the IWO and while working as an adjunct professor at Teachers College, Columbia University. She formulated the essence of her program in her seminal book *Comprehensive Peace Education* with the significant subtitle *Educating for Global Responsibility* (Reardon 1988).

2.4 Reardon's Approach of Global Citizenship in *Comprehensive Peace Education*

Comprehensive Peace Education is not only Reardon's most influential book, it is in my view as well her clearest statement for a global citizenship education informed by peace research and peace education. She describes itself as a "significant landmark" in her own peace learning (Reardon/Snauwaert 2015, p. 96). In her comprehensive approach, Reardon links three ideas:

– She defines peace education as capacity building for a fundamental transformation of an unjust political and economic world order.
– She pleas for a cultural change as a precondition of the structural change (what later came to be called "culture of peace").

- She conceptualizes the global consciousness needed for this "great transformation".

Put briefly, her concept reads:

> The general purpose of peace education [...] is to promote the development of an authentic planetary consciousness that will enable us to function as global citizens and to transform the present human condition by changing the social structures and the patterns of thought that have created it. This transformational imperative must [...] be at the center of peace education (Reardon 1988, p. x).

To my knowledge, she is – beside the already mentioned Elise Boulding – one of the rare peace educators who have elaborated so early and so explicitly the genuine 'planetary' dimension of peace education. In her concept, peace education is grounded in three core values, termed *planetary stewardship, global citizenship* and *humane relationship*. She explains:

> The value of *stewardship* helps students to develop "a consciousness of their relationship to the whole natural order and their responsibility to assure the health, the survival, and the integrity of the planet" (Reardon 1988, p. 59).

> The value of *citizenship* means to educate students "to be capable of creating a nonviolent, just social order on this planet, a global civic order offering equity to all Earth's people, offering protection for universal human rights, providing the conflicts by nonviolent means [...]" (Reardon 1988, p. 59).

> The value of *humane relationship* is "emphasizing a human order of positive human relationships, relationships that make it possible for all to pursue the realization of individual and communal human potential" (Reardon 1988, p. 59).

In the last chapter of *Comprehensive Peace Education*, these three values are confronted with and integrated into four dimensions of education – an attempt that proves a deep philosophical and spiritual grounding of Reardon's pedagogy. The political is not an isolated element, but embedded in an ethical approach, which comprises an awareness and responsibility not only for the fellow humans, but for the whole planet (Table 2.2).

This wide perspective both in global as well as in historical, and beyond, in spiritual dimensions reveals an intellectual kinship to French philosopher Edgar Morin.[3] When Reardon (just eight years younger than Morin) speaks about the aim to support "trends moving us toward the true humanization of the human species" (Reardon 1988, p. x), this reminds of his concept of the "conscious pursuit of hominization", elaborated in the 1970s and summarized in his Manifesto *Homeland Earth* (Morin 1999, French original 1993). The title *Homeland Earth* itself is a perfect summary of Reardon's concept of the planet as a unity. And like Morin, the philosopher of complexity, Reardon underlines the "centrality of complexity" when

---

[3]I found no evidence of any reference to his work in Reardon, even if both worked as authors for important UNESCO publications on education, for instance: *Betty A. Reardon,* Tolerance: the threshold of peace. UNESCO, 1997; and *Edgar Morin*, Seven Complex Lessons in Education for the Future. UNESCO, 1999.

Table 2.2 Four dimensions of Comprehensive Peace Education

The whole person awareness and participation at all levels	*The ecological and the planetary* Natural balance, ecological ethos
The human context Relationships among various systems, social, interpersonal	*The organic and the developmental* Learning as development of the individual, of the human species, and the species in relationship to other species

Source Reardon (1988), pp. 74–75

she speaks about the necessity of a "paradigm shift from an antagonistic, simplified, fragmented, reductionist view of the world, which now conditions our behaviors and institutions, to a complex, integrated, and holistic view of the world and the human society" (Reardon 1988, p. 56). Her concept of *human integrity* is core for the understanding of her idea of peace and peace education, as well as for her approach to the global: "Human integrity in individual persons is related to and part of a social integrity that would permit us to live without doing violence to each other, to other groups, or to our environment, our parent planet" (1988, p. 58). This resonates with Morin's trichotomy *individual – society – species*, resulting in an "Earth awareness" (Morin 1999, p. 44). Thus, we can state another deep connection – peace education, understood as global citizenship education, is as well education for the preservation of our natural environment, as formulated in the *Earth Charter* in 2000 (http://earthcharter.org/). The *Earth Charter* can be considered as both an integral element of a comprehensive peace education and as the spiritual and political grounding of the current *Education for Sustainable Development*.

In an earlier text, on the *Knowledge Industry* (1978), Reardon attacks the system of knowledge production and its ideological outcomes, at the example of the concept of *development*. She pleas for a reform including an "ever increasing popular participation in the creation and transmission of knowledge" (Reardon/ Snauwaert 2015, 74), similar to Morin's demand for a "cognitive democracy". This insistence on a radical reform of knowledge and of our knowledge production is another common feature of these two otherwise so diverse authors. Reardon's sensitivity for these issues is obviously informed by her study of Paulo Freire's pedagogy, as well as by her studies of sexism and patriarchy as a main fundament of the "war system" (see Reardon 1985). She understands the war system as one of the most important factors of all kinds of inequality and injustice. She focuses her studies on the "unchanging nature of the fundamental hierarchical authoritarianism of the global order" and on "patriarchy as the underlying continuing core of this power order" (Reardon/Snauwaert 2015, p. 72).

We have to keep in mind that Reardon developed her concept of peace education mostly before the second wave of postcolonial thinking, marked by Gayatri Chakravorty Spivak, whose seminal essay *Can the Subaltern Speak* was published in the same year 1988, while for instance the English version of Aníbal Quijano's *Coloniality of Power* was only released in 2000. However, Reardon develops already a fundamental critique of not only injustice and inequity of the existent world order, but also of the dominant knowledge production that produces ideologies to justify and legitimate this order. Feminist studies, in general, developed, hand in hand with postcolonialism, an elementary critique of the current world order, but also of its epistemic basic assumptions. Coming from feminist studies, Reardon anticipated the postcolonial insight that "we must recognize how deeply rooted are the assumptions and values of the present system in the worldviews and behaviors of all of us who have been conditioned by it. Much of the educational struggle must take place within even those who most ardently advocate these changes" (Reardon/Snauwaert 2015, p. 78).

Moreover, postcolonial thinking taught us to understand the "present world order" not only in political, economic or cultural, but also in epistemic terms. Authors like Quijano, Mignolo, Grosfoguel and others are tackling the basic concepts of modernity in which they are detecting the "coloniality of power" – a new challenge for critical thinking, including the peace education community: "There is no longer even the possibility of attaining and pretending to be a metacritical voice, from the left, that condemns all the failures of leftist-like discourses, pretending to find a place uncontaminated from the embodiment of existing power relations", states for instance Mignolo (2002, p. 932). He pleas for a "border thinking" as a strategy that helps develop a "critical cosmopolitanism as an intellectual, political, and ethical project." (p. 936). This "border thinking" means a "double consciousness" or 'nepantla' ("being between two worlds", p. 946). It is an attempt to overcome (neo)colonial worldviews even within the existing power structures. While we can observe that Reardon's thinking is open for many of these ideas we have also to state that these more radical postcolonial approaches are, so far, not fully adopted and worked through by today's peace educators (see Zembylas 2018 for a first attempt).

However, the picture of Betty Reardon as a peace educator for global citizenship would not be complete if only based on her writings. I would like to emphasize her global impact due to her activities in so many different countries and continents and her attempts to create a truly global movement of peace educators. She worked as peace educator all over the world, but especially in Japan; most importantly, she founded and led for many years the *International Institute for Peace Education*, which she considers her "major accomplishment in my work in international cooperation in the development of peace education" (Reardon 2015a, b, p. 12) and for which she earned the Special Honorable Mention of the UNESCO Prize for Peace Education. This institute is a self-organized yearly global gathering of peace educators who understand themselves as scholars-practitioners; she was working with intergovernmental organizations, mainly with the UN and UNESCO in the field of peace education, gender issues, human rights and disarmament. Important documents and guidelines resulted from this activity. Furthermore, she inspired and conceived the *Hague Appeal for Peace Global Campaign for Peace Education*, a global network of peace educators, initiated in 1999, at the occasion of the Hague Conference that brought together almost 10.000 peace activists (see Wintersteiner (2013) for the origins of the campaign). In the manual of the Global Campaign, *Learning to Abolish War*, Reardon and Cabezudo speak about a "conceptual framework for peace education for global citizenship", stating that "peace education must become even more action-oriented, educating students for active, responsible global citizenship" (Reardon/Cabezudo 2002, book I, p. 24).

2.5 Peace Education for Global Citizenship – Towards a Postcolonially Informed Discourse

"Cosmopolitanism is a concern of Western scholarship", states Mignolo (2011, p. 252). However, the idea of Global Citizenship (Education) is not exactly the same as cosmopolitanism, since it simply postulates that all people should have a saying in a (not defined) global world order. It is about equal rights to all humans. And in the last decades, Global Citizenship Education has not only gathered momentum (because of its adoption by the UN and UNESCO), but, more importantly, it is, to my knowledge, more informed by postcolonial thinking than any other pedagogy. Therefore, it seems that GCED can really be a key element of the productive discourse between critical (peace) education and postcolonial and decolonial theories proposed by Zembylas (2018, p. 18). This makes GCED even more important for peace educators. Its postcolonial approach helps getting better insight into the limits of Western thinking (which is also underpinning most peace education), and promotes a revaluation of non-Western forms of knowledge, which may lead to a fuller and more complex picture of both global injustices and the idea of peace. Mainly, GCED has the capacity to stimulate:

– Self-criticism of Western educators, reflecting their own position within the whole world system.
– Recognition not only of the current unjust global system, but also of injustices in the past whose consequences are still effective, like colonialism in neo-colonial relationships.
– Deeper understanding of the origins and the impact of ideologies like racism, the concepts of progress and development, Western universalism and metrocentrism etc.
– Recognition and revaluation of other knowledge than Western scientific approaches.

In this very moment, GCED educators are making first steps towards a "making of non-modernity a legitimate locus of enunciation" (Mignolo 2002, p. 942). Thus, GCED opens the door to a radical decolonialization of cosmopolitanism, "questioning the very imperial epistemic foundations of cosmopolitan claims" (Mignolo 2011, p. 262) as well as of education and pedagogical thinking in general. This process has only begun, and not even all global citizenship educators are ready to go this way. My analysis has tried to show that Betty Reardon's work offers a number of entry points to this new approach, primarily because of her radical feminist critique of the war system. Some of the postcolonial concepts are already preformed, but not elaborated in her work; furthermore, some are not yet represented. On the other hand, sometimes her profound analysis of the war system is lacking in many GCED approaches. A fruitful dialogue could help develop both a timely peace education and an up to date global citizenship education. Certainly, these two approaches are, as I tried to demonstrate, two sides of the same coin.

References

Andreotti, V. (2006). Soft versus critical global citizenship education. *Development Education: Policy & Practice – A Development Education Review, 3*, 40–51.

Andreotti, V., & de Souza, L. M. T. M. (Eds). (2012). *Postcolonial perspectives on global citizenship education*. New York: Routledge.

Boulding, E. (1988). *Building a global civic culture. Education for an interdependent world.* New York: Teachers College Press.

Kelman, H. C. (1968, November). Education for the concept of a world society. *Social Education*, 661–666.

Ki-Moon, B. (2012). *Secretary-general's remarks on launch of education first initiative* [as prepared for delivery], 26 September 2012. https://www.un.org/sg/en/content/sg/statement/2012-09-26/secretary-generals-remarks-launch-education-first-initiative.

Marx, K., & Friedrich E. (2010) (= 1848). *Manifesto of the communist party*. Marxists Internet Archive. https://www.marxists.org/archive/marx/works/download/pdf/Manifesto.pdf.

Mignolo, W. D. (2002). The enduring enchantment (or the epistemic privilege of modernity and where to go from here). *The South Atlantic Quarterly, 101*(4), 927–954.

Mignolo, W. D. (2011). *The darker side of western modernity. Global futures, decolonial options*. Durham: Duke University Press.

Morin, E., & Kern, A. (1999). *Homeland earth. A manifesto for the new millennium*. Creskill: Hampton Press.

Nussbaum, M. (1996). *For love of country?* (J. Cohen, Ed.). Boston: Beacon Press.

Pashby, K. (2012). Questions for global citizenship education in the context of the 'New Imperialism'. For whom, by whom? In V. de Oliveira Andreotti & L. M. T. M. de Souza (Eds.), *Postcolonial perspectives on global citizenship education* (pp. 9–26). New York: Routledge.

PISA 2018 Global Competence. http://www.oecd.org/pisa/pisa-2018-global-competence.htm.

Quijano, A. (2000). Coloniality of power, eurocentrism, and Latin America. *Nepantla: Views from South, 1*(3), 533–580.

Reardon, B. A. (1975). A social education for human survival: A synthesis of practices in international education and peace studies. *Social Studies Review, 15*(1), 42–48.

Reardon, B. A. (2015a) (1973). Transformations for peace and survival: Programs for the 70s. In B. A. Reardon & D. T. Snauwaert (Eds.), *Betty A. Reardon: A pioneer in education for peace and human rights* (pp. 47–69). Cham: Springer.

Reardon, B. A. (2015b) (1978). The knowledge industry. In B. A. Reardon & D. T. Snauwaert (Eds.), *Betty A. Reardon: A pioneer in education for peace and human rights* (pp. 71–80). Cham: Springer.

Reardon, B. A. (1988). *Comprehensive peace education*. New York: Teachers College Press.

Reardon, B. A., & Cabezudo, A. (2002). *Learning to Abolish War: Teaching toward a culture of peace*. New York: The Hague Appeal for Peace Global Campaign for Peace Education.

Reardon, B. A., & Snauwaert, D. T. (Eds.). (2015). *Betty A. Reardon: A pioneer in education for peace and human rights*. Cham: Springer.

Röhrs, H. (2000). Deutsche oder weltbürgerliche Erziehung. In *Gesammelte Schriften, Bd. 14. Studien zur Pädagogik der Gegenwart* (pp. 403–415). Weinheim: Deutscher Studien Verlag.

Shultz, L. (2011). Engaging the multiple discourses of global citizenship education within a Canadian University: Deliberation, contestation, and social justice possibilities. In L. Schultz, A. A. Abdi, & G. H. Richardson (Eds.), *Global citizenship education in post-secondary institutions. Theories, practices, policies* (pp. 13–24). New York: Peter Lang.

Spivak, G. C. (1988). Can the Subaltern Speak? In C. Nelson & L. Grossberg (Eds.), *Marxism and the interpretation of culture* (pp. 271–313). Chicago: University of Illinois Press.

UN. (2015). *United Nations Resolution A/RES/70/1, 21 October 2015. Transforming our world: The 2030 Agenda for Sustainable Development.*

Wintersteiner, W. (2013). Building a global community for a culture of peace: The Hague appeal for peace global campaign for peace education (1999–2006). *Journal of Peace Education, 10* (2), 138–156.

Zembylas, M. (2018). Con-/divergences between postcolonial and critical peace education: Towards pedagogies of decolonization in peace education. *Journal of Peace Education, 15*(1), 1–23.

Chapter 3
Peacebuilding Education in Posttruth Times: Lessons from the Work of Betty A. Reardon

Kevin Kester, Toshiyasu Tsuruhara and Tim Archer

Peacebuilding education has grown significantly since the 1970s. It is included within global curricular programs of schools, international agencies, and non-governmental organizations. The trans-disciplinary field draws on theory, research and pedagogy from other similar educational endeavors, including but not limited to: human rights education, intercultural education, sustainable development education, and social justice education (Harris 2004). Transnational conferences and declarations of the United Nations and civil society organizations, such as the Global Campaign for Peace Education and International Institute of Peace Education, both of which Betty Reardon served as a founder, support the movement (Wintersteiner 2013). Key within the development of the academic and pedagogic fields has been the significant scholarly work of Betty Reardon, who remains an instrumental thinker contributing to peace and human rights education after seven prolific decades in the field (Kester 2010; Reardon/Snauwaert 2015a).

Reardon's work has responded to numerous global crises during the period of her foundational contributions. This chapter will examine several of Reardon's seminal works, as archived in the Betty A. Reardon Papers Special Collection at the University of Toledo. Examining how Reardon intellectually tangled with the crises of the Cold War could assist peace scholars today in dealing with the contemporary challenges and contradictions of teaching for peace in the posttruth era. In this chapter, we explore Reardon's work and what her insights might offer for scholars and practitioners today dealing with the crises of posttruth and the potential end of globalization (Peters 2018). Theoretical and pedagogical implications will be offered at the end of the chapter.

Kevin Kester, Tenure-Track Assistant Professor of International Education and Global Affairs at Keimyung University in Daegu, Korea; Email: kevinajkester@gmail.com.

Toshiyasu Tsuruhara, postdoctoral research associate and undergraduate supervisor at the University of Cambridge, Cambridge, UK.

Tim Archer, final year Ph.D. candidate, Hughes Hall scholar at the University of Cambridge, Cambridge, UK; Email: dta30@cam.ac.uk.

The writing of this chapter was supported by a Keimyung University BISA Research Grant 2018–2019.

© Springer Nature Switzerland AG 2019
D. T. Snauwaert (ed.), *Exploring Betty A. Reardon's Perspective on Peace Education*, Pioneers in Arts, Humanities, Science, Engineering, Practice 20, https://doi.org/10.1007/978-3-030-18387-5_3

3.1   Posttruth and the End of Globalization?

Are we living in a posttruth era? Peters (2018) contends that the contemporary era post-2016 has ushered in the end of globalization. He argues that, "It is a chilling realization that Trump's election to power and Brexit are both, in part, reputedly a result of a series of information interventions in the internal democratic political processes of the US and Britain" (p. 1161). He continues, "Today a new Cold War media strategy can easily disrupt internal political processes and events within Western democracies to present 'fake news', build social media constituencies, and cast doubt on the truth status and role of the Fourth Estate" (p. 1162). Peters argues, "information is the new warfare both against civil society and other countries – a new form of the panopticon, after Foucault, or what Deleuze called 'the control society'" (p. 1163). Kester (2018) similarly writes of his concerns that posttruth acceptance of alt-facts represents "epistemological gerrymandering", where "knowledge has been replaced with unsubstantiated opinion, and opinion has become 'fact'" (p. 1330). Thus, we identify at least two keys areas of posttruth: (1) the promotion of belief and feelings on par with or in lieu of expertise, where expertise is devalued and, if grounded in one's individual unsubstantiated experiences, is accepted as truth; (2) The political manipulation of the aforementioned individual truth allows politicians and others to promote traditional values and agendas cloaked in the notion that such truth is unknown because it has been suppressed. Hence, there is an emotional appeal to the underdog. Crilley (2018) insists that these posttruth challenges must be taken seriously, and that education is appropriately placed to offer a response. Peters (2018) too argues that critical pedagogy and critical thinking remain the best defenses of education in this era of posttruth.

Several other scholars also write of the importance of critique and systemic analysis in times of posttruth populism to counter the rise of lies and deception (Higgins 2016; Keyes 2004; Mejia et al. 2018; Zavarzadeh 2003). Zavarzadeh (2003) and Keyes (2004), for example, indicate the linkages of posttruth to media manipulation and intentional public deception, claiming that this posttruth era began in 2003 in response to the US wars in Afghanistan and Iraq. Zavarzadeh (2003) claims that posttruth arose in this time as a "pedagogy of aesthetics – the anti-conceptual and non-analytical teaching" (p. 32) that affectively supports war from both the populist Right and Left through the promotion of emotional deception aimed at uncritical nationalism and colonialism, beating the drums of war. In this, Zavarzadeh offers a 'realist' critique of the pedagogical evocation of emotion over rationality, a key attribute of contemporary posttruth rhetoric. Zavarzadeh radically argues that this attribute hinders crucial – in his words 'objective' – analytical discussions of cause-and-effect and a re-imagination of the material world. He, like Peters, explains it is important to critique the non-analytical and anti-conceptual pedagogies that buttress exaggeration and deception:

The pedagogy of affect piles up details and warns students against attempting to relate them structurally because any structural analysis will be a causal explanation, and all causal explanations, students are told, are reductive. Teaching thus becomes a pursuit of floating details – a version of games in popular culture. Students "seem" to know but have no knowledge. This is exactly the kind of education that capital requires for its "new" workforce: workers who are educated but nonthinking; skilled at detailed jobs but unable to grasp the totality of the system.... (Zavarzadeh 2003, pp. 5–6).

Hence, avoiding structural analysis and attempts at causal and correlational thinking may open a vacuum where epistemological manipulation might flourish (Kester 2018; MacKenzie/Bhatt 2018). Here, the intoxicating aesthetics of affect (which notably are an important aspect of peace education; see Reardon/Snauwaert 2015a, p. 87) may serve to diminish the crucial role of empiricism in understanding the world, opening space for blatant misrepresentations and falsehoods in media, classrooms, and the government, discussed above. Thus, Peters (2018), Reardon/ Snauwaert (2015a), and Zavarzadeh (2003) each call for reemphasizing critical thinking and empiricism rather than rejecting scientific evidence.

Like Zavarzadeh, d'Ancona (2017) traces posttruth back to the Bush administration, but he goes further to include the campaigns of contemporary climate change deniers (including those within the scientific community), and earlier postmodern humanist philosophers. The relation to postmodern thought is unclear here, and, in contrast, Mejia et al. (2018) contest that this contemporary period of alt-facts and posttruth is nothing new. They trace the posttruth era back (even before d'Ancona and Zavarzadeh), throughout US history claiming that to accept posttruth as something new today is to participate in the erasure of the history of colonialism inflicted upon peoples of color by governments around the world. For them, postmodernism is not the gateway to posttruth, racism is. They call into question the very idea that posttruth has heralded in a new era. Taking this approach, scholars must examine the racial and (a)historical dimensions of posttruth. The employment of ahistoricism as a discursive technology is associated with routine and systematic lying aimed at favoring particular social, racial and political groups over others (Baudrillard 1995; Bhambra 2017). MacKenzie/Bhatt (2018) claim that the remedy to posttruth requires rebuilding trust as core to a functioning global civilization, while d'Ancona (2017), like Peters (2018), calls for digital media literacy. Science and education, then, should be enhanced and taken more seriously not as a totality (remembering the foundational critiques from postmodernism), but to challenge false belief and opinion masqueraded as truth across the public media, especially when such false beliefs carry severe racial and civilizational consequences (Crilley 2018; Higgins 2016).

Looking back onto Reardon's work to trace how militarism, sexism and racism are interlinked, and how she proposed to address these gross violations of human dignity and inhibitors to cultures of peace, we have come to understand that Reardon argues for both critical affect *and* critical analysis as important to disrupting oppressive regimes – in this case, the problematic lies and deception of posttruth. We contend this is especially important because posttruth undermines discourses of diversity by grossly essentializing difference (Leonardo/Zembylas

2013). Yet, at the same time, there is a danger in rational counter-responses that may further entrench the posttruth divides if truth is presented as a domain of the academy of science alone. This is, for us, a false dichotomy (that science equates truth); and yet it is one that has been so well essentialized and exaggerated by the posttruth deceptions to bolster the rationale for the political manufacturing of alt-facts (see Hutchison 2016). Thus, drawing on Reardon, we contend two points: (1) it is a moral imperative to counter lying and deception with education for critical inquiry toward new political possibilities; and (2) to do so, peace educators must marry critical thinking with critical affect, empiricism with philosophy, and maintain a keen eye toward the limits of each. In the end, we argue that the way out of the posttruth quandary is not via stricter rationality and righteousness from the academy but through serious engagement with educational affect and theoretical analysis in harmony. We turn now to Reardon's foundational contributions.

3.2 Reardon's Key Contributions to Peace Education

Social and political changes—from the Cold War to globalization to posttruth—provide the backdrop to Reardon's key contributions to peace education. We suggest that her responses to the earlier challenges of the Cold War and globalization offer instruction on how one might respond to the contemporary challenges of the posttruth age. Here, we will review and comment on some of Reardon's primary contributions to peace education. First and foremost, particularly in light of the subject of discussion, we place politics and possibility at the core of peace inquiry. The educational endeavour, drawing on Reardon, should be one that analyzes and critiques violence in all its forms, and offers in its place new possible social arrangements for peaceful societies. We begin with militarism and disarmament.

3.3 Militarism and Disarmament as Core Problematiques in Peace Education

Reardon writes that disarmament should be the core focus of peace education inquiry. She is adamant that peace education that does not propose disarmament as an alternative to militarism and the arms race is not fulfilling the lofty goals of the field. She explains that retreating from the politics of confronting militarism in the classroom in favor of affective learning alone (especially if it is 'peaceful' acquiescence) is insufficient for transformative peace education. Here, it is useful to explain what we mean by affective learning. We understand affective to be grounded in personal experiences encompassing feelings, emotions, intuition, preferences, and values. As such, affective learning muddies concepts common to science and education such as objectivity, distance, control groups, interventions, and linearity. But we do not believe that an affective education rejects such notions of disinterested science and education, as some pundits and educators may claim. Instead, we contend that the affective is part of a holistic education embracing the spiritual and emotional as well as the empirical and rational. Hence, we understand Reardon to be calling for a *both/and* approach to the affective/rational dimensions of learning, where peace learning must not only address students *feelings* about war, violence and peace, but must also address how students *think* about war and peace. Instructively, Reardon argues for a disinterested analysis and critique of the nation-state system to challenge an uncritical and passionate patriotic education that aims to misdirect students from clear political analysis by creating false divisions of 'us' and 'them'. She explains:

> … peace education programs and curricula should include the most central substantive concerns of peace, disarmament as an alternative to the arms race and the present State system which breed war and violence. However, issues regarding the nation-State system and the techniques it uses to maintain the ultimate power position in the world political system have little or no place in current peace education as it is practiced in schools and universities. Until these issues become universal components of the content of peace education, the field cannot be true to its' own purposes (Reardon/Snauwaert 2015a, pp. 82–83).

It is clear here how Reardon thinks about emotions in education; they are important to explore but must not impede clear systematic political analysis. Reardon offers that to reconcile emotions and politics, democratic processes of participation are required both inside and outside the classroom (Reardon/Snauwaert 2015a, p. 87). By extension, we may speculate that Reardon would also call for media literacy and historical analysis, like Peters, as a means to reject posttruth lies and epistemological gerrymandering (Kester 2018).

Finally, Reardon (1982) contends that it is the people power of social movements and global solidarity that offer tremendous power to overcome the destructive international politics of the global military-industrial-academic complex. Global disarmament is achieved through disarming the mind and banding together for social justice. To get there, national social divisions must be bridged at all levels and in all sectors of education. Global solidarity requires social trust and cooperation. A useful starting point for such radical education and political action is at the domestic level. Overcoming patriarchy and gender domination offers a crucial intersectional entry point.

3.4 Patriarchy, Sexism and Education

In *Sexism and the War System* (1985), Reardon pointedly outlines the intimate linkages between militarism and sexism. She highlights how gender pervades every aspect of our lives and that the patriarchal system is the basis of all forms of social injustice and violence, including the mega form of violence: war. In her 1988 monograph, *Comprehensive Peace Education*, and her later 2001 book, *Education for a Culture of Peace in a Gender Perspective*, Reardon provides curricular and pedagogical responses to disrupt the systemic relationship between education, war, and gender domination. Her curricular and pedagogical responses place counter-education at the forefront of challenging and providing alternatives to the patriarchal-militaristic worldview.

Reardon suggests that a gendered perspective provides a critical lens to view the world through. This critical lens makes visible not only the injustices experienced by women, but also brings into focus other injustices present in society and the environment. Reardon also discusses how this gender perspective can convey marginalised knowledges undermined by the patriarchal system. While agreeing with many feminists' calls to not essentialize women as purely motherly carers, Jenkins/Reardon (2007) argue that gender differences are "a primary basis for understanding both multiple ways of knowing and varying perspectives on peace problems" (p. 217). Here, values of care and hope attributed to femininity give women a distinct perspective and can be incorporated towards nuanced ways of perceiving the world and human security within it. These in turn support the holistic approach to education for a culture of peace that Reardon (2001) espouses based upon a moral inclusion of those we differ from to "being within the realm of justice and deserving of fair treatment" (p. 72).

In relation to the aforementioned posttruth era, Reardon's (2007) gender lens and peace education could be seen to be "concerned with developing pedagogies that enable learners to think in terms of complexities beyond the standard curricula on controversial issues that usually teach students to consider little more than the two major opposing positions" (p. 216). Reardon continues that learners may "gain confidence in their own critical abilities and a sense of personal responsibility for the achievement of a just social order" (ibid, p. 227). While specifically focused on challenging the gender order, it may be extrapolated that this could be useful in challenging posttruth manipulations. Similarly Reardon's ethics of care encourage collaboration opposed to the antagonism often seen in posttruth political arenas. In addition, Reardon's thinking, like that of Mejia, Beckermann and Sullivan, opens further lines of inquiry on whether these posttruth times are themselves simply a part of patriarchy as opposed to a departure from it. Writing in 2015 Reardon warns of how "patriarchy adapts to changes in social and political orders, taking on new, alternative forms, such as the corporatization of society" (Reardon/Snauwaert 2015b, p. 145). If posttruth becomes simply an extension of the political tools used to control and dominate the distribution of knowledge, Reardon's critical/analytic, moral/ethical, and contemplative/ruminative reflection (Reardon/Snauwaert 2015a) may provide stalwart ways to continue interrogating patriarchal manipulation.

3.5   Human Rights and Peace Pedagogy

From her analysis of militarism and sexism as the core problematiques of a culture of peace, Reardon centres human rights as the ethical response, and as fundamental toward achieving a human security infrastructure fundamental to achieving sustainable global peace. She argues that human rights are neither a complement, nor a particular component of peace education, but rather integral to constructing peace cultures. In this respect, Reardon argues that the mitigation of economic, social and political violence is far more significant to the realization of human rights than the "non-systemic, aberrant violence of crime, interpersonal conflict, vandalism, etc.", because such aberrant individual violence is "both rooted in and facilitated by the systemic violence of the institutions that uphold the wider culture of violence" (Reardon/Snauwaert 2015b, p. 152). Structural violence inevitably creates the vulnerable.

For Reardon, structural violence is an abuse of human dignity, and human rights can protect against these abuses by mitigating structural violence. Therefore, Reardon calls for raising awareness of human rights in and through education. However, she strictly distinguishes human rights learning from human rights education. Although both intend to increase awareness and the protection of human rights, the former can, at best, mobilize people to oppose public policies, or social, economic, or political structures, while the latter enables people to view human rights as a social purpose. Human rights learning cultivates ethical reflection and assessment for the exercise of social responsibility, where social responsibility is not limited to that of the privileged. Reardon discusses that the intention of human rights learning is "to enable vulnerable communities to become aware of the structural causes of their vulnerability", and "to inspire them to take action to overcome it" (Reardon/Snauwaert 2015b, p. 154). Here, peace pedagogy is integral.

Reardon points out that peace pedagogy must offer methods for reflective, well-reasoned dialogue, and nonviolent conflict resolution strategies, as well as guiding principles for human rights and repertories of problem-solving skills. She clarifies the approaches of peace pedagogy in comparison with that of civic education. Civic education is formative, and has its focus on information and skills accumulation of the learners to enable them to function well within the system. In contrast, peace education is transformative, and assists the learners in developing the capacity to *transform* the existing system. In order to achieve the goal of peace education, Reardon emphasises the role of shared reflective experiences, which she argues contributes to internalising human rights values, and actualising them in their own lives and societies. It is suggested that such internalised and actualised values will motivate learners to acquire the knowledge that is required for the mastery of the political skills to transform the system. Reardon asserts that reflexive inquiry is an appropriate pedagogy for peace learning. Here, she differentiates between queries and questions. According to Reardon, queries are open questions (what, why, how, what if, etc.) that accept a range of possible responses, whereas questions preempt factual or clarifying answers. Reardon points out that there is reluctance both among educators as well as politicians to adopt this type of learning, or dialogical method, because "[w]e are not always so eager to open our own behaviours and values to the critical challenges that may lurk in open inquiry" (Reardon/Snauwaert 2015a, b, p. 158). Such a situation is intimidating, but Reardon takes this as an exhilarating opportunity, because it enriches the learning experiences of the educator and learners. If critical pedagogy and critical thinking remain the best defenses against posttruth political deception, then surely practicing critical inquiry is at the heart of this process.

3.6   New Possibilities

Building on the foundational work of Reardon, we share two points for intellectual and pedagogical development seeking to move peace education forward in our own praxis in response to these posttruth dilemmas. Reardon's thinking, as presented here, provides the impetus for these reflections on peace education today. The first area of concern centers on what we perceive to be the largely underexamined role of first and second-order reflexivity in Reardon's work, and the connection between these prime layers of consciousness and her activism. Here, we argue that reflexivity in peace education is crucial, yet it has been mostly undertheorized and limited to first-order practitioner reflexivity. This presents several hurdles for peace education. Reardon makes several insights here, which we share. We then draw on her thinking, to reflect upon our own praxis as peace educators involved in the field. By doing so, we critique the limitations of psychosocial approaches to educational peacebuilding that locate the individual mind as the site for social change (which has tremendous resonances with the hyper-individualism of posttruth rhetoric). The second concern we raise for peace education focuses on reenergizing the emphasis on gender in peace education as an entry point into action for social justice in other related domains of social difference.

First, as a foundational thinker in peace education Reardon engaged in critiquing not only militarism and patriarchy but also those peace education practices that avoid the explicit political dimensions of peace education. In this, we argue that Reardon offered a second-order critique of the field that is so dear to her. She writes, "Peace education as political education is not a view very widely held in the United States" (Reardon/Snauwaert 2014, p. 84), and she attributes this to two strands of argument. First, she claims that peace is largely practiced as a psychosocial process needing to mitigate individual aggression. Second, she argues that the teaching of explicit values in schools often produces a backlash from administrators and the general public who advocate a 'value-free' curriculum, which is supposedly objective and apolitical (ibid, see pp. 83–88). Yet, the problem here is that education, by its very nature, is political activity; thus, pretending otherwise is to promote indoctrinating education. Reardon explains, "[…] in essence all education is political and that preparation for politics is a major task of education" (ibid, p. 87). Hence, her foundational role in peace education has been to ensure the development of peace education concepts, curricula, and the proliferation of the field around the world, and its intimate relationship with critical inquiry and political action possibilities for more socially just societies. Embedded within her work is a crucial, although unstated, critical reflection on the practices and premises of the field itself. Thus, we argue that peace educators have much to gain from building upon Reardon's second-order reflexivity of the field of peace education (Kester/Cremin 2017).

Second, the focus on gender in Reardon's work opens space and possibility for viewing peace from other nonnormative standpoints, such as the ethic of care from a gender lens (Reardon/Snauwaert 2015b). Methodologically, this is realized through qualitative and arts-based avenues, including autoethnography, autobiography, and decoloniality. Reardon writes about the ethic of care, "within a framework which emphasizes the feminine ethic of care, they start with inquiring into the consequences to the most vulnerable of the human family" (Reardon/Snauwaert 2015b, p. 70). Reardon writes similarly of decolonialism that a starting point for peace education is learning other cultures and languages (Reardon/Snauwaert 2015a, pp. 60–61). In her 1999 review and projection Reardon offered five capacities for 'transitioning' toward a new peace education: cultural proficiency, global agency, conflict competency, gender sensitivity, and ecological awareness (Reardon 1999, p. 37). Her emphasis on the ecological awareness provides a segue beyond the human family and the anthropocene to incorporate the spiritual wholeness of life and interdependence with nature. Given the posttruth crisis, its accompanying climate change denial (see d'Ancana 2017), and the rise in ethnocentrism, these five capacities remain core for critical peace education today. Reardon writes of gender differences, "It is the lens through which the cultivation of human inequalities can be seen most clearly. It is a paradigm through which we can learn how differences in human perspectives conditioned by different experiences can reveal both humanly destructive and humanly enhancing possibilities" (ibid., p. 39). Thus, from gender differentiation and gender (in)equality peace educators can move into other sensitive topics such as the racial climate, sexuality, and cultural logics of posttruth.

Finally, in reflection on our own practices, Reardon's work has assisted our understandings of the effects of violence, masculinity and patriarchy and the importance of peace education to expose and explore these concepts towards critically assessing social structures/possibilities and discovering alternatives. These alternatives must incorporate maligned knowledges from feminist perspectives, but also must explore and give voice to masculine experiences towards finding holistic integration for women *and* men. This peace is concerned with finding balance, and drives our own lives and professional beliefs. In her 2015 epilogue Reardon appears to bequeath a rally cry "contemplating possible futures for gender and peace" (Reardon/Snauwaert 2015b, p. 141). This rally asks for "nothing short of a transformation of the patriarchal global gender order" (ibid, 2015b, p. 144). It is this motivation that inspires us to remain analytical to all information being disseminated and to look through holistic frameworks that help illuminate the complexities and systems at play so as to be able to resist reproducing the pervasive violences. These analytical frameworks will allow us to keep vigil to the possible violences contained in all our work across diverse communities.

3.7 Conclusion

In this chapter, we have inquired into what lessons educators engaged in addressing the challenges of teaching for peace in a posttruth era might learn from the work of Betty A Reardon. Reading through several of Reardon's key works in peace education from the periods of the Cold War and globalization, we have drawn three conclusions that we believe remain salient today. First, peace education must ensure engagement of the rational and affective faculties as crucial to a holistic and inclusive approach to peace learning. Second, peace education that seeks to curtail posttruth tensions should directly critique systems of militarism and patriarchy. Third, peace education that employs a pedagogy of democratic engagement and critical inquiry remains the most promising of pedagogic responses to counter posttruth alt-facts and epistemological gerrymandering. Peace education can play an important role in responding to and offering alternatives to today's posttruth political challenges that affect all our communities. In the end, Reardon's theorizing for peace education remains as timely today as it was for educators in the Cold War and era of globalization.

References

Baudrillard, J. (1995). *The gulf war did not take place*. Bloomington, IN: Indiana University Press.
Bhambra, G. (2017). Brexit, Trump and "methodological whiteness": On the misrecognition of race and class. *British Journal of Sociology, 68*, 214–232.
Crilley, R. (2018). Book review essay: International relations in the age of 'post-truth' politics. *International Affairs, 94*, 417–425.
D'Ancona, M. (2017). *The new war on truth and how to fight back*. London: Ebury Press.
Harris, I. (2004). Peace education theory. *Journal of Peace Education, 1*, 5–20.
Higgins, K. (2016). Post-truth: A guide for the perplexed. *Nature, 540*, 9.
Hutchison, E. (2016). *Affective communities in world politics*. Cambridge, UK: Cambridge University Press.
Jenkins, T., & Reardon, B. (2007). Gender and peace: Towards a gender inclusive, holistic perspective. In C. Webel & J. Galtung (Eds.), *Handbook of peace and conflict studies* (pp. 209–232). Oxon: Routledge.
Kester, K. (2010). Betty Reardon and the international institutes on peace education. In D. Schugurensky (Ed.), *History of education: Selected moments of the twentieth century* (online).
Kester, K. (2018). Postmodernism in post-truth times. *Educational Philosophy and Theory, 50*, 1330–1331.

Kester, K., & Cremin H. (2017). Peace education and peace education research: Toward a concept of poststructural violence and second-order reflexivity. *Educational Philosophy and Theory, 49*, 1415–1427.

Keyes, R. (2004). *The post-truth era: Dishonesty and deception in contemporary life*. New York: St Martin's Press.

Leonardo, Z., & Zembylas M. (2013). Whiteness as technology of affect: Implications for educational praxis. *Equity & Excellence in Education, 46*, 150–165.

MacKenzie, A., & Bhatt I. (2018). Lies, bullshit, and fake news: Some epistemological concerns. *Postdigital Science and Education*. https://doi.org/10.1007/s42438-018-0025-4.

Mejia, R., Beckermann, K., & Sullivan C. (2018). White lies: A racial history of the posttruth. *Communication and Critical/Cultural Studies, 15*, 109–126.

Peters, M. (2018). The information wars, fake news and the end of globalization. *Educational Philosophy and Theory, 50*, 1161–1164.

Reardon, B. A. (1982). The first day of hope. *Teachers College Record, 84*, 255–265.

Reardon, B. A. (1985). *Sexism and the war system*. New York: Teachers College Press.

Reardon, B. A. (1988). *Comprehensive peace education*. New York: Teachers College Press.

Reardon, B. A. (1999). *Peace education: A review and projection*. Peace Education Reports No. 17. Malmo, Sweden: School of Education.

Reardon, B. A. (2001). *Education for a culture of peace in a gender perspective*. Paris: UNESCO.

Reardon, B. A., & Snauwaert, D. T. (2015a). *Betty A. Reardon: A pioneer in education for peace and human rights*. New York: Springer International.

Reardon, B. A., & Snauwaert, D. T. (2015b). *Betty A. Reardon: Key texts in gender and peace*. New York: Springer.

Wintersteiner, W. (2013). Building a global community for a culture of peace: The Hague appeal for peace global campaign for peace education (1999–2006). *Journal of Peace Education, 10*, 138–156.

Zavarzadeh, M. (2003). The pedagogy of totality. *JAC, 23*, 1–53.

Chapter 4
Peace Education Confronting Reality

Magnus Haavelsrud

Peace education is part of the process of *becoming* and *being* politically aware. This means that I agree with the Norwegian philosopher Hellesnes that a useful concept for this process is *politicization* (Hellesnes 1994, p. 136). I see this concept as closely related to the deepening of the attitude of awareness as Freire (1972) describes the concept of *conscientization* – as it integrates reflection and action in *praxis* of changing both self and world. This again is supported by ideals of participatory and dialogic democracy in which relations between lifeworld and system world become part of the content in pedagogic practice. This search for truth is a lifelong process of experimentation and study in which lifeworld experiences remain a testing ground in the investigation of relations between human beings and the world they live in. The process of becoming and being politically aware implies that problems, conflicts, issues, themes, topics, events, and contradictions in our confrontation with reality are at the core when selecting contents and forms in peace education. This process of politicization, however, is not high on the agenda of dominant educational policy-makers in our time. This reality is a paradox in a world that is faced with unprecedented social, cultural and political challenges. It is imperative to develop viable alternatives in meeting these challenges and I shall in this paper revisit some of the ways and means designed by that thought and practice collective under formation already in the 60s – a collective in which Betty Reardon has been to this day one of its core members. After a discussion of what I see as problematic choices in current educational policy-making on the trans-national level, I shall revisit Reardon's call for peace education to confront reality in order to find ways and means of improving it.

Prof. Dr. Magnus Haavelsrud, Emeritus Professor at the Norwegian University of Science and Technology since 2010 and was Distinguished Fellow of the South African Research Chair in Development Education, University of South Africa (2008–2017); Email: magnush@alumni.ntnu.no.

© Springer Nature Switzerland AG 2019
D. T. Snauwaert (ed.), *Exploring Betty A. Reardon's Perspective on Peace Education*, Pioneers in Arts, Humanities, Science, Engineering, Practice 20, https://doi.org/10.1007/978-3-030-18387-5_4

4.1   When Educational Policy-Making Becomes an Obstacle to Peace Education

External forces to educational practices are not always easily detectable in everyday life. In a forthcoming doctoral thesis, Hovdenak analyses the development of transnational educational policy-making in the Organization for Economic Cooperation and Development (OECD) after the 2nd World War. In the following I shall summarize some of his research on how it came to be that current OECD preferences in transnational policy-making in education now is rooted in neoliberal ideology. He concludes that educational policy-making on the transnational level has altered the very concept of education. He traces the history of this educational orientation back to Walter Lippmann's debate with John Dewey in the 1920s. Lippman's work was later celebrated in an international gathering in Paris in 1938 – a meeting that also served as a venue for the preparation and foundation of the thought collective named the Mount Pélerin Society – instigated by the economist Frederick von Hayek. Hovdenak shows that OECD – as a leading agent in the trans-nationalization of policy-making in education – shifted from Keynesian economics in the planning of economic and social development to the neoliberalist Hayek-inspired flexibility paradigm required by free markets that are to a large extent beyond regulation. This market-driven system found strong political bases in the Reagan and Thatcher governments in the 80s. This ideology questions the very concept of planning in that anything that might be thought to be an obstacle to the development and/or maintenance of free markets is not given priority in the planning of future society. Consequently, educational policy-making has to be sensitive to where the market goes implying that a flexible work force must be ready to follow wherever the market dictates – also in learning skills demanded by the market at any time and place. Market preferences influence movements of labour, capital and competence. An epistemology of competence and skills demanded by a market dynamism that cannot easily be either regulated or planned now finds its expression in the everyday life of formal education.

A free market calls for obedience by citizens in accepting the individualism and competition required at the interactional level. This obedience, I believe, depends upon the formation of what Richards (1992, p. 13) call fragmented consciousness, which is the result of the sedimentation of bits and pieces of elite thinking. Richards (2000, p. 136) has coined the concept of *cultural structure* implying, as I interpret it, a causal link between the formation of fragmented consciousness and structural preferences. This causal link reduces the human being's potential in being an historical subject and fits the Lippmannian elitist decision-making. The formation of this mindset may have succeeded to a large extent as we now witness how forms of rightest populism calls for strong leaders with little interest in participatory democracy.

The state is an instrument in developing society according to market principles (Innset 2018) requiring cultural practices that are synchronized with, and obedient to, an ideology in which competition, individualism, privatization and deregulation reign. What is interesting and maybe surprising is that even social democratic governments have adopted neoliberal ideology as witnessed, for instance, under the Blair government in the UK. And in Australia – Burns (2002, p. 4) observes that "a corporate ideology with managerialism as its chief instrument … along with a commitment to economic rationalism and the logic of the market place as its engine" was introduced under a labour government as well. This, she points out, underpins a utilitarian instrumentalism. In Norway social democratic governments from the 80s on also embraced this market driven ideology and introduced the OECD inspired governing tool of New Public Management. No wonder that this ideology collides with educational theories and practices based in politicization and conscientization. A telling example is a conflict arising in that country's *National Institute of Occupational Health* (Haga 2017).

The story describes a manipulative leadership – even involving what Haga (2017) calls '*nettverkskorrupsjon*' *(network corruption)*. This new concept in the Norwegian language connotes persons and/or institutions seeking to further their interests at the same time as they are hiding their actions and critique of same. I think network corruption may be describing the *process* of what Vambheim (2016, pp. 24–29) calls *network violence*, i.e. the violence resulting from interactions among individuals when responsibility of each participant in the network is diluted. It is an interactive phenomenon in that the participants cooperate or reinforce each other even though final common action may not be part of a plan by all the participants in the network. Thus, it may not take a strong will or intention to join such a network. This cultural characteristic of participants demonstrate that network corruption and violence in and by networks relates to the relationship between cultural and structural violence as discussed by Galtung (1996, pp. 199–207).

The actors, however, in network interactions can vary a great deal: Vambheim (2016) analysed interactions in a school bullying network whereas the conflict actors in the *National Institute of Occupational Health* are located at various levels involving colleagues, work place leadership, politicians and government civil servants. In both cases, however, I think Vambheim is right when he notes that some participants may just go with the flow directed by some leader with clear goals. This seems to be the case when Haga (2017) – the self-proclaimed Norwegian *Josef K* (Kafka 2015) – was fired on a Friday and told to vacate his office by Tuesday the following week – and years later arrested in his home suspected of threatening to murder the head of the Norwegian Confederation of Trade Unions! This *Josef K*, however, has analysed these events in light of the collision between his pedagogic work in higher education and the implementation of the government policy of introducing the new governing tool of NPM in the country. He reminds the reader of the tenet in the NPM regime that a leader can lead anything without knowing the subject matter of the institution he/she leads. This understanding of leadership might be well suited in a shop, firm or business enterprise, but can be rather problematic in an institution dealing with education, research, learning, teaching and knowledge production. Haga was a prime mover in the founding of social pedagogy at the University of Oslo in 1974 (Haga 1975) and after thirty years of highly acclaimed educational work he suddenly found himself under the wings of a newly appointed leader whose mission was to introduce this new governing tool rooted in business administration aimed at "regulating efforts to achieve fixed objectives" (Haga 2017). The objectives obviously did not include Haga's dialogic approach aiming at the development of insight and wisdom in both theory and practice grounded in the professional's own experience, knowledge and judgement. His within and below orientation to knowledge production and learning aimed at helping learners (and citizens in general) to become aware of the relations between micro interactions and macro structures. The fate of the Norwegian *Josef K* is explained in terms of relations among both micro and macro actors – the latter involving various ministries responsible for education, labour and administration affairs (www.government.no), the Parliamentary ombudsman (www.sivi-lombudsmannen.no), and the Justice Committee in the Norwegian Parliament (www.stortinget.no). Haga was offered four years' salary on the condition that he would keep silent about what had happened. He refused as he found the offer to be an attempt at bribing and gagging. He chose not to sue anyone after being cleared of the false accusations of threatening to murder the Head of the Norwegian Confederation of Trade Unions. And he continued on the track started in the late 60s in developing a pedagogy of creative resistance in which the better argument is recognized in transparent discourse fitting a democracy – a proof of which is his recent book demonstrating that the Norwegian *Josef K* turns out to be more resilient than the original one.

This story reminds me of the debate between John Dewey and Walter Lippmann and the latter's "… complete pessimism regarding the capabilities of average citizens" (cited in Hovdenak) in participating in developing democratic societies. John Dewey's seminal work on democracy and education was refuted by Walter Lippmann's belief that "Modern society is not visible to anybody, nor intelligible continuously and as a whole. One section is visible to another section, one series of acts is intelligible to this group and another to that." (cited in Hovdenak). Dewey, however, wrote about democracy as a way of life and saw it as an active process of planning futures through collaboration and experimentation. He did not argue that people at large would not be able to deal with even complex issues – in the way Lippmann suggests.

What becomes visible in Hovdenak's analysis is that the heritage of neoliberalism negates the optimism in strengthening the impact of education in creating a socially just and peaceful society. The human being has become an object of free markets and privatization – an object alienated as a subject with other subjects in collectives and collaborative action contributing to building solidarity and empathy. The human being has been reduced to an individual strategic actor aiming at upward mobility under a free market logic – seemingly beyond democratic control – celebrating 'freedom' as competition. Collective actions in solidarity with building the common good is neither rewarded nor desired.

This market-driven educational epistemology is an important part of reality that peace learning faces in our time. Peace education needs to be conscious of this global contextual condition in experiments to be developed from now on and help develop relevant utopias for a future in which human development is put in the front seat again after decades of neoliberalist hegemony. An early warning was issued towards the end of both the Reagan and Thatcher governments when Reardon (1988, p. 54) wrote that "... contemporary education seems very much occupied with excellence in the sense of preparation and capacity to compete, it seems to have little concern with qualities; it is so much obsessed (as is the competitive mode) with quantity and measurement that it is an impediment to transformation rather than a means to it."

This type of 'excellence' has by now – in 2018 – become global with the help of OECD which for years has refined its neoliberalist epistemology in educational policymaking for distribution throughout the world also through the PISA testing regime and follow-up advice to national governments. In Norway, for instance, it has been argued that the government's Directorate for Education has more and more in recent years become a local filial of the OECD Directorate for Education through the adoption of the OECD testing regime (Slagstad 2018). I have compared the OECD PISA test criteria of measuring knowledge of 15-year olds in the three subjects of reading, mathematics and natural science with criteria that would have been included if a peace education perspective had been used. I found that the OECD tests show no interest in specific conditions embedded in neither curricula nor in the external life world of 15-year-olds whose experiences thereby are completely left out in this reductionist view of what constitutes valid knowledge (Haavelsrud 2010). When a neoliberalist pedagogic metaphysics is coupled with a "knowledge industry" coming from above and far-away (Reardon/Snauwaert 2015, pp. 71–79) not much room is left for *creating* knowledge with fellow pupils/students/citizens. The latter have learned to know – and experienced – a world that may be unknown to or not recognized by the test designers hired by OECD.

4.2 Peace Education Contributing to Awareness

Alongside the OECD policy-making, a peace education thought and practice collective has been developing over the last 50 years or so. Assuming that democratic contextual conditions allow for knowledge production about peace and peaceful means in solving conflicts and problems, pupils, students and teachers can learn from this field and at the same time experiment in becoming and being politically aware. I see the freeing of the mind from political indoctrination in thinking about and acting on issues of peace as rooted in the traditions of peace education going back to the 60s in which thinking about, planning and enacting strategies towards preferred futures opposed – and replaced – the scientific paradigm of positivism in which the future was simply regarded as an extrapolation and smooth continuation of past and present. Thus, Clark (1958) ventured to envision *another United*

Nations and the World Law Fund – later the Institute for World Order (later renamed the World Policy Institute) – searched and researched what they called 'relevant utopias', i.e. future models of world order that had some realistic chance (50–70%?) of being implemented. Books on such relevant utopias were researched and written in major corners of the world and the School Program under the leadership of Betty Reardon developed similar cosmopolitan approaches in the learning and teaching of peace. Educational projects made use of simulations and modelling as methods in diagnosing problems arising in existing systems as well as developing ideas about changes in the system or the need for alternative systems to meet the challenges. Reardon later wrote on how this emphasis on learning about the future was part of learning cycles departing and ending with the learner's *confrontation with real life challenges*:

> Each cycle begins and ends with confronting reality and moves through phases, which merge one into the other, of capturing visions, formulating images, articulating preferences, constructing models, assessing possibilities, planning policies, taking action, reflecting on and evaluating change, and, again, confronting reality (Reardon 1988, p. 71).

Educational programs for political education for world citizenship were launched already in the 70s with the purpose to politicize students with regard to world problems (Reardon 1973). It is a call for global learning and politicization confronting the dismal realities of war, racism, hunger, exploitation and ecological breakdown. And most importantly, the proposed programs for the 70s is seen as a condition for the transformation towards peace and survival in the next century! Now that we are in that century time has come to reconsider how this call for transformation has succeeded and to what extent peace education has contributed to the change.

In reference to the neoliberalist turn in educational policy-making noted above it seems that peace education has failed. Individualism and competition are common place and solidarity and cooperation lacking in our neoliberal epoch. The world is moving closer to climate collapse each year, economic growth continues to be the answer in spite of facts informing that the finite planet has limits to growth, and that attaining more equality and basic human rights has to take this into account in moving from economic growth and consumerism to survival and human development. A constant flow of new traumas appears and lack of empathy with past suffering and old traumas result in the lack of healing old wounds as new wounds are being created.

Still, at the same time we do have a discourse in social movements and academies in which futures are envisioned in terms of ecological survival, participation, social justice, transcending conflict transformation, and human rights. This means that the thought collective in peace education rooted in the 1960s is a viable platform for political authorities at all levels when time comes to leave the neoliberal trap in educational policy-making. A core goal of this peace education platform would cultivate the development of political efficacy of future citizens in their participation in political action in developing democracies. Even if refused by the existing OECD regime, this platform or part of it is already adopted by many governments and also institutionalized in domestic and international governmental or non-governmental organizations. So even if the prevention of the impact of neoliberalism in education so far has failed, tackling this obstacle to the institutionalization of peace education policies both at the national and transnational levels depends upon the flourishing of alternatives to it.

4.3 40 Years from Now?

Finally, let me ask the same question that Reardon asked about which educational programs are needed for transformation towards peace and survival in the long range of 40–50 years from now, i.e. 2058–2068. This was Reardon's question in the 70s when she designed her educational programs in that decade. Could we employ the same methodologies as she did then? I think yes – as long as the methodology helps learners in becoming and being politically aware. That means to deal with the current obstacles (consumerism, individualism, competition and manufacturing of consent through propaganda and knowledge industry) discussed above and also take note of the very different communication structure in our time. Peace education projects in formal education may now need to relate more directly to both informal and non-formal communication venues. Growing up we learn from family and friends and nowadays often through social media as well. And these *informal* sources of utility in becoming politically aware are complemented by *non-formal* learning from mass media, voluntary organizations, religion and social media. Becoming and being politically aware in our time, therefore, is the product of an interaction among all these sources of learning in influencing and forming orientations to any issue at any level ranging from local (whether own or others) to global contexts.

Informal, formal and non-formal learning is therefore essential in peace education in our epoch because in all three venues issues and problems of peace are dealt with in some way or other. However, the three venues often give emphasis to – or even specialize – in different contents. And each of them may to varying degrees integrate, separate or relate to contents available in the other two venues. Strong separation of contents between the three venues may be caused by severe disagreements and contradictions whereas integration of contents over venues may be explained by a high level of content agreement. In the case of discrepancies between the sources of information the learner is exposed to a range of content about peace that may be more or less contradictory. Actually, any disagreements and contradictory theses about the diagnosis, prescription and enactment related to any peace problem, conflict or contradiction adds to and becomes part of that problem, conflict or contradiction. Such discrepancies and differences cross all possible sources of communication and learning thereby adds to the original problem and may complicate it further.

4.4   The Special Mandate of Formal Education

It is an important question in peace education to find out how to deal with dis-agreements about diagnosis, prescription and enactment of peace problems, con-flicts and contradictions. This question is of relevance in all of the three venues of informal, formal and non-formal education. But I think that the formal venue rooted in a state's educational policies has a *specific mandate and responsibility* in relating to whatever discrepancies there are in what is recognized as valid knowledge in the other two venues. It is therefore in formal educational systems that knowledge from informal and non-formal sources should be systematically considered, critiqued and evaluated.

Assuming that conditions for democratic public formal education are present in a society, it is to be expected that a major source of valid knowledge may be drawn from the Academy. In a way higher education is an integral part of formal public education and a decisive root in determining knowledge validity – also when it comes to both forms and contents in peace education at all levels in the educational system. This means that the formation of teachers in public education should be exposed to both theoretical and practical knowledge about and for peace in their higher education studies – including the ways and means of learning and teaching peace.

However, even in case higher education and research institutions enjoy academic freedom, they are to varying degrees dependent upon existing political power. And in case democratic contextual conditions are absent in a context, peace education may have to give up on formal education because authorities have decided to use this important venue for indoctrination. Then peace education has to turn to the informal and non-formal venues. This becomes imperative in cases when even the Academy is blindfolded by state ideologies and economic policies. If universities serve hegemonic power more than contributing to meeting criteria of true knowl-edge, their contribution to peace knowledge in the formal system is endangered. Jenkins (2015) has an enlightening discussion on this topic and concludes that political will is needed for peace education to be recognized in spite of dominance from current economic powers. But in case political will for ensuring democratic participation in knowledge production is replaced with hegemonic indoctrination, the Academy has become a vassal to political power. This has been documented and analysed in a 2015 issue of the *International Journal of Development Education and Global Learning* edited by Odora Hoppers. It is therefore no wonder that she has now formed a new initiative aimed at researching and practicing an *applied governance of knowledge systems* aimed at providing safe spaces for even suppressed or marginalized ways of seeing the world into public meaning-making. This implies an obligation to build constructive relations between authorities at all levels in order to safeguard human development. I have asserted that this orientation to governance should be explored as a relevant replacement of the failure of governing as demonstrated in the recent Trojan horse affair in a British school in which the aim was to detect possible violent extremism (Haavelsrud 2018). I think

Odora Hoppers' announced goal is in harmony with the call to practice and institutionalize a type of governance which is based on core values such as respect for life, liberty, justice, equity, care and integrity (*Our global neighbourhood: the report of the Commission on Global Governance* 1995). This agenda, I think, should be embedded in the enactment of *academic freedom* conceived as the pursuit of knowledge without undue influence from political, economic and cultural power elites seeking to use the academy and public education in general for its own and sometimes anti-peace purposes through top-down governing of research and higher education.

4.5 Conclusion

I believe that strengthening academic freedom in combination with ensuring cognitive justice, in the sense of recognizing multiple epistemologies (Visvanathan 1997), opens new possibilities for inclusion of challenges facing humanity today in not only transmission, but also creation, of knowledge at all educational levels. This strong medicine has to be prescribed, I believe, when democracy has been subverted by the dominance of 'rational' systems of control standing in the way of participatory democracy (Saul 1992). A telling example is the fate of the Norwegian *Josef K* referred to above – an almost unbelievable story about the lack of respect for a sound and successful educator. As noted above, he (Haga 2017) has analysed the failure of leadership in light of the government's love for New Public Management – a governing tool in conflict with educational practices contributing to political awareness and conscientization. I therefore conclude that neoliberalism in educational policy-making is an obstacle to designing peace education processes for experimentation aimed at increased political awareness in confronting reality. It is an important challenge to peace education today that neoliberalist epistemology now dominates transnational education policy-making. It forms a serious threat to the development of ideas through people's participation in planning futures – which, I believe, is a must in any transformation of the status quo towards peace and survival. Peace education as politicization, therefore, has to deal with this transnational reality and confront that epistemology which threatens the creativity of the world's peoples in carrying out their historical task of transformation towards peace and survival. This contradiction needs visibility as we realize that a neoliberalist worldview may steer us towards the precipice of Armageddon if not stopped in time. The *very foundation of democracy* may be in danger in cases when extreme right politics combines with neoliberalism – as in the case of recent political developments in Brazil (Safatle 2018).

As noted in the introduction, the purpose of politicization is to lay the ground for becoming and being politically aware – a task including experimental action by individuals as well as collectives in social movements. Peace education is therefore not only an experiment with ideas but includes the goal of acting for transformation of both self and world. This implies "… to promote the development of an authentic planetary consciousness that will enable us to function as global citizens and to transform the present human condition by changing the social structures and the patterns of thought that have created it." (Reardon 1988, p. x). This purpose implies building the capacity to engage in transformative political action and to contribute to the socialization of future citizens' political efficacy. In my view all human beings have the potential of developing greater capacities for not only understanding issues of critical importance, but also in debating issues, participating in decision-making, and enacting decisions – provided that educational opportunities for this to happen are made available.

References

Burns, R. (2002). *The effects of funding sources and the pursuit of new scientific aims in Australian Antarctic Science*. Paper presented at the Conference entitled The Death of the Concerned Intellectual? University of Technology Sydney, Sydney.

Clark, G. (1958). *World peace through world law*. Cambridge, Mass: Harvard University Press.

Freire, P. (1972). *Pedagogy of the oppressed* (M. B. Ramos, Trans.). Harmondsworth, England: Penguin Books Ltd.

Galtung, J. (1996). *Peace by peaceful means: Peace and conflict, development and civilization*. Oslo: International Peace Research Institute; London; Thousand Oaks, CA: Sage Publications.

Haavelsrud, M. (2010). *Education in developments: Volume 2*. Maastricht: Shaker Publishing.

Haavelsrud, M. (2018). Countering extremism in British schools? The truth about the Birmingham Trojan Horse affair. *European Journal of Political and Cultural Sociology, 5*(4), 487–490. https://doi.org/10.1080/23254823.2018.1521033.

Haga, S. (1975). The process of change in higher education. In M. Haavelsrud (Ed.), *Education for peace: Reflection and action* (pp. 137–155). Guildford: IPC Science and Technology Press.

Haga, S. (2017). *Men slikt forekommer da ikke i Norge!* Rånåsfoss: Svein Sandnes Bokforlag AS.

Hellesnes, J. (1994). *Sosialisering og teknokrati: del I og II*. Oslo: Pensumtjeneste.

Hovdenak, S. S. *On the OECD and the transnationalization of policy-making in education*. Forthcoming doctoral thesis. Department of Education and Lifelong Learning. Norwegian University of Science and Technology.

Innset, O. (2018, November 23). Nyliberalismens nytte. *Klassekampen.*

Jenkins, T. (2015). *Theoretical analysis and practical possibilities for transformative, comprehensive peace education*. (Philosophiae Doctor), Norwegian University of Science and Technology, Faculty of Social Sciences and Technology Management, Department of Education and Lifelong Learning, Trondheim.

Kafka, F. (2015). The trial. In N. Gill (Ed.), *Oberon modern plays*.

Our global neighbourhood: The report of the Commission on Global Governance. (1995). Oxford: Oxford University Press.

Reardon, B. (1973). Transformations into peace and survival: Programs for the 1970s. In G. Henderson (Ed.), *Education for peace: Focus on mankind* (pp. 127–151). Washington D.C.: ASCD.

Reardon, B. A. (1988). *Comprehensive peace education: Educating for global responsibility*. New York: Teachers College Press.

Reardon, B. A., & Snauwaert, D. T. (2015). *Betty A. Reardon: A pioneer in education for peace and human rights* (Vol. 26). Heidelberg.

Richards, H. (1992). *Letters from Quebec* (Volume 1: Philosophy for peace and justice). Toronto: Elliott Chapin.

Richards, H. (2000). *Understanding the global economy*. New Dehli: Maadhyam Book Services.

Safatle, V. (2018, November 22). Hvem står bak Bolsonaro. *Klassekampen*.

Saul, J. R. (1992). *Voltaire's bastards: The dictatorship of reason in the West*. London: Sinclair Stevenson.

Slagstad, R. (2018). Når OECD tar makten – om det nye skolepolitiske kunnskapsregime. *Bedre Skole*.

Vambheim, N. V. (2016). *Studies in conflict, violence and peace*. (Doctor of Philosophiae), Norwegian University of Science and Technology, Trondheim.

Visvanathan, S. (1997). *A carnival for science: Essays on science, technology and development*. Delhi; Oxford: Oxford University Press.

Chapter 5
Reardon's Conception of Human Rights and Human Rights Learning

Fuad Al-Daraweesh

Betty Reardon has written extensively on human rights and human rights learning. It is important to mention at the outset that Reardon's conception of human rights (here after HR), and human rights learning (hereafter HRL) are not independent concepts, but interdependent and interrelated within a holistic, comprehensive world view; Reardon is reluctant to atomize and separate fields such as peace, disarmament, abolition of war and sexism, to name a few, from the conceptions of HR and HRL. Perceiving these fields and concepts as interrelated provides a fertile ground for inquiry about human dignity.

The purpose of this paper is to explore and elaborate on Reardon's conception of human rights and human rights learning. To achieve this purpose, this chapter draws on the relationship between human rights and human dignity, and the relationship between human rights and peace, as articulated in Reardon's writings. Reardon's unique conception of human rights learning is discussed through the exploration of related concepts and ideas such as human dignity and peace. The main discussion is focused on accounting for the main characteristics of Reardon's concept of HRL. These characteristics become clear as I discuss the following: the role of HRL in addressing vulnerability through a transformative, critical pedagogy; HRL and the politics of learning; HRL and the holistic approach; HRL and its inclusion of feminist perspective; the contrast between HRL and human rights education; HRL diversification; and changing the current paradigm of HR.

Fuad Al-Daraweesh, staff member of the Center for International Studies and Programs at the University of Toledo, Toledo, OH, USA; Email: fuad.al-daraweesh@utoledo.edu.

© Springer Nature Switzerland AG 2019
D. T. Snauwaert (ed.), *Exploring Betty A. Reardon's Perspective on Peace Education*, Pioneers in Arts, Humanities, Science, Engineering, Practice 20, https://doi.org/10.1007/978-3-030-18387-5_5

5.1 Human Rights and Human Dignity

The fundamental pillar of Reardon's human rights framework is the universal human dignity of all human beings. Human dignity serves as a justification for the content of human rights, and the abolition of all types of discrimination based on labels assigned to humans due to their differences. The concept of dignity supersedes the concept of human rights. Dignity is the umbrella that encompasses for Reardon, all other issues and concerns; the primary subject in her writings is humans and the actualization of human dignity. The idea of human dignity entails 'reverence' as well as "responsibility for" other humans including the actualization and the preservation of their dignity. In her acceptance address for the MacBride Peace Prize at Georgetown University, Reardon (2009b) describes how the concept of human dignity represents:

> the core pursuits of the realization of our common humanity; the repudiation of violence and the realization of universal human dignity, the convergence of the human rights and peace movements, manifested as gender equality and general and complete disarmament, respectively the social and structural transformations from which can emerge the practical possibilities for a culture of peace (p. 3).

In this speech, Reardon articulates the core elements that could potentially pave the way to the preservation and actualization of human dignity. Oppression is a common characteristic of all these concepts. It hinders human flourishing in diverse ways and forms. Ancillary to these elements, Reardon provides the tools to actualize human dignity manifested in the social and political transformation. The concept of human dignity serves two purposes in her writings: first as a justification for human rights, and secondly as a ground in the sense of Kateb (2011) who claims that "it almost seems as if the idea of human dignity is axiomatic and therefore requires no theoretical defense") (p. 1). Reardon uses the concept of human dignity to imply that human dignity is axiomatic, therefore human beings should be treated the same way. The relationship between human rights and human dignity pertain to interdependence. Human rights are justified by the appeal to universal human dignity. Rights are also perceived as tools for the actualization and preservation of human dignity.

For Reardon (1978), human rights pertain to human needs, which are important for preserving and actualizing human dignity. Human rights are divided into three categories based on human needs: basic needs; personal needs; and societal needs. The basic list of needs "reveal that among the basic needs people must satisfy for survival are: sufficient nutritious food; adequate shelter and clothing; protection from disasters; health, sanitation, and education services" (p. 7). Personal needs are "what we need to be a person, unique personality. Our personalities are determined by our special qualities" (p. 7). This category takes into consideration the human potential to pursue what we desire, and who we like to be, and our capacities to develop these needs based on what is offered to citizens by the State in terms of facilities, among other resources. Social needs are based on "the way people organize how they live together. Some aspects of today's society prevent many people from satisfying their human needs" (p. 9). Human rights to the goods necessary to meet people's needs are justified. The justification is based on the grounds that in order for humans to lead a dignified life, these needs ought to be provided.

5.2 Human Rights and Peace

The relationship between peace and human rights is manifested in the relation between vulnerability and violence. The idea of human rights is conceptually interconnected with the idea of peace, in the sense that Reardon conceives peace in terms of the realization of human rights. She argues that

The sum and ethos of the values and principles of human rights taken as a whole *is* – or would be – peace. Human rights standards *are* the specific indicators and particular measures of progress toward and the realization of peace. Human rights puts flesh on the bones of the abstraction of peace and provide the details of how to bring the flesh to life. Putting flesh on the bones is a metaphor for what I believe to be transformation, the substance of profound and lasting change of such a nature as to reconstitute the very body and organic functioning of a person or a society (Reardon 2009a, p. 3).

On a micro level, Reardon (2009a) states "As violence is the central problematic of peace education, vulnerability is at the center of the problematic of HRE and HRL" (p. 16). In other words, vulnerability constitutes the normative ground for human rights as protections. Meanwhile the absence of peace constitutes an invitation to violence. Vulnerability invites violence and human rights provide protections for the vulnerable against violence and abuse. Reardon (2009a) defines violence "as intentional, avoidable harm – usually committed to achieve a purpose. By designating it as intentional harm, I intend to indicate that using violence, especially to achieve economic or political purposes or to maintain social conditions (such as male dominance) is an act of choice, strategic as well as ethical choice. In most situations there are alternatives courses of action toward the ends sought" (p. 14).

Thus, peace addresses violence, while human rights or human rights learning addresses vulnerability and oppression. Vulnerability is defined as "a chronic disadvantage suffered by person or groups at the lower levels of the prevailing social, economic and political structures, women, the poor, the aged, children and minorities. It is a condition in which the vulnerable are the most likely to suffer harm as a consequence of the prevailing structures and policies, as well as, from the periodic disturbances that shake the structures interrupting their normal operation" (Reardon 2009a, p. 16).

5.3   The Role of Human Rights Learning

HRL addresses vulnerability through empowering vulnerable individuals to claim their rights and power. Reardon (2009a) explains that the purpose and intention of human rights learning is to "enable vulnerable communities to become aware of the structural causes of their vulnerability, to help them to understand that it was not the necessary or inevitable consequence of any legitimate social goal and to inspire them to take action to overcome it. Further, the international standards of human rights were both a recognition that their vulnerability should not be accepted by them or their societies and could serve as tools to overcome it" (p. 17). As a result, human rights learning serves a multifold purpose: First, to teach, engage, involve, and reflect critically to change paradigms of injustice embodied in human rights violation. Second, to challenge the current paradigm of internalized oppression and power structure that presents human rights violation in terms of misfortune. For example, a poor individual, whose basic human needs are not met internalizes or views this gross human rights violation as a matter of misfortune. In this context, HRL plays a key role in empowering vulnerable citizens to claim their rights, and from invalidating the understanding of human rights violations as matters of misfortune.

Reardon (2009a) explains that "Human rights learning (HRL) is the conjoined philosophic twin of critical pedagogy, coming to be the preferred pedagogy of peace education, the two united by a common assumption about the relationship between teaching methodology and social and political learning. An even more significant belief that peace educator advocates of participatory, reflective pedagogies share with advocates of human rights learning is that in itself HRL is political in nature" (pp. 3–4). The association between HRL and the critical pedagogy is due to the consistency between the two. HRL provides tools to learners to change the social realities that are antithetical to human rights. The tools, provided, ought to be consistent with the desired outcome. Consequently, HRL becomes the tool of transformation, and it is pedagogically transformative towards a culture of peace. In one of her unpublished papers, Reardon (2009a) argues that "the commitment to human dignity that is the essence of nonviolence inspires the struggle for human rights as the basis for overcoming the many forms of violence that impede a viable, just peace. This commitment requires consistency between means and ends" (p. 9). Reardon believes that the ends should be consistent with the means. If we, as educators, aim to teach about human rights and peace, then we ought to follow a peaceful and humane approach. If our end is to realize human rights and peace, then our approach ought to be consistent with the content of peace, which emphasizes and utilizes a dialogue towards coming to a consensus on issues of concern. Thus, a Freirean pedagogy to HRL becomes of cardinal importance. Reardon (2009a) explains that "the basic argument is a call for the fulfillment of the Freirean promise of education as a means to the realization of human rights through that form of human rights learning defined as *conscientization* – awakening to awareness of the realities of our lives and societies and the interrelationship between these two realms of human experience. It is exactly Freire's focus on the capacity of the inner dynamic of the learning process to illuminate the outer social and political structures that forms the essence of human rights" (p. 7). Thus, HRL, according to Freirean pedagogy, cultivates awareness of the current unjust social realities. This cultivation is based on the process of identifying and conceptualizing the problems that are antithetical to human rights: conscientization. This process is premised on naming the social, economic, cultural, or political conditions that impede or enhance human rights and human dignity.

This awareness leads to engagement to challenge and change these realities. Subsequently, engagement matures to a higher level of activism. Reardon (2009a) adds "The human rights learning goal of their conscientization is their becoming aware of their implication in the structures and the ethical dimensions of their personal circumstances, their political and economic choices" (p. 12). As such, learners reflect on their choices, and consequently become more aware that personal, social, economic, and political daily choices potentially play an instrumental role in contributing to injustice. These choices could strengthen or empower unjust power structures, inequality, or inequity.

Ethical reflection is an important part of HRL. Learners reflect on issues with scrutiny and critical thinking. These issues are examined in the back drop of one one's own positionality in relation to the issues being scrutinized on one hand, and in relation to the power structures that causes the issues on the other hand. In this manner, ethical reflection presents itself in the form of a choice that needs to be made on behalf of the HR learner; either one accepts being an accomplice of the unjust power structure dynamic, or one challenges the structure. Reardon (2009a) states "A process of public conscientization will of necessity involve ethical reflection. It seems to me that what I know of human rights education in its traditional education form does not assure that the ethical issues of complicity with the systemic violence and social responsibility for the suffering of the vulnerable will be considered" (p. 13). One of the goals for HRL is to encourage learners to be socially responsible in rectifying the unjust social realities through engagement.

Challenging the power structure and potentially changing it starts with an awareness of the injustice. It requires the ability to reflect ethically on the social, political, and economic realities of people daily life. Thus, a citizen ceases to view issues related to human rights violation in terms of misfortune or in blaming victims whose rights have been violated. Taking responsibility for human rights learning, in this context, means taking responsibility not only for the cases in which human rights are violated, but also for the social, cultural, political, and economic transformation necessary to describe these visible injustices and the political transformation necessary to revision and refashion the norms, practices, policies, and regulations that cause any human rights violation. This commitment is referenced in Reardon's writing as the development of transformative thinking. Reardon (2009a) states that "human rights learning, at its core, is the cultivation of ethical reflection and assessment for the exercise of social responsibility. Both sets of capacities, ethical reflection and social responsibility, are essential to the development of transformative thinking" (p. 13). As such, critical reflection and social responsibility are important elements of HRL and its pedagogy.

5.4 Human Rights Learning and the Politics of Learning

HRL places emphasis on developing political efficacy for the realization of human rights. HRL employs a distinctive approach to human rights dissemination. Unlike human rights education, HRL aims at a broader audience, such as government agencies. This inclusion is based on the notion that the peace and human rights educators' role is to persuade governments of the possibility of human rights and peace in achieving the full potential of citizens, and in providing a milieu that nurtures capacities, so "governments themselves learn how to do politics" (Reardon 2009a, p. 27). Reardon elaborates: "Our task is to devise a pedagogy for entrenched institutions, new forms of the politics of persuasion, forms that are intentionally designed to be a politics of learning for instructing our governments about peace possibilities and the integral role of human rights in achieving those possibilities" (p. 27). These possibilities include engaging citizens in a dialogue about pressing issues that involve the polity. Maintaining a dialogue between citizens and government officials is crucial in maintaining the social order and consequently the social fabric of a society. The dialogue creates a public space; a platform for citizens to discuss and solve issues related to the way citizens choose to lead their lives.

In this manner, HRL constitutes more than knowledge of rights, but also a way of leading life based on respect, not only to humans across the globe but also to the environment and to other living beings. Reardon explains (2009a) "human rights issues provide the basis for inquiring into how we can work constructively with governments whose policies regarding justice, peace and security we are too often compelled to oppose; and how even in our relations with public authorities whose policies we may oppose, we can live out our fundamental belief in and commitment to learning as the most powerful engine of social and political change" (p. 27). Reardon refers to the transformation that is based on HRL through dialogue as the politics of learning.

The politics of learning is different from the mainstream use and abuse of politics. According to Reardon politics of learning is seeking to learn, challenge, and change power dynamics that are intrusive to human rights and human dignity. During the process of learning, achievement is viewed as a step to improve and advance the well-being of citizens, it is not measured or viewed as a win. Politics of learning is based on Freirean peaceful political processes. Reardon (2009a) describes these processes: "they are Freirean politics of deliberation-action-reflection-renewed deliberation; action and reflection toward the best possible results, all within a process imbued with respect for and guided by the principles and standards of human rights" (p. 28). The politics of learning is the politics of dialogue, informed by knowledge of human rights, and a commitment to address issues related to human rights. These issues are addressed through reflection and deliberation, a dialogue that exhibits the core values of human rights manifested by respect to others, and appreciation of all forms of diversity consistent with the spirit and the core content of rights. Consequently, the purpose of learning in this context is to transform realities that are not conducive to rights and human dignity through empowering the vulnerable.

According to Reardon (2009a) the empowerment of individuals also requires the development of autonomy of thought,. Autonomy of thought is perceived by Reardon to be "*the sin qua non* of preparation for constructive civic participation in an authentically democratic political system" (p. 30). The task of developing autonomy of thinking requires critical thinking, reflection, and action as presented in Freirean pedagogy.

5.5 Human Rights Learning and Other Disciplines

Reardon (2009a) explains that "human rights learning seeks to establish linkages among human rights problems to illuminate the relationships of the problems to the lives of the learners. Personalizing the learning, as did Freire, motivates the learners to engage with the problem and ultimately inspires them to seek alternatives" (p. 5). Although HRL is personal and personalized based on the context, it enriches its own ground by seeking linkage to other disciplines and related themes. Also, the linkage sought between HRL and other disciplines is due to the complexities of understanding the interrelationships between HR, HRL, and justice. Thus, such a linkage, could be helpful in accounting for the meaning of the terms and its uses. Reardon (2009a) maintains that

> the separations and limits of traditional pedagogies imposed by the fragmentation and reductionism of divided subject matter are characteristic of the "political realism" that still dominates current politics – including issues of human rights and peace. The rationalization and tolerance of various forms of economic and political violence as unavoidable in the face of concerns deemed more significant to order and stability is a given in public discourse. In the names of more urgent public priorities such as national security, human rights fall by the policy wayside. Issues continue to be discussed and decisions made without regard to the essential interrelationships among them. (Reardon 2009a, p. 5).

Reardon is aware that addressing injustice is a complex task that requires a holistic outlook concerning all causes and manifestations of injustice. Such a task requires moving back and forth between disciplines to investigate the possibility of offering solutions that address the root causes and not the symptoms. This task, also, is a step closer to understanding the realities suffered by the oppressed. Reardon adds to the discussion: "One of the most promising possibilities of HRL is that it offers the basis for a process of assessing the human condition, which enables us to identify and diagnose the violence of the stable order and the conditions of vulnerability that it perpetuates" (p. 6). In order to understand issues like vulnerability and human rights violation for example, an interdisciplinary approach to these concepts is important. Connecting and contrasting between and across disciplines looking for new meanings to unveil causes of injustice, is rewarding in providing a fertile ground for the researching and finding new ways to address issues related to human rights. The concept of human rights is incomplete if it is not connected to the visible and the invisible factors that contribute either to their realization or their violations.

5.6   Human Rights Learning and Feminism

A feminist perspective is a part of Reardon's conception of HRL. There are two reasons that ground Reardon's rationale for including a feminist perspective to HRL. First, a feminist perspective offers an account of oppression of women by the patriarchal system. As such a feminist perspective offers a counter view to women's vulnerability and violence committed against them. This idea, also, provides a detailed account of the power dynamic between the oppressed (women) and the oppressor (the patriarchal system). Following Reardon, Snauwaert defines patriarchy as "a social, political, and economic system of control and domination structured in terms of a hierarchy of human relationships and value that is based in socially constructed gender differentiation. As such, it bestows unequal power and value onto males who exhibit its most important values and traits, excluding and oppressing those who do not". (Reardon/Snauwaert 2015, p. xii). Reardon maintains that "the patriarchal system is not only a source of gender violence and inequality but of many egregious human rights violations, oppressive to both men and women. We would add to that argument that it also constitutes the most fundamental impediment to peace at all levels of the social order" (Reardon/Snauwaert 2015, p. 106). A feminist perspective adds an important perspective to scrutinize violence in its diverse forms. Also, a feminist perspective provides a fundamental pillar for peace that is based on human dignity for all women and men alike. Patriarchy is an impediment to peace (Reardon/Snauwaert 2015). Instead, Reardon advocates for inclusive human rights learning that include a feminist perspective on human rights which accounts for women's view on vulnerability (Reardon/Snauwaert 2015). Unless a feminist perspective is introduced to human rights and HRL, Reardon is skeptical about the discourse.

Reardon explains that "human rights, as we have seen, are the inspiration and the practical tool for confronting and overcoming injustice. They have provided the most significant progress to date in gender equality. But, in and of themselves human rights, even under stronger possibilities for enforcement, cannot transcend the violence problematic of patriarchy" (Reardon/Snauwaert 2015, p. 107). Including a feminist perspective to human rights and HRL is an integral part of the conception of human rights and human dignity for all. Equality between men and women is the foundation of human rights and peace. The exclusion of feminist perspectives is damaging to both men, women, and the learning process. This exclusion is considered a loss of in engaging feminist perspective in a dialogue. Reardon/Snauwaert (2015) argue "Patriarchy is an 'equal opportunity' destroyer of both women and men. …, an inclusive gender perspective that takes into account patriarchy's disadvantages to both men and women offers a unique opportunity to engage in transformational learning toward a peaceful, just and gender equal global order" (p. 97). As I mentioned earlier, and it becomes clear from Reardon's writings, a feminist perspective to HRL is of great importance for the dialogical transformation of injustice.

5.7 HRL and Human Rights Education

Based on Reardon's writings, there is a difference between human rights learning and human rights education. Reardon places the priority on the former, and is skeptical about the efficiency of the latter. Reardon views human rights learning as continuous field of inquiry; this field has numerous characteristics, including being research-based, interdisciplinary, prescriptive, holistic, open inquiry centered, transformative, and developmental in terms of the autonomy of thoughts and capacities. On the other hand, Reardon seems to view human rights education as static, discipline oriented, descriptive, monolithic, question centered, and lacking the development of autonomous thinking.

According to Reardon (2009a), human rights learning is open for critical challenge and scrutiny which is perceived to be a characteristic of learning in this context. Human rights education might, or might not be open to critical scrutiny, since the pedagogical orientation of education is different. Reardon elaborates: "to risk the consequences of open inquiry and the critical thinking it cultivates that leads some to insist that education and learning are synonymous, opting for education (i.e. transfer of information) as the safer terminology and practice. This reluctance exists among educators as well as politicians. We are not always so eager to open our own behaviors and values to the critical challenges that may lurk in open inquiry" (p. 30). Reardon views human rights education as a tool to transfer knowledge on human rights. The transferred knowledge is divorced from engagement with the social reality. It is packaged in a way that may not generate activism on the basis of what is taught.

In addition, HRL is a developing discipline and concept. Its development is due to the fact that it is an interdisciplinary field which provides a fertile ground for its pursuit of research. Moreover, the field of HRL is holistic. Since its inception, Reardon has connected the field of human rights to peace, sexism, racism, the abolition of war, disarmament, among others. Since HR and HRL draw their concepts from these fields, to view HR separately from the aforementioned fields is to have an incomplete understanding of it. HRL is a prescriptive field in which societal, and political issues are identified, diagnosed, and remedies are prescribed by learners through a development of their capacities to think and act autonomously. Reardon explains.

"Both human rights learning and the pedagogies of peace education are diagnostic and prescriptive and frequently speculative processes – raising queries into issue of what, why, how and what if – that call for communal discourse preceded by individual reflection on the substance of the issue under study. ... The central learning mechanism is a question, a question that engages the learner with the substance, that which is to be changed; describing, assessing, diagnosing and prescribing. The core question or query formulated from the general problematic which is explored through a series of related queries derived from the component sub-problems that comprise the problematic. The inquiry comprises this series of queries and the questions that clarify them. In the construction of an inquiry as a learning process, I distinguish between questions and queries. Questions tend to be narrowly direct and call for answers – usually factual or clarifying" (Reardon 2009a, p. 32). Please see below.

This statement highlights the difference between HRL and human rights education as it relates to the difference in their respective pedagogical orientation; to open inquiry as opposed to question centered approach used in human rights education. The query method enables learners to reflect on the issues being studied. Learners formulate an understanding of the issues based on the queries they pose, and the learning process that occurs as a result of inquiry-based approach. Also, in this excerpt Reardon differentiates between a query and a question. The inquiry is based on a chain of queries, that constitute the pillars to understand the issues being discussed yielding to the development of the learner's capacity to think autonomously. An inquiry is broadly constructed to explore the relatedness and interrelatedness of certain concepts, while a question is a narrowly constructed to elicit direct, factual, and clarifying answer.

5.8 HRL and HR Diverse Forms

Human rights concepts exist in all cultures around the world. Reardon is aware of the diverse cultural concepts that are related to human rights in most countries, cultures, and nations. Such a world-wide recognition pertains to two implications. First, this recognition can serve as a justification to cultivate an agreement, based on an overlapping consensus, on the enactment, preservation, and the actualization of human rights and human dignity. Second, the global embrace of the concept could enrich our understanding of our shared humanity.

Reardon (unpublished paper) argues that "cross-cultural study of human rights concept could be the vehicle for learning about how cultures vary in the structures of human and social relationships and ways of according respect to the human person.... Using human rights concepts and standards in multicultural education can provide the essential basis for teaching reasoned valuing and judgement making. The standards in their derivation and application involve both principles which are universal and practices which are culturally and contextually particular" (pp. 13–14). Reardon believes that the diverse forms of human rights could provide the tools to transform oppression based on the particular context, and according to the universal standards of human rights. In addition, such opportunity could provide insights of great importance to multicultural education.

In *Learning to Abolish War*, Reardon/Cabezudo (2002) explain,

> We believe that such culturally varied and community relevant forms of peace education not only better serve the learners, but greatly enrich the entire field of peace education, increasing the possibilities of its being introduced into all learning environments throughout the world… While we argue for the universal need for peace education, we do not advocate the universalization and standardization of approach and content. We believe that peace education in whatever forms it takes must be a fundamental part of the socialization process in which education plays a major role (p. 17).

Employing different culturally related forms to human rights, human dignity and peace enriches the learning environment and experience. These forms are important for three reasons; the forms have pedagogical, social, and democratic implications. They constitute a pedagogical approach to educate or teach for/about human rights. In this case, educators utilize local (epistemic and ontological) knowledge to transform power dynamic. Relevant forms, also, pertain to information about the social fabric related to the power dynamic that needs transformation. Equally important, such a recognition of other cultures globally is part of the democratic process(es).

Since the concept of human dignity is premised on the claims that humans are morally equal, and consequently their contribution and way of life is ought to be consider as equal. Reardon and Cabezudo seem to be aware of the importance of employing different cultural forms in peace education across cultures. This awareness is based on two factors. First, a liberal society does not adopt one particular substantive view about the ends of life or what constitutes it (Dworkin, as cited in Taylor/Gutman 1994). People are free and equal insofar as they can choose their own conception of the good and make their own plan over a complete life, which might include a conception of the good that draws from a comprehensive doctrine or religion (Rawls 2003, p. 24). Reardon's refrainment from standardization procedure is mainly grounded on the liberal tradition that one pursues his/her own conception of the good. In this example, human dignity could be constitutive of human good, or it could be a human good itself. Based on Reardon's approach, human needs are addressed through local approach and content which is consistent with the notion of dignity in liberal traditions.

Based on the relationship established between human rights and human dignity. It becomes clear that any process that involves human rights dissemination globally ought to be preceded by the consent of local cultures and contexts. Reardon (unpublished paper) argues that "Human rights standards as the concept of dignity and justice that identify and acknowledge social wrongs and cultural faults, as the guidelines through which societies can conceptualize and pursue cultural change…. The People themselves should determine if, when and how their cultures should be changed, and design the learning strategy to devise the changes deemed necessary"

(p. 17). In her writing, Reardon applies the principles of liberalism manifested in human dignity, critical consciousness, and developing the capacities of a learner to autonomous thinking.

The idea of embracing diverse cultural forms related to human rights is of cardinal importance and relevance to Reardon's concept of human rights learning. These forms provide a contextual cultural, social, and political tool to rectify the social wrongs. Disseminating human rights knowledge globally pertains to complexity that stems from the fact some of the cultural knowledge could be perceived as foreign. Reardon (unpublished paper) states "Here, too, women's issues, especially such culturally sensitive questions as marriage and reproductive rights, are good cases in this point. Whereas specific global standards are both necessary and useful, the ways in which they are implemented need to be decided and applied by those directly concerned" (pp. 16–17).

5.9   Paradigms of Human Rights

In "Toward a Paradigm of Peace", Reardon (1989) points to an important factor that contributes to violence and human rights violations "paradigms are perhaps the most important conceptual tools we have and they not only constraint and influence the way we think but also the way we behave, the way we organize our societies, and conduct virtually all human affairs" (p. 16). Reardon in this context refers to the mode and the way we, as humans think, live, process information, and use language. She adds "the present paradigm is at once the source and the product of a war system that, for generations, has been transferred from our minds into experience and from experience back into our minds. We engage in war and violence because we think violently in images and metaphors of war" (p. 16). Reardon believes that current paradigms are not conducive to human rights and peace. Violence infiltrated to our daily life, and is normalized through cultures. Human rights and dignity violations is delivered to homes through media, films, shows, comedy, and even through books and articles. Its repetitive presentation normalizes it. Thus, it becomes part of our daily life, part of a certain culture's construction of its own identity.

The paradigm of violence extends its reach to normalize certain words in the language we use in daily communication. If human rights and peace to be achieved, a new paradigm needs to emerge to replace the current paradigm of violence. In addition to that, educators are in need for a vision to replace current violent reality. Reardon maintains that "If we are to think peace, we need a paradigm of peace. We need not only a vision of peace but also the concepts, the language, the images, and the metaphors" (p. 16). Such change requires envisioning how the world would look like. A first step toward that change is changing ourselves "and our immediate realties and relationships if we are to change the social structures and patterns of thoughts" (p. 17). That explains Reardon's insistence on a critical pedagogy. A learner ought to be aware of language use and the infiltration of violence to the daily use of language that aims at the vulnerable. Some of metaphors that are used ought to be challenged, replaced and that requires as a start to examine one's self and scrutinize certain beliefs, words, or actions that are violent, yet normalized to the extent that one is unaware of them.

5.10 Conclusion

Reardon's concept of HR and HRL is very unique. Its uniqueness is due to the concept's relatedness to other concepts like human dignity, peace, feminism, human security, disarmament, the abolition of war, and the abolition of all forms of discrimination. Human rights learning pertains to some distinctive characteristics according to Reardon. These characteristics include: First, HRL pertains to a specific role that aims at transforming social realities utilizing a Freirean pedagogy. Second, the pedagogy is premised on ethical reflection and social responsibility, and is actualized through the politics of learning. Third, HRL is based on a holistic approach to address not only issues of human rights, but also issues related to vulnerability and violence. Fourth, an authentic approach to HR and HRL ought to take into consideration the perspective of women. Fifth, HRL pertains to a divergence from the established field of human rights education based on the aforementioned characteristics, among other highlighted in this paper. Sixth, HRL takes into consideration the diverse cultural concepts that are related to human rights. In doing, so HRL aligns its core values with the values of liberalism. In order to disseminate, realize, and preserve human rights, a critical transformative pedagogy is of cardinal importance to change the current paradigms of injustice and violence that are aimed at the vulnerable.

References

Kateb, G. (2011). *Human dignity*. Cambridge, MA: Belknap Press of Harvard University Press.
Reardon, B. A. (unknown) *Human rights as education for peace*.
Reardon, B. A. (1978). *Human rights*. Philadelphia: School District of Philadelphia, World Affairs Council of Philadelphia.
Reardon, B. A. (1989). Toward a paradigm of peace. In L. R. Farcey (Ed.), *Peace: Meanings, politics, strategies*. New York: Praeger.
Reardon, B. A. (2009a). Human rights learning: Pedagogies and politics of peace. In *Lecture Delivered for the UNESCO Chair for Peace Education Master Conference at the University of Puerto Rico*. April 15, 2009.
Reardon, B. A. (2009b). Gender and Disarmament: Imperatives for Peace Education and Essentials of a Culture of Peace. Based on acceptance remarks by Betty Reardon at the awarding of the MacBride Peace Prize, Georgetown University.

Reardon, B., & Cabezudo, A. (2002). *Learning to abolish war*. New York: The Hague Appeal for Peace.

Reardon, B. A., & Snauwaert, D. T. (2015). *Betty A. Reardon: Key texts in gender and peace*. Cham: Springer.

Taylor, C., & Gutman, A. (1994). The politics of recognition. In A. Gutman (Ed.), *Multiculturalism: Examining the politics of recognition* (pp. 25–73). Princeton, NJ: Princeton University Press.

Chapter 6
"Learning and Living Human Rights": Betty Reardon's Transformative Pedagogies and Politics of Peace Legacy

Anaida Pascual-Morán

6.1 Human Dignity and a Politics of Peace: "Giving Birth to a New Reality..."

In 2009, reknown peace researcher and educator Betty Reardon visited our UNESCO Chair for Peace Education at the University of Puerto Rico, where she offered the keynote address *Human Rights Learning*: *A Pedagogy and a Politics of Peace* (2010). At the time, I had the honor to comment on her lecture (Pascual-Morán 2010), in which she closely intertwined human rights learning and peace education, giving way to her main argument: Human rights learning comprises both a critical pedagogy and a politics of peace conducive to the respect of human dignity. In other words, Reardon emphasizes that "*learning and living human rights*" is crucial to engage in peace education and solidarity action. Furthermore, she argues that these reciprocal processes are fundamental to making advances and significant transformations toward "giving birth to a new reality... no longer tortured by violence and vulnerability" (Reardon 2010, p. 85).

In the course of her lecture, I truly felt moved to examine Reardon's basic propositions and premises, in order to take on the commitment of forging a new reality, in her words, a world where we can "live in dignity" and realize our "true humanity".[1] In tune with the multiplicity of her provoking explanatory images and analogies, I also felt the urge to engage in a metaphorical reading of her work. In

---

[1]Unless otherwise indicated, Betty Reardon's brief assertions, phrases, and images cited throughout the text and included in the subtitles, belong to the keynote address *Human Rights Learning*: *A Pedagogy and a Politics of Peace*, which she delivered at the University of Puerto Rico in 2009 and was published in 2010.

Anaida Pascual-Morán, Professor at the Graduate Studies Department of the School of Education at the Río Piedras Campus of the University of Puerto Rico, San Juan, Puerto Rico; Email: rivepas@gmail.com.

© Springer Nature Switzerland AG 2019
D. T. Snauwaert (ed.), *Exploring Betty A. Reardon's Perspective on Peace Education*, Pioneers in Arts, Humanities, Science, Engineering, Practice 20, https://doi.org/10.1007/978-3-030-18387-5_6

this reflective inquiry, I not only revisit, but also delve deeper into her interwoven assertions and suggestive images. My reflective stance is also viewed through the lens of some of Reardon's recent writings and undertakings; advances and ongoing research in the field; contemporary emergent pedagogies rooted in Paolo Freire's liberatory vision; and, key current international initiatives from a culture of peace and human dignity perspective. I also address several learnings and challenges that arise from Reardon's foundational work, in light of our own research and educational trajectory in the field and recently lived experiences in Puerto Rico.

6.2   Human Rights Learning: "The Promise of a Transformed, Peaceful, and Just Global Order..."

Reardon affirms that human rights principles and values configure an ethical system that announces "the promise of a transformed, peaceful, and just global order" (2010, p. 47). Specifically, she contends that human rights learning and the critical pedagogies inherent to peace education are conducive to the cultivation of a politics of peace and the respect of human dignity in formative scenarios that include, but nevertheless transcend, schools and universities.

Reardon substantiates the essence of her argument on the basis of a theoretical framework composed of *five premises*. In her *first premise*, Reardon maintains that the "universal actualization of human dignity" through the respect for the totality of human rights and the transformation of worldviews and modes of thought is an essential condition for achieving a sustainable peace. Reardon's *second premise*, notes that holism and critical reflection are crucial to a transformational thinking capable of considering peace and justice issues, while making the respect for human rights possible. Her *third premise* states that a truly democratic and nonviolent politics of peace requires the development of capacities geared to understanding learning as "a process of internalized change". In her *fourth premise*, she depicts human rights learning as an "active learning and learning for action", that requires us to "practice politics as learning and learning as political engagement". And finally, in her *fifth premise*, Reardon invites us to undertake an urgent endeavor: to disseminate a Freirean pedagogy, aimed towards transformative political and social learning.

Based on the framework provided by these five principles, Reardon draws attention to *seven propositions* for human rights learning. The *first proposition*, focuses on the centrality of human rights and a holistic paradigm that ties cognitive and affective domains. While the *second proposition*, alludes to human rights learning as a contemporary Freirean politics, with the potential to give birth to a new social and political reality. Her *third proposition* insists on the dyad "violence/ vulnerability", derived from the critical analysis of the patriarchal origin of fundamental inequities, as a suitable conceptual and ethical tool to foster human rights learning, detect structural injustice, and build a politics of peace. In her *fourth proposition*, Reardon points at pedagogical junctures, such as the *International Year of Human Rights Learning* (2009) and the *Decade for Human Rights Education* (1995–2004), to attain advances and significant transformations. The *fifth proposition*, stresses the pertinence of fostering dialogical "creative-constructive" pedagogies, and generating a persuasive politics of deliberation, action and reflection that challenge those in power and advance human rights. Her *sixth proposition* distinguishes Freirean pedagogy, as the most coherent means to meet the transformative goals of peace education, human rights learning and critical citizenship. Finally, by means of her *seventh proposition*, Reardon calls for individual reflection, shared critique and communal inquiry, as modes of learning conducive to the internalization of human rights values, the respect for human dignity, and the conception of a courageous, hopeful and creative politics of peace.

6.3 Human Rights: "Arbiters of Peace… in the Denial of Human Dignity…"

According to Reardon, both education in general and conventional human rights education based on the transference of information in international documents, "reveal blindness", because they assume learning and education to be synonymous. Furthermore, they both share the premise that socially constructive, critical and holistic learning is an inevitable consequence of education, independent of the reductionist and fragmented "curricular recipes" followed. Moreover, she considers that even though *education* can "plant seeds", it is *learning* that "cultivates the fruit of social and human potential". In this sense, Reardon designates human rights learning as a "generative process", essential to becoming fully human, just "as breathing is to be alive" and "as clean water and adequate food to a healthy society." Thus, Reardon expounds, this learning process requires from us not a "scripted curriculum", but requires us to be competent "high wire performers", "teaching without a net" – which is analogous to "the joys of playing and listening to jazz".

Reardon deliberately distinguishes the critical human rights learning that "conscientization illuminates" from the limited information transference vision, of traditional human rights education. She argues that in this limited conception, the diverse worldviews of learners are not examined or questioned; neither is an "authentic and transparent dialogue with power" present. Furthermore, she expresses that this approach is distant to peace education, which generally adopts a Freirean praxis, with socio-political learning and social justice as pedagogical core. She also indicates, that this central nucleus requires that human rights be integrated in a critical ecological curricular framework as _purpose_ (objectives), *substance* (content), and *process* (methodology). From this perspective, human rights learning fosters significant social and political change, and human rights constitute "the most promising instrument" for a formative process conducive to a politics of peace and respect of human dignity.

Reardon also adduces that human rights as a whole act as "arbiters of peace", since they lead us to identify "the denial of human dignity" in the context of violations, vulnerabilities, and violence. In human rights, she attests, we find the "ethical core" of an education for peace, built upon the value of human dignity, since they provide "enlightening sources" to analyze structural, social and economic oppression. At the same time, they create the appropriate conditions to lessen the impact of violence, understood as "intentional avoidable harm" inflicted upon marginalized populations, due to the ethical failures of the powerful and the complicity of the privileged. Reardon also considers that civil, political, economic, social, and cultural rights for the vulnerable, articulate a holistic transformative vision of a world free of violence and vulnerability. Moreover, they represent a "secular code" for a social, spiritual, and moral ethics, since they provide tools to define and deal with the structural injustices caused by abuses of power.

These injustices, assures Reardon, commonly affect those at the lower levels of the social, economic, and political structures: women, poor, elderly, children, migrants and minorities. In this respect, human rights of the vulnerable constitute "an excellent lens" for determining the violation of human rights. Thus, alleges Reardon, when human rights are denied, they offer indicators of violence and vulnerability. Yet, when they are fulfilled, they provide indicators of progress, since they "put flesh on the bones of the abstraction of peace, bringing the flesh to life" (Reardon 2010, p. 85).

6.4 Human Rights Learning and Peace Education: "The Philosophical Conjoined Twins…"

Pedagogically speaking, Reardon suggests human rights learning is "the philosophical conjoined twin" of peace education, since they share the same pillars: authentic dialogue, the discourse of difference as a crucial value, and close ties between the "reflexive-personal" and the "communal-political". Moreover, it depicts an "impulse toward social justice", since it is rooted in *conscientization*, inspired by the "Freirean liberatory promise". Thus, it requires a "process of internalized change" situated in scenarios such as government programs, community spaces, education ministries, school systems, religious entities, and universities. Said process of change, must be aimed at challenging the limits imposed by "social and political realism", and assuming "idealism as a practical tool".

This approach reminds us that "the most powerful engine" for change, given that its "arena of human rights learning" is lived human experience, as well as ethical and social conscience. Thus, given the diverse and growing forms of violence and vulnerability it requires pedagogies which seek to delegitimize systemic violence and foster an awakening conducive to the sharing of the available "fruits of peoples' resources and talents". Because, at the end, she observes, "just societies" are those that once aware of their vulnerabilities and manifestations of violence, seek to prevent and overcome them.

6.5 Liberatory Pedagogy: "The Conceptual and Methodological Heart of Human Rights Learning…"

Reardon conveys human rights learning as a liberatory pedagogy. Specifically, she points at the valuable contributions of Freirean perspective, in that it leads us to a socially constructive learning and to action in favor of public policies of change. Moreover, she acknowledges that this emancipatory pedagogy is the unquestionable founder of contemporary critical pedagogies and constitutes "the conceptual and methodological heart" of human rights learning.

In Reardon's understanding, three key elements characterize this pedagogical approach: holism, critical learning, and commitment to change. Such critical approach must reclaim the language of education, so that it is conceived as a process geared towards transformational thinking. It also requires ethical reflection and social responsibility leading to a change in values and worldviews to avoid the violation of human rights caused by structural economic, social, cultural, and political violence. As a summary metaphor, Reardon poses the conception-birth processes to image a paradigm shift, from an informative conventional human rights education, to human rights learning as a Freirean pedagogy. She remarks that although there are indicators that this pedagogy is 'aborning' with the potential to "give birth to a new reality", "the labor process" is extremely difficult, since it requires all of the possible "midwifery skills" peace education may provide.

6.6 Freirean Liberatory Pedagogical Advances: "Alternative Possibilities toward Transformative Change…"

Many current pedagogical advances from a liberatory perspective in Latin America and the Caribbean region fundamentally coincide with Reardon's assertions on human rights learning as a politics for peace. Thus, emergent dialogical and participatory pedagogies rooted in this perspective may further strengthen and enrich Reardon's work. From a Freirean viewpoint, "authentic liberation" implies reflection and action upon the world to transform it and education must be aimed at *problematization*, *conscientization* and *humanization* (Freire 1993, 2005, 2006). Likewise, *dialogicity* must be affirmed from the theory and coherently, become *dialogical* in practice, drawing from: a *dialogical pedagogy*, that acknowledges the "educatee's intersubjectivity" and opposes authoritarian forms of teaching; a *dialogical environment*, characterized by a democratic way of communication and a rupture with relations of oppression; and, a *dialogical method*, as a *participatory* and *problematizing* process, capable of illuminating and transforming social, cultural, historic and politic realities of inequity and exclusion (Shor/Freire 1987).

As concrete examples, I would like to single out the pedagogical ideas and key propositions of three Latin American colleagues with a long trajectory in the field of peace and human rights education: Alicia Cabezudo, Abraham Magendzo and Ana María Rodino-Pierri. It is no coincidence that these three peace researchers and educators share with Betty Reardon the distinction of having offered the keynote address at our UNESCO Chair for Peace Education at the University of Puerto Rico. Neither it is fortuitous that most (*if not all*) have shared joint endeavors related to peace and human rights research and education with Reardon. For example, as part of the Hague Appeal for Peace Global Campaign for Peace Education, Reardon and Cabezudo, co-authored a 3-book packet *Learning to abolish war: Teaching toward a culture of peace* (Reardon/Cabezudo 2002). These valuable resource materials, which aim at radically reducing if not eradicating armed conflict, include a theoretical framework, sample lessons, and tools for action related to human rights, humanitarian law, conflict prevention and resolution, disarmament, human security, and a culture of peace.

Fundamentally, Cabezudo (2013) concurs with the nature and scope of Reardon's transformative pedagogies and politics of peace stance. The peace scholar and activist from the University of Rosario in Argentina, stipulates that peace and human rights education's quest for justice is an urgent societal practical need and unquestionable ethical imperative. To this end, she postulates that we have to "build bridges" between peace education and human rights education, revisit traditional constructs, evaluate our pedagogical practices, and jointly elaborate action projects in contexts that may contribute to the construction of more just and equitable societies. Specifically, Cabezudo (2009) recognizes the urgent need to "educate for peace in the city", since it is a geographical space that harbors the majority of the population. Moreover, she likens the city to a "mini world", characterized by a complex ethnic, religious, cultural and socioeconomic diversity, that reproduce all the possibilities and injustices of the wide world. According to Cabezudo, the city is "an ample educational scenario", a privileged "spatial location for peace" that offers extraordinary formal and informal possibilities for pedagogical work towards social justice, equity, solidarity and respect for human rights.

More recently, as vice president of the International Peace Bureau in Geneva, Cabezudo has made inroads in applying the politics of peace to the current "territorial peace" talks and agreements in Colombia – after more than five decades of armed conflict. Particularly, she proposes working from a "social pedagogy" perspective that raises the ethical duty of educational communities to act towards a stable and lasting peace, related to dignification of those vulnerable groups that have been victims of the armed conflict and the recognition of their social, political, economic, and cultural rights (2017). To this effect, Cabezudo is collaborating with various educational entities and communities in the post conflict reconstructive phase in Colombia. For example, she is contributing to the excellent work of our Colombian colleague Benavidez (2016), in the *Schools for Peace Foundation*, geared towards the construction of a national agenda for peace education, with the goal of influencing public policies to combat diverse forms of direct, structural and cultural violence afflicting Colombia.

The Chilean pioneer in the field Abraham Magendzo, asserts that Freirean liberatory and critical pedagogies provide an ideal emancipatory framework for human rights education, while at the same time, human rights education is one of the more tangible expressions of such pedagogies. He reveals that in order to attain its main goal – empowering learners to become "subjects of human rights" – human rights education requires awareness of how "the power component" of certain pedagogies and curriculum interact, so that we can aim at emancipation from all forms of domination and get students involved in actions towards the promotion and defense of the rights of others and their own rights (Magendzo 2005).

From Magendzo's (2006, 2015) perspective, human rights education must be considered an ethical and political education, "a part of life, rather than something separate from and largely irrelevant to other parts of life". In this respect, it must be linked to real problems and issues, such as: poverty, injustices, violence, racism, discrimination, oppression, intolerance, impunity and corruption. Also, it must be conducive to strengthening the students' capacities, so that they can present solutions from an "ethics of human rights". His perspective requires an experiential and active methodology where, after confronting ideas and problematizing their reality, students face their personal and collective life situations and deal with day-to-day conflicts, contradictions, conflicts, tensions and dilemmas.

In his most recent work Magendzo advocates for a *"pedagogy of controversy"*, within a human rights framework and when human rights themselves come in conflict with each other. In essence, he upholds that human rights education must be centered in *'controversialidad'*. Educating in human rights from a controversial perspective implies acknowledging disagreements and dissensions as positive interactions, capable of elucidating a better comprehension of human rights situations and dilemmas. His proposal also accentuates providing students appropriate spaces and opportunities for dialogical reflection and to develop argumentative competencies conducive to conflict management and resolution. Magendzo also summons us to embrace a transformative role and to construct "peace and human rights bearers", inasmuch as education's overall mission is to enlighten the conflictive and contradictory situations that confront us in social, cultural, economic and political scenarios (Magendzo-Kolstrein/Toledo-Jofré 2015a; Magendzo-Kolstrein/Pavéz-Bravo 2015b).

In tune with Reardon, Cabezudo and Magendzo, our Argentinian-Costa Rican colleague Ana María Rodino-Pierri (2016), stands up for cultivating a pluralistic culture of equity, democratic co-existence, and solidarity from three inseparable perspectives: *education as a human right, human rights education*, and *human rights in education*. Rodino-Pierri draws our attention to the fact that the profound and synergic connections between these three constructs denote an embedded complexity, so that no one can disregard the others. For example, we cannot isolate the right to education from the respect for all human rights. Neither divorce human rights education from this interaction, which at the same time is essential for human rights learning (Pascual-Morán 2016).

Rodino-Pierri (2016) recalls that education is, first and foremost, a human right, and that we must avoid the dangers of embracing it exclusively, from an economics-based approach, as "human capital" or "social investment". Metaphorically speaking, Rodino-Pierri envisions the right to education as: 'richness' of economic, social, civil and cultural rights; as 'key' to making our educatee's lives more dignified; and, as a 'bridge' in the transit of every learner towards his or her consciousness about our social realities. She also upholds human rights educations mediating role, legitimized by a broad theoretical, pedagogical and normative corpus, as long as it is geared towards the full exercise of human rights, and the setting in motion of action policies. Furthermore, Rodino-Pierri foresees human rights learning as 'lens', "powerful tool", and "living practice", that urgently needs to be integrated in every educational endeavor (Pascual-Morán 2016).

The assertions that Cabezudo, Magendzo and Rodino-Pierri espouse, can certainly be reconciled with Betty's Reardon's key premise that human rights learning comprises both a critical pedagogy and a politics of peace conducive to the respect of human dignity. And their practical pedagogical approaches, in many ways exemplify Reardon's crucial assertion that only by "*learning and living human rights*" in the context of transformative pedagogies, can we be capable of making possible a politics of peace. Their emergent pedagogical assertions and proposals, rooted in Freire's liberatory perspective from a Latin American and Caribbean contextual experience, also bring forth new stances that certainly may further inspire, advance, and enrich Reardon's foundational and more recent work.

They also portray the "*pedagogy of alternatives*" construct that Reardon (2008) borrows from Mark Webb's "Letter to Naomi Klein" (2008), proposing it as a pedagogical lens to view inequity and injustice in order to strategize options, and bring about "transformed realities" and paradigm shifts. At the heart of City University of New York professor Mark Webb's constructive critique of Naomi Klein's "shock doctrine" and "theory of disaster capitalism", contends Reardon (2008), is the urgency to "break through the sense of the inevitability of violence and injustice" (p. 131). In other words, just as we won't be able to transcend market capitalism unless we consider alternative principles and values of competitive social and economic organization, we will not be able "to effect change that could steer the world toward justice and equity" (p. 133). Thus, concludes Reardon, "the encouragement and facilitation of reflection on alternative possibilities toward transformative change is an essential element of peace education" (p. 133). And so is the underscoring of complementarities and commonalities, rather than the exclusive consideration of the differences, contradictions, and adversarial arguments.

6.7 Synergizing and Joining Forces with Betty Reardon: "Intentional and Avoidable Harm..." – in Puerto Rico

Many coincidences and synergies also exist between Betty Reardon's foundational work and our own research and lived experiences in Puerto Rico. Such is the case with regards to the action-ideas ("*ideas-fuerza*") in our trajectory for human rights and a culture of peace. For example, based on research conducted with professor Anita Yudkin-Suliveres, we identified five principles that have provided the basis for action in Puerto Rico: (1) equity and diversity, (2) intergenerational justice, (3) quality of life, (4) self-determination, and, (5) culture of peace and human rights. We also singled out a driving action-idea of synthesis that the movement "*All of Puerto Rico with Vieques*" has lived for decades, in the struggle for demilitarization, cleanup and sustainable development: *an ethics of solidarity* (Yudkin-Suliveres/ Pascual-Morán 2009).

Many of the assertions and conclusions regarding the action-ideas resulting from this study, are consistent with the central propositions held by professor Reardon. For example, we concluded that human rights education geared towards critical, creative and transformative learning constitutes a core dimension of the diverse and complex field of peace education. Also, that human rights an integrating axis of peace education, while at the same time peace comprises a "human right of synthesis" of our fundamental freedoms. Along the same line, we came to the conclusion that human rights education must aspire to construct, by means of liberatory and critical pedagogies, the scaffold for a new culture based on the values of peace, justice and nonviolence. Another coincidental synergy with our study resides in actual reality, due to the fact that Betty Reardon has publicly denounced for many years that the situation in Vieques exemplifies evident violations of human rights by means of "intentional and avoidable harm". Furthermore, she has argued that our beloved and mistreated '*Isla Nena*', just like Okinawa, embody before the world community a clear instance of military and ecological violence against vulnerable civilian populations.

More recently, we have synergized and joined forces with Betty in addressing two tragic events that unfortunately contextualize our present reality. The first tragic situation is the imposition by the US Congress of the *Junta de Control Fiscal* (Fiscal Control Board) to oversee Puerto Rico's debt restructuring since 2016. The second one is related to the unprecedented devastation that brought about category-5 hurricane 'María'... on that memorable Wednesday of September 20, 2017.

At a local level, the consequential debacle after 'María' was brought about by inadequate emergency plans, logistics coordination difficulties and supplies shortage. It was aggravated, by the negligent contingency plans of the US Government, its delayed and insufficient response, and its underestimation of the magnitude of the catastrophe and death toll. The deaths greatly exceeded the government's official number, an inaccuracy denounced by the *Center for Investigative*

Journalism (CPI) only seven days after the hurricane (Sosa-Pascual 2017). These were deaths that could have been avoided, since most were the product of negligent acts and systemic failures that lasted for many months related to access to energy, health services, and infrastructure. Approximately a year later, the situation was validated by Harvard University and George Washington University studies, which indicated an estimate that ranged from 800 to 8,500 deaths. In this respect, CPI attests to the fact that "most of these deaths occurred in hospitals, which experienced an increase in mortality of 32.3% and were practically inoperative, without electric service, without generators or with deficient ones, and without fuel reserves to operate" (Sosa-Pascual et al. 2018).

Under US federal law "Puerto Rico Oversight, Management, and Economic Stability Act", ironically called "Ley PROMESA", the "Junta de Control Fiscal" currently imposes fiscal planning for the Government of Puerto Rico, thus determining detrimental cuts in key policy areas, such as access to health services, funds for public education, approval of infrastructure projects, and regulation of public employees' pensions. The reality is that this externally appointed governing entity and unelected oversight board fundamentally exists not only to exercise austerity restructuring measures and insolvency proceedings as a result of the debt crisis the Puerto Rican Government is facing, but even more so, in order to protect the bondholders and other financial creditors.

These two inextricably tied realities have affected significantly our recovery efforts after María, not only because of the Junta's budget cuts, but also due to the fact that the US Congress is not setting financial priorities, nor allocating resources for reconstruction consistent with the magnitude of the natural disaster. The unjust situation has led us to make urgent requests to politicians and policy makers, such as demanding that the questionable public debt be audited, and asking the US Congress to repeal the PROMESA Law and to exempt us permanently from the Jones Act. Also known as The Merchant Marine Act of 1920, this unjust law requires that goods shipped between US ports and Puerto Rico be transported on ships that are built, owned and operated by US citizens or permanent residents.

In both tragic situations, Betty's exemplary aphorism of "*learning and living human rights*" materialized in solidarity actions and real contributions. For example, on the aftermath of hurricane María, she actively did networking efforts with congregations in New York, in order to offer relief and build partnerships to help rebuild the Island. At the time, most of us did not have water, electricity or any communication whatsoever; so almost every day I went to areas near hospitals in order to access the internet in order to communicate, not only with close family and friends to see how they were dealing with the emergency, but at her request with Betty, in order to give her updates on the situation and to provide her with information about ecumenical entities and key persons she planned to contact.

Betty never ceased in her efforts to disseminate what was happening to us. For example, I used to send her investigative journalistic articles regarding the devastation and the controversial death count post María by our government, which she proceeded diligently to circulate in the social networks, so that the truth about the situation could be known and gather support. Furthermore, only six weeks after the hurricane Betty authored an article in which she exposes how the whole Island was still in dire condition: most without running water and electricity, enduring shortages and lack of many essentials. In this same article, she also describes how the University of Puerto Rico Río Piedras Campus was severely hit by María, while at the same time she profiles with hope the courage, resilience, and spiritual strength that abounded within our learning community as a whole (Reardon 2017).

Betty even went further in her solidarity action. In this same article, she artfully provided a link to a key document: *"The Cruelest Storm: A Statement for Puerto Rico"* (Latino 2017), convening readers to sign the document and learn more about the circumstances of a "Puerto Rico post María" and the historical and political roots of our current economic and social conditions. The document, which started to circulate only about a week after the hurricane, contained a declaration from a collective of Puerto Rican intellectuals, mostly academics in the diaspora teaching in the US. This is a document that on one hand, denounces "the different legal, political, financial, and logistical predatory forces behind the current second-class-citizenship impasse that is increasing the risk and expendability of Puerto Rican lives after María's catastrophic wake". And on the other, insists upon "an urgent call to politicians and policy makers to exempt Puerto Rico permanently from the Jones Act and repeal the PROMESA Law and other measures and policies that are hampering recovery" (Latino 2017).

But Betty could not be stopped form her desire to support us. Pedagogically she planned and sponsored several formative activities to foster awareness related to both situations – 'María' and 'PROMESA'. In the politics of peace arena, for example, she made lobbying efforts with US Congress leaders in favor of more fairness and justice in the austerity plans of the *Junta de Control Fiscal*. For example, she joined efforts with Hispanic community leaders and members of the Congressional Hispanic Caucus, in the task of delineation of a *10-Point Plan to Address Puerto Rico Humanitarian Crisis* (Espaillat 2017). This plan included, among other demands and recommendations: the enactment of an emergency relief package post María; setting up a task force to coordinate strategic long-term recovery efforts and asses how to mitigate delayed reactions; waiving the Jones Act for diesel and fuel, so that rebuilding efforts were not limited; deployment of an emergency response team to assist local crews; sending more electrical engineers to support efforts in fully restoring the telecommunications system and fix the generators in hospitals; solicit help from US medical institutions to transport children with life threatening conditions and help them get medical attention; deploy more medical personnel on the ground and provide more medicines; restore funding for municipalities that were paying millions for Puerto Rico's debt until the crisis stabilized; deliver necessary supplies in the most remote parts of the Island; and, provide support to prevent epidemics and a public health crisis.

In all the exemplary instances mentioned, Reardon's aphorism of "*learning and living human rights*", as crucial in "*giving birth to a new reality*" free from violence and vulnerability, came to life. For her constant solidarity actions towards our beloved Island… yesterday, today, and for years to come… we have towards Betty Reardon an enormous admiration and debt of gratitude.

6.8 Alongside Betty Reardon… "Learning and Living Human Rights…"

Certainly, Betty Reardon's profound and provocative foundational work and her own existential and practical coherent work in the field, contribute to and enrich our own views of an education for human rights and a culture of peace. Specifically, I will like to succinctly draw attention to *seven key learnings* that we can derive from her work and perspectives:

1. "Learning and living human rights" is crucial to engage in peace education and solidarity action from a transformative and politics of peace perspective.
2. These reciprocal processes are fundamental, if we want to make critical advances and significant transformations towards new realities.
3. Human rights learning and the critical pedagogies of peace education configure an ethical system conducive to the cultivation of a politics of peace and the respect of human dignity.
4. Conventional transference of information human rights education must be replaced by human rights learning integrated in a critical ecological curricular framework, with social justice as pedagogical core.
5. Human rights learning and peace education jointly constitute a powerful instrument in discourse and action to address the diverse and growing forms of violence and vulnerability.
6. Liberatory pedagogy, as founder of contemporary critical pedagogies, constitutes "the conceptual and methodological heart" of human rights learning.
7. The promotion of reflection on alternative possibilities toward transformative change and the consideration of complementarities and commonalities perceived from diverse perspectives are essential elements of peace education.

6.9 Advancing Betty Reardon's Transformative Pedagogies and Politics of Peace Legacy

Harmonizing these key learnings with current advances and ongoing research in the field, and my own trajectory of pedagogical experiences in the field of peace and human rights research and education, I will also like to bring forth *five challenges* to this reflection. Assuming the Freirean *pedagogy of problematizing* (Freire/Faúndez 1986) and Reardon's perspective of the immense value of a *pedagogy of alternatives*, my intent is to affirm, diversify, and enrich Betty Reardon's foundational and recent work.

6.9.1 Education / Human Rights / Integral Peace: Strengthening their Interconnections...

In educating for a culture of peace and human rights, besides prioritizing the interweaving between *human rights* and *education*, it is absolutely essential to strengthen ties with a third key construct in the equation: "*integral peace*". Understanding this notion, just as the United Nations Educational, Scientific and Cultural Organization does: "the presence of social justice and harmony; the possibility that human beings attain their fullest potential and enjoy their right to a dignified and sustainable survival" (UNESCO 1994, p. 4). From my own research and teaching trajectory, I have been able to corroborate that these interactions provide us with a prism to rethink our pedagogical and investigative/creative scaffolds. Furthermore, they bring to life how the perception of education as a universal right may contribute significantly to the construction of "cultures of integral peace" at schools, universities and other formative institutions. Consequently, I reaffirm the urgency of assuming a hopeful stance towards transformative actions, with the interconnections between these constructs as a point of departure.

6.9.2 Pedagogical Advances in Freire's Liberatory Perspective: Asserting a Multidimensional Peace...

Certainly, current and emergent pedagogical advances from a liberatory perspective, may further strengthen, inspire, and enrich Betty Reardon's foundational work and our own initiatives in the field, such as the aforementioned pedagogical proposals posed by Alicia Cabezudo, Ana María Rodino-Pierri and Abraham Magendzo. Such is also the case of other pedagogical ideas conveyed by Spanish pioneers in the field, like Vincent Fisas, Xesús Jares, and José Tuvilla-Rayo. It is extremely relevant, for example, how these renowned authors understand the notion of "positive peace" as an always imperfect and unfinished process; that beyond the absence of war, violence and conflict, demands a comprehensive, dynamic, and "integral peace". So is their assertion of a "multidimensional peace" that requires working towards: (a) "*direct peace*", via constructive conflict management processes; (b) "*cultural peace*", by means of shared values; and, (c) "*structural peace*", through politics of social justice (Fisas 2002; Jares 2002, 2005; Tuvilla-Rayo 2004, 2006).

6.9.3 Pedagogies of Differences … Attending Diversities and Envisioning Unforeseen Alterities…

Educating for peace and human rights also presents the challenge of working from an explicit *pedagogy of differences* perspective. This pedagogical approach entails envisioning equity and inclusion as weaving threads and driving force through culture and education, thus providing a key scaffold towards the eradication of discrimination, exclusion, and violence.

As claimed by Swiss sociologist and educational theorist Perrenoud (2007), the *pedagogy of differences* historically emerges from a 'rebellion' against inequalities, with the aim of contributing to efface discrimination and exclusion. Likewise, Argentinian researcher and philosopher Skliar (2013, p. 2), cautions that a pedagogy of differences involves a pedagogical framework from which we are able to "come close to the encounter with the Other, his or her words, his or her body, his or her gaze", in the context of a "horizon of social equality and difference", that recognizes every singularity and all "unforeseen alterities". This pedagogical framework, as Argentinian education policy specialist Juan Carlos Tedesco suggests (1995), deals with enabling every human being to make a choice on how to construct his or her "multiple identities". Furthermore, as Vignale et al. (2014) from the Centro de Ciencia, Educación y Sociedad in Buenos Aires allege, this is a pedagogy of differences in plural, a multiplicity of pedagogies of singularities, "pedagogies to be born, to come…" – understood as "spaces where the existing relationships stemming from cognitively-based and traditional pedagogical discourses are pulverized, reconfigured, and move through other more singular, airy, and desirable paths".

From the perspective of an ethics of solidarity and an inclusive educational culture of peace and human rights, the pedagogy of differences I propose as an emancipatory pedagogy centered in human dignity and the richness of "that which is different" is no exception. It requires as a general framework of reference and action, a *growth paradigm* that respects diversities and honors strengths and potentialities in every learner. It also entails, acknowledging the singularity of every learner and his or her inalienable human right to optimal development, by means of a *differentiated* teaching approach, geared towards a *personalized* learning process. Therefore, all in all, current pedagogical theories, models and advances in terms of *differentiation* and *personalization* may not only strengthen but also enrich, Reardon's transformative pedagogies and our own work in peace and human rights education (Pascual-Morán 2014a, b).

6.9.4 Systematizing Our "Pedagogical Wisdoms"… Constructing a Culture of Peace and Human Rights

Human rights traverse our formative endeavors and take root as a narrative thread on those principles, practices and projects that define, guide, and inspire us as educators and researchers. Hence, it is essential to recapture, resignify, and reconstruct our pedagogical lived experiences, in order to reappraise those theoretical and investigative/creative constructs that intersect with the construction of a culture of peace and human rights. This requires that we harness the essential systematization tools that enable the coherent articulation of our experiences and practices. And once we have systematized these "accumulated wisdoms", it is essential that we share and socialize them.

Attention should be drawn to the fact that the pioneer proposals for *systematization*, principled on a critical-reflective epistemic base of research and production of knowledge built from practice, emerged in the Latin America and Caribbean region in the sixties – and later extended to other latitudes. They unfolded in the context of diverse popular education, communication and participative action-research initiatives; alongside other pedagogical, social, and theological movements of a liberatory nature. *It's intention and rationale?* To recuperate the richness, plurality, and complexity of 'wisdoms' ('*saberes*'), stemming from emancipatory transformative live-practices and as an alternative to the prevailing hegemonic and reductionist Eurocentric paradigms of "universal knowledge" and "scientific/rationalist" models of teaching, research and evaluation (Mejía 2012; Jara 1994, 2005).

As stated by Peruvian-Costa Rican sociologist and educator Jara (1994, 2005), it is crucial to systematize our experiences and practices, since they are depositories of a wealth of wisdoms that is our responsibility to reconstruct and socialize. It involves, a "dialectic methodological conception", through which we objectify what we have lived and experienced, in order to derive profound learnings. Colombian researcher and educator Mejía (2012) defines systematization in the "terrain of knowledge", as a "way of investigating practices and producing wisdoms". Likewise, our colleague from Venezuela, Díaz-Quero (2004, 2006), indicates that our "pedagogical wisdoms" constitute "action principles", since in our praxis – consciously or unconsciously – we construct "pedagogical wisdoms" of a theoretical, practical, and reflective nature. Díaz-Quero asserts that when we theorize our practice, it becomes an instance of validation of that theory. That is, theory and practice dialectically interact and new wisdoms are constantly produced, that we are called upon to reflect, systematize and share. Thus, we must take on the challenge of evoking and revisiting our "pedagogical wisdoms" in the field from a hopeful perspective – in dialogue with colleagues, students, and our diverse learning communities.

6.9.5 Key Recent International Initiatives: Enlightening Our Work from a Culture of Peace and Human Dignity Perspective ...

Certainly, key recent international initiatives, conventions and policies from a culture of peace and human dignity perspective may enlighten our work in the field.

We are thus called upon to insert our formative endeavors in those international alliances and multisectoral partnerships. Such is the case of three calls to action in recent decades, all of extreme relevance as a working frame of reference: (a) the promotion of peace as human right of synthesis and international ethical directive, with the goal of constructing a new type of education and culture (CIDHP 2010); (b) the culture of peace and nonviolence movement/vision, that summons us to affirm values and principles of social justice, coexistence and respect for life, nature and diversity (UNESCO 2000); and, (c) the 2030 *Agenda for Sustainable Development*, adopted in 2015 by the General Assembly of the United Nations and other sectors of civil society, a comprehensive plan geared towards eradicating "the tyranny of poverty" in all its forms and the empowerment of all women and girls, as indispensable requirements for gender equality and a full lasting peace, that includes 17 sustainable development goals in three inseparable dimensions: the economic, social and environmental spheres (UN 2015).

6.10   Assuming the "Urgency of Now"… Awakening our "Right to Dream"…

Challenges and paradigmatic turns such as those previously mentioned entail – as Martin Luther King advocates and Reardon urges (2010) – that we assume the "urgency of now", guided by a profound faith in human imagination and in our capacity to learn. They also require a redefined educational language, enlightened by a problem-posing pedagogy. In my pedagogical prism, this goes hand in hand, with envisioning "projects of possibility" that call for an integral and sustainable peace resulting from investigative and creative transformative actions. To this end, we must adopt the dreamt profile that Betty Reardon has drawn for us as a starting point: peace educators committed to promulgating human rights learning and generating "a critical, creative and courageous citizenry" (2010, p. 87).

Certainly, Betty Reardon' transformative pedagogies and politics of peace legacy concur with Paulo Freire's liberatory pedagogical perspective, since he compels us to indignantly *denounce* injustices, lovingly *announce* transformations, and hopefully *dream* with the possibilities that "the viable inedited" may bring. In light of Freire's predicament, we understand Reardon's view of peace educators as those who seek to dedicate their talents and energies to *denounce* "the denial of humanity of many by the few", announce the optimal development of our humanity and our learners as fundamental right, and dream with the creation of more just societies premised on solidarity and the respect for human rights. Certainly, Betty Reardon not only embraces the principles and values of the ideal peace educator she profiles, but also personifies her heartfelt aphorism of *"learning and living human rights"*. Moreover, in words and deeds, she incarnates our inalienable right to dream, along the lines the renowned Uruguayan writer Eduardo Galeano poetically portrays it…

Who knows how the world will be in 2025! […] Although we cannot predict the world that will be, we can well imagine the one we would like there to be. In 1948 and again in 1976, the United Nations promulgated extensive lists of human rights; but the immense majority of humanity enjoys only the rights to see, hear and remain silent. Suppose we start by exercising the never-proclaimed right to dream? Suppose we become a bit delirious? Let's set our sights above and beyond the infamy of today, to foresee another possible world… (Galeano 1995, 1996).

References

Benavidez, A. (ed.) (2016). *Pensar en educación para la paz. Apuestas del Encuentro Nacional de Educación para la Paz*, 1ero y 2 de octubre de 2015, Bogotá, Colombia. Retrieved from http://culture-of-peace.info/EDUCACION_PARA_LA_PAZ_FINAL.pdf.

Cabezudo, A. (2009). *Educar para la paz en la ciudad.* Conferencia Magistral 2005–2006, Cátedra UNESCO de Educación para la Paz, Universidad de Puerto Rico, Recinto de Río Piedras. Retrieved from http://unescopaz.uprrp.edu/act/Lecciones/Cabezudo/Cabezudoconfmagistral.pdf.

Cabezudo, A. (2013). *Acerca de una educación para la paz, los derechos humanos y el desarme*: *Desafío pedagógico de nuestro tiempo*. Educação, Porto Alegre, *36*(1), 44–49. Retrieved from http://revistaseletronicas.pucrs.br/ojs/index.php/faced/article/viewFile/12313/8739.

Cabezudo, A. (2017, April 24). *Se necesita más pedagogía social* [Radial interview in Colombia by Tatiana Orozco]. Retrieved from http://www.cacicastereo.com/index.php?option=com_k2&view=item&id=10418:se-necesita-mas-pedagogia-social-alicia-cabezudo&Itemid=560.

CIDHP (2010, December 10). *Declaración de Santiago sobre el Derecho Humano a la Paz*. Congreso Internacional sobre el Derecho Humano a Paz, Santiago de Compostela, España: Foro Social Mundial sobre la Educación para la Paz.

Díaz-Quero, V. (2004). Teoría emergente en la construcción del saber pedagógico. *TELOS. Revista de Estudios Interdisciplinarios en Ciencias Sociales.* Universidad Rafael Belloso Chacín, Maracaibo, Venezuela, *6*(2), 169–193. Retrieved from https://core.ac.uk/download/pdf/158366853.pdf.

Díaz-Quero, V. (2006). Formación docente, práctica pedagógica y saber pedagógico. *Revista de Educación Laurus* 12, pp. 88–103. Retrieved from: Redalyc, Red de Revistas Científicas de América Latina y el Caribe, España y Portugal. Retrieved from http://www.redalyc.org/articulo.oa?id=76109906.

Espaillat, A. (2017). *Congressmember Adriano Espaillat 10-Point Plan to Address Puerto Rico Humanitarian Crisis*. New York's 13th Congressional District.

Fisas, V. (2002). *La paz es posible*: *Una agenda para la paz del siglo XXI*. Barcelona: Intermón/Oxfam.

Freire, P. (1993). *Pedagogía de la esperanza. Un reencuentro con la pedagogía del oprimido*. Madrid: Siglo XXI.

Freire, P. (2005). *Cartas a quien pretende enseñar* (10ma ed.) España: Siglo Veintiuno Editores.

Freire, P. (2006). *Pedagogía de la indignación*. Madrid, España: Ediciones Morata, S.L.

Freire, P. & Faúndez, A. (1986). *Pedagogía de la pregunta*. Buenos Aires, Argentina: La Aurora.

Galeano, E. (1995, July). *The right to dream*. New Internationalist [Blog]. Retrieved from https://newint.org/blog/2015/04/13/galeano-right-to-dream/.

Galeano, E. (1996, December 26). *El derecho a soñar*. Tribuna, El País. Madrid: España [Website]. Retrieved from https://elpais.com/diario/1996/12/26/opinion/851554801_850215.html.

Jara, H. O. (1994). *Para sistematizar experiencias*: *Una propuesta teórica y práctica*. Costa Rica: Alforja.

Jara, H. O. (2005). *Sistematizando experiencias*: *Apropiarse del futuro. Recorridos y búsquedas de la sistematización de experiencias*. Xátiva, Valencia, España: Editorial L'Ullar.

Jares, X. R. (2002). *Educación y derechos humanos*. Madrid, España: Editorial Popular.

Jares, X. R. (2005). *Educar para la verdad y la esperanza… En tiempos de globalización, guerra preventiva y terrorismos*. Madrid, España: Editorial Popular, S.A.

Latino, R. (2017, September 30). *The Cruelest Storm*: *A Statement for Puerto Rico* [Blog]. Retrieved from http://www.latinorebels.com/2017/09/30/the-cruelest-storm-a-statement-for-puerto-rico/.

Magendzo, A. (2005). Pedagogy of human rights education: A Latin American perspective. *Intercultural Education, 16*(2), 137–143. Retrieved from http://citeseerx.ist.psu.edu/viewdoc/download?doi=10.1.1.836.8598&rep=rep1&type=pdf.

Magendzo, A. (2006). *Conversaciones y tensiones en torno a la educación en derechos humanos*. Conferencia Magistral 2002–2003 Cátedra UNESCO de Educación para la Paz. San Juan: Universidad de Puerto Rico, Recinto de Río Piedras. Retrieved from http://unescopaz.uprrp.edu/act/Conferencias/Magendzo/magendzoind.html.

Magendzo, A. (2015). *Construcción del sujeto de paz y de derechos humanos*. Cátedra de Pedagogía, Encuentro "La Paz: Muchas Miradas, un Camino". Bogotá, Colombia, 18 al 19 de marzo de 2013. Organizado por la Secretaría de Educación del Distrito (SED).

Magendzo-Kolstrein, A., & Pavéz-Bravo, J. M. (2015b). *Educación en Derechos Humanos*: *Una propuesta para educar desde la perspectiva controversial*. Comisión Distrital de DDHH de la Ciudad de México.

Magendzo-Kolstrein, A., & Toledo-Jofré, M. I. (2015a). Educación en derechos humanos: Estrategia pedagógica-didáctica centrada en la controversia. *Revista Electrónica Educare, 19*(3), 1–16.

Mejía, M. R. (2012). *Sistematización*: *Una forma de investigar las prácticas y de producción de saberes y conocimientos*. Serie: Educación, Transformación e Inclusión. Ministerio de Educación y Viceministerio de Educación Alternativa y Especial. La Paz, Bolivia. Retrieved from http://www.minedu.gob.bo/files/publicaciones/veaye/dgea/SistematizacionMarcoMejia-Bolivia.pdf.

Pascual-Morán, A. (2010). *Una mirada reflexiva al aprendizaje en derechos humanos como pedagogía crítica y política de paz/A reflexive stance on human rights learning as critical pedagogy and politics of peace*. Commentary to: Betty Reardon's Keynote Address 2008–2009 UNESCO Chair for Peace Education: Human Rights Learning: Pedagogies and Politics of Peace (pp. 73–80 & 81–88). Cátedra UNESCO de Educación para la Paz, UPR-RP. Retrieved from http://unescopaz.uprrp.edu/act/Lecciones/2009reardon/HRLearningBettyReardon.pdf.

Pascual-Morán, A. (2014a, enero-junio). *Pedagogía de las diferencias y la equidad… Desde y hacia una educación-cultura inclusiva de paz positiva e integral*. Revista Ra Ximhai *10*(2), 227–256. Co-edición especial de la Universidad Autónoma Indígena de México y el Consorcio de Universidades Cátedra UNESCO. Retrieved from http://www.redalyc.org/pdf/461/46131266010.pdf.

Pascual-Morán, A. (2014b). *Apuntes y aportes para pensar y practicar una pedagogía de las diferencias*. Revista Pedagogía, *47*(1), 10–30. Facultad de Educación, UPR-RP. Retrieved from http://revistapedagogia.uprrp.edu/wp-content/uploads/2015/10/vol47_01.pdf.

Pascual-Morán, A. (2016). *Develando imágenes, conjugando esperanzas*: *Desde las interacciones entre derechos humanos y educación*. En: Educación y derechos humanos: Complementariedades y sinergias. Conferencia Magistral 2014–2015, Cátedra UNESCO de Educación para la Paz, Universidad de Puerto Rico, Recinto de Río Piedras. Retrieved from http://unescopaz.uprrp.edu/act/Lecciones/2015rodino/confmagistrodino.pdf.

Perrenoud, P. (2007). *Pedagogía diferenciada*: *De las intenciones a la acción*. Madrid, España: Editorial Popular.

Reardon, B. (2008). A pedagogy of alternatives: A peace education comment on Mark Webb's "Letter to Naomi Klein". *In Factis Pax*, 2(1), 131–136. Retrieved from http://www.infactispax.org/volume3/Reardon.pdf.

Reardon, B. (2010). *Aprendizaje en derechos humanos*: *Pedagogías y políticas de paz/Human Rights Learning*: *Pedagogies and Politics of Peace*. Conferencia Magistral/Keynote Address: Cátedra UNESCO de Educación para la Paz, Recinto de Río Piedras de la Universidad de Puerto Rico. Retrieved from http://unescopaz.uprrp.edu/act/Lecciones/2009reardon/HRLearningBettyReardon.pdf.

Reardon, B. (2017, November 9). *Courage, resilience and spiritual strength*: *Peace educators in Puerto Rico*. Global Campaign for Peace Education [Website]. Retrieved from http://www.peace-ed-campaign.org/courage-resilience-spiritual-strength-peace-educators-puerto-rico/.

Reardon, B., & Cabezudo, A. (2002). *Learning to abolish war*: *Teaching towards a culture of peace*. New York: The Hague Appeal for Peace.

Rodino-Pierri, A. M. (2016). *Educación y derechos humanos*: *Complementariedades y sinergias*. Conferencia Magistral 2014–2015, Cátedra UNESCO de Educación para la Paz, Universidad de Puerto Rico, Recinto de Río Piedras. Retrieved from http://unescopaz.uprrp.edu/act/Lecciones/2015rodino/confmagistrodino.pdf.

Shor, I. & Freire, P. (1987). *A pedagogy for liberation*: *Dialogues on transforming education*. Westport, Connecticut: Bergin & Garvey.

Skliar, C. (2013). *Pedagogías de las diferencias*. Buenos Aires: Área de Educación: Facultad Latinoamericana de Ciencias Sociales (FLACSO) & Consejo Nacional de Investigaciones Científicas y Técnicas (CONICET).

Sosa-Pascual, O. (2017, September 28). *Son muchos más los muertos de María*. Centro de Periodismo Investigativo de Puerto Rico [Website].

Sosa-Pascual, O., Campoy, A., & Weissenstein, M. (2018, September 14). *The deaths of hurricane María*. Centro de Periodismo Investigativo de Puerto Rico [Website].

Tedesco, J. C. (1995). *El nuevo pacto educativo*: *Educación, competitividad y ciudadanía*. Madrid: Anaya.

Tuvilla-Rayo, J. (2004). *Cultura de paz*: *Fundamentos y claves educativas*. Bilbao, España: Editorial Desclée de Brouwer, Colección Aprender a Ser/Educación en Valores.

Tuvilla-Rayo, J. (2006). *El derecho humano a la paz en la educación*: *Construir la cultura de la paz*. Retrieved from http://www.aedidh.org/sites/default/files/3-05.pdf.

UN (2015). *Transforming Our World*: *The 2030 Agenda for Sustainable Development*. United Nations Organization. Retrieved from https://sustainabledevelopment.un.org/content/documents/21252030%20Agenda%20for%20Sustainable%20Development%20web.pdf.

UNESCO (1994). Informe final: Primera reunión de consulta sobre el Programa Cultura de Paz. París, 27–29 de septiembre, Organización de las Naciones Unidas para la Educación, la Ciencia y la Cultura.

UNESCO (2000). *Manifiesto 2000 para una Cultura de Paz y No Violencia*. Organización de las Naciones Unidas para la Educación, la Ciencia y la Cultura. Retrieved from https://www.um.es/paz/main2.html.

Vignale, S., Alvarado, M., & Cunha-Bueno, M. (2014). *Pedagogías de las diferencias*. Buenos Aires, Argentina. Centro de Ciencia, Educación y Sociedad (CECIES) [Blog]. Retrieved from http://www.cecies.org/articulo.asp?id=238.

Webb, M. (2008). Letter to Naomi Klein. *In Factis Pax, Journal of Peace Education and Social Justice 2*(1), 137–159. Retrieved from http://www.infactispax.org/volume3/Webb.pdf.

Yudkin-Suliveres, A., & Pascual-Morán, A. (2009). Pensando el quehacer de la educación en derechos humanos y para una cultura de paz en Puerto Rico. En A. Magendzo (Ed.), *Ideas fuerza de la educación en derechos humanos en Iberoamérica* (pp. 278–310). Santiago de Chile: Organización de Estados Iberoamericanos (OEI), Oficina Regional de América Latina de la UNESCO & Ediciones SM Chile.

Part II
Feminism and the Gender Perspective as Pathways of Transformation Toward Peace and Justice

Chapter 7
Exploring Betty A. Reardon's Perspective on Peace

Ingeborg Breines

What a great pleasure and honor to be invited to write on Betty Reardon's work and my connection to it in the context of her 90th birthday! Betty has been a huge inspiration to so many – and still is, at this age – and so also to me. Inspiring role models are rare and important. We need to believe in a person/teacher/instructor in order to want to learn, engage or make improvements in our own life/teaching/behavior. Betty is such an exceptionally inspiring person, not only through her writing and teaching, but also through her personality, her sharing of values, her capacity for friendship and care. She is courageous and consistent. She bridges the personal and the political, the analytical and the practical. She is open to and values other cultures. She manages to *"be the change you would like to see"* to use Mahatma Gandhi's wording. For me personally, I can only ask: Is there any better way of learning than learning by friendship?

My first encounter with Betty was as I was just starting in my new job as deputy Secretary General of the Norwegian National Commission for UNESCO. It must have been in 1984/85. Betty participated in an American – Russian – Norwegian education project. And UNESCO must have been supporting it in one way or the other since I was sent to one of their meetings in Oslo. I felt very fortunate to meet these progressive Russian, American and Norwegian teachers, cooperating intensely over several years in the middle of the Cold War. They impressed me profoundly. How we need such a project today! Eva Nordland, professor and initiator of social-pedagogy at the University of Oslo, was heading the Norwegian group. She later helped me in the development of the UNESCO Associated schools' project (ASP) in Norway. Professionally and ideologically, Betty has since then for me been linked to UNESCO, although we later have shared many other strong and wonderful thoughts and experiences.

Ingeborg Breines, Oslo, Norway; Email: i.breines@gmail.com.

© Springer Nature Switzerland AG 2019
D. T. Snauwaert (ed.), *Exploring Betty A. Reardon's Perspective
on Peace Education*, Pioneers in Arts, Humanities, Science,
Engineering, Practice 20, https://doi.org/10.1007/978-3-030-18387-5_7

7.1   UNESCO

The UN Educational, Scientific and Cultural Organization, UNESCO, was established as the intellectual and ethical body of the UN, to be, "*...a worldwide brain-workers parliament*", as stated at the launching of the organization in 1945, by the then British Minister of Education, Ellen Wilkinson. The UN needs outstanding brain-workers, and preferably those who manage to combine head, hands and heart. That was how Betty came into the equation, and that was why UNESCO had established National Commissions in all Member States with close working relationships to different, relevant, professional, intellectual and creative individuals, institutions and organizations in the respective countries. This was in line with what the predecessor, the International Committee on Intellectual Cooperation of the League of Nations, had done. That UNESCO has later weakened this great asset by letting itself be streamlined with the rest of the UN system including by making the so-called Japanese amendment to its Constitution, is another matter.

The UNESCO Constitution states as its first objective: "*...to contribute to peace and security by promoting collaboration among the nations through education, science and culture in order to further universal respect for justice, for the rule of law and for human rights and fundamental freedoms*". And indeed, UNESCO did outstanding work in helping teachers, cultural workers, artists, scientists, journalists and students meet and bridge disturbing ideological gaps, not least between the East and the West during the Cold War period.

The well-known preamble to the UNESCO Constitution reads*: Since wars begin in the minds of men it is in the minds of men that defenses for peace must be constructed.* How different from a militaristic definition of defense! The organization thereby has a strong peace education mandate, which manifests itself throughout UNESCO's work and within all its fields of competence. A profoundly humanistic education, that naturally includes peace education, is at the core of UNESCO's mandate. This approach to education is echoed in the UNESCO report, *Education for the 21 Century. Learning the treasure within,* which outlines four main educational goals: *Learning to be, learning to learn, learning to do and learning to live together,* the last one considered as basic as literacy. The mainstream educational trends today are unfortunately different, putting emphasis on a more materialistic, instrumental pedagogy of objectives and scorecards.

Betty fitted naturally into the overall UNESCO mission, underlining that intellectual and moral solidarity and the respect for justice and human rights are essential in order to build lasting peace. Her contributions were highly appreciated. She had already a longstanding relation with UNESCO before I joined Headquarters in 1993. She was, for example, an active participant in the important 1980 World Congress on Disarmament Education and even prepared its main working document. She was a member of the Jury of the UNESCO Prize for Peace Education and in 2001 she got the honorable mention of the Peace Education prize. She authored the 3-volume publication: *Tolerance: The Threshold of Peace* (1998) and other publications related to the culture of peace, which we will revert to later.

7.2 The Culture of Peace

My cooperation with Betty in a UNESCO context has been centered around the major UNESCO program *Towards a Culture of Peace*, which, under the guidance of the inspiring Director General, Federico Mayor (1987–1999), became the top priority of the Organization. Betty was not only party to the reflections in UNESCO on the culture of peace, but she was able to help translate the vision into practical educational tools, for different levels of the schools system and teacher training, as well as for adult education and study groups. It is interesting to see how she, in her didactic material, often advised to start the learning process by helping the learners diagnose intolerance among students and teachers. Then she gives the characteristics of a tolerant classroom and indicates learning goals, activities and processes. With her broad orientation she is also able to give the teachers very useful examples and references for further reading.

UNESCO spearheaded the Culture of Peace initiative in the United Nations system and was designated by the UN General Assembly as the focal point both for *the International Year for a Culture of Peace* (2000) and the following *International Decade for a Culture of Peace and Non-violence for the Children of the World* (2001–2010). The UN General Assembly adopted, September 1999, the *Declaration and Program of Action on a Culture of Peace*, as developed by UNESCO. The Program of Action was made to serve as a background document both for the International Year and the following Decade. Member States were encouraged to make their own national action plans.

The Manifesto 2000 on a culture of peace, which was developed by UNESCO in cooperation with some Nobel Peace laureates, was signed by more than 75 million people committing themselves to: "*respect all life, reject violence, share with others, listen to understand, preserve the planet and rediscover solidarity*": www. unesco.org/manifesto2000. This gives evidence to people's longing for peace, and also shows the sometimes, huge discrepancy between people and their governments, also in democracies.

The culture of peace vision emphasizes peace not only as the absence of armed conflict or war, however important that is, but focuses on the content and the conditions of peace. It also requires a positive, dynamic participatory process where dialogue is encouraged, and conflicts are solved in a spirit of mutual understanding and cooperation.

The goals, ideals, and strategies that comprise the initiative and movement from a culture of war and violence to a culture of peace and non-violence are drawn from, and seek to revitalize major international, normative instruments which are basic to the United Nations' mission "*to save future generations from the scourge of war*". The culture of peace concept and program opened up a broad-based reflection on possible new visions/scenarios for the future involving researchers, teachers, artists, activists, organizations and governments who found in the culture of peace a platform for fruitful exchange and mutual inspiration. Highly diverse groups and initiatives dealing with issues such as environment, human rights,

development, disarmament, human security, gender equality and youth empowerment all related constructively to the vision of a culture of peace.

It was considered important to de-learn the codes of the culture of war and
violence that have pervaded our existence in a myriad of ways and to confront not
only the physical violence, but also the structural violence, notably of economic and
social deprivation. In the vision of a culture of peace, dialogue and respect for
human rights would replace violence, intercultural understanding and solidarity
would replace enemy images, sharing and free flow of knowledge and information
would replace secrecy and egalitarian partnership and full empowerment of women
would balance male domination. Such a vision risks to be seen as utopian by those
who align themselves with more predictable, status quo, "tooth-for-tooth"
real-politics.

The culture of peace program analyzed and confronted commonly held beliefs or
myths, such as (i) if you want peace, prepare for war, (ii) nothing can change
because violence is inevitable and intrinsic to human nature, and (iii) violence is an
efficient method for solving problems and disputes.

In the context of the culture of peace program such hypotheses were refuted. It
was stated loud and clear that if we want peace, we must prepare for peace. We
should not only have ministries of defence or security, but ministries of peace or a
culture of peace; not only prestigious military academies, but obligatory peace
education at all levels of the school system; not only peace research that studies the
developments of new weapons, armed conflicts and national security issues, but
peace research that truly helps us understand and solve conflicts creatively and in
non-violent ways. Scientists developed the UNESCO *Seville Statement on Violence*
(Adams 1991), which underlined that: "*It is scientifically incorrect to say that war
or any other violent behaviour is genetically programmed into our human nature*".
And certainly, war and violence are not efficient; experience, and research, proves
the opposite. If arms would bring peace, we would since long have had it!

This major movement of hope and inspiration was unfortunately undermined by
what followed the attacks on the Twin Towers in New York 11. September 2001,
which misled the world to an unsuccessful and seemingly ever-lasting war on terror
with thousands of victims. Long-term peace building was put outside mainstream
politics. Fear and the fight against terrorism has since then dominated both the
international discourse and the use of resources. *The Declaration and Program of
Action on a Culture of Peace* became mainly words on paper or underutilized
guidelines, except in the quarters of the strong, convinced and courageous peace
promoters and pacifists. Now, with provocative militarism and polarisation, when
many get alarmed and afraid of a new cold war or worse, the vision of a culture of
peace seems to get a revival. More people, also more countries, participate in the
yearly High Level Forum on the Culture of Peace in the UN General Assembly.
More institutions and organisations, not least women's organisations, initiate
strategic discussion on how a culture of peace can counter an outdated, but still
dominant, political thinking insisting on the importance of military might.

The question is how do we manage to get rid of this old-fashioned hegemonic masculinity, which continues to influence world affairs so strongly? Betty, who through her writing, has managed to strengthen the links between feminism and anti-militaristic peace building, is an important and inspiring voice. In several of her publications she speaks about "the feminist imperative" as the way to counter what she calls "the militarist-sexist symbiosis". She has helped so many see how eager patriarchy is to avoid gender equality and to legitimate militarism. She has also helped us understand that the vast amounts spent on weapons perhaps are *"more for purposes of status and a sense of national pride than for defence or "security""*. And she continues: *"More than any other manifestation of patriarchy, the compulsive acquisition and excessive use of weaponry demonstrate the abuse of power by the male-dominated state system. Indeed, it seems a destructive* addiction (Reardon 1999, p. 144)."

In the context of the culture of peace program, UNESCO also explored the possibility of a new human right: The right to peace. It was however turned down, primarily by Western countries. The main argument against it was that if all existing human rights were implemented, the sum total would be peace. Some civil society organizations, however, continued the work both in order to keep a visionary process going and with the hope that it eventually could be a legal right. Finally, through a long process, including at the Human Rights Council, the *Declaration on the Right to Peace* (Res 71/189) was approved in December 2016 by the UN General Assembly. The first paragraph reads: "Everyone has the right to enjoy peace".

7.3 Women and a Culture of Peace

Within the overall Culture of Peace Program, I was given the task of establishing and heading the Women and a Culture of Peace Program at UNESCO. The priorities of the program were:

- To support women's initiatives for peace,
- To empower women for democratic participation in political processes and to increase women's capacity and impact in economic and security issues
- To contribute to gender sensitive socialization and training for non-violence and egalitarian partnerships with a special focus on young men and boys.

The cooperation with Betty in this period was particularly intense and fruitful. She was chosen for the Director General's Advisory Group for the Women and the Culture of Peace program, together with two outstanding members of the Executive Board of UNESCO, Ingrid Eide from Norway and Lourdes Quisumbing from the Philippines. Betty participated in specialist meetings and was rapporteur at the

Manila expert group meeting on Women's Contribution to a Culture of Peace, April 1995. She authored the UNESCO publication *Education for a Culture of Peace in a Gender Perspective* (Reardon 2001) and edited the 1999 publication *Towards a Women's Agenda for a Culture of Peace* with Dorota Gierycz from the UN Division for the Advancement of Women (DAW) and myself (Breines et al. 1999). In May 2000 Betty lectured in Norway at the UNESCO conference at the University of Tromsø on *Higher Education for Peace, Transforming a culture of war to a culture of peace*. The aim of the conference was to discuss conditions for peace and the role of institutions of higher education in promoting peace. The conference served as an opportunity to exchange research results and educational strategies that promote creative thinking about peace studies in higher education. I still remember vividly how proud I was of Betty speaking truth to male militaristic power in a big, packed auditorium. It was also interesting to observe how some people not knowing Betty, at the outset got somewhat confused, as they probably expected a less radical and direct way of speaking from this beautiful lady, elegantly dressed with a silk scarf and none of the progressive external attributes.

Many people, so also Betty, gave a lot of their time and energy in the planning of the 4th World Conference on Women in Beijing, September 1995. The overall theme was: Equality Development and Peace, in line with the three preceding UN conferences on women. We were happy from a peace activist point of view when the Beijing Declaration came to include the following: "The *full participation of women in decision-making, conflict prevention and resolution and any other peace initiative are essential to the realization of lasting peace* (United Nations 1995)."

UNESCO presented a Statement on Women's Contribution to a Culture of Peace to the Beijing conference that got signed by women heads of states and governments and other leading women as well as peace activists of both sexes. The statement was based on the report from the expert group meeting in Manila where Betty was the rapporteur. I felt gratified when the term *culture of peace* was used at the Beijing conference for the first time at the UN outside UNESCO. Strategic objective E.4. of the Beijing Platform for Action reads: "*Promote women's contribution to fostering a culture of peace*". It has four operative paragraphs relating e.g. to promoting peace, reconciliation and tolerance and exchange program for young women, women's participation in peace research and consequences of armed conflicts, as well as educational programs focusing on conflict resolution by non-violent means.

7.4   Civil Society

Betty has a prominent role in relation to several peace organizations, not least the International Peace Research Association (IPRA), the Women's International League for Peace and Freedom (WILPF), and the International Peace Bureau (IPB). I have been fortunate to share many civil society activities and events with Betty. In 2009 Betty received IPB's Sean MacBride Peace Prize for her work, her teaching, her writing, her engagement, and for her leading role in the Global Campaign for Peace Education and for establishing and running the International Institute for Peace Education. In 2016 she accepted an important role in IPB's congress in Berlin: *Disarm! For a Climate of Peace. Creating an Action Agenda.* Betty undertook the difficult task of transforming ideas and suggestions presented to the congress into operative peace methodology. Her presentation can be found in the new publication based on the Berlin congress: *Disarmament, Peace and Development*, (Reardon 2018; Archer, Breines, Chatterji and Skilan 2018). In addition, she organized with Tony Jenkins, Janet Gerson, and Dale Snauwaert, from the International Institute for Peace Education, a very well attended and appreciated workshop on peace education (Gerson et al. 2016).

When I was in Pakistan as the UNESCO representative, Betty came to give a workshop on education for a culture of peace. It was so needed, and she was so well received. It gave echoes in the complex context of a post 11. September 2001, Pakistan. Some of the teachers participating continue successfully to this day to use her pedagogy in their teaching. I also felt stronger in my work both in the development of a peace manual for use by Afghan refugees in Pakistan and in the work with the curriculum wing of the Ministry of Education to develop teaching and training material in peace building for Pakistani schools and teacher training institutions. When, several years later, I was invited back to Pakistan to teach peace building at the University of Gujrat, Betty's thinking and teaching was with me, both in the themes I brought up with the students, but also, and not least, in the interaction with them. It was not always obvious how to encourage critical thinking in a system that to a large extent has been promoting a more hierarchical model where especially girls have been subject to norms of obedience. How could I, an older, Western women, get their trust, make them want to be in interaction? How could I manage to make my teaching be of relevance to them? Betty's pedagogy of reflective inquiry was of great help, as it continues to be for so many.

7.5 Peace Education

War and inequality continue to plague humanity, with huge implications for learning possibilities. 65 million people are on the run according to the UNHCR, an unprecedented high number and a disaster for the individual and a potential destabilizing social factor. The right to relevant, quality education for all is far from being fulfilled. We still have a huge difference in learning opportunities, despite globalization or even sometimes due to globalization. It is utterly immoral not to provide learning opportunities to all children. We are not only failing the many young people who are the unreached and who may not be able to develop properly their potential and talents, but we are also depriving society of their contribution. The large majority are girls and women who may have different, constructive and practical problem-solving approaches, so badly needed on the world scene.

The UN Agenda for Sustainable Development (2016–2030), with its 17 universally accepted Sustainable Development Goals (SDGs), to be achieved by all the countries of the world, sees peace, human rights and development as a comprehensive whole. Two of the Sustainable Development Goals are of particular importance to us in this context: SDG 4 on education and SDG 16 on building peaceful societies, justice and functioning institutions. Member States will have to report to the UN High Level Forum on Sustainable Development on both SDG 4 and 16 in the summer of 2019.

UNESCO, which has developed important normative instruments on peace education, has a reporting mechanism by which Member States must e.g. report every fourth year on their implementation of the 1974 *Recommendation concerning Education for International Understanding, Cooperation and Peace and Education relating to Human Rights and Fundamental Freedom*. This reporting mechanism is very important now also in connection with the implementation of SDG 4 target 7 which reads:

> By 2030, ensure that all learners acquire the knowledge and skills needed to promote sustainable development, including, among others, through education for sustainable development and sustainable lifestyles, human rights, gender equality, promotion of a culture of peace and non-violence, global citizenship and appreciation of cultural diversity and of culture's contribution to sustainable development.

SDG 4.7 is particularly important, not least in order to try to counter the ongoing, growing and sometimes aggressive militarization of the mind, in schools, in universities and through mass media. In Norway this type of propaganda was particularly visible in connection with the huge NATO exercise *Trident Juncture* in the autumn of 2018. Among the questions that arise are: How to protect students against unwanted influence from the military when resources are so unequally divided between the military and the civil sector? Since universities are often lacking in official funding, the military industry is sometimes buying its way into academia. Besides the question of brain drain from more productive sectors, this militarization of the mind enhances the need for a code of conduct for scientists like the Hippocratic oath of medical doctors: "*Do no harm*".

Attempting to make a universal code of conduct for scientists, UNESCO researched more than 115 existing ethical guidelines/principles/norms (some 40 international and some 80 national) and in addition looked at the guidelines of some universities and workplaces. German universities are in the forefront of this work. Inspiration could for example be found in the *Russell – Einstein Manifesto* and in Joseph Rotblat's oath: "*I will not knowingly carry out research which is to the detriment of humanity*", which he presented, for example, at the acceptance speech of the Nobel Peace Prize in 1995. Student Pugwash groups echo this:

> I promise to work for a better world, where science and technology are used in socially responsible ways. I will not use my education for any purpose intended to harm human beings or the environment. Throughout my career, I will consider the ethical implications of my work before I take action. While the demands placed upon me may be great, I sign this declaration because I recognize that individual responsibility is the first step on the path to peace.

UNESCO unfortunately failed in its efforts to develop an ethical code of conduct for scientists trying to connect the basic values of science with the ideals of social responsibility and accountability. ICSU, the International Council of Scientists, established by UNESCO, has developed Standards for Ethics in Science. The Commission on Ethics of Science and Technology, COMEST, has since the end of last century guided the work of the Organization in this field. Yet, there is probably so much business to make from production and trade in war material, as well as continued misguided patriarchal pride in military strength, that countries are not willing as yet to sign such a code of conduct.

7.6 Military and Social Expenditure

The world seems to be more willing to pay for war than to pay for peace. Funding the implementation of the two very important UN decisions, the Paris Agreement on climate and the UN Agenda for Sustainable Development, is a major challenge. According to the Stockholm Peace Research Institute (SIPRI), the world presently spends some 1.7 trillion dollars a year on military expenditure, and that is only the official figures. We certainly have not got our priorities right when one year of military costs equals some 615 years of the UN regular budget. *The world is over-armed and peace is under-funded*, said former Secretary General of the UN, Ban Ki-moon. How can the UN manage to do its job with such an imbalance in funding?

The world's oldest functioning international peace organisation, the International Peace Bureau estimates that 10% of the military costs would greatly contribute to reaching the Sustainable Development Goals that most people yearn for. IPB has therefore suggested a 10% reduction in military cost per country and per year over the 15 years of the UN Development Agenda, so far without success.

All efforts are needed in order to move away from unsustainable production and consumption patterns and undertake the green shift required for the survival of the planet and our living conditions. We have to analyze properly what makes us safe and secure in today's world. Prioritizing military force and competition over dialogue and cooperation makes the acute climate- and environmental crisis worse and potentially fatal. We must therefore redefine security from national security to human security and urgently start on the fundamental paradigm shift required. The huge challenge to educators world wide is how to help develop mindsets that would enhance the transition from force to reason and from conflict and violence to dialogue and peace, thus making war and armed conflicts obsolete. Rereading Betty's books right now could help us get stronger and hopefully enable us to make a difference. Perhaps that would also be a 90th anniversary gift that Betty would appreciate.

References

Adams, D. (1991). *The Seville statement on violence: Preparing the ground for the constructing of peace*. Paris: UNESCO Publishing.

Braun, R., Archer, C., Breines, I., Chatterji, M., & Skiljan, A. (Eds.) (2018). *Disarmament, peace and development*. Bingley, UK: Emerald Publishing Limited.

Breines, I., Gierycz, D., & Reardon, B. A. (Eds.) (1999). *Towards a women's agenda for a culture of peace*. Paris: UNESCO Publising.

Gerson, J., Jenkins, T., Reardon, B. A., & Snauwaert, D. T. (2016). Disarmament education: Imperative for peace. In *Workshop Presented at International Peace Bureau World Congress*. Berlin, Germany, October 2.

Reardon, B. A. (1999). *Towards a women's agenda for a culture of peace*. Paris: UNESCO Publishing.

Reardon, B. A. (2001). *Education for a culture of peace in a gender perspective*. Paris: UNESCO.

Reardon, B. A. (2018). Chapter 19: Learning to disarm: Education to realize the IPB action agenda. In R. Braun, C. Archer, I. Breines, M. Chatterji, & A. Skiljan (Eds.), *Disarmament, peace and development*. Bingley, UK: Emerald Publishing Limited.

United Nations. (1995). *Fourth World Conference on Women Beijing Declaration*. http://www.un.org/womenwatch/daw/beijing/platform/declar.htm.

Chapter 8
Peace Education and Gender in Africa: Reflections on the Work of Dr. Betty Reardon

Colins Imoh

The protection of human rights comes with respect for all persons irrespective of their gender. African societies should not be immune to this reality. There is a need to separate Africa cultural values from an oppressive patriarchal restriction on women. Patriarchal hegemony conflicts with the tenets of human rights and the attainment of a just society. The patriarchal system is ingrained in the daily affairs of life, the privileged are not aware of the effect's of this system and the suffering of others. This patriarchal system is assumed to be an inseparable part of the culture of the people; an assumption this paper challenges. What role can peace education play? What role does the work of Reardon play in encouraging practitioners and advocating for breaking the patriarchal system and establishing a more progressive society in Africa? This paper explores these ideas, and the application of peace education in Africa. Peace education has the potential for social transformation. There is a need for collaboration and inclusiveness between all; not the promotion of women against men or the continued domination of women by men, but rather a development of positive traits associated with masculinity and femininity. If we integrate gender equality into peacebuilding, a world where there is no discrimination, where human rights are respected, where freedom is attained, and where the dignity of the human is respected, is possible in Africa.

8.1 Violence, Rethink of the Patriarchal System

In the patriarchal system, males assume authority and privilege compelling women to view their lives within the lens provided by the male. This does not encourage peaceful living and coexistence. This system is dominant in most societies in

Colins Imoh, Doctoral Candidate in the Department of Educational Foundations & Leadership at the University of Toledo, Toledo, OH, USA; Email: imohcolins@gmail.com.

© Springer Nature Switzerland AG 2019
D. T. Snauwaert (ed.), *Exploring Betty A. Reardon's Perspective on Peace Education*, Pioneers in Arts, Humanities, Science, Engineering, Practice 20, https://doi.org/10.1007/978-3-030-18387-5_8

Africa. Reardon has offered a vision of peace and justice that can be achieved in the world through the protection of human rights. These are rights that are attributable to us as humans, irrespective of sex, gender, origin, status, or belief. Everyone is entitled to be respected and honored for who they are; it prevents discrimination and upholds human dignity. Reardon (2015) states that: "Human rights standards are the specific indicators and particular measures of progress toward the realization of peace. Human rights put flesh on the bones of the abstraction of peace and provide the details of how to bring the flesh to life" (p. 3). Human rights are essentially the ethical core of peacebuilding and respect for human rights breeds accommodation and tolerance among people. Conflict is a necessary fact of life because people have differences; however, respect for human rights will lead to the settlement of difference without resort to violence.

Violence according to Reardon/Snauwaert (2015) is the "central problematic of peace education. All violence degrades and denies human dignity … violence as intentional, avoidable harm—usually committed to achieving a purpose" (p. vii). Therefore peace education should inquire into the nature of violence, the structure that supports it, and its effects on society. It should seek to promote the culture of non-violence.

8.2 Need for Peace Education and Human Rights

Peace Education is derivable from a human rights approach, which flows from the lived human experience of the struggle to attain a just and peaceful society. Peace education as Reardon asserts, is an "attempt to bring some cohesion to the multiple and varied forms of curriculum and instruction practiced as peace education" (Reardon/Snauwaert 2015, p. 93). It is an aspect of democratic education closely linked with cosmopolitanism and reflective pedagogy. The capacities of reflective listening, responsibility, risk-taking, reconciliation, recovery, reconstruction, and reverence are needed to properly develop the field (Reardon 1988). For Reardon, peace and justice can be achieved through the protection of human rights.

Human rights are the ethical core of peace education; it is through these rights that the dignity of humans may be restored, and a just and peaceful society established. Human rights are attributable to us as humans irrespective of sex, origin, status, or belief; everyone is entitled to be respected and honored for who they are. In this way, rights prevent discrimination and uphold the dignity of human beings. Reardon states "Human rights standards are the specific indicators and particular measures of progress toward the realization of peace. Human rights put flesh on the bones of the abstraction of peace and provide the details of how to bring the flesh to life" (Reardon/Snauwaert 2015, p. 47). Human rights are essentially the core for peacebuilding. The respect for human rights encourages accommodation and tolerance among people.

Peace education means different things to different people; it serves different purposes based on need, time, and people (Salomon 2007). The conceptualization and development of this field is one of the stories of the life of Betty Reardon. She articulated peace education in her early work within the context of world order. Reardon asserts that the objectives of world order could be achieved through five goals as: "minimization of violence, or war prevention; maximizing of economic welfare, or the providing of better standards of living for more people; increasing of social justice by relieving discrimination and oppression; broadening of the democratic base of public policy making by increasing the participation of minorities and individuals in decision-making processes and improving of the quality of life through restoration of ecological balance"[1] (Reardon/Snauwaert 2015, p. 55). Peace education should empower people to work for a peaceful and just world. It is not an academic discipline but a field; it involves participatory learning that brings about a transformation in society through knowledge, skills and attitudinal change.

This process will lead to living in harmony with each other and nature. Reardon argues that the task of peace education is to "elicit the learning that will enable us to invest our strongest endeavors in moving peace from a preference to a possibility to a probability" (Reardon/Snauwaert 2015, p. 201). This can be achieved when the human rights of all are respected, especially the rights of women. However, women have not had a fair share of the protection of human rights. Betty Reardon's gender perspective on peace education calls for a transformation and inclusion of all voices in the search for peace. She argues that the reinforcement of male-dominated discourses/practices has not solved the problems of the world. The male-dominated system strives towards power, ego, and structure, forgetting or ignoring the human relations needed for peace to strive. There is a need for a conscious effort to change the male dominated situation to an all-inclusive structure for positive change.

The changes required to move societies toward great gender equality rests upon a number of factors that include a change in family structure, legal rights, occupational structure, labor force, power, family division of labor and sexuality, among others (Wright/Rogers 2011). In what follows, the pursuit of gender equality with respect to peace education and peace building will be explored within the African context.

8.3 Gender Inequality in Africa

Africa is not monolithic but a continent of fifty-five countries with diverse communities, including different orientations, values, and culture; perceptions and gendered roles differ considerably. There is the view that most African societies have not made significant progress concerning women's rights. There are a few

---

[1]See also *Education for Peace: Focus on Mankind*, edited by George Henderson, 127–51. Alexandria, VA: Association for Supervision and Curriculum Development, 1973.

shining lights like Rwanda, but the situation is not as encouraging as expected.[2] This can be attributed to the social construction of gender and the nature of patriarchy. Gender is a social construct involving learned identities linked with masculinity and femininity, which also define ways of life entrenched in culture, and other belief systems such as religion. The diverse influence of socially constructed gender roles and patriarchy in Africa is not static but dynamic, differentiating the power, roles, and responsibilities of women from men (Ferris et al. 2012; IFRC 2010; Reardon/Hans 2018), and influencing to a great extent how we think, feel, and what we believe we can and should not do.

Reardon/Hans (2018) defined gender as "a socially derived concept, a culturally varied construct that assigns to men and women a set of cultural roles and social functions, only minimally determined by their respective reproductive and sexual characteristics" (p. 13). In turn, patriarchy can be defined as a "social, political, and economic system of control and domination structured in terms of a hierarchy of human relationships and value that is based on socially constructed gender differentiation. As such, it bestows unequal power and value onto males who exhibit its most important values and traits, excluding and oppressing those who do not. It is a social system that has been almost universally in place throughout the history of human societies, and it constitutes the paradigmatic case of inequality and injustice, and thus structural violence (Reardon/Snauwaert (2015, p. xii)." The interplay between gender roles and patriarchy has greatly influenced the role of women in peace building activities in Africa.

8.4 Different Communities but Similar Issues

The inability to be actively involved in peace education and conflict resolution by women in Africa due to the patriarchal social system and ingrained structural violence has vast implications in the development of the continent. How men and women deal with conflict has gendered implications in Africa based on the structure of society and its impact on traditional practices. The specific conflicts that African communities face are diverse; they can lead to changing roles, but can also lead to limitations of the rights of women, for example concerning decisions regarding school and marriage.

Given the diversity of gender experiences, it is a challenge discussing issues associated with gender in Africa, the communities are different, but they share common realities as Stoeltje (2017) suggests:

---

[2]See: https://www.un.org/africarenewal/magazine/august-2010/african-women%E2%80%99s-long-walk-equality; https://www.afidep.org/africas-progress-gender-equality-womens-empowerment-notable-gender-inequality-persists/; https://en.unesco.org/gem-report/sites/gem-report/files/SSA_Press_Release_English_Gender_Report2015.pdf; and https://www.un.org/africarenewal/magazine/-december-2015/closing-africa%E2%80%99s-%E2%80%98elusive%E2%80%99-gender-gap.

The wide differences in women's experience challenge generalization, but certain features in the organization of African societies can be identified as determining influences on women's lives. Equally relevant are the changes introduced by external forces in the 19th and 20th centuries: colonization and Christianity, the spread of Islam, and the processes of modernization, decolonization, and independence. Together these interactions affected women with both gains and losses (p. 2).

However, within the context of gender and building peace in Africa, there are commonalities in experiences despite changing roles. Gender roles have therefore been in a constant state of flux in response to changing social, cultural, religious, political and economic conditions. The invasion of Africa with the introduction of Christian and Islamic religion which is dominantly patriarchal led to the gradual erosion of the role of women in peacebuilding within the Africa society. The negative masculinity and its promotion of violence have led continuously to the disempowerment of women and the construction of militarism. Women are, in most conflict situations, the frontline responders and bring invaluable resources. Women are active community leaders in most parts of Africa; they are the key that knits the social fabric of society. They are responsible for the transmission and perpetuation of knowledge and are custodians of the customs, tradition, culture, and values of the community. However, they are not holders of political positions, and in this respect, their contribution is most times unrecognized. Nellemann et al. (2011) acknowledged the diverse roles that women play:

Women play a critical role, often bearing significant responsibility for managing critical productive resources such as land, water, livestock, biodiversity, fodder, fuel, and food. They also contribute work and energy towards income generation and carry out a disproportional amount of daily labor compared to men in household and community spheres, such as cooking, cleaning, child care, care of older or sick family members, providing work for collective projects and during weddings, funerals and other cultural ceremonies (p. 29).

Therefore, when conflict disrupts these activities, community life is adversely affected. Women and girls are at more significant risk in conflict; this risk has more to do with socioeconomic differences and inequitable power relations than based on their biological and physiological differences. The patriarchal structures of these societies with their apparent discrimination have increased the plight of women in communities based on the lack of acknowledgment of the unique role women contribute to the growth of communities and the need to provide adequate protection for women in these communities. The lack of recognition of the critical roles and ways women contribute to communities is witnessed in their non-active involvement in peacebuilding and post-conflict reconstruction activities. The implication is that their voice is not heard nor their plight adequately addressed. Their level of education and lack of awareness of their rights has contributed to exacerbating the situation, thereby preventing positive agitation for their rights. A woman should play an active role in empowerment and building peace in the continent for there lies the promise of sustainable development, economic growth, and prosperity in the continent. The United Nations recognizes the role of women in building peace, which has significant implications for peace and justice in Africa.

8.5 United Nations Security Council Resolutions and African Union Instruments

The United Nations recognized the importance of women in peacebuilding leading to the 'Women, Peace, and Security' (WPS) agenda. The United Nations Security Council (UNSC) resolution 1325, adopted on 31 October 2000, is the first resolution on women, peace, and security. It calls for the protection and participation of women in peace processes. The resolution calls for the assessment of the impact of armed conflict on women and girls, the role of women in peace-building and the gender dimensions of peace processes. This resolution was followed by UNSC resolution 1366 on conflict prevention adopted on 30 August 2001, which reiterated its recognition of the role of women in conflict prevention. The United Nations (UN) Security Council has approved eight resolutions (1820, 1888, 1889, 1960, 2106, 2122 and 2422) that recognizes the effect and importance of women in peacebuilding. These resolutions frame the Women, Peace, and Security (WPS) agenda.

Significantly, in African context, the African Union recognized the importance and has similarly called for women's participation. The African Union has shown commitment to women's equality by producing various instruments supporting the role of women in peacebuilding. These include Gender Parity Principle – 2002; African Charter on Human and Peoples' Right on the Rights of Women in Africa – adopted in July 2003 and came into effect in November 2005. Framework for Post Conflict Reconstruction and Development – 2006; African Union Gender Policy – 2009; African Union Convention for the Protection and Assistance of Internally Displaced Persons in Africa – 2009; Africa Union Aide Memoire on the Protection of Civilians – 2013. The enactment of such instruments does not equate to the implementation. The situation on the ground has not changed as anticipated. This is where we have a lot to learn from the wisdom and writing of Betty Reardon.

8.6 Patriarchy and Violence

Reardon sees the perpetuation of violence in the society as a direct result of patriarchy and the war system. Patriarchy is rooted in the collective social and cultural history of people all over the world. It is based on the social construction of gender roles. A common argument is that these roles are biological determined, yet this claim does not have a scientific basis. It is apparent that gender-based role differentiation is a system of subjugation and oppression. It is a social system of control. Furthermore, this control does not only apply to women but extends to all the powerless in society. Reardon calls it "social injustice and cultural violence," a violation of human dignity. It is a system where the powerful construct barriers to prevent others from assessing their potential, while bestowing privilege on those who are deemed to have greater value. They act as gatekeepers; as Achebe (1958) stated in *Things Fall Apart*: "if a child *washed* his *hands* he could *eat* with *kings,*" (p. 6); but the big question is who determines if the hand has been washed correctly? The tragic hero Okonkwo who lived in a patriarchy society killed himself because he could not tolerate change. He was stuck in the past and believed in violence, but his society did change, and he was left behind. Reardon's view is that we have to move from this war mentality driven by patriarchy to the feminist world of balance and relationship. Okonkwo is a reflection of his society, but the change did come. This change will come and is coming to Africa, Reardon's gender perspective can be a starting point.

8.7 A Gender Perspective as a Solution

A gender perspective brings into the public domain the human relationships, values of empowerment, caring, joy, humor, cooperation, sharing, and mutuality. At birth humans are equal and the same, but socialization produces a deep trauma based on roles ascribed to male and female leading to fear and aggressive behavior. Reardon, therefore, described feminism as a

> social movement and a way of looking at the world [that] manifests many cultural and political forms. There is no monolithic, single-minded worldwide feminist movement and no one particular school of feminist thought. Feminists disagree on many issues and policies. So feminism is a rich and varied phenomenon. There is probably only one basic tenet common to all schools and forms of feminism. That is that men and women are of equal human value and all societies should recognize this equality. This does not mean that women and men are the same nor should they always be treated the same. However, it does mean that no one should suffer (Reardon/Snauwaert 2015, p. 64).

This view acknowledges the differences in the appreciation of the feminist framework for transforming society.

Feminism is a holistic all-inclusive system that respects humans for who they are irrespective of their circumstances of birth, sex, belief, origin, among others. This needs to be accepted in societies in Africa. Reardon argues that the escalation of violence in the community can be linked to the exclusion of women in the decision-making process. She feels that the inclusion of women has the effect of reducing and eliminating violence. Reardon acknowledges that this is a challenging task even among women: "[to] convince women of their value and to develop awareness of the denial of that value by present social structures, violent structures, based on a hierarchical view of human value that teaches by experience that some people" (Reardon/Snauwaert 2015, p. 9). Women are the custodians of traditions in Africa, women can play a pivotal role in making a difference, because they are literally in charge. However, women have not used this position of power for transformation, as Reardon acknowledges, it can be difficult to convince African woman of their power. This is where education plays a very pivotal role, as Paulo

Freire acknowledges the oppressed need to realize that they are oppressed, he calls it 'conscientization' the basis of liberation and empowerment.

The 'conscientization' process and the education women receive has been a source of positive change in the society. This is very true from experiences in some parts of Africa, some of the violent practice which dehumanizes women are pressed upon women by their fellow women. Therefore education is a key factor in creating a critical mass of women who can change their situations and liberate themselves. Reardon also sees the education of women as breaking the glass ceiling. She asserts: "The entry of more women into the male world of politics, commerce, and the professions also tends to break the rigid separation of the social functions of men and women, transforming all social functions into human functions" (Reardon/ Snauwaert 2015, p. 10). The remarkable feat of Leymah Gbowee the winner of the 2011 Nobel Peace prize is a reference point of the positive role of women in peacebuilding. Her activism led to the increased role of women as peace activists and advocates of women's rights. The contribution of Gbowee in leading other community women to bring an end to Liberia's civil war is a clear manifestation of how the involvement of women in peacebuilding can achieve positive transformation in the community. Gbowee was educated at Eastern Mennonite University, education is, therefore, a tool to break the shackles of ignorance, exploitation, exclusion and open windows of opportunities for women in Africa and other oppressed people in the world.

This education flows in two ways according to Reardon: "reeducating men to value and perform these 'feminine' functions as it is toward providing women with male competencies" (p. 13). This two-way traffic provides a complementarity that is necessary for the respect of human rights and dignity and the enthronement of a just and peaceful society. However, this is possible only when the beneficiaries of the system are willing to appreciate the transformation and thereby learn; Reardon states that "The conscientization of the elite may be the process upon which the future depends" (p. 15). It is the elites that put up the system and structures that dehumanize; therefore learning and transformation have the potential to change society. This is extremely important in African communities, where men as elites and gatekeepers decide how benefits, opportunities, and burdens are shared. This learning should include the men who should be made aware of the benefit of an inclusive society where women are treated as equal and made aware of the privileges they have. This should form part of the basis of peace education. Reardon/ Jenkins (2015) stated peace education "can play an important role in fostering this perspective through developing critical inquiry that examines various gender identities for both the positive gender attributes that can contribute toward nurturing a culture of peace, and the negative attributes that sustain and promote a culture of violence" (p. 227). It is through this inclusive education that transformation can happen. The transformation of violence in African societies to a more peaceful society, will not occur in a vacuum. It has to be all-embracing, seeking change in how security is conceptualized and promoted. Reardon aims to call for a concentration and focus on human security.

8.8 Feminism: Shift from Security to Human Security

Violence is violence irrespective of where it happens and to whom it happens. It is a product of a society that believes that force should be a method of dispute resolution. This violence dehumanizes people and makes them unable to achieve their potentials. There is a need to change the mindset that produces this violence. Reardon argues that a patriarchy system encourages and promotes violence; therefore there is a need to change such a system. The change she proposes does not and should not lead to the creation of new sets of elites and oppressors but rather the integration of the best of both the masculine and feminine perspective to achieve a just and peaceful society. While the masculine perspective has a tendency to look at negative peace as the absence of war, the feminine looks at positive peace as the establishment of justice. They are both complementary and should not be separated. It is the acceptance and application of the two approaches that can lead to a just and peaceful world. There should be a creation of space for reflection and a redefinition of what security means.

Reardon (2015b) calls for a reconceptualization of the idea security from military-based to human security. She defines human security as "wellbeing made possible through the elimination of all forms of violence, assured by institutions designed specifically to achieve and maintain well-being" (p. 127). Human security focuses on the individual as against security that focuses on the state. It seeks to protect and promote human rights; it focuses on the individual need for human dignity, to be respected and protected from threats that prevent them from achieving their full potential. Today, in Africa, countries spend a disproportionate amount of the state budget on military security and yet there is no peace.

Reardon (2015b) further affirms that achieving human security will not be possible with the current patriarchal militarized system. She claims that the more nations acquire more weapons the more unsafe they become. The acquisition of weapons is borne out of fear. She proposes that:

> Because human security lies as much in the expectation as the experience of well-being, security is greater when the presence or perception of threat is lessened. For human beings and human communities to feel and experience security, they must be able to expect some assurance of well-being in all of the four basic areas of environment, basic needs, human dignity, and protection from avoidable harm. ...If nations are striving for authentic human security, they are not so likely to be preparing for or waging war, but rather working toward peaceful, less costly resolution of conflicts and mutually beneficial solutions to common international problems, building constructive relationships with rather than threatening other nations (p. 125).

Human security is contingent upon the integration of the masculine and feminine internally, and within institutions, which calls for transformation. Human security, based in both a gender analytic perspective, and feminist integration, are very significant within the African context. Is such integration and transformation feasible in the African context?

8.9   Conclusion

Africa women need to be educated for empowerment through both the process and content of their education–the way they learn and what they learn. Education should liberate the mind to appreciate that peace is possible and recognize the profound role of women in making it possible. Education cannot occur in a vacuum; in Africa it has to be context-focused as the reference point, while being linked to recognizing the role of women in building peace. Society reinforces the perception of difference which can lead to fear, conflict, and finally to violence, which we project onto others. Education is a means of changing this perception.

Reardon stated the need to change human relations rather than merely social structures. She claims that "structural change without value change will not necessarily transform the way human beings interact" (Reardon/Snauwaert 2015, p. 23). There is a need to change the structures that promote and enhance dehumanization of the vulnerable, and a human relations component that recognizes the human value needed for deep change in societies. Education can be used as a tool to achieve this objective. Reardon opines that it can be used to dismantle 'coercive force, anonymity, and inequality' that creates 'militarism and oppression, taking the form of imperialism, racism, and sexism' (Reardon/Snauwaert 2015, p. 25).

Finally, African communities have nothing to fear from feminism for it can enhance a peaceful and just society. There is a need for collaboration and inclusiveness; it is not the promotion of women against men or continuation of domination of women by men, instead it is necessarily the integration of the masculine and feminine. "While the masculine perspective looks at negative peace, the feminine looks at positive peace. They are both complementary and should not be separated" (Reardon/Snauwaert 2015, p. 65). Development in African communities will happen where there is no discrimination, where human rights are respected, where freedom is attained, and the dignity of a human is respected. It is possible in Africa when we acknowledge the role of women in our communities and integrate gender into peacebuilding. This is one of the highlights of the work of Betty Reardon.

References

Achebe, C. (1958). *Things fall apart* (Vol. 1, pp. 138–148). Ibadan: Heinemann Educational Books Ltd.

Ferris, E., Petz, D., & Stark, C. (2012). Disaster risk management: A gender-sensitive approach is a smart approach. In *The year of recurring disasters: A review of natural disasters in 2012* (pp. 71–88).

IFRC. (2010). *Gender sensitive approach to disaster management: A practical guide.* Geneva: International Federation for Red Cross and Red Crescent Societies.

Navarro-Castro, L., & Nario-Galace, J. (2008). *Peace education: A pathway to a culture of peace.*

Nellemann, C., et al. (Eds.) (2011). Women at the frontline of climate change: Gender risks and hopes. In *A rapid response assessment* (p. 29). United Nations Environment Programme, GRID-Arendal.

Reardon, B. A. (1988). *Comprehensive peace education: Educating for global responsibility.* 1234 Amsterdam Avenue, New York, NY 10027: Teachers College Press.

Reardon, B. A. (2015a). Human rights learning: Pedagogies and politics of peace. In *Betty A. Reardon: A pioneer in education for peace and human rights* (pp. 145–164). Cham: Springer.

Reardon B. A. (2015b). Women and human security: A feminist framework and critique of the prevailing patriarchal security system. In A. Betty (Ed.), *Reardon: Key texts in gender and peace. Springer briefs on pioneers in science and practice* (Vol. 27). Cham: Springer.

Reardon, B. A., & Hans, A. (Eds.) (2018). *The gender imperative: Human security vs. state security.* Taylor & Francis.

Reardon, B. A., & Jenkins, T. (2015). Gender and peace: Toward a gender inclusive, holistic perspective. In C. Webel & J. Galtung (Eds.) (2007), *Handbook of peace and conflict studies* (pp. 209–230). Routledge.

Reardon, B. A., & Snauwaert, D. T. (2014). *Betty A. Reardon: A pioneer in education for peace and human rights.* London: Springer.

Reardon, B. A., & Snauwaert, D. T. (2015). *Betty A. Reardon: Key texts in gender and peace.* Springer International Publishing.

Solomon, G. (2007). Challenging questions facing peace education in regions of conflict. In S. Clarke-Habibi (Ed.), In *Education for a civilization of peace: Proceedings of the 2007 international education for peace conference* (pp. 67–74). Vancouver, Canada: International Education for Peace Institute.

Salomon, G., & Nevo, B. (2002) *Peace education. The concept, principles, and practices around the world.* Mahwah, NJ: Lawrence Erlbaum.

Stoeitje, B. (2017). *Women, gender and the study of Africa.* In Africa Studies of Oxford Bibliographies. https://doi.org/10.1093/obo/9780199846733-0162.

Webel, C., & Galtung, J. (Eds.) (2007). *Handbook of peace and conflict studies.* Routledge.

Chapter 9
The Letters: An Exchange on Patriarchy, Militarization and Feminist Peace Activism

Swarna Rajagopalan and Asha Hans

Betty Reardon has been a pioneer in making explicit the connection between patriarchy and militarism. This chapter, written together by a pair of activist-scholars as an exchange of ideas and experiences in letters, identifies and reflects upon the ideas and activist themes in Professor Reardon's life work that have had resonance for our work.

October 2, 2018

Dear Asha,

I am writing from the American heartland where the land and the sky appear vast and still, while holding within them furious storms. It's Gandhi Jayanti today, the birthday of the "Father of the Nation." On television in the last week in the US, the allegations of sexual assault against Brett Kavanaugh, Supreme Court nominee, have hogged the headlines. We are told that he—and the accuser to be sure—have faced humiliation, stress and ignominy that could have been avoided by not raising these allegations at all. We are reminded about the tidal waves of revelation and anger that the represents.

I am scheduled to speak this morning in Urbana about our work in Chennai to create awareness about gender-based violence. In the meanwhile, we have just launched the Zone of Peace outreach project, encouraging groups to embrace peace-promoting behavior. I am saying to friends here, as we discuss politics, that the classroom may be the most useful site of resistance in these times. I say this, although academic freedom is under siege too.

Swarna Rajagopalan, Political Scientist, India; Email: swarnar@gmail.com.

Asha Hans, Former Professor of Political Science and Founder Director School of Women's Studies Utkal University, India; Email: ashahans10@gmail.com.

© Springer Nature Switzerland AG 2019
D. T. Snauwaert (ed.), *Exploring Betty A. Reardon's Perspective on Peace Education*, Pioneers in Arts, Humanities, Science, Engineering, Practice 20, https://doi.org/10.1007/978-3-030-18387-5_9

This is the Scrabble tray in my head and I must find and spell the message these words hide: Teaching. Peace. Gender. Equality. Patriarchy.

How does one navigate through moments like this one? How do you find the way to resist so many things at once—a centralizing impulse, arbitrary government, patriarchy, militarism? I understand analytically that peace depends on gender equality and that patriarchy and militarism reinforce each other. But how do I draw out that connection in the venues where we practice our politics? For instance, in the classroom.

What would Betty, foremother of my peace education work, do?

In a classroom of 6 year-olds, I find it easier to talk of peace than gender. In a classroom of 16 year-olds, perhaps they are each on their own easier to broach, but to discuss them as intertwined or symbiotic seems harder. Harder still with older adults, I suspect.

In Betty Reardon's writing, I desperately seek clues about her classroom and political praxis, as much as her theoretical thinking.

Swarna

October 15, 2018

Dear Swarna,

I sit in my room not only writing on disasters in India, but also feeling the change in climate—the heat and the deluge of a flood around me. Coming back to our discussion where do classrooms (6–16 years) fit into this new paradigm?

I go back to Betty and her teaching in the class. Betty is a mentor and I have read what she writes on sex, militarism and patriarchy which has been able to change many of us: our perceptions; our ideologies; and to some extent, our consciousness and the way we live our lives. I have not attended Betty's classes, but while attending the International Institute on Peace Education (IIPE), which she founded, I experienced it as a place of deep learning, and simultaneously a space where we could argue without acrimony.

Exposed to a conference culture in India where the Q&A session is always a battle ground, IIPE was the opposite. IIPE brought together young people not only to learn about conflicts and strategies to mitigate it, but also brought together women from conflict zones like Turkey, Korea and Afghanistan. I was drawn not only to the discussions and opening up of new areas of concern, but also to the process, where each discussion was followed by a reflection on the issues presented. There was no pressure to think up questions, the idea was to reflect on how to take the ideas forward. Peace, I learned, does not only have to be taught; it has to become a way of life.

The importance of the classroom cannot be undermined and as Betty writes, "It boils down to those actual practices, sharing them and guiding educators through practice thereof, and supporting the development of solidarity among those who practice."[1] Using the classrooms of the very young (ages 6–16) provides an

---

[1]Personal communication from Betty Reardon to Asha Hans, September 2018.

opportunity to get young minds to think about peace and explore new under-standings and visions.

Regarding links between peace studies, gender justice, and the #Me Too campaign, an issue has been coming up in the last few days in India about a message sent from a colleague that brought to my notice the 'naming' of a 'peace activist' with whom I have worked. I raised a query in a peace network where we were both members, on what our stand should be about this activist remaining in the network. A well-known feminist peace writer and activist's response to my query was that any action would be difficult to take as: "I am thinking of some of the #Me Too stories being cases of vendetta. That would happen. Worried also that the tools of government would be to dilute and discredit this momentum by getting dubious women to weave some fictitious stories." I ask myself as to what is important at this juncture? Is it our public face or the belief that women's bodies are as important as the peace we advocate? Should peace remain bounded within the pages of the books we write in? By confining our 'ideologies of peace' to the written word, we make invisible the practices of 'humiliation' and 'indignity' associated with the pervasive phenomena which institutionalizes the sites of violence against women and subdues women's voices. For me this is militarism and patriarchy at our doorsteps and reminds me of the ideology of totalitarianism and a silenced people.

Asha

October 16, 2018

Dear Asha,

So many strands in your message, and so many responses in my head!

The Indian edition of #MeToo is very much on my mind too. How could it not be, given that like most women, my life too is full of repressed memories of harassment and stories locked in dead storage, and that I spend a considerable part of each day working to create awareness about gender violence? Could any of us have imagined that change would come like this? In fact, which of us has not thought that it would not come at all in our lifetime? It is hard not to be thinking about this avalanche of stories and revelations all around us.

And in this wonderful teachable moment, we should indeed be reflecting upon how to bring our theoretical understandings into conversations, not just with children but also with the adults around us.

Your point about the kinds of conversations that were possible in the International Institute of Peace Education gathering is so important. How many political conversations today descend into acrimonious ego contests! It is important to learn how to listen to others, with an open mind and without interruption, and it is important to learn how to make your point in a way that is not hurtful, that leaves room for the other person in a conversation and that does not close the door on reconciliation. How hard it is to tell someone about abuse or harassment! No one who has ever listened with care would suggest that it is so simple as to be an instrument of self-promotion or revenge. In fact, as the accusers of prominent men are learning afresh, speaking out is a double-edged sword that hurts you, even if it does not hurt the person you are accusing.

In college, we learned about Gandhi's list of qualifications for a satyagrahi (Gandhi, online); I continue to be impressed by the idea that our peace work begins within us. Gandhi's list included: faith in God and in the innate goodness of humanity; specific personal habits; an ability to master anger; self-discipline and an adherence to truth and non-violence at all times. Contemporary teachers whose organizations claim to do peace work, mirror Gandhi's emphasis; their peace efforts usually include pranayama and meditation techniques that bring individuals to a calmer place from which they are able to develop compassion and nonviolence. A diminution of ego and what we describe in Indian languages as "control over the senses" surely discourage the kinds of unwelcome, persistent sexual overtures of which the peace activist mentioned above, and so many others, now stand accused.

And can you have peace without gender justice? You cannot.

This is the main point that Professor Reardon has made in her life's work, as I understand it. The immediate challenge is to take a teachable moment like this—in our living rooms and classrooms—and use it to illuminate both the iniquitous structures that enable sexual harassment and violence and also the history of resistance to this and other violence. It is essential to ask whether this is the only kind of violence that is gendered, and also, to explore how the gendered violence of patriarchy relates to other kinds of violence in society.

As I write this, it occurs to me that in our work, our gatherings are 'events'. The best peace education is an ongoing conversation—same group, many sessions—a journey undertaken together rather than a message delivered as a courier package. I sign off today thinking about how to get around the gender justice problem in an age when adults juggle too many responsibilities and even children are over-extended.

Swarna

October 22, 2018

Dear Swarna,

I am not sure, because as peace educators/activists we draw our knowledge from multiple locations and forms, from our University teachings, our research, as feminists in the movements and we build our values of justice and non-violence on our experiences and our learnings. Most of the knowledge we apply is from these sources. We bring our hopes and fears, and our ideologies and philosophies to the work. So however disjointed it seems, there is always a strand that unites. Through our documentations of the multiplicity of these strands we are writing the history of our time, of feminism and militarism.

In terms of the theoretical grounding of peace studies and peace research, we have recognized the deep intellectual histories based in a multiplicity of disciplines and human experience. There is also a tenuous global wave spanning across many countries linking militarization and patriarchy with its connected violence; the ecology destroyed by militaristic actions and its gendered effects, and a militarized society where gender differentiations and hierarchy dominate the home front. The task before us as peace educators and researchers is to evolve a paradigm that challenges the military values that distort the learning process, where textbooks are changed to follow nationalist thought built on militarism, and attempts are made to evolve the world into a place filled with hatred and enmity.

The construction of a space for peace is difficult as Indian political culture, like many others, is infused with masculine imagery. This imagery is part of our perceptions strengthened in the absence of any gendered political debate on conflicts in India. Sensationalism by the media reinforces the 'us' and 'them' syndrome and makes heroes and martyrs bolstering misplaced patriotism as well as patriarchy. Violence becomes part of the consciousness of the nation as TV channels and militarist debates, even on use of nuclear weapons, which project the 'should' and not the 'outcome', on humans. War widows are not part of that discourse, and the #Me Too never reaches the women in militarized zones. The press, a safeguard for democracy and secularism, suppresses discussions of gendered identities, except when it highlights women whose role is to sacrifice.

October 24, 2018 (In continuation of the previous letter)

The days are not long enough to find time to write down what I wanted to convey.

Women continue to counter militarization and to promote peace through their networks, despite the dangers posed by militarist structures. Sangat, working across South Asia; the Naga Mothers in Northeast India, and your network, the Women's Regional Network (WRN) are regional examples, as has been the Feminist Scholar Activists Network on Demilitarization (FeDem), a network founded by Betty, had members from Afghanistan, Turkey, Ukraine, Japan, Cyprus, Greece, Philippines and many other countries, all working on countering militarization. FeDem made possible long conversations on sexism and militarism as manifestations of violence that challenged the assumptions of patriarchy in militarized states and took note of women's bold resistance in Okinawa, Afghanistan, Kashmir, Ukraine, Turkey and elsewhere. I felt I was a part of a global movement, moving from my enclosed space to a global site.

Asha

October 25, 2018

Dear Asha,

Your letter gives me a romantic glimpse of transnational feminist peace activism, as I sit here in my corner of India, working in hyper-local mode.

Invited to give a talk, I had offered to speak on the participation pillar of UNSCR 1325, a landmark commitment of the world community to include women in peace building (ahead of its 18th anniversary) and integrate into it a discussion of women in politics in general. In light of the #MeToo revelations in India, the organizers requested me to address that too. I agreed (recklessly?), thinking this was a chance to take that continuum of violence (ergo peace) that we theorize about and narrate it to a general audience.

My narrative at the moment moves from the work women do in conflict, including peace work, to their absence at the peace table, to why it matters, 1325, and then it takes an awkward turn to interpersonal politics. I wonder if moving from the personal to the systemic works better; should I actually work with the teachable moment here, leading from what is closer to their experiences in Chennai, and on top of their minds? But I want to get in my 1325 message before they get distracted by something more topical.

Yesterday, at another discussion on workplace sexual harassment, someone suggested closed circuit television cameras everywhere. One person squirmed (apart from me) but to everyone this was acceptable. "Oh, they are already everywhere and don't interfere with our lives." Militarization, which I struggle to introduce as a topic in Chennai discussions, is so deeply entrenched in our lives that we have made our peace and arrived at a comfortable relationship with surveillance and loss of privacy. Militarization does not need boots and guns, right, as long as we internalize it?

Even as civil rights organizations, those working on land rights, environmental issues and also journalists are targeted for spotlighting unpleasant realities, those of us who work on women's rights remain relatively safe. Marginality is insurance, until our work threatens the patriarchal ground on which a militaristic government stands. This is what is happening today with so many powerful men, in government and society, being called out for sexual harassment and abuse. The volume of these accusations is laying bare the relationship between power-play and sexual violence, and this will be deeply unsettling. Most simplistically, if at the end of this season, most men in the power elite end up accused of harassment, who will be left in power? (Other men, of course!) The ground will shift from beneath the feet of a government whose ministers have been choking on their words of condemnation for sexual harassment. And this would have been true of every party.

If this is the case in the relatively free, peaceful settings of the Mumbai business world and the New Delhi media world, then where militarization is already the norm, like Kashmir or the North-East, sexual violence is inevitable and with AFSPA, the Armed Forces Special Powers Act, impunity unassailable. How much more remarkable is the resistance of women there and their courage in speaking out!

You mention Okinawa. The base has existed since 1957, over sixty years. Three or four generations have lived in its shadow, with militarization as their main reality. Their thinking, culture and gender relations must be shaped by this. After six decades, the military presence must be part and parcel of the way Okinawans live, work and survive. There must be a symbiotic relationship that makes it hard for them to contemplate the removal of the base, even as protests continue. This is what Enloe (2017) means when she writes about patriarchy pushing back.

Everywhere there is a semi-permanent or permanent military presence, you see how deeply enmeshed local lives become with this presence—whether in depending on army doctors to deliver babies or having the army procurement budget ratchet up prices of essential commodities. Security personnel also create insecurity for young girls as they approach girls for phone numbers, photos, or create support jobs for them around bases as cleaners, cooks and laundry workers. If sitting in Chennai, we now accept the presence of cameras everywhere, over six or seven decades, how co-dependent must local populations be to a military presence, and how inured to militaristic thinking!

You can dislodge a military base or installation, you can vote out a government but how do you remove this hard-learned love for strong, militaristic government and dependence on the paternalistic conveniences of a military system from people's hearts and lives? The true challenge is that peace education has to be like Incy-Winsy Spider's efforts—endless and relentless, patient and tenacious.

Swarna

October 31, 2018

Dear Swarna,

You are very right about the difficulty in wiping out from memory militaristic ideas and presence. I was in Turkey for an International Institute of Peace Education at Sabanci University (IIPE) meeting in 2004 where the conscientious objectors and women from the Kurd areas, described the situation of a prevailing militaristic thought and violence even though there was no 'war' in the traditional sense. Such control over people by the State especially its women, exists across the globe. India, for instance, calls its conflict regions in Jammu, Kashmir and North East "disturbed areas," to avoid international interference, and governs them with the help of draconian laws such as the Armed Forces Special Powers Act (AFSPA) which adversely affect women.

You mentioned UNSCR 1325, a resolution which took almost a century of trans-national peace activism by women, and finally achieved ratification as part of the United Nations Agenda. In the time (more than a decade) I have known Anwarul Chowdhury, the man behind this commitment of the world community to include women in peace decision making, he has always said that he believes this resolution is one of the last miles covered in combating militarism. These views are also reflected in the preface he wrote for our book (Hans/Rajagopalan 2016). On the ground, many women working on UNSCR 1325 know that, even though the United Nations Security Council passed it unanimously, the only States that have agreed to implement SCR 1325 do not have conflict on the ground. Most countries, including India, do not even want to discuss it. There are many women however, across the globe trying to change the militarization-patriarchy element by using UNSCR 1325 in a localized version, but few like us have tried to broaden it to a People's Action Plan. Is UNSCR 1325 the answer to ending patriarchy, or do you think we need to try other avenues?

Patriarchy, we have come to understand is difficult to eradicate, as it has been embedded in social structures for millennia. It has situated men in a controlling position so powerful that across centuries women have not been able to dislodge the patriarchal hierarchy. I am fascinated with Cynthia Enloe's book 'The Big Push' where, in the preface she confesses that when the word Patriarchy was used at a picnic table she had fled. She acknowledges that it was because the word sounded so heavy so blunt, so ideological ... instead she was interested in nuances. She concedes that she was wrong as she found that Patriarchy does not blot out nuances. She suggests that Patriarchy is a searchlight, a concept that can enable us to see what we otherwise might miss: the connective tissue between large and small; subtle and blatant forms of radicalized sexism; gendered misogyny; and masculinized privilege (Enloe 2017: pp. ix–x).

I learned about patriarchy early in life from my mother's poetry. She moved from Pakistan to India, leaving behind her sisters and friends, and remaining linked to them in spirit. Yearning for peace, she wrote:

...Sometimes man-made borders divide us

Borders of religion sometimes keep us apart

Separated from our sisters

Yearning for peaceful encounters

We look across walls separating us

I call them from my lonely universe...

Betty Reardon, ties up all the voices from FeDeM and elsewhere (including mine) and looks at the whole organization of world society, and sees it as one big patriarchy with a hierarchical structure. As I look at these issues, the images of my mother, Cynthia and Betty are before me; three very different people but with one aim: to see militarism obliterated from the lives of women on this planet.

Asha

November 1, 2018

Dear Asha,

Always so many threads in your letter to which I could respond!

I wonder if our failure as feminist peace educators is in story-telling. We understand this patriarchy-violence-militarization link instinctively, but are not able to translate it smoothly and palatably. I often say in workshops that I did not use the word patriarchy for a long time—in common with Enloe but without her slow coming to feminism—because I always wanted to be sure I used it correctly. We have a way of bandying about words, careless about their full historical weight. It is finally by reading my Chennai colleague V. Geetha's lucid writing that I began to feel comfortable using the word (Geetha 2007). Now, I see it everywhere, like particles in air.

On the other hand, patriarchy has mastered the art of the parsimonious, easy-to-follow, don't-strain-your-brain narrative. There are men and women, strong and loving, bold and beautiful, and as long as they follow the official script, the story is brilliantly easy to narrate. "A place for everything, and everything in its place." Our stories are messy; our conceptual leaps are not fully explained; our sub-plots leave loose ends—and mostly, when we do try to tell these stories through academic or activist settings, they are too complex at best, and can be too tedious for people to follow along.

I read your mother's poem and wondered: Should we rely on the arts to make this point that patriarchy reinforces militarization which in turns reinforces patriarchy? Should we string stories together to illustrate this rather than do what we do?

But then patriarchy plays its other card—gravitas. When you paint, or sing, or narrate, or act, are you serious about your content? That which is delivered in a deadpan tone, and a deep voice, and in words that mystify to explain—that is what we must take seriously, is it not? So here we sit, trapped.

So, this Sunday, I did start at 1325 and I finished at #MeToo and I am not sure how much sense my story made, but I tried. I asked the audience to take away an understanding that interpersonal violence and systemic, structural violence lie on one continuum and the privileges and entitlement we inculcate at one end manifest at the other. But there are many missing pieces on the continuum I sketched between the sexual violence in conflict and workplace sexual harassment.

Two of these are domestic violence and identity-based gender violence (aka 'honor killing').

There is now evidence of the link between militarization and increased levels of domestic violence (Adelman 2003; Rehn/Sirleaf 2002, for instance). It comes from greater access to and comfort with weapons and violence as a way of dealing with the world. It comes from men and boys being brutalized by their experience as soldiers. It comes from the greater vulnerability of women, girls, boys, the elderly and people with disability in uncertain times. It comes from a confidence about impunity—to whom are we accountable in times of war? Adding this narrative to the continuum clarifies the patriarchy-militarization link, as well as the lack of safety in public spaces.

In a state like Tamil Nadu, where I live, 'conflict' is not local. The conflict across the Palk Straits, and its spillover, are as close as we have come to it in our lifetime. The structural violence of inter-caste hierarchies and their deployment of violence to police community borders by punishing couples who defy them, is where we find a place on this continuum. The enforcement of a system-defined boundary through interpersonal violence actually captures exactly what militarization is about, I think. The system maintains itself first by limiting the mobility and life-choices of girls, and then by punishing mainly the boys for transgressions. When we talk about gender and militarization, this is the example closest to home. This example will help people understand that these are not remote issues that happen in Kashmir or Manipur, but our own concerns. Comfort with violent rule enforcement is militarization, and it creeps into every part of our lives.

Once we make this argument, picking up our role as civil society and feminist peace educators is a little easier. Then, in a place like this, 1325 read with the Universal Declaration of Human Rights (UDHR) and the Convention on the Elimination of all Forms of Discrimination Against Women (CEDAW) reminds us that we have actually been raising the level of urgency in our advocacy on women's human rights, full citizenship and participation, and freedom from violence. But how much time this takes! And what a cumbersome, Mahabharata-like story to tell! When will we get through this story, and get people to visualize a peace plan of their own?!

Swarna

November 3, 2018

Dear Swarna,

As I sit in Berlin in a hotel in Check Point Charlie, it is not surprising to look outside the window and visualize the changes the world has seen. The Berlin Wall has fallen and the end of the Cold War has been declared. But despite the changes in Europe, with not only the unification of Germany and the end of the USSR, why does the strong national security paradigm that emerged out of the Cold War still exist? Why did BREXIT emerge or how can patriarchal leaders like Trump still strengthen national security to the detriment of the peace system?

I have been wondering if we can challenge this process through new alternatives to the existing national security system? A system built on our conviction that there has been a failure of the traditional approach to security, so we need to look at security based on human and ecological needs, a security that provides for human dignity and fulfills people's basic needs, that Betty has been promoting for so many years. Men are important to the process as they also endure the outcome of militarism as you yourself have mentioned.

Since the 1960s, the peace movement has been suggesting different plans and methodologies to do away with war. This discourse however rarely included the most virulent part of the war system, i.e., nuclear weapons. The objections to banning nuclear weapons are at their core patriarchal and racist (Cohn 1987; Hill/Ruddick 2006). One of the few writers who has continued to highlight the issue has been Ray Acheson who links nuclear weapons, gender and human security. She recently quoted US ambassador to the United Nations, Nikki Haley, who when opposing negotiation of the treaty prohibiting nuclear weapons, said that: 'First and foremost I'm a mom, I'm a wife, I'm a daughter' and this is what she would want for her children/family, but then ended her speech by saying that 'we have to be realistic' This argument, says Vanessa Griffin a Fijian activist, was a slap in the face of every woman who had given birth to 'jellyfish' babies as a result of US or French or British nuclear weapons testing in the Pacific Islands or Australia (Acheson 2019, p. 392).

An emerging trend which makes State power in the global arena visible to the eyes of the public, is the importance given to the indicator of economic power: Gross Domestic Product (GDP). Each morning television viewers wake up to see how well their economy is improving, not understanding the inequality underlying this new bastion of patriotism (Oxfam International 2018).[2] The issue of nuclear weapons remain important, but in this new euphoria of global economic ranking, it loses visibility in the public perception. My question is, would this be a moment to seize and create a move for change?

---

[2]Oxfam India reported in 2018 that in India, the richest one percent bagged 73% of wealth created in 2017 which is equivalent to the total budget of Central Government in 2017–2018.

While arms trade continues to make countries like China rich, and Russia remain a big, if not great power, in this changing system can our suggestion that we adopt the concept of human security based on people's interests, and not state interests, work? I visualize that the human security paradigm would need to be broadened to include our understanding of the changing economic processes of militarization. If State responsibility in militarization is shared with the market economy, which has non-State actors leading it, then our analyses on demilitarization should also be more cognizant of these dynamics.

Asha

November 4, 2018

Dear Asha,

How apt—or perhaps inevitable—that you should be writing near Checkpoint Charlie, reflecting on the obsolescence of Cold War security thinking and nuclear weapons!

You are right to point to the priority of economic well-being in this age, and that this might be a moment to seize; to point to the guns and butter, swords and ploughshares arguments for disarmament. The 2017 and 2018 Nobel Peace awards explicitly point to this thinking—the importance of nuclear disarmament and the link between ending sexual violence. It has taken over a century of peace activism, including feminist peace work, to create this moment. So, yes, should we not seize it?

Non-proliferation arguments have in the past presumed some state actors to be more stable, rational and rule-abiding than others; but those with nuclear aspirations do not see themselves as unstable or rogue regimes, and the very implication that they might be, fuels their determination. Arguments that nuclear installations are costly and run safety risks have been countered by the fact that once set up, nuclear energy is cheap and there are reactors that are safe. But in an age when everyone, including states and civil society are encouraged to think like merchants and ask, what will be my return, the cost-benefit argument for nuclear disarmament may finally work.

However, as you point out in your letter, citing Ray Acheson, Carol Cohn and others, the ultimate barrier to dismantling these weapons may be their association with masculinity and the machismo of a state. This is why patriarchy will tolerate and even patronize the women's movement as long as it speaks of equal wages and better workplaces and even gender-based violence, as long as it leaves security and defense to "the boys."

This cuts many ways. Women grow up thinking that these issues are too hard for them. Even in a country like India, women attending engineering and science colleges in large numbers tend to think about defense applications purely as research projects, largely unwilling to contend with public policy and ethical ramifications. While we are comfortable with critiquing traditional or Cold War security thinking, and ready to formulate and generate empirical support for alternative paradigms, there are still too few women willing (and given the opportunity) to learn about and speak about weapons systems and defense policy.

Our nuclear critiques take moral and humanitarian positions—no argument about their validity—but we leave the nuts and bolts, and therefore, at the end, we are shut out of those decision spaces as not really being knowledgeable.

In 2001, I attended the Women Waging Peace conference in Boston. Thandi Modise, the African National Congress leader and Parliamentarian then serving on the South African Parliamentary Committee on Defense, pointed out in a discussion that while women might enter government through mass movements, deprived of other opportunities, they found it hard to deal with technical issues. One could argue that most male politicians also lack technical training on law, budgets and defense issues, but male privilege cancels this out in their case. No one points to their lack of skill or experience; "is man, can do" seems to be how we still think. Our consciousness-raising and peace education must also have a technical turn so that women are comfortable with the technical ideas and vocabulary of defense issues and can confidently hold their own.

If peace activists want to address nuclear disarmament, feminist or not, they are going to have to pick up where Betty Reardon's arguments leave off—coming to terms with pointing to patriarchy, its flaws, and then separating ideas of security from the possession of relative privilege (by virtue of gender or nuclear weapons). This is not an easy road and if you consider that we always seem to be hurtling towards conflict, we are in a race we seem bound to lose. How dismal!

Perhaps here too a change of perspective matters. We have had atomic and nuclear weapons available for almost a century, and yet, they have been used only twice. We have used other lethal weapons more often, to be sure—chemical, biological and now most insidious, cyber-attacks. But maybe our hesitation to use the weapons we have stockpiled means we have a little more time than we dare hope?

Writing this makes me feel like I need to be in a classroom or a public conversation every single day, no time to waste. And of course, to keep learning so that I can teach and write.

Swarna

November 5, 2018

Dear Swarna,

It is a catch twenty-two situation, we have had a long discourse on small armaments, trade of armaments for a long time, and its impact on women, but I wonder if we still stand where we started. We had begun with the multiple strands of militarization and obviously as our discussion developed, we found them anchoring in patriarchy. Its existence in 'peacetime' and a strengthening economic global base were other situations that emerged.

My question is how do we pull these strands into a common theme of a sustainable peace that brings women together to take further our discourse on a global, gendered culture of peace? We are aware that in this disparate world looking for change, the United Nations which was created to end the "scourge of war", is becoming less relevant to the aims of an increasingly militarized world of States and a state system, whose thinking underpins the ideology of security associated to "our territory" and "our sovereignty." It is a state system where a just gender order is yet to be established.

Despite these enormous obstacles I think it is a time we push for change. The Women's March in Washington, the youth getting together globally, Indian farmers on the move in millions, all show that the international world order is ready for an alternative system based on the fundamental value of human rights started by Eleanor Roosevelt 70 years ago by the promotion of the Universal Declaration of Human Rights. It is time to reassert in our writing and our actions the principles of nonviolence and reach our aspirations started by women like Betty Reardon, Elise Boulding and Cora Weiss, who are the precursors to these efforts.

We need to speak and write about the cost and risks of wars, to attract more young feminists into the fold. We need to attract young people from peace and women's movements, and also from larger social movements, and find different ways to create radical thinking in government, for instance by the mundane act of linking the SDG goals (for example, SDG 5 on gender equality and SDG 16 on peace).

I am sitting in my room in a hotel in Helsinki looking out into a dark world changing to the light of a morning, and thinking of my wandering yesterday, surrounded by malls in the shrinking market square where people from surrounding regions gather to sell their products. Marjaana Jauhola who teaches in Helsinki University, recounts the history of the cold war and its struggle with communism and capitalism. The Market Square in Helsinki reflects people's continuing faith in their ability to protect their shrinking spaces, even though the economic challengers are formidable.

Asha

November 9, 2018

Dear Asha,

I read our exchange and think how different our perspectives and how complementary! You ask the big questions and reflect on societal and global trends. I seem to be obsessed with nuts, bolts and the hyperlocal, like the ant and the earthworm. The synergy of the two levels of work, which of course, both of us do otherwise combine, makes our work effective—or so I hope!

My big day-to-day concerns as a feminist peace educator are as follows.

First, how do I get people to realize and acknowledge that the large security issues are as important to their lives as today's power outage and rising prices of onions?

Second, how do I get them to see that you do not need a degree or an office to take an interest and care about these issues? In fact, citizenship, or even humanity, is justification enough for engaging with questions about war, peace, militarization and social justice. How do I persuade women, convinced by patriarchy that their place is at home and their intelligence inadequate to consider public issues, that this is their problem?

Third, children get it intuitively but how do I convince adults that because peace depends on social justice, human rights, sustainable development, public health and education are all part of peace work?

Fourth, how do we remind people that our lives are intertwined, our futures mutually dependent? Perhaps this is easier than the others, ironically, because we can access the arsenal (pardon the war word) of spiritual teachings from every tradition humanity has nurtured.

Fifth, how do we persuade women that they can be thought of as policy leaders on peace and security without special inheritance or office, even as we give them that training?

Sixth, what is the place of sexual and gender-based violence in discussions about peace and security? As feminists of course, we would say that peace is incompatible with insecurity and impunity. But what does it mean when we only raise issues relating to violence and reproductive rights? Are we not more than our bodies? We should mindfully balance, drawing attention to vulnerability and violence while stressing less physically immediate concerns such as the right to freedom of expression, choice and political participation.

Seventh, all these concerns return me to first-order political agendas. At the political level, this means that talking about 1325 to people around me makes most sense if I can link it to the Universal Declaration of Human Rights and CEDAW. At the personal level, I think about raising and educating girls to become confident citizens, to see themselves as possessing leadership qualities and equally entitled to opportunity. This work is done one girl or one small group of girls at a time. Peace work for me begins with reminding human beings that they too are citizens of equal value.

Perhaps I ask these questions because I live so far away from traditional conflict zones. Desperate to do my share for peace, maybe I invent these anxieties to occupy myself?

There is such a sense of urgency today. It seems as if negative forces—divisive, post-factual, undemocratic and violent—are coming at us faster than we can marshal the strength to resist. Every election, every court case, every debate, every day is fraught with the sense that if we lose this one, we lose it all. Every now and then, however, I think of everything humanity has survived and overcome. We wait so long for change and then it comes suddenly and quickly. This too will pass and we shall overcome.

When I focus on structural issues like patriarchy and caste, then the work is both easier and harder—easier, because I know not to expect instant response, and harder because I cannot be sure to see change in my lifetime. The ant and the earthworm inspire me because their efforts are patient, untiring, quiet and ultimately, over time, they do move mountains and shift the earth. They epitomize the Gita's teaching that one should act without expectation of, or entitlement to, outcomes or rewards.

All this will add up. We shall overcome, one day.

Swarna

References

Adelman, M. (2003). The military, militarism, and the militarization of domestic violence. *Violence Against Women, 9*(9), 1118–1152.

Acheson, R. (2019). Patriarchy and the bomb: Banning nuclear weapons against the opposition of militarist masculinities. In B. A. Reardon & A. Hans (Eds.), *The gender imperative: Human security vs state security* (2nd ed., pp. 392–409). New York: Routledge.

Akibayashi, K., & Takazato, S. (2019). Gendered security under long—Term military presence. In B. A. Reardon & A. Hans (Eds.), *The gender imperative: Human security vs state security* (2nd ed., pp. 37–58). New York: Routledge.

Cohn, C., Hill, F., & Ruddick, S. (2006). *The relevance of gender for eliminating weapons of mass destruction.* The Weapons of Mass Destruction Commission No. 38. Stockholm.

Enloe, C. (2017). *The big push: Exposing and challenging the persistence of patriarchy.* Oxford: Myriad Editions.

Gandhi, M. K. (n.d.). *The selected works of Mahatma Gandhi, Vol. V—The voice of truth*, Part II-Section II: Means and ends. Qualifications and training of a Satyagrahi. Retrieved October 16, 2018, from https://www.mkgandhi.org/voiceoftruth/satyagrahi.htm.

Geetha, V. (2007). *Patriarchy.* Kolkata: Stree-Samya Books.

Hans, A., & Rajagopalan, S. (2016). *Openings for peace: UNSCR 1325, women and security in India.* New Delhi: Sage Publications.

Oxfam International. (2018). *Richest 1 percent bagged 82 percent of wealth created last year—Poorest half of humanity got nothing.* Retrieved November 1, 2018, from https://www.oxfam.org/en/pressroom/pressreleases/2018-01-22/richest-1-percent-bagged-82-percent-wealth-created-last-year.

Reardon, B. A., & Hans, A. (2019). *The gender imperative: Human security vs state security* (2nd ed.). New York: Routledge.

Rehn, E., & Sirleaf, E. J. (2002). Women, war, peace: The independent experts' assessment on the impact of armed conflict on women and women's role in peace-building. *Progress of the World's Women, 1*, 14–15.

Chapter 10
Dehumanization and Trauma in Palestine: Representations of the Occupation and the Great March of Return in the Patriarchal War System

Tina Ottman

Violence, says Betty Reardon, is the core problematic for our times, and 'there may be no more significant responsibility and challenge' than 'the search of a new paradigm of peace to replacement the present paradigm of war' (Reardon 2015, p. 110). Reardon defines violence not simply as war, but as that which 'degrades and/or denies human dignity ... intentional, avoidable harm—usually committed to achieve a purpose ...' (economic, political, or 'to maintain social conditions') (Reardon/Snauwaert 2015a, b, p. 152). It is 'an act of choice, strategic as well as ethical choice' and a deviation from the 'core value of human dignity and respect for the living Earth; and from the concomitant human responsibility to honor them' (Reardon/Snauwaert 2015a, b, p. 153).

The 70-year old control of Palestinian lives, especially the current blockade of the Gaza Strip, which has produced egregious psychological, economic and ecological distress, represents an ongoing instance of this particular form of overarching violence; the search for regional peace remains one of the century's most high-profile and highly-contested challenges. This chapter attempts to examine the nature of how, in the overarching context of the patriarchal war system highlighted throughout the lifetime's work of Betty Reardon, violence occurs in this conflict as a result of *dehumanization* (degradation plus the refusal to acknowledge human dignity) and *trauma* in the case of the Palestinians living in historic Palestine, and has culminated in the highly symbolic, currently ongoing 'Great March of Return' in Gaza.

Tina Ottman, Associate Professor at Doshisha University's Faculty of Global and Regional Studies, Kyoto, Japan; Email: etottman@yahoo.com.

© Springer Nature Switzerland AG 2019
D. T. Snauwaert (ed.), *Exploring Betty A. Reardon's Perspective on Peace Education*, Pioneers in Arts, Humanities, Science, Engineering, Practice 20, https://doi.org/10.1007/978-3-030-18387-5_10

10.1   Symmetries of Health and Human Security

Reardon's assertions about violence cited above, have been supported by the World Health Organization [WHO] (WHO 2001, 2002, 2003, 2010, 2011, 2012, 2013a, b, c, 2017) and other international agencies, who routinely note the traumatic impact of war and violence on health, specifically on the mental health of individuals and groups. Health in the occupied Palestinian territories in this chapter will be viewed from the perspective of the WHO's 'positive peace' description of 'a state of complete physical, mental and social well-being and not merely the absence of disease or infirmity' (WHO 1946). As Sharpe (2010, pp. 351–352) explains, health (in which I include mental health) is 'fundamental to the human experience,' a barometer of positive peace and thus human security, and societies that are health-deficient are almost certainly societies suffering from systemic violence.

The dovetailing of health and human security may be witnessed through the Commission on Human Security's 'working definition', 'to safeguard the vital core of human lives from critical pervasive threats while promoting long-term human flourishing' (Alkire 2008, p. 2). Such repeated observations on health as a critical symbol of human insecurity are common sense; for Reardon this presents 'a comprehensive security system that would seek to reduce all forms of harm to … citizens and keeps [States] from doing all in their power to mitigate the damage of what are still unavoidable harms' (Reardon 2010, p. 26). Where chronic ongoing conflicts are concerned, over a long trajectory the effects of war trauma have the potential to saturate the ethos of the health of societies, widening their locus of suffering to manifest as a form of collective (societal) trauma. In the case study at the heart of this inquiry, Palestine (specifically the Gaza Strip) is a typical example of a society that is '"trauma organized" … where violence is tolerated as a normal way of life' (Hallaq 2003).

10.2   Violence as Sacred Narrative

In the case of the Palestinians, the sources of violence are multiple and complex, spinning out from the continuing Israeli occupation, and in origin emanate largely from the *sacred foundational narrative* (Litvak/Webman 2009, p. 35) of the 1948 Nakba that de-centered the Palestinan world; around 800,000 men, women and children were forced into exile or internal displacement with the foundation of the State of Israel. This has constituted the initial defining or 'chosen trauma' of Palestinians—to adopt the terminology of Turkish Cypriot psychiatrist Vamik Volkan (see Volkan 1996, 2001, 2004, 2013, 2018).

Yet while Palestinians define themselves by the very real rupture of their existence caused by the Nakba, it seems, at times, as if they would be adrift without this unwelcome yet resounding self-image. In fact, however, it points to the need for further inquiry into structural vulnerability, which Reardon (2015, p. 153) explains as creating 'the impulse to violence'. Resulting from 'chronic disadvantage suffered by persons or groups at the lower levels of the prevailing social, economic and political structures', those who are vulnerable 'are the most likely to suffer harm as a consequence of the prevailing structures and policies' (Reardon 2015, pp. 153–154). Snauwaert, commenting on Reardon's envisioning of how violence is encoded in the patriarchal war system, identifies how the encoding is 'inherent in various social structures and *modes of thought*' (my emphasis) (Snauwaert 2015, p. xi). These include '*ways of thinking and believing that justify and normalize these structures*' (for example patriarchy, which we can observe in highly mili-tarised, on-edge, macho Israeli Jewish society, is 'in symbiotic relation with mili-tarism (the war system)' and 'constitutes the basic structure of a violent society'. Such 'ways of thinking', indeed, are 'so insidious as to convince normally demo-cratic societies [among which Israel classifies itself, my comment] that the exi-gencies of security permits a nation to violate internationally agreed standards of human rights' (Reardon 2010, p. 9).

10.3 A Human Geography of Trauma

The societal, cultural, political and historical losses of Palestinians literally repre-sent a human geography of trauma, punctuated by the absence of the 'present absentees' in the towns and countryside of contemporary Israel. This was the official terminology of the Israeli Custodian of Absentee Property, who in 1950 compiled lists of their 'some 94,000 residential rooms, 9,700 shops and 1,200 offices, worth in total some 11,800,000 pounds sterling' and in villages, 'tens of thousands of buildings … real estate assets belonging to refugees amounted to nearly a quarter of all buildings in the country at the time', not to mention personal and livelihood possessions, livestock and vehicles, valued at 'twenty million pounds sterling' by the UN Conciliation Commission for Palestine (Kadman 2015, loc. 473/5416). 'The geography is such that without knowledge of the Palestinian villages' existence in the past, it would be impossible to know that they were once there,' writes Davis (2011, p. 1) of two such villages, Suba and Bayt Mahsir, today subsumed inside Kibbutz Tzova and Beit Meir in the Ya'ar HaK'doshim (the Forest of the Martyrs, established in the Jerusalem hills in 1951 by the Jewish National Fund in memory of the Holocaust's six million perished European Jews). In one of those cruel juxtapositions of history, Yad Vashem (The World Holocaust Remembrance Center, https://www.yadvashem.org/) also outlooks onto this scenic forest, whose less than picturesque symbolism includes the site of the former village of Deir Yassin (Dayr Yasin), infamous as the scene of one of the worst atrocities on April 9th of the 1948 war, in which an estimated and highly contested number of villagers (between 94 and 254) were massacred (Brooks 2008, p. 297; Morris 2006; PalestineRemembered.com; Sharvit n.d.). Israelis are encouraged to go hiking the forest trails, which constitute 'the green lung of the residents of Israel's capital. The forest has a variety of trees, flowers and wildlife, remains of ancient farming implements and burial caves' (Jewish National Fund n.d.).

In common with most 'chosen trauma' victims, the Palestinians perceive their suffering through the Palestinian Nakba (and the later 'setback' or *Naksa* of 1967) to be 'unsurpassed in history' (Abu-Sitta 2000, p. 5)

As with the Jewish Holocaust, the broad strokes of the Nakba are both familiar and contested: the details of the 1948 war that pre-empted the flights, expulsions and atrocities (Morris 2007, loc. 729/4448; Abd al-Jawad 2007) remain the subject of intense historiographical controversy (Ottman 2008; Picaudou 2008). In the 'traumatic rupture' (Masalha 2012, p. 13), the Palestinian Central Bureau of Statistics [PCBS] suggests 'more than 800,000' [PCBS 2017] became internally displaced or exiled abroad from their towns and villages in 1948 (and more again in 1967).

Studies such as Sami Hadawi's monumental *Palestinian Rights & Losses in 1948* (Hadawi 1988), Michael Fischbach's *Records of Dispossession* (2003), the critical mapping work of Abu-Sitta (2000, 2007, 2010) the photographic records of pre-Nakba Palestine published by the co-founder of the Institute for Palestine Studies, Khalidi (1984, 2006), Rochelle Davis's examination of Palestinian village books that emerged from the 1980s on, *Palestinian Village Histories* (2011) and Noga Kadman's account of the Palestinian strata upon which Israel has been established (Kadman 2015) provide comprehensive evidence of the fabric of the world that was lost.

As with many of the past century's major unresolved historical traumas, the further the event recedes in terms of the lived memory of survivors, the more its living memorialization grows. This is heightened by the phenomenon identified by Marianne Hirsch as 'post-memory' whereby 'descendants … connect so deeply… that they need to call that connection memory and … memory can be transmitted to those who were not actually there to live an event' (Hirsch 2008, pp. 105–106). Thus although 2018 marks 70 years since the Nakba, these events are entirely present in Palestinians' lives, a 'society crystallized as a "community of memory"' whose narrative spans the 'continuum between past and present' (Milshtein 2009, pp. 48–49). This feature is particularly acute for those enduring ongoing repression and loss, as regular reports from regional NGOs and medical teams regularly attest:

> Palestinian security has deteriorated rapidly since 2000. More than 6000 Palestinians have been killed by the Israeli military, with more than 1300 killed in the Gaza Strip during 22 days of aerial and ground attacks ending in January, 2009. Israeli destruction and control of infrastructure has severely restricted fuel supplies and access to water and sanitation. Palestinians are tortured in prisons and humiliated at Israeli checkpoints. The separation wall and the checkpoints prevent access to work, family, sites of worship, and health-care facilities. Poverty rates have risen sharply, and almost half of Palestinians are dependent on food aid. Social cohesion, which has kept Palestinian society intact, including the health-care system, is now strained. More than US\$9 billion in international aid have not promoted development because Palestinians do not have basic security. International efforts focused on prevention of modifiable causes of insecurity, reinvigoration of international norms, support of Palestinian social resilience and institutions that protect them from threats, and a political solution are needed to improve human security in the occupied Palestinian territory. (Batniji et al. 2009, p. 1113)

Reardon, who was a signatory to Code Pink's 'End Gaza Blockade' campaign (https://www.codepink.org/303665) to petition then Secretary of State Kerry to 'ask that you stop enabling the blockade with US military assistance' has repeatedly expressed support for non-violent conflict resolution in Palestine-Israel, in particular praising Palestinian and Israeli women's groups that together challenge the oppression of Palestinians' lives, such as Women in Black, Machsom (Checkpoint) Watch and New Profile (see, for example, Reardon 2010, p. 32).

10.4   Palestine – Trauma as Historical Narrative and Lived Condition: The Construction of Memorial Days

The 1948 catastrophe did not immediately become 'the Nakba', just as the Jewish Holocaust required a period of time until it acquired its sacrosanct and tragic stature and nomenclature through a process of iconic construction, as Jeffrey Alexander has commented (Alexander 2004, p. 197).

Amal Jamal also affirms that 'Any form of coherent self-image was challenged by the differing existential conditions in which the various Palestinian communities lived after their expulsion and dispersal from Palestine' (Jamal 2003, p. 2). Their widely diverse circumstances 'led to a growing discrepancy in Palestinian practices of subjective self-constitution'. This produced 'multiple and diversified self-images that did not cohere and/or even contend with the official national discourse ... intensified by the internal differences regarding the future political vision that Palestinians foresaw for themselves,' (Jamal 2003, p. 2).

Thus it was that in 1998, despite considerable opposition to the Oslo Process, the time had come to come to terms with the collective trauma in a less diffuse fashion, in the form of a PNA-sanctioned Nakba Day on May 15th, 1998, when a Supreme National Commission for Commemorating the Nakba guided the outpouring of events that were to counter Israel's 50th anniversary of independence. The official entry of May 15th into the canonical calendar connects the 'forgotten Palestinians' living within Israel with those outside of it and marks a growing similarity in their commemorative practices (Sorek 2015, loc. 1437).

The PNA commemorations were marked by the 'million people' *masirat al-milyun* rallies in the Occupied Territories, processions of young people holding signs of destroyed villages and keys to houses, speeches, art and photography exhibitions and performances of traditional arts that have characterized Nakba Day commemorations ever since then, together with outbreaks of violence against participants whenever Israeli troops attempt to disperse crowds.

Then there are the daily mnemonic practices that are common to Palestinians, regardless of geographic location (whether in *al-karij*, the diaspora, or *al-dakhil*, the Occupied Territories and the Gaza Strip) or political control (PNA, Hamas, or neither), such as retaining property deeds from Ottoman times, keys to former homes, and naming streets, businesses and public and educational institutions after former villages, cities and towns; maintaining associations that preserve the memory of lost homes (including the publication of village books, and narration of personal and familial stories).

The commemoration of Nakba Day within Israel itself has suffered from the state's further rightward turn: in March 2011, a bill (the 'Nakba Law') was passed in the Israeli Knesset 'prohibiting any activity "which would entail undermining the foundations of the state and contradict its values"' (Ma'an News 2011) and seeking to impose fines on any organizations or institutions (particularly state-funded ones, such as foundations, schools or universities) that participate in Nakba commemoration (Adalah 2012a; Kestler-D'Amours 2011; Kremnitzer/Fuchs 2011; Sofer 2011; Stoil 2011). The human rights organization Adalah (the 'legal center for Arab minority rights in Israel') and the Association for Civil Rights in Israel (ACRI) campaigned vigorously (Adalah 2012b) against the intervention.

The legislation aimed at reining in those publicly-funded institutions and preventing Nakba commemoration has discouraged Arab mayors and municipal representatives from participating in the March of Return (Sorek 2015, Loc. 3300) but in general, it has had precisely the opposite effect on the numbers of people attending these rallies. Journalist Jonathan Cook correctly sums up the 'effect' of the Nakba Law as a 'backfire', claiming that there is 'greater attention on the Nakba than ever before. Recent [return] marches have been among the largest in the event's history, and have increasingly attracted a younger generation of Israel's Palestinian citizens' (Cook 2018). With increasing amounts of racism, oppression and hopelessness following the failure of the Oslo Peace Process and the drift towards the right in Israeli Jewish society, the extent of collective trauma for Palestinians living both within Israel and the oPTs is mirrored by the expansion and intensity of commemorative practices; for Palestinians, the past is definitely not a 'foreign country'. To paraphrase Pierre Nora, Palestinians speak so much of memory because there is so little of theirs left—and so few Nakba survivors remaining to carry the struggle forward (Nora 1989). As Reardon suggests, 'Neither holidays, nor statues honouring these "sacrifices for the nation", can make the nation secure. Neither can the mythology that sanctifies war provide authentic solace for the loss of what was and what could have been' (Reardon 2010, p. 22).

10.5 Encroaching Upon Memory: Collective Trauma and the Politics of Return

As Ben-Ze'ev and others have observed (Ben-Ze'ev 2004; Sorek 2015), the pilgrimage to former sites of abode for Palestinians was formerly a private and ad-hoc event. Nevertheless, the '48 IDPs' within Israel (the largest group of whom are those descended from refugees expelled from the village of Saffuriya in northern

Israel) have maintained a tradition of the March of Return to depopulated villages on Israel's Independence Day for the past three decades, representing a critical infusion of 'post-memory'; a handing-on of collective trauma to young Palestinians as part of their cultural education (Social TV 2018). Jonathan Cook reports:

> 'The annual march is now by far the largest event in the calendar of Palestinians inside Israel. ...Our march to the destroyed villages is closely followed by all Palestinians but especially by the refugees in the camps,' said Awaisi [an organizer]. 'It shows them that they are not forgotten and that we continue to stand with them.'
>
> ... 'It is a heavy responsibility for those of us inside '48,' added Awaisi. ... 'We march on behalf of all the refugees, to represent them because they are denied the right to attend.' (Cook 2018).

Despite the introduction of the Nakba Law, the commemorative practice of return has nevertheless grown enormously in size, symbolic power and politicization, as the result of a combination of a range of factors: political desperation (indicated above), together with more liberal approaches to citizenship within certain sectors of Jewish Israeli and Palestinian society; the eruption of the Israeli revisionist historians into public discourse, and critically, the development of both Arab print and online media and satellite television channels such as the highly influential Al Jazeera in the 1990s, followed by social media in the 2000s and the emergence of a new generation of citizen journalists armed with cellphones and later, drones. There can be little doubt that the internet has changed everything as far as how young Palestinians receive and disseminate cultural knowledge, and by association, how they are drawn to commemorative practices such as the March of Return and Nakba Day. Khoury (2018) notes that in northern Israel, over 20,000 people marched this year in a 'procession of return'. Clearly for Palestinian participants, the March of Return is more than a ceremonial 're-enactment ... a simulacrum of the scene or situation recaptured' (Connerton 1989, p. 72); it represents a very present collective action, a challenge to the status quo that has resulted in confrontations with existentially-threatened right-wing Israelis from the 2000s onwards (Sorek 2015, Loc. 3134–3203). From a feminist peace perspective, such as that championed by Reardon and Jenkins, the significance of this non-violent social action is that it represents an upending of an oppressive hierarchy, grounded in patriarchal oppression that forms a thick and critical part of militarization:

> ... actions of resistance and opposition ... taken within an analytic framework ... termed military violence – violence committed by military against civilians or outside the realm of combat – [locates itself] within a framework of patriarchal militarization. A similar analysis of the militarization of society informed the resistance efforts of the Israeli women who organized New Profile ...[who] continue to resist as the Israeli occupation of Palestinian territory continues... New Profile also facilitates men's nonviolent resistance in its support of conscientious objectors' refusal of service in the occupied territories of Palestine. (Reardon/Jenkins 2007, p. 215)

10.6   The Great March of Return: Acute Trauma Politics

At the time of writing, the most politicized form to date of the March of Return has been adopted to protest along the borders of the heavily blockaded Hamas-controlled Gaza Strip, as activists originally scheduled 45 days of non-violent demonstrations to run from Land Day on March 30th 2018 until the 'million person' climax on Nakba Day on May 15th, 2018 (one day after the opening of the U.S. Embassy in Jerusalem) although it now appears that there is no precise end-date. The demonstrations are at their most intense on Fridays, the Muslim day of prayer; however, their larger context derives from the historic deprivation of its citizens, 70% of whom are descendants of 1948 refugees, whose freedom of movement beyond the densely-populated Strip is heavily restricted by Israel and who face increasingly untenable living conditions since the 2006 election of Hamas, followed by three violent wars in 2008–2009, 2012 and 2014 in which Israel heavily bombed Gazans in response to rocket fire. Suffering from radical economic de-development and over 40% unemployment, Gazans do not receive constant supplies of electricity and are almost entirely lacking in uncontaminated potable water or sewage treatment (Gisha n. d., 2016; OCHA 2018a; United Nations Conference on Trade and Development 2015; United Nations Country Team 2012, 2017; UNRWA 2015; World Bank 2016). This impacts the ecological health of their environment, since untreated sewage is discharged into the sea (from which Gaza fishers attempt to make a living).

In an interview with the progressive Israeli news site, *972mag*, one of the 20 organizers, Hasan al-Kurd, expressly declares that the aim of the 'Great Return March' is to roll back Gazans' situation to a time of greater freedom:

> We want to send a message that we want to live in peace — with the Israelis. We're against stone throwing or even burning tires. ...The situation in Gaza has become unbearable and we absolutely can't live in Gaza anymore – that's what prompted us to plan this march and that's why we anticipate so many people to attend the protest. ... The whole idea is based on UN Security Council Resolution 194 (the right of return) and the current unbearable living conditions in Gaza. It is actually a peaceful act. (Younis 2018)

The organizers claim that they desired the protests to include cultural events and to attract families (Younis 2018); Ahmad Abu Artema, an originator of the Great Return March, and other organizers 'agreed they would pitch tents and have meals, traditional dabke dancing, football games and even weddings hundreds of metres from the perimeter', (Holmes/Balousha 2018). Fadi Abu Shammalah's emotive *New York Times* Op-Ed, 'Why I march in Gaza', a cry for human dignity, also stresses the cultural nature of the event:

> The resistance in the encampments has been creative and beautiful. I danced the dabke, the Palestinian national dance, with other young men. I tasted samples of the traditional culinary specialties being prepared, such as msakhan (roasted chicken with onions, sumac and pine nuts) and maftool (a couscous dish). I sang traditional songs with fellow protesters and sat with elders who were sharing anecdotes about pre-1948 life in their native villages. Some Fridays, kites flew, and on others flags were hoisted on 80-foot poles to be clearly visible on the other side of the border. (Abu Shammalah 2018)

This is far from the portrayal of events in Israeli media, both broadcast and print, which do not examine the issues being protested, nor the troublingly youthful age of victims and mostly focus on sensationalist description of 'riots'. With the exception of the left-liberal newspaper *Ha'aretz*, they do not query the IDF's use of lethal force against demonstrators, which may be the subject of an independent UNHRC investigation (Al-Hussein 2018; Miles 2018; UN Watch 2018). Reports and analysts emphasize the use of burning kites that have set fire to fields and forestry over the border (Ben Zikri 2018; Khoury/Kubovich 2018; i24 News 2018; TOI Staff and Agencies 2018; The Tower Staff 2018; Weber Rosen 2018), 'incendiary' balloons (Tzuri/Levi 2018), Judah Ari Gross's *Times of Israel* article 'Condoms, kites, birthday balloons: 'Silly' Gaza weapons could lead to real war' emphasizes how 'Palestinians in the Gaza Strip are relentlessly flying a variety of airborne arson and explosive devices into Israel, causing hundreds of fires, millions of shekels in damage' (Gross 2018); burning tyres, weaponized drones, anti-Semitic chants, slingshots, homemade firebombs and Molotov cocktails, wire-cutters and knives are also detailed (MEMRI TV 2018a, b); among the goals are to 'kidnap Israeli civilians and murder soldiers' (Marcus/Zilberdik 2018). Israeli media also views the protests as largely or entirely Hamas-orchestrated (Beck 2018; Gilboa 2018; Lenarz 2018; Lev Ram/Okbi 2018; Ragson 2018; Siryoti et al. 2018; Yemini 2018; Zitun 2018). It has widely publicized Hamas' official admission that 50 of its members are among those killed (MEMRI 2018c, d). Jonathan Halevi, a retired lieutenant colonel, writing in *Jerusalem Issue Brief*, concurs, 'The Great Return March' is the Hamas codename for its campaign that is striking against Israel's existence. … Attempts are being made to tear down the fences to enable infiltration into Israel' (Halevi 2018).

Jerusalem Post journalist Khaled Abu-Toameh, reporting also on the website of the right-wing Gatestone Institute, credits the demonstrations as being entirely 'organized by Hamas and other Palestinian factions' (no mention of non-violent origins) with an entirely different aim in mind, one that is sure to stir extreme existential fear among Israeli Jews:

> … the 'March of Return' is hardly about a 'humanitarian crisis' in the Gaza Strip. Instead, it is a campaign designed to put the issue of the Palestinian refugees at center stage and let the world know that the Palestinians will not give up what they call their 'right of return.'
>
> The 'March of Return', as Hamas leader Ismail Haniyeh said a few days ago, marks the beginning of a new Palestinian intifada, or uprising, against Israel. As Haniyeh and other organizers of the campaign have clearly stated in recent weeks, the Palestinian protests are aimed at thwarting US President Donald Trump's yet-to-be-announced plan for peace in the Middle East. (Abu-Toameh 2018)

Indeed, the Palestinian Information Center website, reporting Haniyeh's speech, affirms that the aim of the march is not to protest against humanitarian conditions ('a matter of bread, bread and electricity' but rather a 'battle for independence and confronting apartheid … a political issue for a people displaced from its land and an illegal state has been established on its land. The issue of a people who wants

independence and a return to their land... no retreat, no concession and not com-
promise, and that Hamas and Gaza will not recognize Israel' [researcher's trans-
lation]) (Palestinian Information Center 2018). Meanwhile, Anshel Pfeffer looks at
the struggle between Hamas and the PA, and sees the Great March of Return as a
strategic move by Hamas not merely to marshal Gazans' frustrations at their
deprivation, but also to buttress their power and appeal against the waning influence
of the PA:

> Hamas has recognized its limits and a historic opportunity to grasp the leadership of the
> Palestinian cause from its rivals in Fatah, as Palestinian President Mahmoud Abbas at 83,
> with his popularity plumbing new depths, may soon be leaving the scene. That's why
> Hamas in the last three and a half years has stuck to the cease-fire with Israel, tried to
> enforce it on other factions in Gaza, and searched for a diplomatic way out of its and Gaza's
> isolation.

> ... The Hamas leadership will never say so publicly but it realizes it has lost every single
> round since the bloody coup in which it took over Gaza in 2007. With few options
> remaining, it has changed tactics, and its behind-the-scenes organizing of the "Great March
> of Return" that began Friday reflects this, more than a sudden embrace of nonviolence.
> Sinwar and his comrades who came of age in the early days of the first intifada are returning
> to that ethos of 'popular uprising', not because they plan on dismantling their impressive
> arsenal but because they understand the old ethos is more effective at present. (Pfeffer
> 2018).

Yet Abu Shammalah disagrees that Hamas is at the heart of the Great March of
Return:

> Representatives of the General Union of Cultural Centers, the nongovernmental organi-
> zation for which I serve as executive director, participated in planning meetings for the
> march, which included voices from all segments of Gaza's civil and political society. At the
> border, I haven't seen a single Hamas flag, or Fatah banner, or poster for the Popular Front
> for the Liberation of Palestine, for that matter — paraphernalia that have been widespread
> in virtually every other protest I have witnessed. Here, we have flown only one flag — the
> Palestinian flag.

> True, Hamas members are participating, as they are part of the Palestinian community. But
> that participation signals, perhaps, that they may be shifting away from an insistence on
> liberating Palestine through military means and are beginning to embrace popular, unarmed
> civil protest. But the Great Return March is not Hamas's action. It is all of ours. (Abu
> Shammalah 2018)

The demonstrators, groups of whom moved increasingly closer into the ARA
(access restricted areas) buffer zones along the border, and in some cases, beyond it,
have inevitably been met with a sharp response from the IDF, who have inflicted a
huge number of casualties (OCHA 2018b, c; Palestinian Center for Human Rights
2018). The peak day of casualties, May 14th, when 60 Palestinians were killed and
at least 2,771 injured (Dabashi 2018, citing figures from the Gaza Ministry of
Health; different figures reported by the Palestinian Centre for Human Rights
[PCHR 2018]), coincided with the opening of the American Embassy in Jerusalem.
At the time of writing (December 2018), the numbers are of course still rising: 175

killed, among them 33 children and six persons with disabilities; 9621 wounded including around 200 people requiring amputations (PCHR 2018).

The IDF also fired gas canisters at encampments far from the buffer zone, which were 'set up specifically for the demonstrations at a distance of 400 to 600 m from the fence' (B'tselem 2018a). These tents included 'field clinics, food vendors and various activities for children and adults, such as clown shows, poetry readings, live music shows and soccer matches,' explains B'tselem, adding, 'Many families gathered inside tents where they ate and talked.' (B'tselem 2018a).

It is not only the abnormally large quantity of persons injured, but the grave nature of the injuries caused by IDF live-fire sniper tactics that have earned international condemnation (Hass 2018; UNHR: OCHR, 2018b, 2018c). Medècins Sans Frontiéres (MSF) reported that their clinics are 'overwhelmed' (Patel et al. 2018) and they have treated more patients already than during the 2014 Gaza war" 'MSF surgeons in Gaza report devastating gunshot wounds among hundreds of people injured during the protests over recent weeks. … MSF medical teams note the injuries include an extreme level of destruction to bones and soft tissue, and large exit wounds that can be the size of a fist,' (Medècins Sans Frontières 2018).

This action has resulted in an admonition of Israel, together with a threat of further investigation of the Israeli military from the International Criminal Court (ICC) (International Criminal Court 2018); three NGOs (Al-Haq, Al Mezan and the Palestinian Centre for Human Rights) jointly submitted further sets of complaints to the ICC (Abunimah 2018). Meanwhile, B'tselem took the unusual tactic of openly urging IDF soldiers in Gaza to refuse orders to shoot (B'tselem 2018b) and carried out a media campaign in which the names and ages of victims who had lost their lives were published (Fig. 10.1[1]). Despite a petition filed in Israel's High Court of Justice by human rights NGOs (Yesh Din, the Association for Civil Rights in Israel, Gisha and Hamoked: Center for the Defense of the Individual) querying the army's rules for live fire and requesting that it be made illegal (Kubovich 2018a), the IDF refused to reveal its rules of engagement and the Court ruled the Gaza situation constituted a state of war and therefore, "The state opposes the applying of human

---

[1]B'tselem executive director Hagai El-Ad wrote to UN Secretary General António Guterres sharing the names of the victims (publicized in this campaign) and condemning 'the 35 Palestinians killed and 1,500 injured by live ammunition … the predictable outcome of the manifestly illegal rules of engagement implemented during the demonstrations, of ordering soldiers to use lethal gunfire against unarmed demonstrators who pose no mortal danger. These orders are unlawful under both international law and Israeli law. Responsibility for these fatal outcomes rests with the policy makers and – above all – with Israel's prime minister, defense minister and chief of staff.' El-Ad called for the UN to 'do all in its power – and its responsibility – in order to protect Palestinian lives and uphold international norms.'

As a result, according *Israel Hayom*, Israel's 'national service program suspend[ed] the organization's eligibility for volunteers, saying campaign violated the law'. (Altman and Israel Hayom Staff, 2018; 'Rights group B'Tselem loses volunteers after calling for IDF insubordination'.

Jihad Ahmad Muhammad Fareinah, 34

Ahmad Ibrahim 'Ashur 'Odeh, 18

Amin Mahmoud Hamad Abu Mu'amar, 25

Mahmoud Sa'di Yunes Rahmi, 34

Abd al-Fatah Bahajat 'Abd al-Fatah 'Abd a-Nabi, 18

Naji 'Abdallah Shehdeh Abu Hjeir, 24

Jihad Zuheir Salman Abu Jamus, 29

Muhammad Na'im Muhammad Abu O'mar, 26

Muhammad Kamal Muhammad a-Najar, 25

Bader Fayeq Ibrahim a-Sabagh, 20

Abd al-Qader Mardi Suliman al-Hawajri, 41

Fares Mahmoud Muhammad a-Raqab, 25

Ahmad 'Omar Muhammad 'Arafah, 25

Shadi Hamdan 'Ali al-Kashef, 33

Muhammad Sa'id Musa al-Haj Saleh, 32

Thaer Muhammad 'Abd a-Ra'uf Rab'ah, 30

Alaa a-Din Yihya Isma'il a-Zamli, 15

Ibrahim Salah Ibrahim Abu Sh'ar, 17

Ibrahim Ziad Salameh al-'Ur, 20

Ousamah Khamis Muslem Qdeih, 38

Majdi Ramadan Musa Shabat, 37

Sedqi Taleb Muhammad Abu 'Ateiwi, 44

Hussein Muhammad 'Adnan Madi, 13

Yasser 'Abd a-Rahman Mustafa Murtaja, 30

Hamzah 'Eid Ramadan 'Abd al-'Aal, 22

Marwan 'Awwad Hamad Qdeih, 44

Abdallah Muhammad 'Abdallah a-Shihri, 28

Islam Mahmoud Rushdi Hirzallah, 28

Ahmad Nabil Muhammad 'Aqel, 24

Ahmad Rashad 'Abdallah al-'Athamneh, 24

Muhammad Ibrahim Ayub Ayub, 14

Sa'ed 'Abd al-Majid 'Abd al-'Aal Abu Taha, 31

Abdallah Muhammad Jebril a-Shamali, 19

Tahrir Mahmoud Sa'id Wahbah, 18

Ahmad Muhammad Ashraf Hassan Abu Hussein, 24

35 people were shot and killed in Gaza demonstrations under manifestly illegal orders issued under the direction of the Israeli government and the senior military command. More than 1,500 others were injured by live fire.

The order to shoot at civilians who pose no danger is manifestly illegal. Use of lethal force is permitted only when there is a clear and present danger to life, as a last resort. The responsibility for issuing manifestly illegal orders lies primarily with the policy makers, including the prime minister, the defense minister and the chief of staff. Giving or obeying such orders is forbidden.

Fig. 10.1 Soldiers, hold your fire! Israeli media campaign by B'tselem. [*Source* B'tselem 2018b]

rights law during an armed conflict," (Kubovich 2018b; Winer and TOA Staff 2018).

What can be inferred from the ongoing protests is that they have returned the focus back to the issue of non-compromise on the 1948 refugees, of course central to Nakba commemoration and at the core of the collective trauma. They have also highlighted the efficacy of non-violent action. Observes Khalidi (2018):

> Instead of futile diplomacy and pointless (and easily exploited) armed resistance, nonviolent grassroots movements are growing stronger. They range from the boycott, divestment, and sanctions (BDS) movement to the kind of marches we've seen for the past several weeks in Gaza. …Such an approach terrifies the Israeli security establishment, which depends on demonizing any Palestinian resistance … As retired Maj. Gen. Amos Gilad said of Israel's response to Palestinian nonviolence, "We don't do Gandhi very well."

Finally, not all Gazans meet the demonstrations against Strip's collective punishment with a response that speaks only of collective distress. At the time of writing, the Gaza Peace Doves initiative (Figs. 10.2[2], 10.3[3] and 10.4[4]), a classic

---

[2]The post appears on May 3rd, 2018 at https://www.facebook.com/gershon.baskin/posts/10160275190200366.

[3]The message on Israeli peace activist Gershon Baskin's Facebook page is:
Gaza sends messages of peace to Israelis
We want freedom
We want peace
We want to live in safety
We want to lift the siege
We want justice and democracy
We want to live equally
We want to live in dignity
The right to travel and travel
Right to treatment
Right to education
The post appears on May 4th, 2018 at: https://www.facebook.com/gershon.baskin/posts/10160279975250366.

[4]The post appears on May 5th, 2018 at: https://www.facebook.com/gershon.baskin/posts/10160281225100366.
One of the commentators, Rachel Ben-Shitrit, attempted to translate the clip (from Arabic to Hebrew):
'I'll try to translate.
The first woman to speak: the message is a message of peace.
We came here to the border and flew 150 pigeons to send a message to the world and to Israel. We are teenagers with no connection to a political party, sending a message of peace and love. We don't want wars, we don't want people to be killed, we don't want blood. We want to go back to our country through justice.
The second woman: the pigeons represent peace, and so we want to send a message to the other side via these pigeons that people in Gaza are a democratic people, seeking freedom and peace. We want to live in freedom like the rest of the Arab nations.
- sorry for my inaccuracies, my Arabic is not fluent. But I tried as well as I could.'
[Researcher's translation, from Hebrew to English.]

Fig. 10.2 Gaza peace doves initiative. [*Source* Gershon Baskin, Facebook 2018a]

peace action reflective of Reardon's lifelong promotion of youth engagement with peace education focuses on the original non-violent aims of the Great March, with a symbolic call for peace that attempts transcendence over collective trauma. It is documented through social media and comments under the postings subject it to accusations of 'fake news'. Nevertheless, the initiative appears as a series of posts by Israeli-American peace educator and long-time friend and colleague of Betty Reardon, Dr. Gershon Baskin (co-founder of the NGO and think-tank Israel/ Palestine Center for Research and Information, [http://www.ipcri.org/]) on his Facebook page and was broadcast on Palestinian television (see Fig. 10.4). The action, consisting of the release of doves across the border, bearing peace messages by Gaza youth, reflects one of Reardon's '9 Gifts of Peace Education,' namely 'Preparing citizens to practice nonviolent methods and strategies in political and social movements and in campaigns for change, striving together with diverse others in constructive and transformative conflict resolution and social and political change' (Global Campaign for Peace Education 2018).

Fig. 10.3 'Gaza sends messages of peace to Israelis.' [*Source* Gershon Baskin, Facebook 2018b]

Fig. 10.4 AlGhad TV: Gaza Peace Doves. [*Source* Gershon Baskin, Facebook, 5 May] (Baskin 2018c)]

10.7   Concluding Remarks

This chapter has endeavoured to show how Palestinians' empirical experience of historic and continuing loss and violence is a critical manifestation of Reardon's assertion that 'militarized national security systems have been the principal source of many denials and violations of human rights and civil liberties' (Gibson and Reardon 2010; Jenkins and Reardon 2007, p. 50). Palestinians' absence of human security have been encoded into cultural and contested historiographical narratives, and gradually given shape and iteration through commemorative practices, in particular through days of memory (primarily Nakba Day) and the March of Return, the corollary of which is to be observed in the current Great March of Return in Gaza, perhaps the most political attempt of all to redress the issue of the return of Palestine's 1948 refugees and descendants. Their absence of human security and human dignity is unlikely to be ameliorated within what Reardon aptly describes as 'the present highly militarized, war prone, patriarchal nation-state system' (Reardon, cited in Snauwaert 2015, p. xviii).

Finally, it is the unresolved and ongoing nature of Palestinians' suffering adds the qualitative (and cumulative) intensity of immediacy and damages their capacity for life-enhancement. The re-traumatising re-enactments involved in annual Nakba marches and visits to abandoned villages are reminiscent of Jenny Edkins' non-linear 'trauma time', which, unlike 'historical, narrativised time ...has [no] beginnings and ends'. In such cases, 'Events from the period of the trauma are experienced in a sense simultaneously with those of a survivor's current existence' (Edkins 2003, p. 40). For Palestinians living under occupation, whether in the oPTs or as IDPs within Israel, their 'current existence' contains sufficient daily stress and humiliation on top of the collective revisiting of historical injury, with significant impact on their health status, a further circular indicator of their absence of human security (Batniji et al. 2009). The acknowledgement of their 'human dignity' is a key factor in the restoration of their human rights, as Reardon indicates in a reflection on the topic:

> Human dignity is intrinsically part of all human beings, but it has to be realized, and to be realized, it has to be actualized. What I mean by that is we must come to the awareness, the realization that as human beings we are endowed with dignity, which at its essence means that we are worthy of life, we are worthy of respect and we are responsible to give respect and affirm life, so that it might be actualized.

> ... I would argue that many people are denied dignity... I see that there is a component of the peace process that should be related to the realization of human dignity. That is, when we say we are about building or making or negotiating peace, we should be about building, making and negotiating the realization and actualization of human dignity. (Global Campaign for Peace Education 2016)

It would seem that possibilities for a peaceful solution to the Israel-Palestine conflict lie strongly with such an 'actualization of human dignity,' as part and parcel of with the restoration of human security, of which health is one of the critical barometers, as was mentioned at the beginning of this discussion. Ascertaining that a people's 'natural and constructed environments …[are] able to sustain life and health' is, says Reardon, 'the first and primary fundament of human security' (Reardon 2010, p. 19) and such an approach appears key to the amelioration of Palestinians' lives. Finally, echoing Reardon's analysis, I concur with Giacaman et al, who maintain that, 'Hope for improving the health and quality of life of Palestinians will exist only once people recognise that the structural and political conditions that they endure in the occupied Palestinian territory are the key determinants of population health,' (Giacaman et al. 2009).

References

Abd al-Jawad, S. (2007). Zionist Massacres: The creation of the Palestinian refugee problem in the 1948 war. In E. Benvenisti, C. Gans, & S. Hanafi (Eds.), *Israel and the Palestinian Refugees* (pp. 59–127). Berlin, Heidelberg, New York: Springer.

Abunimah, A. (2018, April 30). New Gaza war crimes evidence sent to ICC. *The Electronic Intifada.* Retrieved April 30, 2018, from https://electronicintifada.net/blogs/ali-abunimah/new-gaza-war-crimes-evidence-sent-icc.

Abu Shammalah, F. (2018, April 27). Why I march in Gaza. *The New York Times.* Retrieved April 27, 2018, from https://www.nytimes.com/2018/04/27/opinion/march-gaza-friday-palestinian.html.

Abu-Sitta, S. (2000). *The Palestinian Nakba 1948: The register of depopulated localities in Palestine.* London: Palestinian Return Centre. Retrieved April 2, 2018, from http://www.plands.org/en/books-reports/books/the-palestinian-nakba-1948/pdf/the-register-of-depopulated-localities-in-palestine.

Abu-Sitta, S. (2007). *The Return Journey: A guide to the depopulated and present Palestinian towns and villages and holy sites in English, Arabic and Hebrew.* London: Palestine Land Society. Retrieved April 2, 2018, from http://www.plands.org/en/maps-atlases/atlases/the-return-journey.

Abu-Sitta, S. (2010). *Atlas of Palestine, 1917–1966.* London: Palestine Land Society. Retrieved April 2, 2018, from http://www.plands.org/en/maps-atlases/atlases/the-atlas-of-palestine.

Abu-Toameh, K. (2018, May 2). Palestinians: The real Gaza blockade. The Gatestone Institute. Retrieved May 2, 2018, from https://www.gatestoneinstitute.org/12244/gaza-blockade.

Adalah. (2012a). 'Nakba Law' - Amendment No. 40 to the Budgets Foundations Law. Retrieved March 4, 2018, from https://www.adalah.org/en/law/view/496.

Adalah. (2012b). Adalah & ACRI: Do not bar Nakba commemoration at Israeli universities. Retrieved March 4, 2018, from https://www.adalah.org/en/content/view/7770.

Alexander, J. C. (2004). On the social construction of moral universals: The "Holocaust" from war crime to trauma drama. In J. C. Alexander, R. Eyerman, B. Giesen, N. J. Smelser, & P. Sztompka (Eds.), *Cultural trauma and collective identity.* Berkeley: University of California Press (pp. 196–263).

Al-Hussein, S. (2018). Special Session of the Human Rights Council on the deteriorating human rights situation in the Occupied Palestinian Territory, including East Jerusalem, May 18. Retrieved May 19, 2018, from http://www.ohchr.org/EN/HRBodies/HRC/Pages/NewsDetail.aspx?NewsID=23100&LangID=E.

Alkire, S. (2008). A conceptual framework for Human Security: Working Paper 2. Centre for Research on Inequality, Human Security and Ethnicity, CRISE. Retrieved November 29, 2018, from https://www.researchgate.net/publication/242201569_A_Conceptual_Framework_for_Human_Security.

Baskin, G. (2018a) [Untitled photograph.] Facebook, 4 May. The post was available to Baskin's Facebook friends on 4 May 2018 at https://www.facebook.com/gershon.baskin/posts/10160279975250366.

Baskin, Gershon. (2018b) [Untitled video.] Facebook, 5 May. The post was available to Baskin's Facebook friends on May 5th 2018 at https://www.facebook.com/gershon.baskin/posts/10160281225100366.

Baskin, Gershon. (2018c) From Gaza - Like and Share this Message All Over Israel, Palestine and the World! Facebook, 3 May. The post was available to Baskin's Facebook friends on 3 May 2018 at https://www.facebook.com/gershon.baskin/posts/10160275190200366.

Batniji, R., Rabaia, Y., Nguyen–Gillham, V., Giacaman, R., Sarraj, E., Punamaki, R-L., et al. (2009, March 5). Health as human security in the occupied Palestinian territory. *The Lancet, Health in the Occupied Palestinian Territory, 4*(373), 1133–1143. https://doi.org/10.1016/s0140-6736(09)60110-0.

Beck, N. (2018, May 2). The Great Deception March on Gaza's borders. *Arutz Sheva* (Israel National News). Retrieved May 2, 2018, from https://www.israelnationalnews.com/Articles/Article.aspx/22089.

Ben-Ze'ev, E. (2004). The politics of taste and smell: Palestinian rites of return. In B. Nerlich & M. E. Lien (Eds.), *The politics of food* (pp. 141–160). Oxford and New York: Berg.

Ben Zikri, A. (2018, May 2). Kite terrorism: Massive fire after kite with Molotov cocktail attached sent from Gaza explodes. *Ha'aretz*. Retrieved May 2, 2018, from https://www.haaretz.com/israel-news/massive-fire-after-kite-with-molotov-cocktail-attached-sent-from-gaza-1.6052362.

Brooks, S. (2008). Deir Yassin Massacre. In S. C. Tucker (Ed.), *The encyclopedia of the Arab-Israeli conflict: A political, social, and military history. Volume 1.* Santa Barbara, California; Denver, Colorado, and Oxford, England: ABC Clio.

B'tselem. (2018a, April 20). Military fired teargas at family tents far from fence during Gaza protests, injuring hundreds. Retrieved May 2, 2018, from https://www.btselem.org/gaza_strip/20180419_military_fires_tear_gas_at_gaza_protest_tents.

B'tselem, the Israeli Information Center for Human Rights in the Occupied Territories. (2018b, April 26). Soldiers, hold your fire. Retrieved May 2, 2018, from https://www.btselem.org/gaza_strip/2180426_soldiers_hold_your_fire.

Connerton, P. (1989). *How societies remember* [Kindle edition.]. Cambridge: Cambridge University Press.

Cook, J. (2018, April 19). 'A place I do not recognise': Palestinians mark 70 years of Israeli injustice. *Middle East Eye*. Retrieved April 20, 2018, from http://www.middleeasteye.net/news/nakba-palestine-israel-1948-palestinian-citizens-out-cold-israel-celebrates-70-years-427471332 and https://www.jonathan-cook.net/2018-04-19/a-place-i-do-not-recognise-palestinians-mark-70-years-of-israeli-injustice/.

Dabashi, H. (2018, May 22). Palestine after the May 14 massacre. *Al Jazeera.com*. Retrieved May 23, 2018, from https://www.aljazeera.com/indepth/opinion/palestine-14-massacre-180521110715978.html.

Davis, R. A. (2011). *Palestinian village histories: Geographies of the displaced* (Kindle edition.). Stanford, California: Stanford University Press.

El-Ad, H. (2018, April 26). Letter to Mr. António Guterres, Secretary General of the United Nations. B'Tselem.

Fischbach, M. (2003). *Records of dispossession: Palestinian refugee property and the Arab-Israeli conflict.* (Kindle edition.). New York: Columbia University Press.

Giacaman, R., Khatib, R., Shabaneh, L., Ramlawi, A., Sabri, B., Sabatinelli, G., et al. (2009, March 5). Health status and health services in the occupied Palestinian territory. *The Lancet. Health in the Occupied Palestinian Territory, 1*(373), 837–849. https://doi.org/10.1016/S0140-6736(09)60107-0.

Gibson, I. R., & Reardon, B. A. (2010). Human security: Towards gender inclusion. In G. Shani, M. Sato, & M. K. Pasha (Eds.), *Protecting human security in a Post 9/11 world* (pp. 50–78). Basingstoke: Palgrave Macmillan.

Gilboa, E. (2018, April 22). The 'March of Return': Hamas' dirty war against Israel. *The Jerusalem Post*. Retrieved April 23, 2018, from https://www.jpost.com/Opinion/The-March-of-Return-Hamas-dirty-war-against-Israel-552445.

Gisha. (2016). Dark grey lists. Retrieved May 21, 2018, from http://gisha.org/UserFiles/File/publications/Dark_Gray_Lists/Dark_Gray_Lists-en.pdf.

Gisha. (n.d.). Fifty shades of control. Retrieved May 20, 2018, from http://gisha.org/50shades/50_Shades_Of_Control_EN.pdf.

Global Campaign for Peace Education. (2018, December 21). 9 Gifts peace education gives year round (and a note of thanks from Betty Reardon!). https://www.peace-ed-campaign.org/9-gifts-peace-education-gives-year-round-and-a-note-of-thanks-from-betty-reardon/.

Global Campaign for Peace Education. (2016, September 13). Making peace real: An interview with Betty Reardon. https://www.peace-ed-campaign.org/making-peace-real-interview-betty-reardon/.

Gross, J. A. (2018, June 20). Condoms, kites, birthday balloons: 'Silly' Gaza weapons could lead to real war. *The Times of Israel*. Retrieved June 20, 2018, from https://www.timesofisrael.com/condoms-kites-birthday-balloons-silly-gaza-weapons-could-lead-to-serious-war/.

Hadawi, S. (1988). *Palestinian rights & losses in 1948: A comprehensive study*. London: Saqi Books.

Hallaq, E. (2003). An epidemic of violence: Trauma organized and producing environments rule our lives. *Palestine-Israel Journal of Politics, Economics and Culture, 10*(4), 2003: Two Traumatized Societies. Retrieved December 25, 2013, from http://www.pij.org/details.php?id=59.

Halevi, J. (2018, May 1). Hamas' warfare tactics in the "Great Return March". *Jerusalem Issue Brief, 18*(6), 1–8. Retrieved May 2, 2018, from http://jcpa.org/pdf/JIB_vol18_no6_1may18.pdf.

Hamas. (2018, April 28). Hamas: Palestinians' right to return to homeland is inalienable. *Hamas website*. Retrieved April 29, 2018, from http://hamas.ps/en/post/1286/hamas-palestinians-right-to-return-to-homeland-is-inalienable.

Hass, A. (2018, April 22). Gaza doctors: Israeli fire at border protests causing wounds not seen since 2014 war. *Ha'aretz*. https://www.haaretz.com/middle-east-news/palestinians/.premium-gaza-doctors-injuries-in-border-protests-worst-since-2014-war-1.6014013.

Hirsch, M. (2008). The generation of postmemory. *Poetics Today, 29*(1), 103–128. Retrieved March 9, 2015, from http://poeticstoday.dukejournals.org/content/29/1/103.full.pdf+html. https://doi.org/10.1215/03335372-2007-019.

Holmes, O., & Balousha, H. (2018, April 6). Time for peaceful resistance, says Gaza's new movement. *The Guardian*. Retrieved April 7, 2018, from https://www.theguardian.com/world/2018/apr/06/time-for-peaceful-resistance-says-gazas-new-movement.

Humaid, M. (2018, March 31). We want to return to our lands without bloodshed or bombs. *Al Jazeera*. Retrieved March 31, 2018, from https://www.aljazeera.com/indepth/features/return-lands-bloodshed-bombs-180330170242175.html.

i24 News. (2018, May 16). Firebombs tied to kites launched from Gaza spark fires in Israel near border. *i24 News*. Retrieved May 16, 2018, from https://www.i24news.tv/en/news/israel/172425-180416-firebombs-tied-to-kites-launched-from-gaza-spark-fires-in-israel-near-border.

International Criminal Court. (2018, April 8). Statement of the Prosecutor of the International Criminal Court, Fatou Bensouda, regarding the worsening situation in Gaza.

Jamal, A. (2003). Palestinian dynamics of self-representation: Identity and difference in Palestinian nationalism. *HAGAR: Studies in Culture, Polity & Identities, 4*(1/2), 65. Retrieved August 10, 2018, from http://people.socsci.tau.ac.il/mu/amaljamal/files/2018/02/Amal-Jamal-Palestinian-Self-Represent.pdf.

Jenkins, T., & Reardon, B. A. (2007). Gender and peace: Towards a gender inclusive, holistic perspective. In J. Galtung & C. Webel (Eds.), *Handbook of peace & conflict studies* (pp. 209–231). London and New York: Routledge.

Jewish National Fund [Keren Kayemeth leIsrael]. (n.d.). Jerusalem Forest - Nature in Jerusalem. Retrieved April 28, 2018, from http://www.kkl-jnf.org/tourism-and-recreation/forests-and-parks/jerusalem-forest.aspx.

JLBWC Staff. (2018, April 26). Hamas: March of return to continue through Ramadan, spread to West Bank. *The Jewish Link*. Retrieved April 27, 2018, from https://www.jewishlinkbwc.com/index.php/world-us/10050-hamas-march-of-return-to-continue-through-ramadan-spread-to-west-bank.

Kadman, N. (2015). *Erased from space and consciousness: Israel and the depopulated Palestinian villages of 1948*. (Translated from the Hebrew by Dimi Reider.) Bloomington and Indianapolis: Indiana University Press.

Khalidi, R. (2018, May 10). The Palestinians have not forgotten, they have hot gone away. *The Nation*. Retrieved May 11, 2018, from https://www.thenation.com/article/after-the-nakba-the-persistence-of-palestine/.

Kestler-D'Amours, J. (2011, March 29). Israel criminalizes commemoration of the Nakba. *The Electronic Intifada*. Retrieved April 30, 2018, from https://electronicintifada.net/content/israel-criminalizes-commemoration-nakba/9289.

Khalidi, W. (1984). *Before their diaspora: A photographic history of the Palestinians 1876–1948*. Washington DC: Institute for Palestine Studies.

Khalidi, W. (2006). *All that remains: The Palestinian villages occupied and depopulated by Israel in 1948*. Washington DC: Institute for Palestine Studies.

Khoury, J. (2018, April 19). Over 20,000 march in Northern Israel to mark 'catastrophe' of Israeli independence. *Ha'aretz*. Retrieved April 20, 2018, from https://www.haaretz.com/israel-news/.premium-20-000-march-to-mark-catastrophe-of-israeli-independence-1.6012681.

Khoury, J., & Kubovich, Y. (2018, May 4). Palestinians set fires at Israel-Gaza crossing; 70 wounded by Israeli fire in border protests. *Ha'aretz*. Retrieved May 5, 2018, from https://www.haaretz.com/israel-news/gaza-protests-weekly-border-march-begins-1.605447.

Kremnitzer, M., & Fuchs, A. (2011, March 21). The Nakba Bill: A test of the democratic nature of the Jewish and democratic state. The Israel Democracy Institute. Retrieved March 9, 2018, from https://en.idi.org.il/articles/6894.

Kubovich, Y, (2018a, April 29). Israeli army refuses to disclose open-fire policy for Gaza border protests. *Ha'aretz*. Retrieved April 29, 2018, from https://www.haaretz.com/israel-news/.premium-israeli-army-refuses-to-disclose-open-fire-policy-for-gaza-protests-1.6035708.

Kubovich, Y, (2018b, May 3). Israel to top court: Gaza protests are state of war, Human Rights Law doesn't apply. *Ha'aretz*. Retrieved May 3, 2018, from https://www.haaretz.com/israel-news/.premium-israel-gaza-protests-are-state-of-war-human-rights-law-doesn-t-apply-1.6052794.

Lenarz, J. (2018, May 4). TIP Backgrounder: Hamas-led "March of Return" is not for independence, but for end of Israel. *The Tower*. Retrieved May 5, 2018, from http://www.thetower.org/6226-tip-backgrounder-hamas-led-march-of-return-is-not-for-independence-but-for-end-of-israel/.

Lev Ram, T., & Okbi, Y. (2018, May 4). *Shnei rachfanei Tsahal noflu ba'retzua, hazatatot ba'tsadoh shel ha'Falestinai shel maavar Kerem Shalom*. [Two IDF drones fell in the Gaza Strip, arson on the Palestinian side of the Kerem Shalom crossing.] *Ma'ariv*. Retrieved May 5, 2018, from http://www.maariv.co.il/news/military/Article-636705.

Litvak, M., & Webman, E. (2009). *From empathy to denial: Arab responses to the Holocaust*. New York: Columbia University Press.

Ma'an News Agency. (2011, March 23). Israel bans events commemorating Nakba. *Ma'an News*. Retrieved March 6, 2018, from http://www.maannews.com/Content.aspx?id=371548.

Marcus, I., & Zilberdik, N. J. (2018, May 18). 'Bring a knife, dagger, or handgun,' kidnap Israeli civilians, and murder soldiers and settlers - Instructions on Facebook to Gazans for 'March of Return'. *PMW* (Palestinian Media Watch).

Masalha, N. (2012). *The Palestine Nakba: Decolonising history, narrating the subaltern, reclaiming memory*. London & New York: Zed Books.

Medècins Sans Frontières. (2018, April 19). Palestine: MSF teams in Gaza observe unusually severe and devastating gunshot injuries. Retrieved May 19, 2018, from http://www.msf.org/en/article/palestine-msf-teams-gaza-observe-unusually-severe-and-devastating-gunshot-injuries.

MEMRI TV. (2018a, April 27). Clip #6545. Members of Gaza 'Fence Cutters' Unit' Proclaims: Victory or Martyrdom!' - Scenes from Gaza 'Return March'. [Video.] Retrieved April 28, 2018, from https://www.memri.org/tv/fence-cutters-unit-gaza-proclaims-victory-or-martyrom. Transcript at https://www.memri.org/tv/fence-cutters-unit-gaza-proclaims-victory-or-martyrom/transcript.

MEMRI TV. (2018b, April 28). Clip #6547. At rally held by 'Tire-burning unit' in Gaza, demonstrators brandish wire-cutters, chant anti-Semitic slogans - Scenes from Gaza 'Return March'. [Video.] Retrieved April 28, 2018, from https://www.memri.org/tv/rally-of-tire-burning-unit-in-gaza. Transcript at https://www.memri.org/tv/rally-of-tire-burning-unit-in-gaza/transcript.

MEMRI TV. (2018c, May 16). Clip #6575. Hamas Political Bureau member Salah Al-Bardawil: 50 of the martyrs killed in Gaza were from Hamas, 12 regular people. [Video.] Retrieved May 16, 2018, from https://www.memri.org/tv/hamas-politburo-member-bardawil-fifty-martyrs-were-hamas-members.

MEMRI. (2018d, May 18). The 'Great Return March' Campaign: An initiative sponsored by Hamas, whose goal was to breach the Border Fence, penetrate Israeli territory. Special Dispatch #7476. Retrieved May 18, 2018, from https://www.memri.org/reports/great-return-march-campaign-initiative-sponsored-hamas-whose-goal-was-breach-border-fence.

Miles, T. (2018, May 18). UN sets up human rights probe into Gaza killings, to Israel's fury. *Reuters*. Retrieved May 18, 2018, from https://www.reuters.com/article/us-israel-palestinians-un/un-sets-up-human-rights-probe-into-gaza-killings-to-israels-fury-idUSKCN1IJ0UU.

Milshtein, M. (2009). The memory that never dies: The Nakba memory and the Palestinian national movement. In M. Litvak (Ed.), *Palestinian collective memory and national identity* (pp. 47–69). New York: Palgrave Macmillan.

Morris, B. (2006). The Historiography of Deir Yassin. *Journal of Israeli History, 24*(1), 79–107. Retrieved May 2, 2018, from https://doi.org/10.1080/13531040500040305.

Morris, B. (2007). Revisiting the Palestinian exodus of 1948. In E. L. Rogan & A. Shlaim (Eds.), *The war for Palestine: Rewriting the history of 1948* (2nd ed., Kindle version, pp. 37–59). Cambridge: Cambridge University Press.

Nora, P. (1989). Between memory and history: Les lieux de mémoire. *Representations, 26*(Special Issue: Memory and Counter-Memory) (Spring, 1989), 7–24. Retrieved May 1, 2018, from http://www.jstor.org/stable/2928520.

OCHA. (2018a). Gaza electricity supply. Retrieved May 2, 2018, from https://www.ochaopt.org/page/gaza-strip-electricity-supply.

OCHA. (2018, May 18). 56 Palestinians reported injured during demonstrations in Gaza on first Friday of Ramadan. Retrieved May 19, 2018, from https://www.ochaopt.org/content/56-palestinians-reported-injured-during-demonstrations-gaza-first-friday-ramadan.

OCHA. (2018c, May 11). One Palestinian killed and hundreds injured in Gaza during ongoing demonstrations. Retrieved May 12, 2018, from https://www.ochaopt.org/content/one-palestinian-killed-and-hundreds-injured-gaza-during-ongoing-demonstrations.

Ottman, E. T. (2008). A question of historiography: The 'new historians' of Israel. *Ritsumeikan Annual Review of International Studies, 7*, 55–67.

Palestinian Center for Human Rights. (2018, May 15). The final toll for bloodiest day since beginning of return and Breaking Siege March in the Gaza Strip.

Palestinian Central Bureau of Statistics. (2017). Ms. Ola Awad, President of the PCBS, reviews the conditions of the Palestinian people via statistical figures and findings, on the eve of the sixty ninth annual commemoration of the Palestinian Nakba. Retrieved February 3, 2018, from http://www.pcbs.gov.ps/post.aspx?lang=en&ItemID=1925.

Palestinian Information Center. (2018, April 29). Haniyeh announces the inauguration of a new stage … the March of Return continues. *[Haniyeh yuelin tadshin marhalatan jadida… masirat aleawdat mustamira.]* PIC. https://tinyurl.com/yaj4yqlz Accessed on 30 April 2018.

Patel, Y., Al-Wa'ra, A., & Wuheid, N. (2018, May 4). Video: Médecins Sans Frontières clinic overwhelmed by Palestinians wounded during March of Return. *Mondoweiss*. http://mondoweiss.net/2018/05/frontieres-overwhelmed-palestinians/. https://youtu.be/2vru8MaWkTA

Pfeffer, A. (2018, April 2). Israel beat Hamas. Now it may lose its victory. *Ha'aretz*. Retrieved April 3, 2018, from https://www.haaretz.com/israel-news/.premium-israel-beat-hamas-now-it-may-lose-its-victory-1.5964194.

Picaudou, N. (2008). The historiography of the 1948 wars. Retrieved April 2, 2018, from http://www.sciencespo.fr/mass-violence-war-massacre-resistance/en/document/historiography-1948-wars.

Ragson, A. (2018, March 31). IDF: Don't believe Hamas propaganda. *The Jerusalem Post*. Retrieved March 31, 2018, from https://www.jpost.com/Arab-Israeli-Conflict/Did-an-IDF-sniper-gun-down-a-Palestinian-running-from-the-border-547579.

Reardon, B. A. (2010). Women and human security: A feminist framework and critique of the prevailing patriarchal security system. In B. A. Reardon & A. Hans (Eds.), *The gender imperative: Human security vs state security* (pp. 7–37). Abingdon and New Delhi: Routledge.

Reardon, B. A., & Snauwaert, D. T. (2015a). *Betty A. Reardon: A pioneer in education for peace and human rights*. Springer Briefs on Pioneers in Science and Practice 26. Heidelberg, New York, Dordrecht, London: Springer Books.

Reardon, B. A., & Snauwaert, D. T. (2015b) *Betty A. Reardon: Key texts in gender and peace*. Springer Briefs on Pioneers in Science and Practice: Texts and Protocols, 27. Heidelberg, New York, Dordrecht, London: Springer Books.

Sabbagh-Khoury, A. (2011). The internally displaced Palestinians in Israel. In A. Sabbagh-Khoury & N. M. Rouhana (Eds.), *The Palestinians in Israel: Readings in history, politics and society* (Vol. 1, pp. 27–46). Haifa: Mada al-Carmel–Arab Center for Applied Social Research. Retrieved May 27, 2018, from http://mada-research.org/en/files/2011/09/ebook-english-book.pdf.

Sharpe, A. (2010). Public health and patriarchy: Militarism and gender as determinants of health insecurity. In A. Hans & B. A. Reardon (Eds.), *The gender imperative: Human security vs state security*. Abingdon, Oxon and New Delhi: Routledge (pp. 351–383).

Sharvit, A. (n.d.). Historian Benny Morris: Was mistake not to complete transfer in '48. *Survival of the fittest (an interview with Historian Benny Morris)*. DeirYassin.org. (Extracted from *Haaretz*, Magazine Section, January 8, 2004; https://www.haaretz.com/1.5262454). Retrieved January 2, 2016, from http://www.deiryassin.org/bennymorris.html.

Siryoti, D., Guttman, N., Reuters and Israel Hayom Staff. (2018, April 29). IAF strikes 6 Hamas targets in response to Gaza border riots. *Israel Hayom*. Retrieved April 29, 2016, from http://www.israelhayom.com/2018/04/29/iaf-strikes-6-hamas-targets-in-response-to-gaza-border-riots/.

Snauwaert, D. T. (2015). Preface. In B. A. Reardon & D. T. Snauwaert (Eds.), *Betty A. Reardon: Key texts in gender and peace*. Springer Briefs on Pioneers in Science and Practice 26. Heidelberg, New York, Dordrecht, London: Springer Books.

Social TV. (2018). The return to Safuria. [Video.] Published on 25 April. Retrieved May 3, 2018, from https://youtu.be/dqCSqbbhDi0.

Sofer, R. (2011, March 23). Knesset passes 'Nakba bill'. *YNet News*. Retrieved September 24, 2015, from https://www.ynetnews.com/articles/0,7340,L-4046440,00.html.

Sorek, T. (2015). *Palestinian commemoration in Israel: Calendars, monuments, and martyrs* (Kindle edition.) Stanford: Stanford University Press.

Stoil, R. A. (2011, March 23). 'Nakba Bill' passes Knesset in third reading. *The Jerusalem Post*. Retrieved November 28, 2014, from http://www.jpost.com/Diplomacy-and-Politics/Nakba-Bill-passes-Knesset-in-third-reading-213396.

The Tower Staff. (2018, May 2). Watch: Fires started by kites from Gaza carrying burning fuel scorch Southern Israel. *The Tower.org*. Retrieved May 3, 2018, from http://www.thetower.org/6218-watch-fires-started-by-kites-from-gaza-carrying-burning-fuel-scorch-southern-israel/.

TOI Staff and Agencies. (2018, April 21). Liberman says Hamas to blame for death of 15-year-old in Gaza. *The Times of Israel*. Retrieved April 21, 2018, from https://www.timesofisrael.com/liberman-says-hamas-to-blame-for-death-of-15-year-old-in-gaza/.

Tzuri, M., & Levy, E. (2018, May 7). Incendiary balloons from Gaza cause damage to Israeli fields. *YNet News.com*. Retrieved May 8, 2018, from https://www.ynetnews.com/articles/0,7340,L-5253939,00.html.

United Nations Conference on Trade and Development. (2015, July 6). Report on UNCTAD assistance to the Palestinian people: Developments in the economy of the Occupied Palestinian Territory. UNCTAD. Retrieved April 3, 2018, from http://unctad.org/meetings/en/SessionalDocuments/tdb62d3_en.pdf.

United Nations Country Team in the occupied Palestinian Territory. (2012). Gaza in 2020: A livable place? Retrieved April 9, 2018, from https://www.unrwa.org/userfiles/file/publications/gaza/Gaza%20in%202020.pdf and https://reliefweb.int/sites/reliefweb.int/files/resources/104094048-Gaza-in-2020-A-livable-place.pdf.

United Nations Country Team in the occupied Palestinian Territory. (2017, July 11). Gaza 10 years later. UNSCO. Retrieved April 6, 2018, from https://unsco.unmissions.org/sites/default/files/gaza_10_years_later_-_11_july_2017.pdf.

United Nations Relief and Works Agency. (2015). Gaza: Eight years of blockade. Retrieved May 2, 2018, from https://www.unrwa.org/sites/default/files/gaza_eight_years_of_blockade.pdf.

UN Watch. (2018, May 18). Full Text: UN draft resolution on Gaza omits Hamas. Retrieved May 19, 2018, from https://www.unwatch.org/full-text-un-draft-resolution-gaza-omits-hamas/.

Volkan, V. (1996). Bosnia-Herzegovina: Ancient fuel of a modern inferno. *Mind and Human Interaction, 7*, 110–127. Retrieved May 10, 2018, from https://www.researchgate.net/publication/323769004_Bosnia-Herzegovina_Ancient_Fuel_of_a_Modern_Inferno.

Volkan, V. D. (2001). Transgenerational transmissions and chosen traumas: An aspect of large-group identity. *Group Analysis, 34*(1), 79–97. Issue published: March 1, 2001. Retrieved May 9, 2018, from https://doi.org/10.1177/0533316012207773.

Volkan, V. D. (2004). *Blind trust: Large groups and their leaders in times of terror.* Charlottesville, VA: Pitchstone Publishing.

Volkan, V. D. (2013). *Enemies on the Couch: A psychopolitical journey through war and peace* (Kindle edition.) Durham, N.C.: Pitchstone Publishing.

Volkan, V. D. (2018). *Immigrants and Refugees: Trauma, perennial mourning, prejudice and border psychology* (First published 2017 by Karnac Books.) (Kindle edition.). Abingdon, Oxon: Routledge.

Weber Rosen, J. (2018, May 2). Farmland in flames as Gaza protests give way to 'kite terrorism'. *The Jerusalem Post*. Retrieved May 3, 2018, from https://www.jpost.com/Israel-News/Farmland-in-flames-as-Gaza-protests-give-rise-to-kite-terrorism-553329.

Winer, S., & TOA Staff. (2018, April 29). State says use of live fire in Gaza protests within Israeli, international law. *The Times of Israel*. Retrieved April 30, 2018, from https://www.timesofisrael.com/state-says-use-of-live-fire-in-gaza-protests-within-israeli-international-law/.

World Bank. (2016, November 22). Water situation alarming in Gaza. Retrieved April 5, 2018, from http://www.worldbank.org/en/news/feature/2016/11/22/water-situation-alarming-in-gaza.

World Health Organization. (1946). Constitution of the World Health Organization: Principles. Retrieved November 29, 2018, from https://www.who.int/about/mission/en/.

World Health Organization. (2001). The world health report 2001: New understanding, new hope. Retrieved April 20, 2011, from http://www.who.int/whr/2001/en/whr01_en.pdf.

World Health Organization. (2002). The world health report 2002: World report on violence and health. Retrieved April 20, 2011, from http://www.who.int/violence_injury_prevention/violence/world_report/en/introduction.pdf.

World Health Organization. (2003). Mental and social aspects of health of populations exposed to extreme stressors. Retrieved April 20, 2011, from http://www.who.int/mental_health/emergencies/MSDMER03_01/en/.

World Health Organization. (2006). Commission on Social Determinants of Health. Retrieved April 28, 2011, from http://www.who.int/social_determinants/resources/csdh_brochure.pdf.

World Health Organization. (2010). Mental health and development: Targeting people with mental health conditions as a vulnerable group. Retrieved January 2, 2013, from http://www.who.int/mental_health/policy/mhtargeting/en/index.html.

World Health Organization, War Trauma Foundation and World Vision International. (2011). Psychological first aid: Guide for field workers. Retrieved January 3, 2013, from http://www. who.int/mental_health/publications/guide_field_workers/en/.

World Health Organization and United Nations High Commission for Refugees. (2012). Assessing mental health and psychosocial needs and resources: Toolkit for humanitarian settings. Retrieved January 5, 2013, from http://www.who.int/mental_health/resources/toolkit_mh_ emergencies/en/index.html.

World Health Organization. (2013a). Building back better: Sustainable health care after emergencies. Retrieved January 6, 2014, from http://www.who.int/mental_health/ emergencies/building_back_better/en/.

World Health Organization. (2013b). Investing in mental health: Evidence for action. Retrieved January 3, 2014, from http://www.who.int/mental_health/publications/financing/investing_in_ mh_2013/en/.

World Health Organization. (2013c). Mental health action plan 2013–2020. Retrieved January 2, 2014, from http://www.who.int/mental_health/publications/action_plan/en/.

World Health Organization. (2017). Mental health and psychosocial support in emergencies. Retrieved May 10, 2017, from http://www.who.int/mental_health/resources/emergencies/en/.

Yemini, B.-D. (2018, April 27). As global press ignores swastika kites, Hamas is winning propaganda war. *YNet News.com*. Retrieved April 28, 2018, from https://www.ynetnews.com/ articles/0,7340,L-5240805,00.html.

Younis, R. (2018, March 27). Gaza 'Return March' organizer: 'We'll ensure it doesn't escalate to violence—on our end'. *972mag.com*. Retrieved March 28, 2018, from https://972mag.com/ gaza-return-march-organizer-well-ensure-it-doesnt-escalate-to-violence-on-our-end/134104/.

Zitun, Y. (2018, May 5). WATCH: Hamas fakes injuries, uses children in Gaza border protests. *YNet news.com*. Retrieved May 5, 2018, from https://www.ynetnews.com/articles/0,7340,L-5252107,00.html.

Chapter 11
Some Questions from Popoki to Betty Reardon About Human Security, Gender and Teaching/Learning/Creating Peace

Ronni Alexander

Popoki is a cat, and is the main figure in the Popoki Peace Project. Among Popoki's human friends is one named Betty Reardon. She knew him as a live cat, but perhaps grew closer to him in his work with the Popoki Peace Project, a grass roots group begun by this author in 2006. The Project uses creative and critical skills to work for peace.[1] Like many human peace educators, Popoki thinks inquiry, critical thinking and reflection are important. Popoki lives in the real world, but also in the world of creativity, critical expression and reflection. He communicates with words and sounds, but understands the importance of silence, listening and hearing. Whether with or without words, Popoki loves stories and honors each story as unique and important. As a cat, Popoki is not human, but at times he takes on, and/ or is assigned, human qualities. At the same time, Popoki's difference opens the door for exploration of diversity and inclusion.

Popoki loves peace. He sees the creation and maintenance of peace as a process in which each person and creature has a role; it is a process which begins from our bodies and encompasses our total capacity for thinking, feeling and being. To create peace, we need to analyze and understand what Reardon calls "militarized patriarchy" and the system of institutionalized misogyny. We also need to envision how a truly peaceful world might be different from the peace we have learned about in school and elsewhere, and to imagine how our hearts and bodies might experience peace. Popoki tries to envision the smells, tastes, textures, sounds, and appearance of that world. He dreams of a feminist world free of violence to other living creatures, our home the earth, and ourselves.

Popoki's friend Betty Reardon is a brilliant theorist, thinker and practitioner of peace. As she engages in the process of identifying the patriarchal, militarized and

---

[1]For more on the Popoki Peace Project see for example, Alexander (2016, 2018a, b), Wada (2011).

Ronni Alexander, Professor in the Graduate School of International Cooperation Studies, Kobe University, Kobe, Japan; Email: alexroni@kobe-u.ac.jp.

© Springer Nature Switzerland AG 2019   151
D. T. Snauwaert (ed.), *Exploring Betty A. Reardon's Perspective on Peace Education*, Pioneers in Arts, Humanities, Science, Engineering, Practice 20, https://doi.org/10.1007/978-3-030-18387-5_11

misogynist systems that obstruct the creation of a peaceful world, she has never hesitated to embrace peace, nor to deconstruct it. One of the things that Popoki loves about her is that even as she outlines the configuration of our violent and turbulent world, she leaves us not only ready to commit to peace but also with a feeling of hope. Popoki tries to give hope, too.

Popoki is a precocious cat; he asks questions about peace: What color is peace? What are its scents and flavors, or its textures and shapes? If we reach out to touch it, how might it feel? Would you like to embrace it, or keep your distance? These simple questions are intended to help people to think more deeply about peace and to discover what they can contribute to the creation and maintenance of a more peaceful and gentler world. The origins of the Popoki Peace Project do not come directly from Betty Reardon's work, but Popoki and his friend Ronni have learned much from her about peace pedagogy, and share many of her ideas. Using stories, this essay will first explore some of the ways Popoki and Reardon converge, and then pose three big questions and a few smaller ones from Popoki about human security, gender and teaching/learning/creating peace.

11.1   The Popoki Peace Project

I am Ronni, a friend of Popoki's and in 2006 I began the Popoki Peace Project. The immediate purpose was to publish and then use my book of illustrated questions about peace, *Popoki, What Color is Peace?* (Alexander 2007) in community work and education for peace. The idea grew out of my general frustration with not only the focus of peace education in Japan, but also with what I saw as the teaching and learning of peace in unpeaceful ways. The following story from the early eighties, well before the Popoki Peace Project was even conceived, is illustrative of the negative side of peace education that focuses overwhelming on war in general and Hiroshima/Nagasaki in particular.

On a trip to Okinawa with junior high school students from Hiroshima, we visited the Okinawa Peace Memorial Museum. A student called me over to explain a photo showing rows of crosses marking the graves of Allied soldiers who had died in the Battle of Okinawa. He was unable to grasp the meaning of the photo because until that moment he had thought the only people who died in World War II were Japanese.[2]

The horrific reality of the atomic bombs is without question an important component of peace education, but the lessons we need to learn are not only those

---

[2]Today, not only is peace education in school less widespread in Japan than it was in the eighties when this incident occurred, but the content is increasingly skewed toward promoting nationalistic emotions and denying/erasing anything that puts Japan in a poor light. For example, references to the so-called Comfort Women and Japanese war atrocities are being taken out of history books. This trend is leaving students poorly educated, e.g. unaware of and misinformed about many important and controversial issues.

pertaining to fear, or even those about the strength and courage necessary for survival. It is essential that students learn about the complex web of processes and relations that led to the development and use of nuclear weapons in 1945 and understand how they relate to our present-day world with its present-day wars and crises. Needless to say, lurking behind all of these forms of visible violence are the invisible ones, such as patriarchy, sexism and militarization as shown first by Reardon in *Sexism and the War System* (1996). Popoki's challenge in this regard is how to address the visible problems of the real world while at the same time making their connections with the past and their invisible aspects accessible, relevant and interesting. One way that Popoki does this is through thinking with stories.[3]

The second source of frustration was the practice of teaching peace through lectures and rote learning, as well as the way the subject matter was increasingly becoming sanitized, depoliticized versions of peace processes for use in supposedly apolitical classroom settings. Reardon, reflecting on an essay she had written earlier, speaks to the latter point, referring to "the 'ideological reductionism' that currently defies reasoned political discourse and the lack of civility in that discourse that violates human dignity, the core and fundamental value of peace and peace education that animates the philosophy of cosmopolitanism" (Reardon/Snauwaert 2015, p. 181). Peace education without political discourse, critical thinking and critical expression might provide important information, but is much more likely to reproduce the war system than contribute to peace making.

Popoki, like Reardon, has Freirean beginnings; critical inquiry and thinking are essential for peace teaching and learning. Popoki asks questions, but also understands the importance of reflective listening, verbal and non-verbal critical expression and attentive silence.[4]

Along with reflective listening and critical skills, perhaps the point where Popoki and Reardon converge the most is with what Readon identifies as the three manifestations of imagination for peace making: envisioning, imaging and modeling (Reardon/Snauwaert 2015, p. 101). For Popoki, and for most human beings, our engagement with the world begins with our bodies, complex "brain-body-world entanglements" (Blackman 2012, p. 1) that are assemblages of human and non-human processes.[5] Our physical understanding of the world underlies our ability to think and to imagine; it is essential to the development of affect and of our

---

[3]Popoki's friends are encouraged to not only to think about stories, but also to think with them. Thinking with stories requires thinking relationally, a process that exceeds the boundaries of the way stories are generally used in Western approaches that focus on thinking about stories (Clandinin 2016, pp. 29–30).

[4]While educators and activists emphasize 'raising our voices,' sometimes that is not possible or desirable. Silence can be a form of resistance or communication, as in the case of some forms of empathy and active listening. (See Parpart/Parashar 2019).

[5]Feminist scholars provide multiple understandings of bodies as, for example, discursively reproduced (Butler 1993), as inscribing (Vaittinen 2017), and as gendered and tied to a two-gender binary (Repo 2016) and differentially grievable (Butler 2004). Significant to this is that "the human body can be *simultaneously all this*, and much more" (Vaittinen 2019, p. 246, italics in the original).

perceptual becoming (Blackman 2012). Without the restrictions of the 'reality' of the experienced world, children are able to be fabulously creative. Popoki's young friends draw gardens of peace with flowers, space ships, animal friends and delicious foods. All the creatures are friends and space travel is available to anyone who wants a little adventure. As adults, we learn to restrict our imaginations and creativity. As a result, we become unable or unwilling to fully imagine how things might be, which of course greatly impedes our ability to create something new and different.

Along with the growing interest in bodies, emotion and affect, feminist scholars of international relations have begun to focus on the importance of narrative, media and art for helping to identify and bring to light the 'invisible' aspects of world politics (Shepherd 2013; Sylvester 2011; Wibben 2011). Emotion and affect have become a focus of attention for the role they play in politics (Ahmed 2014; Åhäll 2015; Crawford 2000, 2014; Hutchison and Bleiker 2008, 2014; Lutz/Abu-Lighod 2008; Ling 2014; McDermott 2014; Mercer 2014).[6] Popoki, and his friend Ronni, are particularly interested in these new approaches, but also emphasize non-verbal aspects of expression.

The emphasis on bodies, emotions and alternative modes of expression is not only to envision peace but also important in the analysis of social relations and violence. Popoki calls on humans to identify the invisible and to give it a name, and perhaps a color or shape. Here too, he shares with Reardon the understanding that we need to make visible the social relations that, for example, produce and re-produce militarization in all its forms. Popoki uses stories – story-telling, story-making and art-making – especially that done by non-professionals or so-called "citizen artists", urging his friends to think with stories in a variety of settings.

There are many ways to tell and create stories. Popoki invites people to create their own stories on particular themes such as human rights or decolonization. Sometimes he provides a situation to help them get started, such as telling them that Popoki is crying and asking them to make stories about why he is crying, what can be done to comfort him now, and what can be done to change the underlying causes of his tears. The creation of these stories requires the artist to engage in various cognitive tasks: reflective listening (what does Popoki say about the reason), critical analysis (what is the immediate reason for the tears, what are the underlying causes, and why are those causes a problem), empathy (what Popoki is feeling), strategic thinking and planning (what can be done now and in the long term), and creative expression (putting it into a story and pictures). In other words, the stories are not only about a particular issue, but they provide a way to think and analyze that issue from various perspectives.

---

[6]Both emotion and affect are difficult terms to define. Åhäll (2015) and Ahmed (2014) discuss emotion in terms of the extent to which it can be understood as socially and culturally constructed; a place where bodily sensation, emotion and thought interact. Affect, on the other hand, is often used to denote what happens inside and therefore is very much related to embodiment, and seen as something that happens before emotion (Åhäll 2015, p. 5).

None of us has experienced a truly peaceful world. Popoki believes that without the ability to imagine the peace we have not experienced, we are hard pressed to create it. Popoki's work, therefore begins with creativity, and with Popoki himself. Popoki is a cat, but he might have been some other creature. Although many people like cats, what is most important is not Popoki's cat-ness but his non-human status which puts him beyond the intricate and often difficult nuances of human relationships. Human participants often assign him roles in accordance with social norms and understandings of gender, age, status, etc. but sometimes they break the rules and/or transcend them. Popoki becomes whatever they want him to be. And he even has many friends who claim that they dislike cats.

Popoki is a cat. He is at times lazy or frivolous. He can be old or young, gendered or genderless, and his striped tail is colored, but the colors are constantly changing. In other words, Popoki is anyone we want him to be.

Popoki's questions and stories help to put into perspective the issues of our day, and to help people to look for strategies and solutions on a personal scale, but also on a global one. One such strategy is the idea of human security or, to replace military security with policies that provide both "freedom from want and freedom from fear" (UNDP 1994). There are various intrinsic problems with this idea, not the least of which is that most understandings of human security continue to call on states to be the provider of security, whether it be economic, political, lifestyle or national/military. Reardon questions this, suggesting that first, "If human security is to be achieved, patriarchy must be replaced with gender equality and second, war as an institution must be abolished in favour of non-violent structures and processes for resolving conflict and achieving national policy goals" (Reardon/Hans 2019, p. 7). What would the world look like without patriarchy and the institution of war? How can we imagine, and then create that world? This involves both pedagogical and theoretical aspects.

In the following pages, Popoki and I will try thinking about this task with stories from our work together. We will address three big questions and a few small ones about human security, gender and peace to our friend, Betty Reardon.

Question 1: Does elimination of patriarchy and the institution of war mean by definition the elimination of other 'isms' such as colonialism and racism too? Do you think using an intersectional approach is useful in this context?

Story 1: Popoki has a friend named E. E. is from Guåhan/Guam, a territory (e.g. colony) of the United States, and among those who were given U.S. citizenship under the 1950 Organic Act of Guam.[7] She enlisted in the military as a U.S. citizen to perform what she understood as her responsibility to protect her country. Like many others on Guåhan/Guam, E. comes from a military family with expectations for their children to join the military. By enlisting, E. fulfilled her 'duty' as both a citizen and a family member. In fact, she was the first Chamoru woman to serve in

---

[7]Guåhan is the indigenous Chamoru name for the island generally known as "Guam". American citizens on Guam are not allowed to vote for president and have a non-voting representative in Congress.

the U.S. military. She has many stories about the misogyny she experienced while in the military, but among all her stories, perhaps the most hurtful and shocking one, she told me, was when she was asked by other soldiers when she had begun wearing clothing (2018.5 interview). The implication of this racist question was that as an indigenous person, she would have had to become 'civilized' in order to join the military. It might have been asked differently if she had been a man, but there are many examples of racism directed at men in the military, too.

Colonialism, in its most visibly violent form as conquering territory and in what may be its less visible forms as control of economic, social and political resources, is dependent on militarism, militarization and 'othering' for its continuation. Some, but not all of that 'othering' involves binary thinking that denigrates one side of the binary in order to affirm the other. Military enterprises rely on gender binaries to affirm 'masculine' attributes considered to be necessary for soldiering such as strength, power and rationality through the denigration of 'feminine' characterizations such as weakness and impulsiveness. In asserting the legitimacy of their presence, colonial powers use similar gender binaries with respect to local populations; the unpredictable 'feminine' is reproduced in the uncontrollable 'native'.

As an indigenous woman from a U.S. territory, E. posed a multifaceted challenge to the gendered and racialized military status quo, even as she tried to support the military and all that it represents. Certainly E.'s story exemplifies the most odious aspects of what Reardon would call sexism and the war system, but adding consideration of other categories of oppression such as race (Chamoru), or background (from a territory rather than a state) would provide opportunities for a more nuanced analysis of not only what E. has experienced but why she represents such a threat to the military institution itself. Eliminating patriarchy and sexism might change E.'s situation, but would it completely solve the problem?

Question 2: Gender equality presumably means equality for all genders, including but not exclusive to women and men. How can we imagine that equality without re-creating and/or depending on gender(ed) binaries?

Story 2: One of Popoki's friends, N., participated in a roleplaying session about gender sensitive disaster recovery support. N. was assigned the role of Popoki, which entailed provision of psycho-social support. N. wrote about the experience of observing "the world and the importance of thinking about what is peace through Popoki, who is neither male nor female or LGBT. ... (W)e never knew the gender of Popoki, and it made me think about what is genderless. I discovered that when I was thinking about which gender, male or female, was suited for each of the roles in our disaster mitigation plan" (N. in "Popoki News" 2018.11).

Popoki may, or may not be 'genderless', but the question of how to think about gender without thinking about male/female binaries is important. What does it mean to be a woman, or a man, or neither, or both? How do we know? Around 1999, shortly after I had publicly come out as lesbian, I was working on the proofs of an essay on why the consideration of gender was necessary for the understanding of international relations. I realized that while I recognized that there is undoubtedly a category of 'women' who are marginalized and oppressed in multiple ways, I could not find a way of defining who was, or was not, a part of that category without relying on binaries, gendered or otherwise. In that article I left it to self-identification, but there is a much larger issue here of discourse and the way we envision, express and acknowledge gender diversity.

Sexism rests on a hierarchal binary that prioritizes the masculine over the feminine in general and particular masculinities over particular femininities. The denial/rejection of sexism employs similar binaries. Our language, knowledge and understanding of the world rests on such binaries; they are an important component of how we know ourselves and our world. The addition of categories is helpful, but not sufficient if it reproduces gender/gendered binaries in a different form. Gender equality that honors gender diversity needs to rest on ways of knowing, expressing and experiencing that are not rooted in a female/feminine/male/masculine binary. At the same time, gender equality should not mean the end of gender performativity or gendered expressions. Gender equality ought to offer more choices, but what are those choices and how can we express them?

Popoki is a cat, and Popoki's human friends seem to be able, sometimes, to give Popoki relative gender freedom. But in so doing, they reproduce a human/ non-human binary. Once again, equality and freedom become possible only through particular inequalities or lack of particular freedoms. How can we transform our language and understanding to overcome such binary thinking?

Question 3: Human security, like most other conceptualizations of security, invokes 'fear' in a variety of contexts, generally stated either in terms of fear *of* something or freedom *from* fear. How can we express the absence of fear in a way that is proactive, positive and does not reproduce a safe/unsafe binary?

Story 3: About a year after the 2011 nuclear accident and tsunami that destroyed much of the coastline in northeastern Japan, plans were being drawn by the government and contractors to build a 14.5-m sea wall along hundreds of kilometers of coastline. Popoki and his friends were in a bar in a temporary shopping mall in one of the decimated towns. They brought up the topic of the proposed wall asking, "Will it make you safe?" The reply was, "That's what they tell us...." "But will it make you feel safe?" "Absolutely not! We won't be able to see the ocean or know if anything changes, and it will give us a false sense of security. We'll think we are safe, but we might not be!".

Since this conversation, Popoki and I have focused not only on being safe but also on feeling safe. What began as a discussion of the politics of wall and wall-building grew into a more general discussion of what it means to feel safe and why that is important. This touches on many aspects of Reardon's work in terms of the importance of recovery, both transcending trauma and also regaining what has been lost (Reardon/Snauwaert 2015, pp. 100–101). Recovery is also related to what makes us able and/or willing to continue to work for peace in the face of overwhelming odds, and to be caring, empathetic and perhaps even to be creative.

If we understand peace to have many dimensions, some within a person's own heart and/or mind and others involving various aspects of the external world, then we can perhaps say that it is possible to be at peace in unpeaceful circumstances and also to not be at peace even in peaceful surroundings. Part, but not all of this involves the subjective feeling of safety, both for internal and external peace. What is and is not safe, or feels or does not feel safe, is at least in some ways socially constructed; our dependence on violence for 'security' is a clear example of this. To the extent that we seek to increase our feelings of safety through unsafe means, we will neither be safe nor feel safe, and will not be at peace.

How can we imagine safety in ways that are not harmful to ourselves or threatening to others? When our understanding of what is safe and what feels safe are both dependent on violence, then we have no basis to challenge a person who claims to feels safer with a gun. Global demilitarization is important for our safety and that of the world, but demilitarization of our minds is equally important.

Creative resistance is also a way that people assert their feelings of being unsafe. Famous examples involving war include such works as Picasso's *Guernica* and the Maruki Hiroshima murals, but we can find them everywhere. There is even a drawing of Popoki on the Separation Wall outside of Bethlehem. These can be extremely powerful political tools, but for precisely that reason, many people, including artists and citizen-artists, maintain silence. As peace scholars, educators and activists, we need to be able to hear silence. Popoki sits quietly beside those who do not speak, offering his soft, warm fur and listening carefully with his ears and with his heart, waiting to catch any silent message they may send. Sometimes it is effective, other times not, but he understands affirming and respecting silence to be important for long-term, non-violent solutions to violence in all its forms. Under what circumstances is it necessary, or possible, to hear silence or to make silence heard? Will doing so make us safer? Will it make us feel safer?

11.2 Conclusion

Popoki is a precocious and curious cat. He can be joyful and frivolous, but also serious and sad. He wants to be friends with everyone, even those who do not desire to know him, because he believes that connection with others is important for peace. He identifies as a cat, but enjoys going beyond catlike performativity. He uses the personal pronoun 'he,' except when he uses 'she' or 'they.' Popoki loves stories. When he thinks with them, he discovers different strands and threads of other stories. And when he follows those, he finds even more. Those threads are paths that lead him inside his own body and far away into the realm of history and that of imagination.

Popoki shares with Betty Reardon a feminist commitment to peace learning and peace making. Like Reardon, he understands the need to envision peace and to empathize with those who are in unpeaceful situations, as well as the need to be supportive of those engaging in efforts for recovery. He condemns violence and seeks to create and maintain peace using only non-violent means. Popoki recognizes that in order to create peace it is essential to make patriarchal relations and institutionalized misogyny visible, and to eliminate both. He seeks to do this using critical thinking, critical expression, art, stories and reflection. Popoki asks simple questions that have difficult answers; one of his favorite words is 'why'. Popoki is not human, and often wonders why human beings have so much difficulty respecting human rights and understanding that peace must be holistic and organic, fully incorporating all life on our planet.

Popoki is grateful to Betty Reardon for providing so many strands and threads to his peace story. He hopes she shares his, too, and that together they will make many more.

References

Åhäll, L., & Thomas, G. (Eds.). (2015). *Emotions, politics and war*. New York: Routledge.

Ahmed, S. (2014). *The cultural politics of emotion* (2nd ed.). Edingurgh: Edinburgh University Press.

Alexander, R. (2007). *Popoki, what color is peace? Popoki's peace book 1*. Kobe: Epic.

Alexander, R. (2016). Living with the Fence: Militarization and military spaces on Guahan/Guam. *Gender, Place and Culture, 23*(6), 869–882. First published on-line in 2015.

Alexander, R. (2018a). Drawing disaster: Reflecting on six years of the Popoki Friendship story project. *Journal of International Cooperation Studies, 25*(2), 59–96.

Alexander, R. (2018b). Teaching peace with Popoki. *Peace Review, 30*(1), 9–16. https://doi.org/10.1080/10402659.2017.1419669.

Blackman, L. (2012). *Immaterial bodies: Affect, embodiment, mediation*. Thousand Oaks, CA: Sage.

Butler, J. (1993). *Bodies that matter: On the discursive limits of 'Sex'*. New York: Routledge.

Butler, J. (2004). *Precarious life: The powers of mourning and violence*. Verso.

Clandinin, D. J. (2016). *Engaging in narrative inquiry—Developing qualitative inquiry* (Vol. 9). New York: Routledge.

Crawford, N. C. (2000). The passion of world politics: Propositions on emotion and emotional relationships. *International Security, 24*(4), 116–156. Posted Online: March 29, 2006.

Crawford, N. C. (2014). Institutionalizing passion in world politics: Fear and empathy. *International Theory, 6*(3), 535–557. Published Online: October 09, 2014.

Freire, P. (1996). *Pedagogy of the oppressed* (M. B. Ramos, Trans.). New York: Penguin.

Hutchison, E., & Roland, B. (2008). Fear no more: Emotions and world politics. *Review of International Studies, 34*, 115–135.

Hutchison, E., & Roland, B. (2014). Theorizing emotions in world politics. *International Theory, 6*, 491–514.

Ling, L. H. M. (2014). Decolonizing the international: Towards multiple emotional worlds. Forum: Emotions and world politics. *International Theory, 6*(3), 579–583. Retrieved May 20, 2017, from https://www.cambridge.org/core/services/aop-cambridge-core/content/view/026BC7C8D8B25151DB4862D3E6F08DFA/S175297191400030Xa.pdf/decolonizing-the-international-towards-multiple-emotional-worlds.pdf.

Lutz, C. A., & Abu-Lighod, L. (2008). *Language and the politics of emotion*. Cambridge: Cambridge University Press.

McDermott, R. (2014). The body doesn't lie: A somatic approach to the study of emotions in world politics. *International Theory, 6*, 557–562.

McSorley, K. (Ed.). (2013). *War and the body: Militarisation, practice and experience*. New York: Routledge.

Mercer, J. (2014). Feeling like a state: Social emotion and identity. *International Theory, 6*, 515–535.

Parpart, J. L., & Parashar, S. (Eds.). (2019). *Rethinking silence, voice and agency in contested gendered terrains*. New York: Routledge.

Popoki News 2018.11. No. 159. Retrieved December 25, 2018, from http://popoki.cruisejapan.com/pdf/Popoki_News_No159.%202018.11.pdf.

Reardon, B. A. (1996). *Sexism and the war system.* Syracuse: Syracuse University Press.

Reardon, B. A., & Hans, A. (2019). *The gender imperative: Human security vs. state security* (2nd ed.). New York: Routledge.

Reardon, B. A., & Snauwaert, D. T. (2015). *Betty A. Reardon: A pioneer in education for peace and human rights.* Heidelberg: Springer.

Repo, J. (2016). *The biopolitics of emotion.* Oxford: Oxford University Press.

Shepherd, L. (2013). *Gender, violence and popular culture: Telling stories.* New York: Routledge.

Sylvester, C. (Ed.). (2011). *Experiencing war.* New York: Routledge.

United Nations Development Programme (UNDP). (1994). *Human development report.*

Vaittinen, T. (2017). The global biopolitical economy of needs: Transnational entanglements between ageing Finland and the global nurse reserve of the Philippines. Dissertation.

Vaittinen, T. (2019). Embodied in/security as care needs. In C. E. Gentry, L. J. Shepherd, & L. Sjberg (Eds.), *Routledge handbook of gender and security* (pp. 241–251). New York: Routledge.

Wada, K. (2011). Conversations with Ronni Alexander: The Popoki peace project: Popoki, what color is peace? What color is friendship? *International Feminist Journal of Politics, 13*(2), 257–271.

Wibben, A. (2011). *Feminist security studies.* New York: Routledge.

Chapter 12
Media, Sexism and the Patriarchal War System: Why Media Literacy Matters to Peace Education

Sally McLaren

We live in media-saturated societies, and media organizations now have unprecedented power to shape our world views, influence our behavior and provoke extreme reactions. Reading Betty Reardon's groundbreaking monograph, *Sexism and the war system* (1996), in the context of 2018, I was struck by the parallels between what she identified as the 'patriarchal war system' and what I contemporarily refer to as the 'global patriarchal media system'. This is how I would describe the male-dominated media ownership system that produces content and communications infused with stereotypical representations of gender, sexuality, race, ethnicity, age, socio-economic status and abilities, whilst concurrently reinforcing and normalizing inequalities and injustices. The conceptual framework for analyzing the integral interrelationship between sexism and the war system put forward by Reardon in her book can be applied to understanding how contemporary media works in tandem with the war system in maintaining the sexist and patriarchal global order.

This chapter reflects on Reardon's work on sexism, patriarchy, militarism and the war system, and how it applies to the contemporary media landscape. It is also an appeal to peace educators to include media literacy with a gender perspective in their scholarship and teaching in order to strengthen critical thinking and increase their understanding of "the deep-rooted connections between sexism and the war system" (Reardon 1996, p. 83) and the increasingly mediated nature of this system. I discuss Reardon's work on the role of patriarchy in the war system as it applies to the media system. I also note some specific mentions of the role of media and popular culture in her writing and assess its relevance in the current context. Finally, I discuss the practical applications of Reardon's work – in particular, her call for a consideration of the transformational possibilities (1996, p. 83) and

Sally McLaren, Adjunct, School of Humanities and Communication Arts, Western Sydney University, Australia; Email: sallyjmclaren@gmail.com.

© Springer Nature Switzerland AG 2019
D. T. Snauwaert (ed.), *Exploring Betty A. Reardon's Perspective on Peace Education*, Pioneers in Arts, Humanities, Science, Engineering, Practice 20, https://doi.org/10.1007/978-3-030-18387-5_12

strategies for change (p. 84) evolving from an understanding of the relationship between sexism and militarism, and how media literacy can contribute to and compliment Reardon's work.

12.1   Reardon's Conceptual Framework

The "many-headed, ubiquitous monster" that is sexism, says Reardon, is deeply-rooted in all human cultures and social organizations and is "as complex and pervasive as the war system itself" (1996, p. 16). Based on misogynistic attitudes and assumptions that men are superior to women, both biologically and intellectually, sexism strengthens the control and dominance of patriarchal elites (p. 10) that work to exclude women from "the realms of power, particularly technology and politics" (p. 16). Reardon employs two definitions of patriarchy in *Sexism and the war system*. Firstly, that it is "a set of beliefs and values supported by institutions and backed by the threat of violence," which imposes structures and divisions between women and men (Reardon 1996 citing Elster 1981, p. 15). Secondly, patriarchy is a "system of dualisms" that relegates women to lesser and ostensibly weaker roles, because it is a "system of values developed through male experience" (Reardon 1996 citing Zanotti 1979, p. 37). Patriarchy is, therefore, the solid foundation of the war system.

War, according to Reardon, is "a legally sanctioned, institutionally organized armed force, applied by authority to maintain social control, pursue public objectives, protect vital interests, and resolve conflicts" (1996, p. 13). Significantly, she says, it has been the "exclusive prerogative" of privileged political elites, and since these elites have been predominantly male, the legal justification for and theological rationalization of war has been an overwhelmingly patriarchal concern throughout human history (p. 13). Reardon refers to the war system as "our competitive social order, which is based on authoritarian principles, assumes unequal value among and between humans, and is held in place by coercive force" (1996, p. 10). Similar to the context of our media-saturated contemporary societies, she argues that "the war system pervades our lives and affects every aspect of society from the structural to the interpersonal" (p. 11). With the development of digital media and the ubiquity of smart phones and other sophisticated personal media devices, our lives have truly become mediated to an unprecedented extent. This is a dangerous and significant outcome because patriarchal and misogynist values remain entrenched, yet reinvented in troubling and sophisticated ways, in our hi-tech global media environment.

Since the publication of *Sexism and the war system*, there have been several major international conflicts in the Middle East, with ongoing wars in Syria and Yemen, and violent conflict and unrest in Venezuela, Kashmir, Sudan and West Papua, for example. During this time, the role of media organizations, as well as the way in which armed violence has been represented and reported (or sometimes –

just as tellingly – ignored), has changed and evolved (Tehranian 2004; Vavrus 2017). However, Reardon's work, which demonstrated "the fundamental symbiosis between sexism and the war system" (1996, p. 5) remains relevant because the patriarchal war system must now sustain itself with the cooperation of the global patriarchal media system. In 2018, Reardon noted that this system persists because "the war system is the maintenance mechanism of the patriarchal power order" and is still "deeply embedded psycho-socially and structurally" (Reardon 2018). In the same way, the media messages that we are bombarded with daily also systematically and simultaneously function to maintain patriarchy, normalize violence and emphasize how to be a woman or a man in narrow and stereotypical ways. In particular, these binary gender role expectations are socially and culturally defined and constantly produced and re-produced within a system of social practices (Wharton 2012, p. 9). These continue to be crucial to the technologies of patriarchy. They are so embedded in modern society that they frequently pass unnoticed, or are seen as 'normal' (Gallagher 2001; Vavrus 2002; Gill 2011; Connell/Pearse 2015).

12.2 Media, Sexism and Patriarchy

Decades of feminist media research has shown that media representations, particularly the way in which images of people and places are constructed in visual media, are "connected to patterns of inequality, domination and oppression" (Gill 2007, p. 7). The role the media play in perpetuating gender stereotypes directly benefits patriarchy. This inherent sexism is, as Reardon has stated, a major impediment to achieving peace and justice (1996, p. 26). Though narrow and stereotypical representations of women have been consistently challenged, changes in media representations resulting in the visibility and diversity of "non-stereotypical roles" for both women and men have often been framed in the media as feminist victories "at the expense of men's potency" amidst a "crisis of masculinity" (Ross 2010, p. 5).[1] Even when we see media representations of 'diversity', for example, people of color or gender minorities, they are often included as mere entertainment or a token presence. The structures and decision-making processes also do not reflect this diversity. Compounding this situation is the global increase in militarism (Enloe 2016) and the increasingly complicated role that media and sexism play in maintaining, legitimizing and popularizing the war system (Thomas 2009, p. 98).

---

[1]In January 2019 this was exemplified by the sensational backlash against the Gillette television commercial, which had aimed to draw attention to toxic masculinity and the sexual harassment of women. Instead, rightwing political groups, conservative media and men's rights activists called for a boycott of the brand, prompting some to show images of themselves on social media platforms symbolically destroying their razors. Gillette did not withdraw the commercial and it has been viewed more than 14 million times on Youtube.

12.3 Media and the War System

Images of war and violence are dominant in both news and entertainment media. There is nothing new about this phenomenon in itself but, as technology develops, the relationship between war and media is constantly changing and sometimes difficult to track (Schubart 2009, p. 2). Applying a gender perspective to the relationship between war and media reveals the multiple ways that femininities and masculinities are constructed, coopted and managed in order to maintain the patriarchal status quo. This status quo includes the normalization of violence and conflict, the exclusion of women from decisions on war and peace, as well as the romanticization and popularization of military service.

Reardon has addressed obstacles to abolishing sexism and the war system and the role of media since the 1990s. In *Women and peace: Feminist visions of global security* (1993), she recognized that "popular media are replete with violent images and incidents" (p. 41) whilst noting that,

In films, textbooks, and newspapers, and on television, women are portrayed as sacrificing mothers, servile domestic workers, sweet homemakers, brainless fashion plates, unbearable shrews, evil temptresses/sex objects, and objects of violence. Even in the case of women heads of state, the media frequently find it necessary to comment on their garb or family status (p. 45).

These stereotypical media images remain, but as I write above, in the current media environment the power of these gendered representations to reach large global audiences has increased exponentially through digital and social media. As Reardon discusses in detail in *Sexism and the war system*, the entry of women into military service has been controversial, with the sexist assumption that the mere presence of women "could serve to mitigate the savagery of warfare" (p. 55) and the idea that the acceptance of women into the military is a cooptation rather than concession to women's rights (p. 56) because these women must conform to militarized masculinity. Mainstream Hollywood films such as *Courage Under Fire* (1996), *GI Jane* (1997), *Zero Dark Thirty* (2012) and *Megan Leavey* (2017) have idealized women who battle chauvinist objections to their presence in the military, yet fulfil male expectations of their roles, all without questioning the sexist foundations on which the war system is based and maintained. Essentially, these films are propaganda for the fake empowerment of women in the military.

In *Sexism and the war system*, Reardon argues that the continuation of sexism in politics is an indication of the extent to which our contemporary political institutions and practices remain "rooted in patriarchy" (p. 32), with the result that "women's exclusion from political power…. is a significant factor in maintaining the war system" (p. 33). The equal participation of women in politics is also seen as a threat to what Connell terms "hegemonic masculinity" – "the pattern of practice (i.e., things done, not just a set of role expectations or an identity)" that has allowed the male subordination of women to continue (Connell/Messerschmidt 2005, p. 832), as part of "the combination of the plurality of masculinities and the hierarchy of masculinities" (p. 846). Hegemonic masculinity also provides a 'solution' to tensions surrounding gender relations, "tending to stabilize patriarchal power or reconstitute it in new conditions" (p. 853). It is in the context of stabilization and reconstitution that the media representation of the participation of women in politics and other patriarchal institutions, such as the military, is highly relevant.

12.4 Mediating Gender and the Male Chauvinist Backlash

Byerly (2013) notes that much "media coverage still conforms to a deeply engrained patriarchal ideology of women in both elective office and within the broader public sphere" (p. 8). Discriminatory media practices persist: "despite a global women's media movement that has lasted more than three decades and made gains in both legal and cultural fronts in most nations of the world, sexist media representations have endured" (Ross 2010, p. 91). Reardon (1993) also noted that these efforts to induce positive change were by both women and men, "but women have been among the most numerous of the voices raised against stereotyping and violence in the media, and in favor of education for peace and non-violence" (p. 48). Whilst it is beyond the scope of this chapter to assess all the factors involved in the persistence of patriarchal and sexist media practices, it is important to emphasize that powerful media organizations, many of which are controlled and managed by men, disseminate ideas and attitudes about gender relations in our societies. According to Riordan (2004), "this particular worldview is one that minimizes the achievements of feminism, constructs women in opposition to one another rather than as supportive of each other, and creates women as desirable objects for men" (p. 99). This is certainly evident in entertainment media, such as in the films mentioned above, but also reinforced through news and advertising. The commercial imperative (Ross 2010, p. 86) that contributes to the continued objectification and sexualization of women in media needs to be considered here. As arms manufacturers profit from the continuation and threat of war, media companies also benefit from the commercialization of gendered images. Thus, the war system and the media system do nothing to improve the human condition – instead, they perpetuate oppression, misery and inequality.

Consequently, we can see how feminist challenges to abolishing the war system, along with demands for "economic equity, social justice, ecological balance, political participation, and peace" (Reardon 1996, p. 26), for example, are perceived as threats. Furthermore, Reardon has theorized that these challenges are connected to "the possibility that both increased militarization and the male-chauvinist backlash are symptoms of an authoritarian system responding to a threat to its continuation" (ibid.). This idea is more pertinent than ever, as the emergence of 'strongman' type leaders in the United States, the Philippines, Brazil, Turkey and Poland (Hirsch 2019), to name just a few. These men have perverse and chauvinistic attitudes towards gender equality, pose a fundamental threat to women's reproductive rights, and in the case of Hungary, even the academic study of gender (Redden 2018). The outcomes of this disturbing trend are already visible –

continuing conflict, increased militarization, rising socio-economic inequalities and inaction on climate change.[2]

Reardon's assertion that the media "glorification of violence and denigration of women serves to perpetuate the acceptance of both warfare and women's status as second-class citizens" (1993, p. 45) remains relevant. In the context of the global increase in militarization and the chauvinist backlash toward gender equality, patriarchal war and media systems are finding new ways to romanticize and popularize the military. Two examples from East Asia – a region characterized by increasing militarization and transnational flows of popular culture and media – exemplify current trends in reconfiguring patriarchy through media. Firstly, the Japanese Self-Defense Forces (JSDF) have launched a series of successful public relations campaigns since 2015, when Prime Minister Abe pushed new security legislation through the Diet and advocated changes to the constitution that effectively moved Japan from a "peace state" to a "war-capable state" (McCormack 2016). The focus has been on utilizing Japanese popular culture, such as manga, anime and idols, to create images of military service as cool, fun and joyful. Young girls dressed as 'sexy schoolgirls' are prominent in this imagery, but they are also heavily armed. As Fruhstuck (2017) point outs out, this is significant because now the JSDF "are newly equipped with the legal means to cause mass destruction in the context of war" and these fighting girls feature prominently in their publicity campaigns (p. 198).

Secondly, the 2016 South Korean television drama *Descendants of the Sun* garnered huge audiences not only in South Korea but other Asian countries such as China. The drama is focused on the romance between a male special forces captain and a female doctor. They meet in a civilian situation, but soon find themselves together as part of overseas peacekeeping operations in a fictional Middle Eastern country. Their romance develops in the context of war and disaster but is constantly interrupted due to the 'duties' of war. The drama's narrative emphasizes not only the gender binary but also its associated norms – men as warriors and potentially killers, and women as carers and protectors of life. The BBC reported that the Chinese Communist Party's newspaper, the People's Daily issued praise for the drama – as "an excellent advertisement for conscription" and a great way to showcase South Korea's "national spirit", but later the government issued a warning on the dangers of watching Korean dramas, "which it said could lead to marital trouble and criminal behavior" (Wong 2016). As these two examples show, the mass appeal and audience reach of popular culture normalizes the war system whilst utilizing gendered images of women and men.

---

[2]A European environmental activist and academic recently said to me that fighting for gender equality is not as urgent or important as dealing with climate change. I responded that perhaps we would not be in this mess if we had gender equality. Gender equality does not necessarily preclude war and natural disaster in a patriarchal system, but this anecdote illustrates the failure of some educated Western elites to consider the relevance of gender in policymaking, conflict resolution and peacebuilding.

12.5   Transforming the System and Ourselves

Finally, I would like to respond to Reardon's call in *Sexism and the war system* for a consideration of the transformational possibilities (1996, p. 83) and strategies for change (p. 84) evolving from an understanding of the relationship between sexism and militarism through a reflection on some of my classroom experiences teaching about gender, war and media. I also emphasize how media literacy, which is the ability to critically analyze and evaluate media, can contribute to and compliment Reardon's work.

In *Women and peace: Feminist visions of global security* (1993), Reardon wrote that,

> Promoting consciousness of the negative aspects of sex-role separation, developing sensitivity to the emphasis of media on violence, and calling attention to the excessive focus of history of war, can make a significant contribution to peace (p. 45).

The emphasis on consciousness and sensitivity here are key to understanding the way media construct war, violence and gender relations. If we are to envision and work towards more just, equal and indeed feminist futures, then a thorough understanding of how media organizations construct reality and shape our world views is crucial. However, we have to pay attention to pedagogy as we debate and discuss solutions and alternatives. As Reardon writes in *Education for a culture of peace in a gender perspective* (2001), moving "the discourse of argument and controversy out of the 'win or lose' realm into that of mutually conducted searches for the best solution" (p. 168) is a constructive and creative teaching approach.

In courses I have taught on global politics and gender, for example, I have emphasized the role of media in shaping our understanding of global conflicts and how different kinds of hierarchies and privileges – in particular gender, race and ethnicity – reinforce each other. Gender is an organizing principle of every society (Wharton 2012, p. 9), and is extremely significant in the global political order, yet it has been largely excluded from the academic study of international politics (see Tickner 2001). Similarly, media texts such as films and news reports are often used uncritically in the classroom to show certain situations or illustrate particular points, often with just a basic discussion of the narrative, rather than how image and sound work together to create reality, or what kind of production decisions were made to emphasize a certain point. Furthermore, mainstream media texts can often contradict academic research. For example, the research literature on female combatants in civil wars paints a complex picture of agency, coercion, nationalism and gender norm transgression (Alison 2004; Parashar 2009). However, media representations of women fighters are often based on simplistic stereotypes and their success at emulating male fighters. The actual conflict is not fully explained and diverse viewpoints are rarely included.

In my classes, I have used a 2014 *60 Minutes Australia* report on Kurdish women fighters in Iraq and Syria battling against Islamic State as an example of this. The report shows women fighters on the front line shooting a variety of weapons. At night they are filmed relaxing by a campfire singing traditional songs. The reporter embedded with the group describes them as having a "bond of blood and gender" (60 Minutes Australia 2014). Before viewing the media text, the students also read research by Alison (2004) and Parashar (2009). We then discuss what we know of the conflict and how we know it before viewing the media text. The viewing of the media text is an analytical exercise based on media literacy learning. The students make notes about the visual images and sound: who appears, how they appear and what we hear them saying. In this way, we are not only looking at the content because the detailed breakdown of visual and sound editing techniques helps us to see the extent to which there is nothing 'natural' about media representations. From the camera angles to the background music, a series of production decisions have been made to present an issue to an audience in a particular way. This learning outcome is significant to students, who often say that when they develop these types of media literacy skills, they are more questioning of media reports and less likely to accept images of people and places as 'normal' or 'natural'.

Obviously, academic texts are also subjective constructions of societies and issues, and they should be read critically too. However, as hooks (2010) argues, critical thinking can be a survival skill – a way to survive racist, sexist and class elitism (p. 183). This can be a good strategy for challenging the symbiotic relationship between sexism, the war system and media, and using our critical skills creatively to envision new futures.

12.6   Conclusion

For more than three decades, Reardon has paid feminist attention to the relationship between sexism and militarism (Reardon 2019, p. 7). This chapter has discussed how the conceptual framework for analyzing the relationship between sexism and the war system put forward by Reardon in her 1996 book, *Sexism and the war system*, as well as her other work, is significant in understanding how contemporary media works in tandem with the war system. The patriarchal war system cannot function in the twenty-first century without the cooperation of the patriarchal media system. Examples from different parts of the world mentioned here show that news and entertainment media continue to normalize war and emphasize stereotypical gender norms.

Reardon's consistent focus on and dedication to achieving a peaceful and gender equal society helps us to keep inquiring, analyzing, and educating for peace. As the persistence of women in politics, feminist activism and the #metoo movement, for example, have all recently shown, change is happening despite concerted efforts to defend the "patriarchal gender order" (Connell/Pearse 2015, p. 90). There is transformative potential in critical responses to sexism and the war system. Since we live in media-saturated societies, media literacy is also an important critical skill that helps us to make sense of the world, as well as to continue envisioning more creative and peaceful futures.

References

Alison, M. (2004). Women as agents of political violence: Gendering security. *Security Dialogue, 35*(4), 447–463. https://doi.org/10.1177/0967010604049522.

Anderson, R. (2005). Gendered media culture and the imagery of war. *Feminist Media Studies, 5* (3), 367–370.

Byerly, C. M. (2013). The geography of women and media scholarship. In K. Ross (Ed.), *The handbook of gender, sex, and media* (pp. 3–19). Malden: Wiley.

Connell, R. W., & Messerschmidt, J. W. (2005). Hegemonic masculinity: Rethinking the concept. *Gender & Society, 19,* 829. https://doi.org/10.1177/0891243205278639.

Connell, R. W., & Pearse, R. (2015). *Gender in world perspective* (3rd ed.). Cambridge: Polity Press.

Enloe, C. (2016). *Globalization and militarism: Feminists make the link* (2nd ed.). Lanham: Rowman & Littlefield Publishers.

Fruhstuck, S. (2017). "…And my heart screams": Children and the war of emotions. In S. Fruhstuck & A. Walthall (Eds.), *Child's play: Multi-sensory histories of children and childhood in Japan* (pp. 181–201). Oakland: University of California Press.

Gallagher, M. (2001). *Gender setting: New agendas for media monitoring and advocacy.* London: Zed Books/World Association for Christian Communication.

Gallagher, M. (2005). Beijing's legacy for gender and media. *Gender and Media Monitor.*

Gill, R. (2007). *Gender and the media.* Cambridge: Polity Press.

Gill, R. (2011). Sexism reloaded, or, it's time to get angry again! *Feminist Media Studies, 11*(1), 61–71. https://doi.org/10.1080/14680777.2011.537029.

Hirsch, A. (2019, February 13). Nationalist strongmen are bent on controlling women's bodies. *The Guardian.* Retrieved from https://www.theguardian.com.

hooks, B. (2010). *Teaching critical thinking: Practical wisdom.* New York: Routledge.

McCormack, G. (2016). Japan: Prime Minister Shinzo Abe's agenda. *The Asia-Pacific Journal: Japan Focus, 14*(21). Retrieved from https://apjjf.org.

Parashar, S. (2009). Feminist international relations and women militants: Case studies from Sri Lanka and Kashmir. *Cambridge Review of International Affairs, 22*(2), 235–256. https://doi.org/10.1080/09557570902877968.

Reardon, B. A. (1993). *Women and peace: Feminist visions of global security.* Albany: State University of New York Press.

Reardon, B. A. (1996). *Sexism and the war system.* Syracuse: Syracuse University Press.

Reardon, B. A. (2001). *Education for a culture of peace in a gender perspective.* Paris: UNESCO Publishing.

Reardon, B. A. (2018). On frameworks and purposes: A response to Dale Snauwaert's review of Jeffrey Sachs' "The age of sustainable development": Patriarchy is the problem. *Global Campaign for Peace Education.* http://www.peace-ed-campaign.org/patriarchy-is-the-problem/.

Reardon, B. A. (2019). Women and human security: A feminist framework and critique of the prevailing patriarchal security system. In B. A. Reardon & A. Hans (Eds.), *The gender imperative: Human security vs state security* (2nd ed., pp. 7–36). New York: Routledge.

Redden, E. (2018, October 17). Hungary officially ends gender studies programs. *Inside Higher Ed.* Retrieved from https://www.insidehighered.com.

Riordan, E. (2004). The woman warrior: A feminist political economic analysis of Crouching Tiger, Hidden Dragon. In K. Ross & C. M. Byerly (Eds.), *Women and media: International perspectives* (pp. 81–103). Malden: Blackwell Publishing.

Ross, K. (2010). *Gendered media: Women, men and identity politics*. Lanham: Rowman & Littlefield Publishers.

Schubart, R. (2009). Introduction. In R. Schubart, F. Virchow, D. White-Stanley, & T. Thomas (Eds.), *War isn't hell, it's entertainment: Essays on visual culture and the representation of conflict* (pp. 1–10). Jefferson: McFarland & Company.

60 Minutes Australia. (2014). *The brave female fighters winning the war against ISIS* [Video file]. Retrieved from https://www.youtube.com.

Tehranian, M. (2004). War, media, and propaganda: An epilogue. In Y. R. Kamalipour & N. Snow (Eds.), *War, media, propaganda: A global perspective* (pp. 237–242). Lanham: Rowman & Littlefield Publishers.

Thomas, T. (2009). Gender management, popular culture, and the military. In R. Schubart, F. Virchow, D. White-Stanley, & T. Thomas (Eds.), *War isn't hell, it's entertainment: Essays on visual culture and the representation of conflict* (pp. 97–114). Jefferson: McFarland & Company.

Tickner, J. A. (2001). *Gendering world politics: Issues and approaches in the post-Cold War era*. New York: Columbia University Press.

Vavrus, M. D. (2002). *Postfeminist news: Political women in media culture*. Albany: State University of New York Press.

Vavrus, M. D. (2017). The challenge of warrior women: Gender, race and militarism in media. In R. A. Lind (Ed.), *Race and gender in electronic media* (pp. 72–88). New York: Routledge.

Wharton, A. S. (2012). *The sociology of gender: An introduction to theory and research* (2nd ed.). Malden: Wiley.

Wong, T. (2016, March 27). Descendants of the Sun: The Korean military romance sweeping Asia. *BBC News*. Retrieved from https://www.bbc.com.

Chapter 13
Language, Gender and Power: Possibilities for Transformation of Political Discourse

Michele W. Milner

Betty Reardon's work as an activist and feminist peace scholar (2015), has contributed to the field of peace education by defining the central problematic of peace and justice as the violation of human dignity. Reardon identifies how the many forms of violence; direct, structural and cultural (Galtung 1969) have a symbiotic relationship to the current military war system and how this is derived from patriarchal ideologies that privilege and maintain gender differences. She introduced the feminist concept of human security (2019) as way to transform the existing militarized state security system rooted in patriarchal structures and values. Reardon sees patriarchy as a particularly complex ideology and set of beliefs that sustains and maintains the durability of the war system and violence in all of its forms. The transformative concept of human security that she conceptualized, recognizes the fulfillment of human rights as a prerequisite for creating conditions for a comprehensive peace.

Coming from the disciplinary background of applied linguistics, specifically critical discourse analysis, I was immediately drawn to the lens offered by the analysis of language and its dialectic relationship to power, and how it could be used to increase awareness of the ways language maintains key aspects of patriarchal ideology, such as stereotypical gender differences and inequitable power relationships. Reardon's contribution to our understanding of the core problematic for peace and human security point us towards possibilities for transformation in terms of realizing a holistic feminine perspective. The scale of this task is all-encompassing, and this chapter asserts the power of language as a necessary component of this process to examine how gender identities and relations are

Michele W. Milner, Principal Fellow of the Higher Education Academy, PFHEA, is the Director of Learning and Wellbeing at the Royal Veterinary College (RVC), University of London, London, UK; Email: mmilner@rvc.ac.uk.

© Springer Nature Switzerland AG 2019
D. T. Snauwaert (ed.), *Exploring Betty A. Reardon's Perspective on Peace Education*, Pioneers in Arts, Humanities, Science, Engineering, Practice 20, https://doi.org/10.1007/978-3-030-18387-5_13

constructed and maintained through social interaction. Language is one of the sites where attention needs to be focused in order to recognize the transformative possibilities of conceptual reframing as part of Reardon's alternative paradigm for a positive global future.

The intersections and connections between language, gender and power have been an area of interest for academics since the mid-1970s, coinciding with the changes around women's roles in society that had begun to take place in the previous decade. Much of the earlier work on language and gender focused on systematically exploring differences in how women and men used language in specific social and cultural contexts (Trudghill 1974). However, this early descriptive work also began to question 'why women find some communicative practices more accessible and relevant than others (Cameron 1996) in terms of the roles that they occupy within social structures.

At the same time, and across many areas of the social sciences, the 'linguistic turn' as it's known, began to explicitly probe the link between language and ideology. Researchers began to examine how social relations are created and maintained through language and the analysis of real-time language data, began to show the need to raise awareness of how language mediated and reinforced relationships of power. Critical discourse analysis (CDA) explored how the conceptual frameworks that constitute ideology and belief systems are given legitimacy and power through communicative patterns that emerge in discourse produced by power elites and state structures (Chilton 1996). CDA examined how aspects of the social world (people, places, actions) and structures (organizational and institutional) interacted with one another in terms of their relations to power structures and how this was discursively expressed (Fairclough 2010). From a CDA perspective, language use is understood as being fluid rather than fixed, and therefore needs to be unpacked and questioned in order to challenge the underlying ideological assumptions that lie behind how concepts are expressed. Importantly though, CDA also points out the transformative possibilities of language by recognizing it as a site that can illuminate how power is constituted, and also its potential to shape social relations.

This type of analysis shows that language choices made by social actors to express concepts are not merely symbolic or trivial sources of ornamentation, but are consequential in how they create and sustain conceptual frameworks for how issues are considered and debated. The gendered identities and relations maintained by these conceptual frameworks also intersect with race, ethnicity, class and nationality in hierarchical arrangements of power that limit the influence of the voices depending on where they sit on the rungs of the hierarchy. The durability of patriarchy is sustained through these social structures, which limit access to the benefits of the market economy through systemic structural discrimination or structural violence.

13.1 Language as a Part of Peace Education

The analysis of how language is used in public discourses offers another vantage point from which to more fully understand how gendered identities are normalized. An understanding of the relationships between language and power provides 'a critical perspective on unequal social arrangements sustained through language use, with the goals of social transformation and emancipation' (Lazar 2005). This forms another important critical/analytical tool from which to unpack how ideological concepts such as patriarchy are so durably maintained.

Patriarchy as defined by Reardon (2015) is 'a socially derived concept, a culturally varied concept that assigns to men and women a set of cultural roles and social functions only minimally determined by their respective reproductive and sexual characteristics' (p. xii). It is binary in nature and maintains gender exclusivity and privileges for what is considered to be 'masculine'. As Gilligan (2018) notes 'patriarchy exists as a set of rules and values, codes and scripts that specify how men and women should act and be in the world' (p. 6).

Language mediates these actions and behaviors and is used to normalize gender differences and the resulting differential relations to power. The conceptual frames created by language to report on and discuss political issues, uphold inequity (i.e. poverty, security) and naturalize stereotypical notions of gendered roles and behaviors for women in power. As feminist scholar Enloe comments (2017), patriarchal dynamics are evident in the political arena through the 'privileging of certain sorts of masculinities in both the distributions of power and the distributions of status and material rewards … and when anything that is deemed feminine is positioned either on a pedestal to be admired, but not wield authority or on the lower rungs of the system's ranked order' (p. 55).

Peace education has an important role to play in better understanding how the ideology of patriarchy persists. Reardon (2015) points to the normative aims of peace education to shine a light on normalized gendered relations and to move towards an inclusive gender perspective,

> Peace education can play an important role in fostering this perspective through developing critical inquiry that examines various gender identities for both positive gender attributes that a contribute toward nurturing a culture of peace, and the negative attributes that sustain and promote a culture of violence (p. 105).

This type of inquiry is crucial in order to understand the resistance, resilience and tenacity of the ideology of patriarchy and how it is normalized in mainstream political discourse. The following examples illustrate the importance of understanding the connection between language and political thinking firstly, by looking at an example of how gendered identities and physical violence against women is normalized through language in the mainstream media. The second example identifies conceptual frames that influence the terms of the debate around the issues of security and poverty. These frames continue to support unequal social structures and attitudes, which constitute structural violence.

13.2   Language and Political Thinking

One of the ways in which language can be seen to normalize physical violence against women while sustaining unequal gender roles is through the increase of the use of violent rhetoric in political discourse to describe women in positions of power. An example of this can be seen in the UK during the very divisive and heated responses to the UK government's preparations for Brexit. Prime Minister Theresa May has been widely criticized both within her own party and by the opposition, for the steps she has taken in the Brexit preparations as the deadline to exit the EU approaches for the UK. During one period of heated opposition to May's Brexit planning in the fall of 2018 the following utterances were made by members of her own party as a reaction to her actions (*Huffpost* 2018):

> A former Tory minister told The Sunday Times: "The moment is coming when the knife gets heated, stuck in her front and twisted. She'll be dead soon."
>
> "Assassination is in the air," one Tory MP told the paper.
>
> Another source described as an ally of former Brexit Secretary David Davis said May was now entering "the killing zone".

Confrontational rhetoric is nothing new to the British House of Commons and is an expected challenge for any PM to face during Prime Minister's question time. Yet the extremely violent nature of these remarks is stunning as it takes opposition to a visceral level of violence. This method of expression is all the more shocking considering the murder of the female MP Jo Cox in 2017 by an outraged constituent that showed that this kind of sentiment could, tragically be translated into physical violence against women.

The threat of this type of violence has also been seen in the reaction on social media to the BBC's first female political editor, Laura Kuenssberg. From the start of her tenure in 2016, she has endured abuse and threats of violence on a regular basis prompting the BBC to hire a security guard for her when attending political events. As was noted in the *Guardian* (2017, September),

> Some of it is doubtless rooted in a refusal to accept her professional judgment, an almost subconscious rejection of the idea that a woman – even a woman whose life's work is covering politics might know what she's talking about. It's striking that neither previous male holders of her job, nor the largely male political editors of titles overtly hostile to Corbyn have been so singled out.

While opposition to political views is to be expected, it would seem that the level of personal cruelty and extreme violence demonstrated in these reactions to women in positions of power has become socially tolerated if not entirely acceptable. While there was negative reaction in the mainstream media against the types of comments made about Theresa May, social media abuse against female academics and political figures continues due to less stringent controls on acceptability and in platforms where this type of expression is often encouraged.

The continued use of violent tropes in public discourse can be linked to the ideology of patriarchy and is part of the cultural violence that Reardon sees as degrading to human dignity. As Reardon (2015) explains:

All violence degrades and/or denies human dignity. This is why I assert that the substance of the field should comprise an inquiry into violence as a phenomenon and a system, its multiple and pervasive forms, the interrelationships among the various forms, its sources and purposes and how it functions and potential alternatives for achieving the legally sanctioned, socially accepted, or politically tolerated purposes commonly pursued through violence (p. xi).

The normalization in public discourse of stereotypical conceptions of masculinity/femininity and inherent difference reinforces a diminished sense of physical, and by extension, intellectual strength in women, which sustains patri-archal ideologies. When these types of violent utterances are used by men in positions of power, such as former MPs, and are then repeated in the mainstream media this reinforces violence against women as being socially acceptable. The attacks are cloaked in the guise of free speech and therefore not considered to be breaking social norms about direct violence. However, this begs a larger question as to why it is necessary to discredit women in this manner when they inhabit roles traditionally occupied by men. Who benefits from men and women maintaining traditional roles and power relationships and the status quo? Why is it necessary to damage the credibility of the women who inhabit traditional male positions in ways that refer to force rather than by challenging the intellectual merit of their ideas and work?

Another way that discourse sustains and maintains the ideology of patriarchy is through the conceptual framing of issues in public discourse and the metaphors that map to those frames. The cognitive linguist Lakoff (2004, 2008, 2016) has examined the cognitive aspects of framing in political communication and has shown how specific language choices and metaphors, can influence the terms of the public debate about complex issues and ideological positions, and also where there is potential for reframing in order to challenge assumptions and the status quo. Lakoff contends that strategically considered language use including conceptual metaphors, are necessary elements for the reframing of social issues.

Language gets its power because it is defined relative to frames, prototypes, metaphors, narratives, images, and emotions. Part of its power comes from its unconscious aspects: we are not consciously aware of all that it evokes in us… If we hear the same language over and over we will think more and more in terms of frames and metaphors activated by that language (2008, p. 15).

According to Lakoff (2008, 2016) this powerful connection between language and ways of thinking about concepts is largely unconscious, but is activated in our minds by familiar words, phrases, metaphors or narratives in public discourse. This cognitive configuration predisposes our emotional response to concepts and ideas, in effect structuring our world knowledge and telling us what to pay attention to and what to ignore. This means that each time a frame or metaphor is unconsciously activated it becomes strengthened and becomes part of our 'common sense' understanding of an issue. Similarly, alternative perspectives that are not part of this conceptual apparatus and that may pose a challenge, are not maintained or easily considered.

The framing in public discourse of the concepts of state security and peace has been explored from this perspective. A consistently used framework of image schema for the concepts of national security, defense and international relations was found used in media and policy discourses (Chilton 1996). Security is often characterized through the image of a 'container' usually defined by national borders, which has implications concerning both the nature of the container (how, where and by whom it is constructed?) and the ability for movement both within and, into/out of the container. How this image persists in framing the issue can be seen vividly in recent debates about immigration control and the need for walls to protect national security in the US, or in the desire of the UK to 'secure its borders' as part of the rationale for Brexit. Another image that is part of this schema is the 'path' image concept. The idea that there is a 'path to peace' that is part of an overall 'journey' associated with the concept of attaining peace, privileges attention on the purpose or endpoint of the 'path' or 'journey' as opposed to the process. This is often used in security and peace discourse such as "path to peace" or "roadmap to peace" which places importance on a set of actions to achieve the stated purpose, often the cessation of direct violence, but with little attention paid to the ongoing creation of conditions conducive to creating and maintaining peace. Another aspect of the conceptual framework for security discourse is the 'link' schema. This is of particular relevance to peace discourses as it links movement in/out of various locations or conditions by an agent and as can be seen in expressions such as 'developing ties' 'shoring up allegiances' or 'representation in'. Chilton comments, "the link concept tends to be absent from realist and neorealist discourses, since states are conceptualized as separated, while it will be often presupposed in discourses concerned with cooperation and interdependence between states" (1996, p. 55).

This set of framings for security and peace located within a realist paradigm, sustain concepts of the nation state as the dominant instrument of security and limit consideration of the holistic and interdependent concept of human security that Reardon sees as a necessary imperative of her ethical framework. This means that the pervasive patriarchal ideology embedded in the use of these metaphors and this conceptual framing of security in public discourse, continues to reinforce divisions while also limiting the consideration of alternative narratives. This is antithetical to the description of a feminist concept of human security described by Reardon as necessary for the achievement of human dignity.

Poverty is a ubiquitous concept in public discourse, yet it is also a 'contested term' as its definition is related to divergent ideologies on economic systems and social structures. Sen (1999) questioned the validity of the standard income-based measure used to define poverty to appreciate the impact of diminished capabilities as a result of inequity. He notes,

> ... there is strong case for judging individual advantage in terms of the capabilities that a person has, that is, the substantive freedoms he or she enjoys to lead the kind of life he or she has reason to value. In this perspective poverty must be seen as a deprivation of basic capabilities rather than lowness of income (1999, p. 87).

A central element of Reardon's conceptual framework (2015) is the concept of human rights as the 'inspiration and the practical tool for confronting and over-coming injustice'. Yet the ways in which poverty is conceptually framed discur-sively locates it within an individualistic framework that sees the issue as either being the result of 'natural' market forces or the lack of human ability to participate in the market economy.

The concept of poverty sustained in much of public discourse is as a 'disease' that needs to be 'eradicated', 'tackled' and 'alleviated' in order to find 'relief from' (Milner 2014). The verbs that are used when discussing poverty are usually found in discourses related to disease, and therefore metaphorically represent poverty as a natural or organic phenomenon rather than as by-product of economic policies. By conceptualizing poverty in this way, it means that the responsibility for poverty is subverted away from human agents, onto natural forces, which could be more difficult to control. If poverty is conceptualized as a natural phenomenon, like a disease, then the response to the problem shifts from the need to explain potential causes, such as structural discrimination, to the responsibility for 'treatment' as a response. Although the disease metaphor can bring attention to the issue in order to find a 'cure', this becomes located within the framework of the market economy and sees poverty as a natural and unavoidable by-product. It is not viewed as the result of intentional economic practices and policies that create and maintain inequity.

The container schema is also part of how poverty is conceptually framed, as a kind of 'trap' to be 'climbed' or 'lifted out of' or demarcated by a 'line' to 'fall below'. As with security, the concept of a 'container' specifically brings up questions of agency for both the line and trap metaphors, in terms of how the boundaries that form the edges of the container are created and maintained. This then raises the question of agency and responsibility for 'who' or 'what' has set the 'trap'; if it can be avoided, and how do those caught in it, get out. While the 'trap' metaphor does little to link causality or responsibility for 'who' or 'what' has set the trap, it does confer a degree of agency on those who live in poverty since they 'fell into' the trap. It casts them in a negative role since they have become a victim of a presumably avoidable situation by falling into the trap. The trap conceptualization and questions of who or what has created it, diverts attention away from how policies and social institutions create the structure of the container, and how the line, that creates the threshold of poverty, is maintained. A view of poverty as structural violence, and therefore as a situation that is avoidable, would question the boundaries of the container or trap, in terms of a lack of access to resources (either through scarcity or power imbalances which deprive capabilities) and therefore an ethical failure in society. This dominant conceptual framework for poverty takes a market orientation to the issue and sees the boundaries of the container as being formed by a lack of will on the part of the people who could not avoid it, thus constituting a moral failure on the part of the individuals in the trap, not a reflection of structural barriers within society.

These two conceptual metaphors of a 'disease' and 'container' frame poverty as a natural outcome of economic forces with 'the market' as the animating force, which can cause people to be trapped by poverty, and which can also alleviate it. This conceptualization maintains that if open markets are allowed to function freely then people could be "lifted out of poverty" by market forces, or they could avoid poverty entirely. The trap of poverty could then be interpreted as a function of market forces. In this scenario, poverty can be seen as a problem of scarcity that is a function of markets that are not open which support free market ideologies. The idea of poverty as either a natural phenomenon, or as some type of container, does not allow it to be seen as an issue of structural violence based on conditions of inequity that are counter to human rights and dignity. By representing poverty as something natural it does not connect causal responsibility to social policies, which limit access to resources and diminish an individual's capabilities to benefit from the current market economy system. When poverty is seen as a lack of equity instead of an issue of scarcity, it fundamentally becomes an issue of human rights, but this conceptualization is limited in the dominant public discourse framework used to express and debate poverty.

The ubiquitous nature of these conceptual frames for security and poverty in policy and media discourse shows the durability of patriarchal ways of understanding and constructing issues, which emphasize divisions and hierarchical relationships. As Reardon points out (2015),

> Through the tenacity of patriarchal thinking hierarchical arrangements of society based on race, class, and gender and buttressed by inequitable access to the benefits of production based on what has become global, corporate, free market capitalism psychologically reinforced by the fear of others....patriarchy as the basic paradigm of human institutions continues to prevail (p. 115).

The repeated activation of these concepts makes the associated frames stronger over time. The terms of the debate are pre-structured and therefore the possibilities for issue framing and actions that are truly transformative, such as human security, and which fall outside of these frames are limited. The potential for these frames to determine the terms of the public debate is further highlighted by Lakoff's findings (2016) that it is cognitively difficult to consider simultaneously frames that seemingly contradict each other.

13.3   Conclusion

The function of language to mediate social interactions locates it firmly as a source of evidence of the issues that need to be challenged, but more importantly as a site of transformation towards an inclusive gender perspective on issues of human security and human rights. It can achieve this as one of the tools that support the normative aims of peace education to illustrate forms of hierarchy and a relational view of gender. Language should 'play a continuing part in the emancipatory aims of feminism as a political movement (Mills/Mullany 2011, p. 161).'

The discursive construction of social issues has a role to play in challenging conventional beliefs that maintain and normalize aspects of the war system and gendered notions of power, which support structural violence such as poverty and discrimination. In fact, feminist linguists, Holmes and Meyeroff (2013) have stressed the need to,

.... draw attention to and challenge unquestioned practices that reify certain behaviors as being morally, or aesthetically better than others. We should never cease to engage actively with and challenge assumptions about gender norms and loudly draw attention to the way power, privilege and social authority interact with and are naturalised as properties of independent social categories (p. 14).

A pioneer of gender and language, Cameron (2009) questioned some of the traditions of linguistic research for contributing lengthy descriptive accounts of language difference but wondered if these were truly able to affect some kind of societal change and answer the question 'What is to be done?' Reardon (2015) answers this question by identifying the important role of peace education,

A major task is raising awareness regarding the gender peace problematic and how all are implicated in it. Women need not perceive themselves as subjects of discrimination or oppression to understand their subordination in their patriarchal hierarchy. Most men do identify themselves, nor do they perceive their actions as sustaining gender disparities. Education should elicit understanding of the complex realities of gender inequality. Men do not need to contribute to or behave in ways that sustain patriarchal society to be the beneficiaries of male privilege. Building awareness of the patriarchal structures that account for gender disparities and male privilege are core learning goals for an inclusive gender perspective in peace education (p. 104).

The resilience and prevalence of patriarchal modes of thinking in public discourse which reinforce the status quo are tenacious, and Reardon (2015) herself questions whether the socio-political structure of patriarchy is likely to change due to the 'strong influence on reportage and the way in which the information media manage public security discourse to the continued advantage of the dominant security paradigm'. This observation lends credence to Lakoff's (2016) view of how deep-seated cognitive frames are in fact issue defining, and continue to structure the terms of the debate. The frames provide a short-cut link to ways of reasoning about social issues that support certain world-views, such as the war system which Reardon links to patriarchy. When these frames are evoked they not only strengthen the validity of the reasoning behind them but also limit our ability to think in different ways about an issue. Importantly this also means that facts that do not fit into the dominant frames are more easily ignored. A vivid example of this can be seen in the inability of the constant fact-checking of President Trump's statements, done by the New York Times and other mainstream media outlets, to challenge the conceptual frames of white, privileged masculinity that President Trump has continually communicated through his tweets. Trump's rhetoric states the need for personal security against immigrants and new modes of industrial production while reinforcing how stereotypical white, male identities are under siege. The importance of rhetoric as a divisive tool can be seen only too clearly over the past two years in the political contexts of both the USA and UK. In both countries, conceptual frames that depict immigration as an urgent crisis that threatens national security have bitterly divided the countries and left little room in public discourse for facts that contradict these frames.

However, this also means that consciously challenging these conceptual frames is an important site for transformational change to address the core gender peace problematic. As Lakoff (2016) notes, facts will rarely change the world; 'conceptual change occurs through the activation and strengthening of alternative frames'. The challenge for transformative language use is to break the cycle of repetition and to start to reframe. When language is seen as merely ornamental or inconsequential it ignores the pervasive conditioning effect of privileged conceptual frames that are linked to patriarchal ideologies. These are indicative of how we construct value around issues and structure the terms of the debate. One need look no further than at the corrosive and divisive effect of the rhetoric emanating from the Trump White House and how quickly the terms of the debate have hardened around issues of social justice, challenging what were once considered to be established norms for human rights and the rule of law.

This points to language as an important site in the urgent struggle to articulate Reardon's concept of human security and the need to carefully consider how the concept can be uniquely framed and understood as essential to a comprehensive understanding of peace. The reframing of complex issues in order to promote systemic social change has the ability to subvert existing stereotypes, and to articulate and promote alternative solutions as more than merely liberal reactions that seeks to negate (and thus inadvertently reinforce) entrenched patriarchal frames and ways of seeing the world. New discourses that promote and communicate new frames of understanding will enable an empowered and equitable future as part of a holistic feminist perspective that values and maintains the dignity of all humans.

References

Cameron, D. (1996). The Language-gender interface: Challenging co-optation. In V. Bergrall, J. Bing, & A. Freed (Ed.), *Rethinking language and gender research: Theory and practice* (pp. 31–53). London: Longman.

Cameron, D. (2009). Theoretical issues for the study of gender and spoken interaction. In P. Pichler & E. Eppler (Eds.), *Gender and spoken interaction* (pp. 1–17). Basingstoke: Palgrave.

Chilton, P. (1996). *Security discourses: Cold War metaphors from containment to common house.* New York: Peter Lang.

Enloe, C. (2017). *The big push: Exposing and challenging the persistence of patriarchy.* Oxford: Myriad.

Fairclough, N. (2010). *Critical discourse analysis: The critical study of language* (2nd ed.). London: Pearson.

Galtung, J. (1969). Violence, peace, peace research. *Journal of Peace Research, 6*(3), 167–191.

Gilligan, C., & Snider, N. (2018). *Why does patriarchy persist?* Cambridge: Polity.

Hinsliff, G. (2017, September 25). Laura Kuenssberg hiring a bodyguard was depressing. Then it got worse. *Guardian.* Retrieved from https://www.theguardian.com/.

Holmes, J., & Meyerhoff, M. (2003). Different voices, different views: An introduction to current research in language and gender. In *The handbook of language and gender* (pp. 11–17). Oxford: Blackwell.

Lakoff, G. (2004). *Don't think of an elephant!: Know your values and frame the debate.* Vermont: Chelsea Green Publishing.

Lakoff, G. (2008). *The political mind: A cognitive scientist's guide to your brain and its politics.* New York: Penguin Books.

Lakoff, G., & Wehling, E. (2016). *Your brain's politics: How the science of mind explains the political divide.* Exeter: Imprint Academic.

Lazar, M. (2005). *Feminist critical discourse analysis: Gender, power and ideology in discourse.* Basingstoke: Palgrave.

Mills, S., & Mullany, L. (2011). *Language, gender and feminism: Theory, methodology and practice.* London: Routledge.

Milner, M. (2014). *The discursive construction of global poverty: Social responsibility in patterns of reporting* (unpublished doctoral thesis). Lancaster University, Lancaster, UK.

Reardon, B., & Hans, A. (2019). *The gender imperative: Human security vs state security* (2nd ed.). London: Routledge.

Reardon, B., & Snauwaert, D. (Eds.). (2015). *Betty A. Reardon: Key texts in gender and peace.* New York: Springer.

Sen, A. (1999). *Development as freedom.* Oxford: Oxford University Press.

Simon, N. (2018, October 21). Backlash against 'disturbing' language used about Theresa May. *Huffpost.* Retrieved from https://www.huffingtonpost.co.uk/.

Trudghill, P. (1974). *The social differentiation of English in Norwich.* Cambridge: Cambridge University Press.

Part III
Peace Education Pedagogy and Applied Peacebuilding Practices

Chapter 14
Toward a Just Society: An Account

Janet Gerson

A just society is not a static given. The problematic of injustice continually provokes renewed efforts for individuals and societies; for theorists, educators, political activists, and for all those who strive for a more just world. Betty Reardon and Rainer Forst are two leading thinkers who have devoted their work to conceiving of *justice* as dynamic, morally based, critical, and relational. Each is deeply concerned with how to challenge injustice, especially as it is replicated in the structures of thinking, invalid justifications in communication, and invalid societal narratives. Their mutual affinity is evident in their shared *conception of the person* and their understanding of political power. Reardon's pedagogical practice of *reflective* inquiry (Reardon 1988a, 2001, 2013; Reardon/Cabezudo 2001; Reardon/Snauwaert 2011, 2015a; Gerson 2014; in press) is complemented by Forst's theory of the *right to justification* (2012, 2013, 2014, 2017; Allen 2014).

Reardon is arguably an organic intellectual. Her peace pedagogy of *reflective inquiry* is derived from five decades of practice as an educator, theorist, and global civil society activist, especially in supporting gender, ecological, and human security and in countering militarism. Her ground-breaking work is foundational for the field of peace education. Forst is a political theorist and philosopher. His theory, based on the principle of the *right to justification*, is a cognitive analytic approach that builds upon Kantian theorists of justice, particularly Rawls (1971, 1992) and Habermas (1984, 1987, 1991; Finlayson/Freyenhagen 2013). With Habermas (1992, 1996), he continues the lineage of the Frankfort School's critical theory (2014, 2017).

In these times, populist authoritarianism is on the rise. The promises of the welfare state and democratic rule are losing vitality. Democracy has been characterized as "in chains" (McLean 2017), dying (Levitsky/Ziblatt 2018) and threatened

Janet Gerson, Education Director, International Institute on Peace Education, New York, NY; Email: gerson@i-i-p-e.org.

© Springer Nature Switzerland AG 2019
D. T. Snauwaert (ed.), *Exploring Betty A. Reardon's Perspective on Peace Education*, Pioneers in Arts, Humanities, Science, Engineering, Practice 20, https://doi.org/10.1007/978-3-030-18387-5_14

by fascism (Stanley 2018; Albright 2018) and tyranny (Snyder 2017). Although enough food and other material needs are currently produced for every person in the world to be sufficiently clothed, fed and housed, this is not happening. In fact, the number of poor is growing as wealth is concentrated into the hands of an increasingly tiny few. At the same time, climate catastrophe is afflicting, especially in the most vulnerable, impoverished regions. The richest cities located on coasts must consider how to cope with destructive flood emergencies and possible complete submergence. Migrants are fleeing states of perpetual war and climate-caused disasters.

Our governments and international institutions appear to be inadequate to respond, characterized by "(t)he near total lack of reasoning and reasonable discourse in contemporary American politics", as Reardon states (Reardon/Snauwaert 2015a, p. 190). In the face of all these real-world problems, there is a great need to challenge political leaders' and official authorities' use of lies, "fake news", and other kinds of invalid justifications for their own consolidation of wealth and power.

For those concrete thinkers who want deliverables, for those who see power as resting primarily with the 'sovereign', for those in contentious politics who demand direct action, my response will not satisfy. Justification will be not be described as an "end-driven activity of basically problem-solving" but instead as "intersubjective…the practice of offering justifications that are answerable to others within a practice of offering and evaluating and responding to reasons" (Laden 2014, p. 110). As Habermas has outlined, there will always be those people and organizations that have no interest in cooperating, who operate covertly and deceptively for their own strategic self-interests by engaging in "manipulative action" and "systematically distorted communication" (1998, p. 93). These are among the most important purveyors of invalid justifications, obfuscations, ideologies and other unjust narratives. What follows addresses people who know they need other people and for whom accountability is an imperative. To these people working for a more just, peaceful and accountable world, I direct you to the work of Betty Reardon and Rainier Forst.

I see Reardon and Forst as having similar aims, directed towards different but overlapping audiences. Both aim to challenge injustice while also showing how just relations can be generated. Reardon aims at social-political transformation cultivated within peace education – an education for learning *how to think* in order to critique and challenge structural violence and ideologies, to generate legitimate co-created norms and visions, and to cultivate relationships for *acting in concert with others* (1996, 2013; Reardon/Nordland 1994; Reardon/Cabezudo 2001; Reardon/Snauwaert 2011, 2015b). Her vision of a just society would entail processes that facilitate webs of relationships, societies, and institutions that can support, protect, and provide well-being, dignity, and inclusion for all living systems in our planetary society (1988a, b, 1995; Reardon/Snauwaert 2015a). She has theorized and engaged in *reflective inquiry* as a philosophical, pedagogical, and political practice for that broad vision (Reardon, Reardon & Snauwaert; Gerson). As evidenced in the quote above, politics demands "reasoning and reasonable discourse" (Reardon/Snauwaert 2015, p. 190) as central to the dialogical and democratic processes necessary for a functioning, inclusive political order.

Forst would most probably not disagree. He would, however, describe reason, a means of *philosophical thinking in a discursive mode*, as central to a just society. He understands the foundations of justice as the *right to justification*. Practical reason is the "faculty of justification" (Forst 2017, p. 22). Reason is more than rational, analytic thinking – it is normative and binding. Reason "connects us with others in the light of principles and values that it examines with a view toward their justification" (p. 22). Justification is a means to elaborate, validate, legitimize, and to recognize. Justification also means to challenge invalid, unjust, arbitrary claims. Politics for Forst entails both *philosophical* and *practical inquiry*. Forst's work is more theoretical and abstractly described than Reardon's. He addresses philosophers and political theorists, as well as other scholars and citizens who would advocate for and demand justification for invalid social narratives and social-political dis-orders.

Forst asserts the need to re-articulate core concepts of political theory in relation to practical reason. He aims to de-reify them, detach them as code words for political ideologies, and re-interpret them "in a 'dialectical' way that understands them as having the character of social processes" (Forst 2017, p. 8). Reardon also aims to enliven concepts through re-articulations as they arise in processes of reflective inquiry, and other notable activists, educators, and scholars have also sought to de-reify and re-interpret invalid social narratives. For example, Augusto Boal, Brazilian drama theorist and political activist, used theater techniques to open space for public reason. He used *dynamizing* theater techniques to enliven the static, reified, or 'stuck' aspects of oppressive relations (2002). To *dynamize* means to de-stabilize what seems intractable or insurmountable. Justice is not a state that is put in place and stays; it must be revisited as each new injustice, conflict, or problem of structural violence becomes an obstacle or danger. Thus, a social, process-oriented understanding of justice requires a *recursive* methodology (2017, p. 155), one for revisiting, reconsidering, de-reifying. Both reflective inquiry and the right to justification are recursive. Both are means for practicing justice and challenging injustice.

14.1 An Emancipatory Conception of the Person

Reardon and Forst conceive of the person in much the same way. For both, every person *counts*. Dignity is "moral autonomy" (Forst 2017, p. 29) and is inherent in each person. Both Reardon and Forst reference Kant's insight that each person is not the means to an end, but always an end in herself. Each person can be recognized as the *author* of his own story. Each person – every one – is recognized as the *subject* of their own story, their own *account.* As we know from human history and from our current moment, individuals are at risk to be *subjected* to domination, suppression, manipulation; in contrast, Reardon's and Forst's conception of the person supports an emancipatory intention. At the same time, this conception is not one of solely supporting individual identities or needs. The person is not only a center in herself, but also a center that is itself centered in the context of other human beings, all of whom are equally, inherently worthy of respect among each other. This autonomous yet relational conception of the person is the foundation for the following discussion of how humans can challenge injustice.

For both Reardon and Forst, humans have the capacity for *reason,* the ability to think and to justify. Forst's theory of justification – *practical reason* – applies to challenges that "arise in concrete contexts, and equally beyond them" (Forst 2017, p. 3). Forst's theory of justice is grounded in ethical, moral, and critical justification, as is Reardon's reflective *thinking* inquiry (1988a, 2001, 2013; Reardon/Cabezudo 2001; Reardon/Snauwaert 2011, 2015a; Gerson 2014, in press). These lines of reflection and justification form a *normative framework* (Forst 2017). For both thinkers, practical reason gives fundamental support to human agency – the ability to act. And, the ethical, moral, and critical dimensions of practical reason in relation to each other provide guidance for individuals and societies to act justly. Forst calls the weaving of these ethical, moral, and critical means in their relational contexts, the tying of the *normative knot* (Forst 2015, p. 28).

Finally, for both Reardon and Forst, humans have capacities related to communication. With regard to justice, these communicative capacities enable individuals and groups to assert rights by making claims; to demand reasons from others, especially for apparent obstacles to those claims; and, more generally, to be responsible to respond to the assertions and considerations of others. These communicative and relational dimensions of practical reason are combined in *social orders of justification* and *justificatory narratives.* Orders of justification "consist of a complex web of different justifications, some of which have congealed into justificatory narratives,, that exercise hegemonic power – and provoke counternarratives" (Forst 2017, p. 34). These accounts may be dominating and repressive, closing off space for practical reasons, or dialectically expressed, they may be emancipatory. For both Reardon and Forst, critical theory has an emancipatory intention. Their practices put forth ways to challenge unjust, invalid justificatory narratives – "one *basic claim* is fundamental…the claim not to be subjected to any form of rule that cannot be adequately legitimized toward those who are subjected to it" (Forst 2017, pp. 34–35).

Forst expresses this dynamic within the conception of the person as one who has dignity, voice, and can demand space for authorship and agency – "in the struggles of those affected, the call for the right no longer to count as a social nullity but instead to have rights to co-determine and self-determine is at once the moving force and the norm proper to political practice" (p. 35).

Grounded in this conception of the person, I will now explore Forst's and Reardon's insights into how a just society might be practiced, at least on the social-political level. My focus will not be justice on the reified level of institutional and official authority; the concern here is: How do the right to justification and reflective inquiry complement each other? How do these conceptions help to rethink and practice justice? And, as critical theory and practices, how can these help us counter injustice?

14.2 Forst's Theory of the Right to Justification

Forst maintains that the *right to justification* is the fundamental principle of justice. It is the right to demand reasons. In the relational paradigm of justice (2017), the *right* to justification is simultaneously the *duty* to justify claims, narratives, and actions. Justification, then, is the demand for validity and also for responsibility. As I understand it, justifications that are demonstrated to be valid and for which actors take responsibility constitute *accountability*. Justificatory practices challenge *arbitrariness*, which Forst equates with domination, the "rule of some people over others without legitimate reason" (Forst 2017, p. 154). The practice of making claims and demands, and the reciprocating duty of justification are central to both cooperation and conflict processes. Justificatory practices are central to the co-construction of a just social-political order and achieving legitimacy. They are even more important than the use of force, or the implied use of force, in maintaining social stability.[1]

For Forst, power is *noumenal*, an "intersubjective, social power" of one agent to influence another to do something they "would not otherwise have thought or done…[as] a result of a good and convincing discourse, a recommendation, a lie, an act of seduction, a command, or a threat" (2017, p. 63). In this conception, power is neutral, but in context or intention power can be either negative or positive – unjust or just.

14.3 Reardon's Pedagogy of Reflective Inquiry

Reardon's reflective inquiry is a pedagogy of comprehensive and critical peace education. Reflective inquiry is a *practice* for addressing justice-challenging issues that can be used in public settings as well as classrooms. The practice has developed from Reardon's global civil society activism, her formation of working groups such as Women's International Network for Gender and Human Security (WINGHS), Feminist Scholars and Activists Working for Demilitarization (FeDem), and the

---

[1]Thanks to Frank Brodhead for making this point on noumenal power and domination.

International Institute on Peace Education (IIPE),[2] three examples that I have participated in. Even as a formal classroom educator, Reardon continuously introduced learners to activists grappling with complex injustices of indirect, structural violence and also direct violence. In all settings, she has regarded herself as a co-learner, an 'edu-learner' (1988a, b), an equal participant in processes of learning from and with others. In this way, she consciously aims to supplant hierarchy with relational connectedness. I see the *conception of the person* as the foundation for her philosophy of reflective inquiry, and through the practice of reflective inquiry, we learn how to think as authors and agents of political efficacy.

As discussed above, Reardon's reflective inquiry takes place in a *learning community*, a community of inquiry – a classroom, a global network of activists, a local community group. The facilitated community inquiry serves as a kind of container for the pursuit of learning. Welcoming and *uniting* are facilitated through processes of introduction and convivial exchange (see Coleman et al. 2006). The aim is to offer recognition and space for each and every participant. The dialogic practice elicits participants' input. Thus, a *space of communication* is opened, inviting active participation.

Reflective inquiry uses question-formation to open thinking, participation, and discussion. Inquiry shapes the pursuit. Inquiry circumvents lecturing; lecturing tends to create a hierarchy of 'experts' above learners which can obstruct speaking and deep listening reciprocally. Reflective inquiry is "in essence a process of thinking by interrogation" (Reardon 2011, p. 7), a dialogic exchange, a delving and grappling into a challenging issue, an "encountering [of] the subject of the inquiry as the entry point into the process of examination" (p. 7). Thus, Reardon's methodology generates a *space of communication*. Based on my experience as a facilitator in classrooms and a coordinator of contexts for its use such as IIPE, I will lay out a generalized description of how this works.

First, as equals, participants articulate and refine the inquiry topic, a current *problematic*, that is, a complex of related challenges. The second task is to formulate the *question* that both drives and guides the inquiry through the processes of reflection. Third, relevant concepts are defined and put in relationship to the problematic, the case study, thereby forming a *conceptual framework* that sets the parameters and scope of the inquiry. Empirical and experiential input are contributed by the participants and facilitators to ground the collective reflection in actual, real, researched content. These procedural steps *dynamize* the problematic.

---

[2]"The International Institute on Peace Education (IIPE) is a weeklong residential experience for educators. IIPE is at various universities and peace centers throughout the world. IIPE facilitates exchanges of theory and practical experiences in teaching peace education and serves to grow the field. In serving the field, the IIPE operates as an applied peace education laboratory that provides a space for pedagogical experimentation; cooperative, deep inquiry into shared issues; and advancing theoretical, practical and pedagogical applications…in its intensive residentially based learning community." Retrieved November 29, 2018, from https://www.i-i-p-e.org/about/ (As Education Director of IIPE and as co-author of this text, I have somewhat rearranged this text for clarity here).

Through the whole process, participants contribute their reactions, experiences, beliefs, visions. They grapple with ethical, moral, and critical dimensions of the problematic. From the reflective discussion, insights are gleaned. These are then used to formulate actions to challenge and transform unjust power relations, including ideologies and illegitimate rationalizations for the use of violence. Possible actions are formulated by individuals, small groups, and the whole group collectively.

For example, there are many dimensions to the problematic of climate crisis that can be brought together in a reflective inquiry – scientific, diverse geographic challenges, industrial and governance concerns. Normative assumptions that form the justificatory narrative of humans' relationship to Earth's living systems must be reconceived. The human narrative that the Earth's abundance of good land, air, and water exist infinitely for our own use—and only as a means for our ends – cannot continue. Must our normative framework, our scope of moral inclusion, expand to include all living beings and systems? If so, how can we as individuals and as societies transform in both our thinking and our actions? How might our normative framework be regenerated to include *ecological justice*?

The learning communities sense of interconnectedness and interrelatedness gives some resilience to the difficult interactions that emerge. The learning from and with each other enables insights and outcomes that would not have been reached without the dialogical interactive experience. The whole is greater than the parts, constituting a *relational and intersubjective* practice that complements Forst's philosophical theory. Reardon emphasizes moral/ethical and critical modes of reflective inquiry. She states that

> [t]he sequence and mode of instruction most effectively emerge from the learners' question, *"What does this subject have to do with me, my life, and the society in which I live?"* In a peace learning inquiry that question will ultimately involve a query, *"What has the subject to do with us as a community, our common welfare and the kind of society in which we would prefer to live?"* (Reardon 2015, p. 190) (emphasis added).

Reardon links moral and ethical inquiry. In what follows, I explore Forst's elaboration of these normative dimensions.

14.4 Ethical and Moral Reflection and Justifications for Building Justice and Community

As Reardon explains, in e*thical reflection*, each individual asks himself the question *"What does this subject have to do with me, my life, and the society in which I live?"* (Reardon 2015, p. 190). In relation to an issue, conflict, or decision to be made, a person asks, *What is valuable to me? What is good in my esteem? What kind of person do I want to be? Ethical reflection* holds the dignity of the person as author and agent of his own life. At the same time, ethical responses must reflect the individual *within the context* of relationships and community. Importantly, the

J. Gerson

individual must take responsibility for his own decisions. He, in the end, is accountable for his stance and his reasoning and for how these will guide his actions. He must provide justifications for his stance and/or actions. Thus, the person is autonomous and also responsible both to himself and simultaneously to others. In reflective inquiry, these types of responses are shared and reflected upon, often in small groups. Insights, further questions, and the reflective reasoning itself – the justifications – are shared from all groups to the whole community. This way each and every individual contributes to the accumulated insights and challenges faced by the whole group.

Questions in reflective inquiry are not simply "yes or no" types; for the most part, they do not have answers. These reflective contexts differ from planning meetings, decision and policy-making, and laying out plans of action, where answers are necessary outcomes. Often, the inquiry question is more complex and without any definite answer. The investigations may actually lead to many *more* questions. To be sure, some of these questions may remain unanswered for a lifetime. This is true of many inquiries in peace learning and in social-political contexts. Reardon calls these *queries*, for example the one above, "*What has the subject to do with us as a community, our common welfare and the kind of society in which we would prefer to live?*" (Reardon 2015, p. 190). We may hold this query for a lifetime, visiting and revisiting it recursively as our lives unfold and the contexts shift.

In other words, commonly held understandings must shift. There are many contexts locally and globally where people are subjugated as slaves or servants, where they are held as means to others' ends. There are multiple types of structural violence where hierarchies value some while subordinating others. But there are also examples of profound normative shifts, for example, in gender relations where women were previously viewed as property of men, now women can participate as citizens, own property, and have more autonomy.

In our complex and globalized world, the power of states is pressed into service by multinational corporations, favoring their wants over the demands and expectations of their citizens and residents. Bureaucratic obstacles to more justice are amplified by technology – layers of mechanical and bureaucratic filtering that block ordinary people, customers, clients, patients, constituents from reaching a person who can respond to requests, demands, complaints. When it comes to the challenges of climate crisis, justice, and well-being, social and political officials and institutional authorities seem incapable of truly facing the threat of human extinction. We may be past the point where humanly coordinated power can withstand the force of nature. However, we must try. Moral reflection and justifications must be applied to these struggles of ecological justice as well.

Moral reflection is focused on what can be claimed as universally valid for everyone. While *ethical reflection* focuses on the life-choices confronting an individual, *moral* norms rest on a "categorical, unconditional, reciprocal and general claims to validity – *nobody* is allowed to violate a moral norm and everyone can expect everyone else to observe the norm" (Forst 2017, p. 28). Moral justifications differ from ethical justifications where the individual must answer finally to herself. In moral reflection, "the mode of justification is strictly *intersubjective* from the onset" (p. 28). Moral reflections and justifications must satisfy the criteria of *reciprocity* and *generalizability*. Forst explains that the criterion of reciprocity has two types, first of all, that

> no one may raise claims that she refuses to grant to others (reciprocity of contents) and [second,] that no one may simply assume that others share her own evaluative conceptions and interests so that she could claim to speak in their name or in the name of higher values (reciprocity of reasons), (p. 28).

The criterion of *reciprocity of contents* holds the challenge of both equality and inclusion. Reciprocity of contents evaluates the question of application of the *who*, the *how*, and the *how much* of justice. *Reciprocity of reasons* evaluates claims and justifications based on beliefs "perspective, evaluations, convictions, interests, or needs" (Allen 2014, p. 68) and systems of thinking. I see reciprocity as what we owe each other (although I do not necessarily mean contractually) as equal yet interdependent beings.

Generalizability is the criterion that "nobody may be excluded from the community of justification" (Forst 2017, p. 28). This means that justifications are morally valid if no one can reasonably reject them (Scanlon 2000; Forst 2017), if a moral justification applies to one, then it applies to all. I understand generalizability to be grounded in the recognition that we need each other.

These criteria for valid moral justifications leave room for a diversity of perspectives and in this way they go beyond *consensus* in discourse theory "because the criteria permit a judgment of which claims can or cannot be reciprocally or generally rejected in a specific conflict" (Forst 2017, p. 29). Those involved do not *have* to agree. They can reach understandings in which each justification offered may not be *accepted* by all. They are 'shareable' but do not necessarily move to the level of being 'shared' by all (p. 29). This is a profound point for resisting homogenization and protecting the diversity and plurality of our communities – local, national, and international.

The prohibition of torture is an example of a moral principle, one that has been codified in International Law through the United Nations Convention against Torture and Other Cruel, Inhuman or Degrading Treatment or Punishment (https://www.ohchr.org/en/professionalinterest/pages/cat.aspx). The Convention (a treaty in international law) contains the same conception of the "inherent dignity of the human person" with "equal and inalienable rights of all members of the human family" as Reardon and Forst. The principle of the immorality of torture was previously encoded in the Universal Declaration of Human Rights - a statement of principles - but the Convention states *as law* that "no one shall be subjected to torture or to cruel, inhuman or degrading treatment or punishment." The principle of generalizability is encoded in the clause: "No exceptional circumstances whatsoever, whether a state of war or a threat of war, internal political instability or any other public emergency, may be invoked as a justification of torture" (1984, https://www.ohchr.org/en/professionalinterest/pages/cat.aspx).

The criteria of reciprocity and generality in justification are relevant to the assessment of validity. Criteria that justifications are reciprocal and general are applications of *critical assessment*. The practices of ethical and moral justification and reflective inquiry pull out ethical and moral reasons that weave societal relations into what Forst calls a *normative knot*. He states that ethical justification are threads that tie the "normative knot between me, concrete others, social expectations, and general considerations" (Forst 2015, p. 28). Moral justifications are the threads that are tied by

> the acting and reflecting moral person who must answer to concrete others who are affected morally by her actions…but in such a way as to transcend this relationship and be universalized: the others are at once concrete and generalized others, at once irreplaceable individuals and members of an *all-inclusive human community*" (p. 29) (emphasis added).

Thus, ethical and moral reflective inquiry and justification are processes through which human beings and communities are woven together in relationships of interconnectedness and interdependence. But it must be obvious that the ethical and moral dimensions of justificatory practicing are not sufficient in themselves. *Critical theory* and *critical reflective inquiry* constitute another set of threads pulled into the normative knot.

14.5   Critical Reflective Inquiry

Thus far, ethical and moral justification and reflection have been presented in a positive, co-constructive light. Forst's theory of the right to justification has been explained as foundational to the normative knot. This normative framework holds the understanding that humans are responsible to themselves and to others, and that we recognize that we need each other to think through and practice justice together. Amy Allen critiques this positive constructive dimension of Forst's theory. She claims that it is *not sufficiently* critical in challenging dominant power; specifically, she argues that reason itself is central to *invalid justifications* and oppressive ideologies. Arguing in defense of marginalized groups, Allen critiques Forst's theory as emphasizing positive, empowering traits without sufficient emphasis on how reason, the centerpiece of European Enlightenment, has been used to *legitimize* domination. Allen, a philosophy, women's and gender studies scholar, argues that this challenge "figures prominently in the critique of reasons offered by many feminist, queer, critical race, and postcolonial theorists" (Allen 2014, pp. 66–67).

Forst responds that the power of practical reason is neutral in and of itself, and agrees with Allen that justifications can be used *invalidly* to suppress, obfuscate, mislead, manipulate, and turn parts of populations against others. At the same time, he stresses the emancipatory intention of any *critical theory of justice*. Critical theory, Forst asserts, must be

> based on the *principle of criticism itself*. Its medium is justifying reason understood as critical, public reason… Progress in the spirit of emancipation occurs where this

principle becomes established and social spaces of justification are opened up (Forst 2017, p. 18).

Reason, as Forst explains it, must be applied to actual issues, contradictions, problems, and conflicts that arise in real life, that real people face. This is also why Reardon's reflective inquiry always starts with actual problematic, actual cases of injustice. As Forst affirms

> [t]he question of justification always arises in concrete contexts and equally points beyond them. It sets in train a dynamic that cuts specifically into question 'ethically reasonable' standards of justification in an intensified reflective process that concerns not only the… context of justification, but is also able to subject the latter to general scrutiny (Forst 2017, pp. 3–4).

Forst responds further to Allen's critique by expanding his understanding of justification as persuasion that can be embodied, affective, perhaps even multi-modal. As I understand it, reason is more than the rational, purely thinking capacity associated with the Enlightenment tradition. Forst places this notion of reason within the context of a relational conception of power.

Power for Forst is *noumenal*, a power of recognition and persuasion, a relational form of power. He explains that power is '*the capacity of A to motivate B to think or do something that B would otherwise not have thought or done*' (Forst 2014, p. 179). Forst is clear that this power can be exerted for any range of intentions – good, bad, dominating, or for someone's own good, or not. This type of power is in contrast to coercion by physical force or violence, when "the noumenal character vanishes" (p. 179). Power, he says, is "what goes on in the head…and what goes on is a recognition of a reason (or…reasons) to act differently than one would have without that reason" (p. 179).

Furthermore, Forst challenges the realist account of politics and power by claiming that the noumenal account has a more encompassing explanatory range.

> …a noumenal account of power relations is more 'realistic' than theories that locate power in physical means, be it money or weapons. For it explains all forms of power that cannot be explained by recourse to such means – the power of speech, of (again: good or bad) arguments, of seduction, of love, of 'acting in concert', of commitments, of religion, of morality, of personal aims, etc. (Forst 2014, p. 180).

What is important about noumenal power is that it is the predominant means of perpetuating unjust relations. It is not clear to me that Reardon would agree with this. For her, both invalid justifications and also brute force are the injustices that she includes in the obstacles and problematics of peace. What is really important is that the intention of her practice of reflective inquiry is to generate engagement with noumenal power. Reardon's reflective inquiry and Forst's right to justification are both methods that illuminate the way to use noumenal power to counter injustice and simultaneously build and bind social-political relationships, a complementary, perhaps integral, dimension of noumenal power. As Forst suggests:

Reason, in other words, is the ability and the power that normatively binds us – it *connects* us with others in the light of principles and values that it examines with a view to their justification (Forst 2017, p. 22).

Noumenal power, then is the "force more powerful" that underlies nonviolent action theory (Sharp 1973, 2003, 2012; Snauwaert 2018; Ackerman/Duvall 2001). It involves critically analyzing both *justificatory narratives* of domination (ideologies) and also *social orders of justification*, the social-political structures of authority. "[I]t is only in understanding noumenal power, of, say, patriarchy, the idea of the free market and other *ideological complexes* that we understand the power they have over people" (Forst 2014, p. 181). This applies in subordination as well as empowerment. The social process of critical analysis that takes place in critical reflective inquiry supports the processes that *reweave* normative ethical and moral ties.

The reconstruction of the contextual logic of justification is the reconstruction of the use of reason, and here, reason counts as something essentially normative, not as a pure instrument. It binds us (Forst 2017, p. 23).

The reconstructive reweaving using critical and co-constructive practical reasons opens the discursive space, facilitating a means for generating alternative justificatory narratives and social orders of justification. This is how normative change can happen. This constitutes a *foundational* potential of reflective inquiry as a discursive non-violent relational practice. As Forst acknowledges, reason itself cannot stand alone; it requires the social dimension.

14.6   Conclusion

Rainer Forst's theory of the right to justification complements Betty Reardon's pedagogy of reflective inquiry. Together they demonstrate how political processes can be not only philosophical and practical, but also democratic in a dynamic sense, beyond the reified institutional form. Brought together in this exploration, these two perspectives form a scaffolding for the theory and practice of an *intersubjective relational paradigm* of justice (Forst 2017, p. 154; Laden 2014, p. 112; Gerson et al. 2018). As a facilitator of reflective inquiry, I wonder how we might organize spaces of justification more demanding than what can be attained in classrooms or communities, even intensives such as the International Institute on Peace Education. More investigations should be done to apply Forst's model to public deliberations in which "justification of the political order" (2017, p. 148) is demanded. As it stands now, Reardon is correct in her critique of the "near total lack of reasoning and reasonable discourse in contemporary American politics" (Reardon 2015a, p. 190). She is speaking of what we demand of our politicians. Discursive critical practices, such as the right to justification in combination with the democratic processes of reflective inquiry, are needed to counter the proliferation of invalid justifications, unjust social orders, unjust narratives, and anti-reasonable political argumentation.

References

Albright, M. (2018). *Fascism: A warning*. New York: Harper Perennial.

Allen, A. (2014). The power of justification. In R. Forst (Ed.), *Justice, democracy and the right to justification: In dialogue* (pp. 65–86). London: Bloomsbury Press.

Ackerman, P., & Duvall, J. A. (2001). *A force more powerful: A century of nom-violent conflict*. New York: Palgrave Macmillan.

Boal, A. (2002). *Games for actors and non-actors* (2nd ed., A. Jackson, Trans.). New York: Routledge.

Coleman, S., Raider, E., & Gerson, J. (2006). Teaching conflict resolution skills in a workshop. In M. Deutsch & P. T. Coleman (Eds.), *Handbook of conflict resolution* (2nd ed., pp. 695–725). San Francisco, CA: Jossey-Bass.

Finlayson, J, G., & Freyenhagen, F. (2013). *Habermas and Rawls: Disputing the political*. New York: Routledge.

Forst, R. (2012). *The right to justification: Elements of a constructivist theory of justice* (J. Flynn, Trans.). New York: Columbia University Press.

Forst, R. (2013). *Justification and critique: Toward a critical theory of politics*. Cambridge: Polity Press.

Forst, R. (2014). *Justice, democracy and the right to justification: In dialogue*. London: Bloomsbury Press.

Forst, R. (2017). *Normativity and power: Analyzing social orders of justification* (C. Cronin, Trans.). Oxford, UK: Oxford University Press.

Gerson, J. C. (in press). *Reclaiming common bases of human dignity: Honoring Evelin Lindner*. Lake Oswego, OR: World Dignity Press.

Gerson, J. C. (2013). *Democratizing global justice: The world tribunal on Iraq, 7*(2), 86–112. http://www.infactispax.org/journal.

Gerson, J. C. (2014). *Public deliberation on global justice: The world tribunal on Iraq*. Doctoral dissertation. New York: Teachers College Columbia University.

Gerson, J., Snauwaert, D., & Warnke, J. (2018, September 29). *Rethinking power & democracy in destructive times*. Peace & Justice Studies Association Conference, Philadelphia, PA.

Habermas, J. (1984). *Theory of communicative action, volume one: Reason and the rationalization of society* (T. A. McCarthy, Trans.). Boston, MA: Beacon Press.

Habermas, J. (1987). *Theory of communicative action, volume two: Lifeworld and system: A critique of functionalist reason* (T. A. McCarthy, Trans.). Boston, MA: Beacon Press.

Habermas, J. (1991). *The structural transformation of the public sphere: An inquiry into a category of bourgeois society* (T. Burger with F. Lawrence, Trans.). Cambridge, MA: MIT Press.

Habermas, J. (1992). *Moral consciousness and communicative action* (C. Lenhardt & S. W. Nicholsen, Trans.). Cambridge, MA: MIT Press.

Habermas, J. (1996). *Between facts and norms: Contributions to a discourse theory of law and democracy* (W. Rehg, Trans.). Boston: MIT Press.

Habermas, J. (1998). *The pragmatics of communication*. Edited by Maeve Cooke. Cambridge, MA: MIT Press.

Laden, A. S. (2014). The practice of equality. In R. Forst (Ed.), *Justice, democracy and the right to justification: In dialogue* (pp. 102–126). London: Bloomsbury Press.

Levitsky, S., & Ziblatt, D. (2018). *How democracies die*. New York: Crown.

McLean, N. (2017). *Democracy in chains: The deep history of radical rights*. New York: Viking.

Raider, E., Coleman, S., & Gerson, J. (2000). Teaching conflict resolution skills in a workshop. In M. Deutsch & P. T. Coleman (Eds.), *The handbook of conflict resolution: Theory and practice* (pp. 499–521). San Francisco, CA, US: Jossey-Bass.

Rawls, J. (1971). *A theory of justice*. Cambridge, MA: Harvard University Press.

Rawls, J. (1992). *Political liberalism*. New York: Columbia University Press.

Reardon, B. A. (1988a). *Comprehensive peace education: Educating for global responsibility* (p. x). New York: Teachers College Press.

Reardon, B. A. (1988b). *Educating for global responsibility: Teacher-designed curricula for peace education, K-12.* New York: Teachers College Press.

Reardon, B, A., & Nordland, E. (1994). *Learning peace: The promise of ecological and cooperative education.* Albany, NY: SUNY Press.

Reardon, B. A. (1995). *Educating for human dignity: Learning about rights and responsibilities.* Pennsylvania Studies in Human Rights. Philadelphia: University of Pennsylvania Press.

Reardon, B. A. (1996). *Sexism and the war system.* Syracuse, NY: Syracuse University Press.

Reardon, B. A. (1999). *Peace education: A review and projection.* Sweden: School of Education, Malmo University.

Reardon, B. A. (2001). *Educating for a culture of peace in a gender perspective.* Paris: UNESCO.

Reardon, B. A. (2013). *Meditating on the barricades: Concerns, cautions and possibilities for peace education for political efficacy.* Springer Netherlands.

Reardon, B. A., & Cabezudo, A. (2001). *Learning to abolish war: Teaching toward a culture of peace.* Retrieved December 3, 2018, from http://www.peace-ed-campaign.org/learning-to-abolish-war-teaching-toward-a-culture-of-peace/.

Reardon, B. A., & Snauwaert, D. T. (2011). Reflective pedagogy, cosmopolitanism, and critical peace education for political efficacy: A discussion of Betty A. Reardon's assessment of the field. *In Factis Pax, 5*(1), 1–14. http://www.infactispax.org/journal/.

Reardon, B. A., & Snauwaert, D. T. (2015a). *Betty A. Reardon: A pioneer in education for peace and human rights.* SpringerBriefs on Pioneers in Science and Practice.

Reardon, B. A., & Snauwaert, D. T. (2015b). *Key texts in gender and peace.* SpringerBriefs on Pioneers in Science and Practice.

Scanlon, T. M. (2000). *What we owe each other.* Cambridge, MA: Belkamp Press.

Sharp, G. (1973). *The politics of nonviolence: Three volume set.* Manchester, NH: Extending Horizons Books.

Sharp, G. (2003). *There are realistic alternatives.* Boston, MA: The Albert Einstein Institute.

Sharp, G. (2012). *From Dictatorship to democracy: A conceptual framework for liberation.* New York: The New Press.

Snauwaert, D. T. (2010). Democracy as public deliberation and the psychology of epistemological world views and moral reasoning: A philosophical reflection. *In Factis Pax, 4*(1), 120–126. Retrieved December 15, 2010, from http://www.infactispax.org/journal/.

Snauwaert, D. T. (2011, November). Democracy, public reason, and peace education. *Global Campaign for Peace Education Newsletter* (88). http://www.peace-edcampaign.org/newsletter/archives/88.html.

Snauwaert, D. T. (2012, November). Betty Reardon's conception of "peace" and its implications for a philosophy of peace education. *Peace Studies Journal, 5*(3). Retrieved November 24, 2018, from www.researchgate.net/publication/233907030_Betty_Reardon's_Conception_of_Peace_and_its_Implications_for_a_Philosophy_of_Peace_Education/download.

Snauwaert, D. T. (2018a, May 15). *Power and a sustainable just peace: A response to Reardon's "On Frameworks and Purposes—Patriarchy is the Problem".*

Snauwaert, D. (2018b, September 29). *Revolutionary nonviolence and Rainer Forst's critical theory of justice.* Presentation, Peace and Justice Studies Association Conference, Philadelphia, PA.

Stanley, J. (2018). *How fascism works: The politics of us and them.* New York: Random House.

Synder, T. (2017). *On Tyranny: Twenty lessons from the twentieth century.* New York: Crown.

United Nations Human Rights Office of the High Commission. (1984). *Convention against torture and other cruel, inhuman or degrading treatment or punishment.* Retrieved February 18, 2019, from https://www.ohchr.org/en/professionalinterest/pages/cat.aspx.

Chapter 15
Reardon's Edu-learner Praxis: Educating for Political Efficacy and Social Transformation

Tony Jenkins

Betty Reardon emphasizes that the social and political purposes of peace education should be directed toward nurturing political efficacy for social transformation. What does this look like in practice? How might we actually go about educating for political efficacy without falling prey to pedagogies of indoctrination? Throughout her career, Reardon developed conceptual frameworks and explicitly and implicitly identified modes of learning and teaching practices that can be adapted to these purposes. Understanding these practices in theory is very different from being able to apply them. In this sense, developing the educational-political-efficacy of the teacher shares a dilemma with developing the political efficacy of the student: how do we facilitate transformative modes of learning that support the development of those inner capacities that are the basis for external action? How do we help learners step over the lines of knowing, to doing, to being? While many modes of transformative learning can be identified that may contribute to political engagement, no singular or combined pedagogical approach can assure effective outcomes. Political engagement is an active disposition. It is active, requiring ongoing ethical reflection connected to action. It is a disposition grounded by an effort to remain consistent between personal ethics and action. It is the pursuit of integrity. Political efficacy is thus tied to and made more consistent through a reflective praxis. As peace education is itself a politically efficacious act, preparation for transformative pedagogical practice should be similarly rooted in a reflective, teaching praxis. This praxis is manifested in Reardon's vision of teacher as 'edu-learner.' As a student, co-teacher and mentee of Betty Reardon, I've witnessed this praxis in action and have sought to make it my own. I hope the following reflections, culled from reading, learning and co-teaching with Betty, may provide insight and practical wisdom for other educators to develop their own reflective teaching praxis.

Dr. Tony Jenkins, Lecturer of Justice and Peace Studies at Georgetown University, Adjunct Professor of Peace Studies at University, Managing Director of the International Institute on Peace Education (IIPE), and Coordinator of the Global Campaign for Peace Education (GCPE), Washington, DC, USA; Email: jenkins@i-i-p-e.org.

© Springer Nature Switzerland AG 2019
D. T. Snauwaert (ed.), *Exploring Betty A. Reardon's Perspective on Peace Education*, Pioneers in Arts, Humanities, Science, Engineering, Practice 20, https://doi.org/10.1007/978-3-030-18387-5_15

15.1   Pursuing Transformation

> The purpose of learning, as peace education seeks to cultivate it, is transformative, drawing
> from within learners' capacities to envision and affect change and helping them develop the
> capacity to transform that existing system. The determining factor in most formal education
> is the intent of the educating agent. In learning it is the intent of the learner. The most
> influential factor in transformative learning is the conscious, reflective experience of the
> learner. (Reardon 2015a, p. 159)

Peace education is an ambitious political undertaking. It's overarching social
purposes are directed toward system change, shifting the needle from a culture of
violence to a culture of peace. Culturally embedded violence shapes individual
worldviews, which in-turn influence individual attitudes and actions. Individual
citizens are the micro units upon which all social systems are dependent. There can
be no effective or sustainable transformation of the system without also transforming individual actors.

> Among the changes that have to be made for the achievement of such a [transformative]
> shift, the most significant ones are within ourselves. The way which we move toward these
> inner changes, the way in which we envision and struggle for peace and try to construct that
> new paradigm, is the most essential means through which we will be enabled to make the
> larger structural changes required for a peace system. Thus the journey is really more
> personally meaningful to us than the destination. What we are about, on a day-to-day basis,
> is actually how we change paradigms. We must change ourselves and our immediate
> realities and relationships if we are to change our social structures and our patterns of
> thought. (Reardon 2015b, p. 112)

Process matters. How we come to inner change is as important as the resulting
outer change itself. It is through the struggle of seeking to change our everyday
reality that we begin to challenge patterns of thinking and action that lead to
paradigm shifts and system change. Engagement in everyday action for change is
premised upon establishing lifelong, reflective learning practices. Paulo Freire
viewed this as a form of "praxis: reflection and action upon the world in order to
transform it" (Freire 1970, p. 51). Learning for social change and political efficacy
cannot be narrowed to a singular pedagogical experience. The learning called for
should lead to the development of reflective practices that support a sustained,
lifelong praxis. It is learning that extends beyond the classroom or the particular
moment.

15.2   Edu-learning Our Way to Change

The development of such praxis is as relevant to the educator as it is to the student.
Reardon proposed that this praxis could be rooted in the development of an
'edu-learner' disposition - a disposition she actively adopted.

An edu-learner is "a practitioner/theorist whose primary activity is learning
while trying to help other people learn... The most fundamental aspect of the

edu-learning process is the role of the teacher as learner and the view of learning as a lifelong process of experience reflected upon and integrated into new learning in an organic, cyclical mode, a mode that is conscious of the relations between the inner experience and the outer realities" (Reardon 1998, p. 47).

Teaching, as an edu-learner, is a process of reflective learning. Edu-learning as a teaching praxis, also requires a meta reflective practice upon the various dimensions and relationships at play in the teaching and learning processes – within and between the teacher, the student, the institution of education, and society at large. Teachers minds are deeply colonized by the educational paradigm in which they are shaped and by the spaces and institutions in which they teach.

> Without such reflection [of deep inner questioning that is essential to personal change], learning cannot be fully integrated into the thinking and worldviews that condition our personal interpretations and assessments, from which we make the choices that lead us to action. (Reardon 2015b, p. 117)

An edu-learning praxis is rooted and nurtured via intentional reflective practices. Co-teaching, a practice I engaged in with Betty on many occasions, is a particularly democratic mode of transformative learning that supports and fosters communal pedagogical reflection (among the educators) and models communal reflective learning for and among the students. Developing a reflective praxis, independent of other learners, limits the holistic repertoire of questions and queries necessary for critical reflection on one's reality. Co-teaching and co-learning support consideration of multiple points of view. This dialogical, communal approach to reflective inquiry invites internal worldview deliberation that is less likely to happen in isolated reflection. Co-teaching with Betty is an authentic, dialogical experience. It begins with a collaborative, deliberative, intentional and reflective process of co-planning that includes (1) identifying the social purposes the learning is intended to contribute to, that are rooted in the realities of the learning community, the institutions in which the learning takes place, and society at large; (2) discerning the educational goals and focused learning objectives to be pursued; and (3) designating the contents and modes of learning most relevant to the goals and objectives. These "best laid plans" are not meant to be prescriptive, but rather assure intentional reflection in curricular planning. The real fun begins with the teaching itself:

> The true art of teaching lies in the capacity of the teacher to draw out the intent of the learner, to bring it to the consciousness of the individual learner and co-learners in the learning setting, as well as that of the teacher. (Reardon 2015a, p. 159)

> Peace educators seek to devise pedagogies that enable them to draw out the learners' intentions, then to discern the point of engagement at which the learner can undertake critical reflection on the subject matter as the basis on which to enter into dialogue with others for shared critique and communal inquiry into responses to the problems being addressed. (Reardon 2015a, p. 160)

Drawing forth or eliciting the intention of the learner is made possible through varying modes of reflection on experience. Critical consciousness requires intentional reflection on reality – explored via both internal and communal inquiry.

Hearing others' reflections on reality can support an individual's own pursuit of internal critical reflection. My early co-teaching experiences with Betty were intimidating, due in large part to worldview assumptions I held about learning and education. When Betty would ask for my input, I responded with trepidation. My formative education trained me to meet such questions with anxiety, assuming judgment would be passed based upon my responses. Did I possess the correct knowledge according to authorities? Am I making the correct interpretations? Is my thinking naïve? How we acknowledge our students' responses to our inquiries can easily lead to existential anxiety. Students trained in a hierarchal knowledge paradigm are tacitly aware that any response they provide to an inquiry from an academic authority is a reflection on their self as rooted in their experience of the world. If the authority responds in the negative, it can be invalidating of existence and can turn-off a student's desire to learn. Betty's responses were more than validating; they were the beginning of a dialogue between co-learners. It became quickly evident that her reflections upon my reflections led to new learnings for us both.

Edu-learning also requires engaging in a meta-reflection of our roles as educators and how these roles shape and inform learning outcomes. How do our general attitudes toward learning and teaching shape how we show up in the classroom? Are we modelling reflection and learning or are we reproducing hierarchies of knowledge? Are we eliciting learning from students, or are we feeding our egos by seeking to impart our knowledge upon them? Edu-learning draws upon elicitive learning culled through reflective inquiry and supported by reflective and empathic listening to discern the intentions of the autonomous learner. The edu-learner uses these dialogic methodologies to facilitate subjective teacher-student encounters, cull interpretations of a student's worldview, and to support the learner in making their own interpretations.

In nurturing my own edu-learner disposition, I've sought to develop a praxis rooted in intentional reflection upon the many relationships in the teaching and learning process. My reflections have led to the development of a framework I utilize in the preparation of educators in the intentional application of transformative peace pedagogy. I describe this framework as a "Pedagogy of Relationships." Initially developed via my work with the International Institute on Peace Education, and later refined in my doctoral dissertation (Jenkins 2015), the Pedagogy of Relationships establishes an inquiry framework for considering six fundamental relationships in the teaching and learning process through which the values and principles of peace can be modeled and nurtured. These include: (1) the relationship between the teacher and the student, (2) the relationship of the student to the self, (3) the relationship of the student to existing knowledge, (4) the relationship of the student to emergent knowledge (or creation of new knowledge), (5) the relationship of the student to others, and (6) the relationship of the student to society (the world). Developing a conscious and reflective awareness of the ways in which we enter into each of these relationships, and how the nature of these relationships shapes to a significant degree student outcomes and agency, is critical to efficacious and ethical peacelearning pedagogy.

15.3 Pedagogies for Political Engagement

Political agency is generated internally. We take external action upon those things that we hold dear and meaningful. Justice and peace, learned as abstract concepts and goals, will not be acted upon. Peacelearning pedagogy is pursued through inquiry that connects abstract concepts to the learner's experience of the world. The first step in meaning making is asking how is this issue or problem of injustice relevant to my experience of the world? We amend this inquiry by adding an ethical reflection: what is my role in creating and sustaining this problem, and what is my responsibility to address it? Political agency is further premised upon playing an active role in creating knowledge and the solutions to problems. If learners are able to imagine how their actions contribute to the solution of problems, they are more likely to take those actions. The pedagogical framework developed by Betty via her work with the World Order Models Project establishes a praxis model for a pedagogy of engagement:

> Each cycle [of learning experience] begins and ends with confronting reality and moves through phases, which merge one into the other, of capturing visions, formulating images, articulating preferences, constructing models, assessing possibilities, planning policies, taking action, reflecting on and evaluating change, and, again, confronting reality. (Reardon 2015c, p. 106)

This particular learning cycle demonstrates the future orientation of peace education. Such learning is pursued through "authentic inquiry," a mode of inquiry in which there are no predetermined answers, and teacher and student pursue the inquiry together.

> Thus, a primary mode of peace education should be authentic inquiry. Such a method would be derived from posing of queries, which would perform three functions: reveal apparent obstacles to peace, open avenues for exploring the causes of and alternative approaches to transcending the obstacles, and assess the alternatives according to criteria which would result in the most life enhancing choices. (Reardon 2015b, p. 117)

Reardon's more recent pedagogical scholarship identifies three modes of reflective inquiry, critical/analytic, moral/ethical, and contemplative/ruminative (Reardon 2013). Together, these modes of reflective inquiry can operate a reflexive learning praxis that can be applied to formal and non-formal learning for peace and social change. Critical/analytic reflection supports the development of a critical consciousness (Freire's 'conscientization' or 'conscientização') that is necessary for disrupting worldview assumptions critical to personal change (Mezirow, Boulding) and political efficacy. This mode of reflection also invites initial consideration of alternatives and approaches to change. Moral and ethical reflection invites consideration of a range of responses to a social dilemma raised during critical/analytic reflection. It invites the learner to consider an appropriate ethical/moral response. Contemplative/ruminative reflection provides a futures orientation, requiring the learner to consider how one's response might be received by others. Amongst other intentions, this latter form of reflection also invites the learner to consider how they might change their self. These modes of reflective inquiry, pursued first sequentially (and later adapted to a circular praxis) establish an intentional framework for transformative curricular design for political agency.

I've adapted these modes of reflective inquiry as a framework and pedagogical sequence for teach-ins and other non-formal political learning fora. One practical way I've applied this framework is via a peace education seminar I teach at Georgetown University that culminates in a teach-in experience designed and facilitated by the students. The teach-in is an opportunity to apply pedagogical learnings in a political forum with their peers. The holism of the reflective inquiry framework is applied by the students to guide peers through a multi-stage process of personal change that begins with critical consciousness connected to personal experience. This consciousness is deepened by reflection on more preferred alternatives, personal responsibility, and ethical duty. The final call to consciousness is a reflection upon personal integrity: how am I to be in the world based upon this new awareness? In facilitating this inquiry, the students have adopted an edu-learner disposition, modeling humility, reflective listening, and co-learning that is instrumental to facilitating learning for political and social change. The learning with and from one another is itself a preferred political process.

15.4   The Classroom as a Mirror of Society

The classroom conjures up images of symbolic, institutionalized power. Symbolic assumptions about instruction, knowledge, power, and social hierarchy are shaped by our images of neatly ordered desks and a teacher standing in front of a chalkboard. The classroom is an imagined space, based on a social invention, created by those in power who envisioned formal education as a socializing tool to prepare citizens to participate in a world designed by others. Peace education calls for a different vision, one in which the classroom is seen as a space for freedom pursued through open and authentic inquiry. A space where students find meaning and are invited to co-create their future. We need a paradigm shift in the classroom that supports a shift to a peace paradigm outside the classroom.

As edu-learners, what we are about on a day-to-day basis in the classroom, is how we support and facilitate that paradigm shift. The disposition that we take as educators in the classroom is political. It is the modeling of a political relationship that is extended outside of the classroom. As such, we need to be ever mindful of how our teaching praxis informs and shapes political externalities.

Education is our most political institution. Regardless of its form and content, it shapes political agency. The current paradigm fosters political complacency. We can challenge that norm. Thomas Jefferson advocated that "wherever the people are well informed they can be trusted with their own government; that whenever things get so far wrong as to attract their notice, they may be relied on to set them to rights" (Jefferson 1789). Jefferson got it partially right. Being well informed is insufficient for the call to action necessary to challenge injustice. Justice and freedom is dependent upon an education that fosters critical consciousness through open authentic inquiry. This is a vision of education that was likely even too dangerous for Jefferson's established goals of governance.

I think we are all familiar with the metaphor of the classroom as a mirror of society. While this may be factually correct, it is metaphorically and pedagogically limiting. The image we see when we look in the mirror is flat and two-dimensional. It is a subjective image of how we see the world in the current moment; it is not an image of what is preferred or can be. We tend to dote on this present image and obsess with its flaws, making it very difficult to see what's beyond those imperfections. The educator as edu-learner looks in the mirror and considers the reflected image's subjectivity, as well as their own. Then, with intention and awareness that a more authentic view of the world can only emerge from bringing these subjective realities into relationship, the edu-learner engages their self in authentic inquiry and a new, never before seen image begins to emerge. This is the learning that the edu-learner models for her pupils, her co-learners who are equally engaged in shaping new, collective images of a preferred future. This is the politically efficacious learning of the transformative edu-learner, and one of the greatest lessons I learned from Betty Reardon, my mentor, friend and co-teacher.

References

Boulding, K. (1956). *The image: Knowledge in life and society.* Ann Arbor, MI: University of Michigan Press.

Freire, P. (1970). *Pedagogy of the oppressed.* New York, NY: Herder and Herder.

Jefferson, T. (1789). *Thomas Jefferson to Richard Price.* Retrieved from https://www.loc.gov/exhibits/jefferson/jeffrep.html#060.

Jenkins, T. (2015). *Theoretical analysis and practical possibilities for transformative, comprehensive peace education.* Thesis for the degree of Philosphiae Doctor, Norwegian University of Science and Technology. Trondheim, Norway: NTNU.

Mezirow, J. (1991). *Transformative dimensions of adult learning.* San Francisco, CA: Jossey-Bass.

Reardon, B. (1988). *Comprehensive peace education: Educating for global responsibility.* New York, NY: Teachers College Press.

Reardon, B. (2013). Mediating the barricades: Concerns, cautions, and possibilities for peace education for political efficacy. In P. Trifonas & B. Wright (Eds.), *Critical peace education: Difficult dialogues* (pp. 1–28). New York: Springer.

Reardon, B. (2015a). Human rights learning: Pedagogies and politics of peace. In B. Reardon & D. Snauwaert (Eds.), *Betty A. Reardon: A pioneer in education for peace and human rights* (pp. 145–164). New York: Springer.

Reardon, B. (2015b). Toward a paradigm of peace. In B. Reardon & D. Snauwaert (Eds.), *Betty A. Reardon: A pioneer in education for peace and human rights* (pp. 109–120). New York: Springer.

Reardon, B. (2015c). The fundamental purposes of a pedagogy of peace. In B. Reardon & D. Snauwaert (Eds.), *Betty A. Reardon: A pioneer in education for peace and human rights* (pp. 93–108). New York: Springer.

Chapter 16
Practicing Peace Education: Learning Peace and Teaching Peace with Betty Reardon

Ian Gibson

In the early 2000s a friend suggested that I enroll in a peace education class in Tokyo organized by Teachers College Columbia University. I was interested in improving my teaching skills and saw this as an opportunity to possibly expand my teaching scope. I had little or no knowledge of peace education but was intrigued by the premise outlined in the course handout. The course was modular, including perceptions of poverty and development, education for peace in a gender perspective, peace education perspectives on security, human rights and dignity, education for a culture of peace and justice, conflict resolution, and an introduction to the concepts of violence and non-violence. The courses were taught mainly by Professor Betty Reardon along with a group of peace educators she had assembled, among them, Kozue Akibayashi, Tony Jenkins, Michelle Milner and Janet Gerson.

I soon discovered that Betty's style was very unlike other teachers I had encountered. For one she hardly lectured (although occasionally we did press her) but insisted on group work based around homework, readings, and set "questions of inquiry" on the readings for discussion. She would then clarify our discussion results by writing them out on a white board, all the while elucidating comments and constantly challenging the students to critically engage with the tasks. Betty was very focused on 'systems', for example in our module centered on Human Security, she led us through a series of questions such as "What should a security system do? Is it necessary? Do we need it? Is it Just? Does the system meet the basic needs of the people? Is equality assured by the proposed system and does it protect the environment?" We were also repeatedly asked to examine our own values in relation to issues. Focusing on values allowed a building of consensus of opinion. With many differing nationalities in the room it was a way of examining "the other" and realizing, as Betty was wont to stress, that difference is just that, different, and not something to be feared or ridiculed.

Ian Gibson, Associate Professor at Kyoto University of Foreign Studies and Director of the Kyoto University of Foreign Studies JUEMUN (Japan University English Model United Nations) program, Kyoto, Japan; Email: irgibson12@yahoo.com.

© Springer Nature Switzerland AG 2019
D. T. Snauwaert (ed.), *Exploring Betty A. Reardon's Perspective on Peace Education*, Pioneers in Arts, Humanities, Science, Engineering, Practice 20, https://doi.org/10.1007/978-3-030-18387-5_16

Betty was very much driven by what she explained was the Freirian concept of "learning from the learner", adapted from Freire's seminal text *Pedagogy of the Oppressed* (Freire 1970/2006) where Freire as a literacy teacher discovered through his work with so called 'peasants' that their insights were in turn illuminating to Freire. Reardon insisted that classes should be learner centered where the teacher should speak the least and students should speak the most. We all have something to offer and share with others, she said, and our voices are of equal importance. Her dislike of debate and competition meant that the classroom atmosphere was very relaxed, and we worked together in what she termed "mini societies" in our ever-changing discussion groups, engaged in problem solving, role-play and simulations, and poster presentations. Again and again she would underline our 'intentionality' as educators to "surface the possibilities" in our own classes, our goals being to "kindle compassion", "cultivate mutual respect", "host open mindedness", "advance clarity of thought" and "empower knowledge in people to exercise their own rights and responsibilities", all this through eliciting responses by inquiry and getting students to recognize their own capacities (Betty was very fond of the word 'capacities'). As we grew as peace actors, so we grew involved in capacity building, both for ourselves and for others.

In these classes, and often when we went out to bars and restaurants after the classes, I was very much taken by her good nature and humor. War, organized and sporadic violence, patriarchal systems and a myriad of human rights abuses are not the most light of subjects to deal with but Betty insisted always on a 'rationale', a reasoned approach, and one that avoided over-emotional responses and struck at the heart of the matter. This of course was critical thinking at its most exact and this was Betty's expertise as an educator, to guide us and show how one could pare apart problems, examine the specific details and construct reasoned solutions to extremely complex issues. She built ideas through structured frameworks, piece by piece and showed us the way to construct viable alternatives ("multiple alternatives") to imprecise and ill-informed systems of control. At no point did we ever feel as a class that we were being talked down to, or our voice was not important and that we had nothing to contribute, something that an upbringing in the British education system had left in me. Once during a Sunday afternoon (the classes were mostly held over weekends in Tokyo) a colleague, let's call him Phil, in a very broad New York accent responded to something that Betty was clarifying for him in front of the class as "Is that what I was trying to say?" and I just loved the fact that her fierce intellect could elucidate such a warm reaction and raise a laugh. Laughter is a wonderful alleviation to anxiety (as is the chocolate that she used to pass around when we were flagging!) and is so important in establishing a safe learning environment. Indeed, she always taught with a twinkle in her eye, something I never forget when teaching my own classes.

Over the course of the three or so years I spent attending her classes in Tokyo I was able to develop my own particular skills as an educator. One key point that Betty never stopped reminding us was that even though we were dealing with peace education issues, the principles of peace education practices could be extended to any classroom. That is, even if one was teaching a history class or a civic engagement class or even a mathematics class, the same teaching styles learnt in peace education could be used. Problem solving, discussion groups, clarification of issues, facilitating instead of directly leading a class, setting an example of how one would want to be treated as a learner ("teaching by example" was her expression) and generating a classroom atmosphere that was conducive to elucidating the best responses at that particular moment. Another of her teaching points that stuck with me was that facilitators should try to give "questions not statements", critical education is important not for the opinion being put forward but by asking a simple question such as 'How?' After all, once students are engaged, the higher the engagement, the more the involvement in the transformation of the person and the changing of the process. She constantly told us to "challenge the attitude" and of course she was asking us to do just that to ourselves, to challenge our attitude, to examine our own beliefs and to reassess our own opinions in light of the data and documents and readings we were presented with, stressing that when reading anything we should "Have a conversation with the text" and constantly challenge the author's discourse with question such as "Is this right?" or "Do I believe this?"

It was only much later that I started to see strong links in her theory and pedagogy of peace with an often-neglected section of ancient Graeco-Roman philosophy known as the Stoa. Of course, Betty was influenced by Dewey and Freire but her methods of inquiry, her cosmopolitan beliefs, and stress on truth, tolerance, courage, justice, wisdom and value ethics rightfully travelled far back to the universal truths promoted by Socrates and his predecessors in the Stoa.

The Stoa took its name from the *Stoa Poikile* (or "Painted Porch") where its founder, Zeno of Citium (c. 301 BCE) discussed his teachings. Stoicism then differed from its modern understanding of "small 's' stoicism" – the "stiff upper lip" form. It emphasized virtue ethics, where virtue, or "excellence of character" (following on from Socrates' teaching) was the highest good (http://www.plato. stanford.edu/entries/stoicism/). Later teachers, such as the ex-slave Epictetus (c. 55–135 CE) during the Roman period of Stoicism, would stress our role as social actors and our place in a common universal humanity (plato.stanford.edu/entries/ Epictetus) and urge us to strongly examine our own cognitive processes instant by instant and be aware of how these 'impressions' were key to our experience of the world (these days alluded to as 'mindfulness'). Epictetus believed "when we do things for the good of the polity, we are actually (perhaps indirectly) bene-fitting ourselves" (Pigliucci 2017, p. 59). Another of the Stoa theorists, Hierocles (active around 430 CE) also proposed centering ourselves in a system of concentric circles that linked us to others in the universe where one who endeavors to conduct themselves correctly in each connection merges the circles into one center. In so doing this was one of the first examples of cosmopolitan thought, or that of adopting a "citizen of the world" perspective (see also Pigliucci, ibid., 59–60). Betty emphasized the processes of 'implicit' and 'ex-plicit' knowledge in her own teaching practice and theories, constantly asking us to evaluate and examine our perspectives of our world, and once one read the teachings and theories of the Stoa, be they those of Seneca (c. 4 BCE–65 CE), for his sins the tutor of the Tyrant Nero, Epictetus, or the Roman

Emperor, Marcus Aurelius (121–180 CE) one is again and again struck by the parallels between what Betty was teaching and the social truths of cooperation and peaceful existence these ancient scholars were putting forward (even Marcus!).

Indeed, Seneca's *De Ira (On Anger)* (www.sophia-project.org) is one of the most powerful treatises on understanding and combating violence ever, and once read one will understand just how anger and violence arises and how it stems from rational ignorance (which makes the perpetrator(s) irrevocably, morally, suspect). Seneca like the other Stoics, following Socrates, realized that people commit violence through ignorance, i.e. a lack of rationality or wisdom. In other words, no one willingly does wrong, it is their ignorance or misguided perception of the 'good' that leads them to do vice. Hannah Arendt brilliantly identified this in her coverage of the trial of Eichmann in Jerusalem (Arendt 1994) where Eichmann, a key mechanic in the Final Solution, was seemingly unable to grasp his complicity and remained oblivious to the facts presented. The Stoics reiterated time and again the role of reason and rationality in our thinking, much as Betty did in her own teaching, believing that if one stripped everything back to the rational soul this would provide considered solutions to any problematic; in the words of Marcus Aurelius, Book 5, 20, "An obstacle in a given path becomes an advance" (Hammond 2006, p. 42) the obstacle becomes the way.

Turning from what Reardon taught to how I used her teachings in practice, I recently developed a peace education class in Kyoto and will now outline what I believe are its salient points taken from Reardon's instruction. Choosing issues for discussion in a peace and conflict class is challenging. The world offers up many areas of concern on micro and macro levels. Often it is best to jump right in with the merry issues of war and peace as an opener for day one. Discussion questions in the first class could be general: What is understood by peace? If someone said to you that Japan is still a country of negative peace what do you think that means? What do you understand by violence? What forms of violence can you identify? Is war inevitable? Can you say why violence occurs? By what means is violence resolved? What forms of non-violence are you aware of? Is non-violence as a concept, viable? And so on. By such inquiry the facilitator can swiftly gauge "the knowns and the unknowns", what areas are needed to be covered.

Another way to start a new class with a bang is to show a controversial image. Reardon often stressed the concept of "constructive controversy" that is a guided discussion based on an area of controversy. One image I often show to an opening class is the celebrated frontispiece of Thomas Hobbes' *Leviathan* (Hobbes 1651/ 1968). The image, composed of bodies forming the sovereign state, has innumerable possibilities for questions of 'othering', patriotism, nationalism and peace and conflict, such as, why do states form? What is meant by soft and hard power? What is the social contract in the state? What keeps societies stable or why do societies fragment?

In the first class in a peace education driven course it is also important to establish and clarify (Reardon again) the expectations of the facilitator. Because peace education is inclusive in practice, the first class must demonstrate its cosmopolitan underpinnings and how these are crucial for the foundations of cosmopolitan well-being in our world. In teaching peace and conflict studies through peace education a certain amount of advocacy (Betty explained this as "gentle persuasion") comes into play and the facilitator must be extremely careful, particularly in the early stages of the instruction that certain criteria are understood. First, when the matter of values are examined, especially in a class that is comprised of many different cultures such as the one under discussion, different values must be treated as just that, different. This, in other words, is an explication of cosmopolitanism. Kwame Anthony Appiah of Princeton University, for example, sees cosmopolitanism beginning with the essential idea rooted in the human community as in national communities of the need to develop ways of coexistence, based on dialogue. Appiah views this idea as being the oldest sense of conversation; one that fosters the art of living together and in turn acknowledges a mutual association with one another (Appiah, in Gibson 2011, p. 88). Appiah has investigated in detail the concepts of cosmopolitanism, isolating key influences such as toleration, a system of values and a respect for difference, arriving at a succinct summary that cosmopolitanism is "universality plus difference", that is a moral duty to the protection of others directed by the consideration and acknowledgement of the inherent biological and social constructions of each person (Appiah, quoted in Gibson, ibid.). Because the learning of peace encourages critical inquiry and discussion the above points must be clearly prescribed to the class before any active discussion takes place, underlining that one might not always agree but the learning objective is to see difference as just that, different, and not tied with a value judgment of it being categorically wrong.

So, in a one-semester course what issues can be explored? Because this is a peace and conflict course offered in a Japanese University the A-bomb attacks and Japan's wartime record will probably be addressed at some point. Now this offers up a delicate matter, one that calls for extremely sensitive handling when presenting the issue, because the subject can often form a dichotomy of opinion between Japanese students and overseas students, particularly participating Chinese or Korean students. One nuanced study by the Japanese historian Asada (1998) used primary sources that documented the discussions in the Japanese Emperor's underground bunker to terminate the Pacific War at the time of the two A-bomb attacks in late summer 1945. The discussions took part between the "peace party" consisting of Emperor Hirohito himself, the Lord Keeper of the Privy Seal, the Foreign and Navy Ministers, and (with some reservations) the Prime Minister Suzuki Kantaro who were strongly opposed around the table by the military chiefs, the Army Minister Anami Korechika, the Chief of the Army General Staff Umezu Yoshijiro, and Chief of the Naval General Staff Toyoda Soemu, all of whom refused to capitulate insisting on a decisive homeland battle against invading American forces (Anami 1998, p. 478). A careful reading of the paper reveals the all too human decisions behind armed conflict and the consequences of these decisions. Because peace education stresses a balanced critique of issues, Asada's paper can be juxtaposed with an article written by Henry Stimson (1985) in which the former Secretary of War under Presidents Roosevelt and Truman gave the decision to spare Kyoto (where this course is taught) and approve four other targets for the A-Bomb including the cities of Hiroshima and Nagasaki. Stimson's action, influenced by a prewar visit to Kyoto, poignantly illustrates the human face behind extreme decisions in conflict, often overlooked in somewhat broad statements in International Relations studies regarding war. To which the caveat can be carefully added when reading Asada and Stimson's accounts that a past event is just that, past. Nothing can change the event, but in this moment the important point is to critically analyze the causes, actions taken, and consequences of those actions, and to identify what can be learned from these fateful decisions.

The last point incidentally, is also a key point in Reardon's instruction when facilitating a peace education class. Because sensitive issues are raised, and often students (especially on a "hot topic" such as the deployment of the A-bomb in Japan or the continued U.S. military presence in Okinawa) will vociferously and sometimes forcefully argue points, it is a very good policy to defuse potentially hot arguments by asking very calmly and non confrontationally, "That's an interesting point, would anyone else care to comment?" or by giving a time out by asking students to reflect on what could we learn from the matter under discussion, setting this as an assignment perhaps. These moves also display a very practical demonstration of conflict resolution if handled correctly, the right moment for a "time out". With any issue entailing peace and conflict it is often how the subject is presented that can influence its outcome. Again, gentle persuasion is sometimes necessary in order to make sure that both sides of a subject are fully examined. Thesis, antithesis and synthesis are the order of the day in peace education. Students are instructed that all opinions and judgments are valid, but they remain opinions and judgments, and therefore must be carefully measured and examined and supported by careful analytical reasoning and evidence.

As with Asada's paper above, carefully selecting relevant papers and sources are essential. An issue that is rarely explored in peace and conflict studies is a gender perspective to peace. The recent interest in Human Security, although contested, has allowed such a perspective to be discussed (see Gibson/Reardon 2007). Japan was one of the main financial contributors to the Commission on Human Security (CHS) chaired by Sadako Ogata and Amartya Sen (established in January, 2000) which of course becomes of relevance to a class in Japan, and Human Security is an excellent way to explore the myriad of concerns that affect both women and men on our pale blue dot. For example, the issue of security affects migration, post war recovery, food security, health security, education for the girl child, environmental sustainability (see also the UN Sustainable Development Goals [SDGs]) and economic and human development. The United Nations has many documents detailing Human Security and gender issues and gender security such as Security Council Resolution 1325 (October, 2000) and the Convention on the Elimination of All Forms of Discrimination against Women (December, 1979) which are pertinent and relevant to the study of gender perspectives. Another extremely good source is the Hague Appeal for Peace's *The Hague agenda for peace and justice in the 21st century*, arising from the efforts of 10,000 conference attendees at The Hague Appeal for Peace, May 1999. Both the CHS and the Hague Agenda are very useful for student presentations and discussion where students can be asked to present on these topics and also set the discussion questions. Often students when presenting will be asked to include questions in their presentations that allow pause for thought as well as open up discussion to the floor, thus avoiding a rather dry non-interactive presentation. Again, it is essential that interaction is foremost in these classes and that everyone in the class is able to feel involved while gently ensuring that while all comments are welcome no student is allowed to dominate proceedings.

Even with large classes of over a hundred students it is still possible to engage in effective discussion. A simple rule is to group students randomly in numbers no less than three and no more than six at the beginning of every class. For one thing students get the opportunity to mix with students they otherwise would never have met and placing Japanese students with overseas students together encourages them to open up rather more than usual. Japanese students are often (in my opinion) rather reticent when placed with overseas students so one way to overcome this is to ask students to of course make sure that all readings are completed before the class and for the facilitator to set a list of questions to accompany the readings to be also completed before class. That way all students are prepared for the class and have their reading responses ready for class discussion (peer pressure is gently encouraged here). Then each group can prepare its collective responses and present them to the class. The facilitator collects these responses and clarifies and paraphrases them on a board (old school but very effective) and often these responses will form new areas of inquiry. Again, Freire's idea of "Learning from the Learner" proves a very applicable method for making the classes inclusive and productive. It is often also pertinent to stress (*pace* Reardon) that the study groups are in effect mini societies that are negotiating and exploring their way through problems and at the same time students have to remain respectful of the differing opinions of others in the group.

From some of the points made above it can be seen that Peace Education methodology is very much a practical approach to teaching peace and conflict studies and that the teaching and interactive nature of the class should demonstrate the *act* of peace, that is, exemplary ethical and moral treatment of fellow human beings and the external world. Reardon has made this adequately clear in her teacher training classes over the years and echoes consummate teachers like John Dewey and the Stoic ex-slave Epictetus who through his *Discourses* (Dobbin 2008) stressed the importance of vigilant ethical practice over mere reading: walk it like you talk it. To elaborate, one can teach human rights but one has also to practice human rights, one can also teach the issues surrounding nationalism and patriotism (areas of key interest and discussion in Japan) but these are of no use unless one is also prepared to examine one's own attitudes and beliefs carefully, and from moment to moment, in class and outside, demonstrate the principles of peace education in practice: that of universal tolerance, universal human dignity and universal moral inclusion. As Reardon writes: "What more comprehensive definition of peace education could we offer than learning to learn about, and functioning in and with complexity, so as to enhance the richness and diversity of life" (Reardon in Reardon/Snauwaert 2015, p. 116).

16.1 Conclusion

Reardon's ground-breaking work with Teachers College Columbia University produced some of the most effective ways that peace education is now taught and understood. Interactive classes are key. Reardon was (and still is for that matter) very unequivocal on this point. In her teacher trainer seminars, she purposely avoided lecturing, (she of course recognized its place) preferring to elicit comments from students and use them to further the discussion. She followed Freire in overriding the traditional "mug and jug" (Freire, ibid.) of simply pouring education into the student and explicitly allowed the class to actively engage in a subject, suggesting multiple responses to a set of problematics. As a result, students learnt to be aware both of the inclusive nature of peace education and aware that they are active contributors to the process of problem solving and peaceful resolve. This remains a key factor in peace education's instruction of peace and conflict studies: fostering ability to resolve conflict rationally, constructively, and non-violently.

References

Arendt, H. (1994). *Eichmann in Jerusalem: A report on the banality of evil.* New York, NY: Penguin Books.

Asada, S. (1998). The shock of the atomic bomb and Japan's decision to surrender: A reconsideration. *Pacific Historical Review, 67*(4), 477–512.

Commission on Human Security. (2003). *Human security now: Protecting and empowering people.*

Epictetus. (2008). *Discourses and selected writings* (R. Dobbin, Trans.). London: Penguin Classics.

Freire, P. (1970/2006). *Pedagogy of the oppressed.* New York: Continuum Press.

Gibson, I. R. (2011). Human Security: A framework for peace constructs, gendered perspectives and cosmopolitan security. *Journal of Peace, Conflict and Development, 7*, 85–101.

Gibson, I. R., & Reardon, B. A. (2007). Human security: Towards gender inclusion. In G. Shani, S. Makoto, & M. Pasha (Eds.), *Protecting human security in a post 9/11 world: Critical and global insights* (pp. 50–63). London: Palgrave Macmillan.

Hague Appeal for Peace. (n.d.). *The Hague agenda for peace and justice in the 21st century.* UN Ref A/54/98.

Hobbes, T. (1651/1968). *Leviathan.* Baltimore: Penguin Books.

Marcus Aurelius. (2008). *Meditations* (M. Hammond, Trans.). London: Penguin Classics.

Pigliucci, M. (2017). *How to be a Stoic: Ancient wisdom for modern living.* London: Rider Books.

Reardon, B. A., & Snauwaert, D. T. (2015). *Betty A. Reardon: A pioneer in education for peace and human rights.* Cham: Springer International Publishing.

Reardon, B. A., & Cabezudo, A. (2002). *Learning to abolish war: Teaching for a culture of peace.* New York: Hague Appeal for Peace.

Reardon, B. A. (2001). *Education for a culture of peace in a gender perspective.* Paris: UNESCO.

Seneca *De Ira (On Anger).* (n.d.). Retrieved from http://www.sophia-project.org/uploads/1/3/9/5/13955288/seneca_anger.pdf.

Stanford Encyclopedia of Philosopphy. (2017). *Epictetus.* Retrieved from https://plato.stanford.edu/entries/epictetus/#LifWor.

Stanford Encyclopedia of Philospophy. (2018). *Stoicism.* Retrieved from https://plato.stanford.edu/entries/stoicism/.

Stimson, H. L., & Truman, H. S., (1947). The decision to use the atomic bomb. *Bulletin of the Atomic Scientists, 3*(2), 37–67.

UN General Assembly. (1997). *Convention on the elimination of all forms of discrimination against women.* Retrieved from http://www.un.org/womenwatch/daw/cedaw/.

UN Security Council. (1997, October). *Security Council Resolution 1325 on women, peace and security.* Retrieved from http://www.un.org/womenwatch/osagi/cdrom/documents/Background_Paper_Africa.pdf.

Chapter 17
Shared Reflections and Learnings from Betty Reardon—Action Planning Models: National and International Partnerships in Asia

Kathy R. Matsui

The minds of the leaders of the world are set in thinking that national security is about being equipped with military arms and strength, that violence can be prevented by violence, and that violence can be resolved by violence. But is that so? Does it really work that way?

Reardon (1988) contended that the ultimate goal of peace educators as global citizens is to preserve this beautiful earth and all living creatures. War is devastating to human beings and to the environment, and yet nations have failed to find alternatives to war. Peace education programs endeavor to construct a mechanism of prevention rather than preemption. The philosophy of peace education is to educate and transform the social structure of society which would include the benefit of the less privileged. The outcome of the education may not resolve the tense situations in war zones of the world, but it may be that education for the young is to realize that every individual has a choice to resolve conflict nonviolently and that choice rests upon us. We can choose to have war, but we can also choose to have dialogue and transform structures without violence. We can dismantle the structure of the society we live in to make it a safe and secure place where we can enjoy peace and adequate standards of living. Transformation needs to be done at all levels of every institution, from the individual to the highest level of government.

This chapter introduces peace education activities conducted in Asia as well as the peace building aspirations sought after for the future of Northeast Asia. As the result of the many years of experience with the International Institute on Peace Education (IIPE) and shared reflections and learnings from Betty Reardon, it is clear that there is a need for strategic ways of educating for a culture of peace.

From this experience we came to understand that peace education is a personal teleology, a personal lifework. This chapter pursues the significant impacts and how

Kathy R. Matsui, Professor at the Department of Global Citizenship Studies, Seisen University, Tokyo, Japan; Email: matsuikathy@hotmail.com.

© Springer Nature Switzerland AG 2019
D. T. Snauwaert (ed.), *Exploring Betty A. Reardon's Perspective on Peace Education*, Pioneers in Arts, Humanities, Science, Engineering, Practice 20, https://doi.org/10.1007/978-3-030-18387-5_17

a peacebuilding program can transform the negative feelings and mindsets of the people of Northeast Asia towards the Japanese people and government.

There is a need to identify peaceful methods for establishing a foundation for reconciliation and diplomatic relations, and peace education can be this peaceful method. The issues presented here will first introduce the vision for a culture of peace that came out of Reardon's peace education theory and methods; and describe what Northeast Peacebuilding Institute (NARPI) is and the purpose of its establishment. The chapter further discusses in what ways NARPI is designed to educate peace leaders to build a culture of peace and to transform the potential sources of conflict in Northeast Asia into a resourceful region of collaboration and peace.

17.1 Vision for a Culture of Peace

The United Nations defines the Culture of Peace as "a set of values, attitudes, modes of behavior and ways of life that reject violence and prevent conflicts by tackling their root causes to solve problems through dialogue and negotiation among individuals, groups and nations" (UN Resolutions A/RES/52/13: Culture of Peace and A/RES/53/243, Declaration and Programme of Action on a Culture of Peace). In this world, where violence still prevails, there is a need for education that teaches the citizens of the world to achieve a culture of peace.

In 1899, like-minded people who believed that peace was possible met at the Hague, Netherlands. A hundred years later in 1999, hundreds of peace educators, peace builders, NGO's and lawyers working for peace gathered at The Hague and discussed how peace can be achieved and came up with what is now known as The Hague Agenda. Among the many action plans on the agenda, peace education was one of the topmost priorities. Soon afterwards, the Global Campaign for Peace Education was launched. The campaign stated:

> A Culture of peace will be achieved when citizens of the world understand global problems, have the skills to resolve conflict constructively, know and live by international standards of human rights, gender and racial equality appreciate cultural diversity (which includes various faith and spiritual foundations) respect the integrity of the Earth. (The Hague Appeal for Peace Global Campaign for Peace Education Campaign Statement)

Such positively impactful learning is not possible without peace education programs. Thus, exploring the process to overcome post war historical trauma to the victims and atrocities of the Japanese military through peace education and leadership is presented here. Furthermore, in order to prevent such atrocities from happening again in history, an effort to transform the mindset of maintaining war as a lawful way to achieve national security, to focusing on the needs of human security. Reardon (2010) argues that "If nations are striving for authentic human security, they are not so likely to be preparing for or waging war, but rather working toward peaceful, less costly resolution of conflicts and mutually beneficial solutions to common international problems, building constructive relationships with rather than threatening other nations" (p. 31). Thus, peace education can develop leaders to strive for human security as a criterion to reach the peace education ultimate goal and a culture of peace. For the well-being of Asia, transforming the culture of militarism to a culture of peace and nonviolence is mandatory. Adams (2017) defines that "A culture of peace is an integral approach to preventing violence and violent conflicts, and an alternative to the culture of war and violence based on education for peace, the promotion of sustainable economic and social development, respect for human rights, equality between women and men, democratic participation, tolerance, the free flow of information and disarmament." Reardon (2001) suggested that:

> Building a culture of peace depends very much on education, because education in our contemporary world is the main carrier of culture. Only education can enable societies to understand the culture of violence which has blighted our past, debases our present and threatens our future. It is through education that the peoples of the world will be able to derive and prepare to pursue the vision of a culture of peace (49–50).

What emerged from the learnings offered by Reardon, was the establishment of The Department of Global Citizenship Studies at Seisen University, the Global Campaign for Peace Education, Japan, Global Citizenship and Peace Education Certificate Program, as well as the Global Citizenship Studies, Graduate Program at Seisen University, and Northeast Asia Regional Peacebuilding Institute (NARPI). This chapter will focus on how NARPI develops peace leaders to build a culture of peace and the impact the program brought to the participants of Northeast Asia.

17.2 The Need for a Peacebuilding Institute

More than seventy years have passed since the end of World War II, yet to this day, the Japanese government has been the focus of criticism for not taking adequate responsibilities for the military atrocities committed in the past (Field 1997, p. 2; Honda 2000, p. 34; Koschmann 2000, p. 741; Ogawa 2000, p. 42). Er (2002) stated that "grudging offers of deep reflection and remorse (but not amounting to a genuine apology) to its neighbors (from Japan), coupled with Chinese and Korean refusals to forgive and forget past atrocities, have led to profound distrust among the countries involved" (p. 34). Furthermore, Er argued that Japan's refusal to officially apologize for the wrongdoings done during occupation and military aggression would be an obstacle to establishing a good relation between Japan and its neighboring countries (p. 33). Japan would have to acknowledge the wrong doing, articulate sincere sorrow, and apologize for the harm done, if peace was to be obtained.

There is a need to reconstruct and reframe diplomatic relations to collaborate in realizing an improved and rewarding system of spiritual, educational, and economic growth. This is indeed a contribution NARPI can offer for the spiritual, educational, and economic growth of Northeast Asia. Thus, as stated by Barr (1998, para. 5), "Overcoming these 'hurt feelings' is the price of admission to a brave new world of diplomatic linkages around the Pacific." Once the issue has been addressed properly and sincerely, Japan and the countries in Asia-Pacific will be able to come to an agreement for a renewed positive relationship.

Peace can be cultivated, learned and put into practice through peace education. The pedagogy of peace education includes the knowledge, skills, and attitude needed to develop adequate leadership with the appropriate characteristics to conduct reconciliation and peace-building processes. Reardon (1988) noted that, "many forms of peace education seek to be, in practice and consequence, vehicles for global transformation which implies change of the widest possible breadth in social organization and the greatest possible depth in personal perspectives and behaviors" (p. 47). Leadership also seeks for an activity that leads people to this transformation. Heifetz (1994) defined leadership as an activity, "the activity of any citizen from any walk of life mobilizing people to do something … It allows for the use of a variety of abilities depending on the demands of the culture and situation" (p. 20). Peace education is one means to nurture and develop various skills and abilities for our future responsible global leaders.

Thus, peace education can teach people how to take leadership roles and mobilize themselves and others through the process of healing the past and building peace in the present and future. Reardon (personal communication, October 3, 2006) stated that it is possible to teach toward the capacity to forgive by following the process of resolution, responsibility, remorse, reciprocity, reconciliation, and reconstruction. This learning process is important in the past and current situation in Northeast Asia, a fertile ground for peacebuilding can be practiced through peace education.

17.3   Developing Leadership Qualities for Peacebuilding

The situation in Northeast Asia is a sensitive and complex social issue that requires education through moral decision-making and social responsibility. It is important to establish ethical standards for leadership through peace education. Moral education can assist in the construction of a foundation for people seeking a better and positive future as defined by Reardon (1997). Reardon continues that moral education is "an education in which they are helped to see that many of the problems of intolerance and derivation they face can be resolved through the application of ethical standards to social relations and public policy" (p. 44). This definition resonates with the description of moral leadership as introduced by Wren (1995):

The understanding of the nature and processes of leadership must be coupled with a clear sense of the moral and ethical overtones of leadership; that is to say, the group goals which are the objective of leadership must be moral, and the process of achieving these goals must be ethical. (p. 481)

Therefore, research on the role of leadership in peace education may be significant and necessary to educate the young and upcoming leaders and carries a host of potentials and capabilities strewn with moral education. The values and attitudes of a person are identified by the moral and ethical standards of the culture each individual is raised with. Freire (1970) highlights the need and importance of ethical virtues in dialogue, "Founding itself upon love, humility, and faith, dialogue becomes a horizontal relationship which mutual trust between the dialoguers is the logical consequence" (p. 91). These virtues are crucial in achieving a just and peaceful world. Reardon (1997), argued that, "The degree of human suffering tolerated in the world is evidence of our failure to insist on the fulfillment of the moral standards nations have agreed to in the covenants and treaties intended to bring a tolerable level of civility to world society" (p. 44). Prince (1988) described, "Moral development is to a great extent determined by the cultural standards of the larger society from which organizational members come...Individuals are prepared by their previous experiences to behave in accordance with societal standards of right and wrong" (p. 484). Thus, the collaboration of peace and leadership may contribute to the development of moral and ethical standards of an individual and the surrounding society as well as the development of a culture of peace.

Reardon (1988) described that the ultimate goal of peace educators as global citizens is to preserve this beautiful Earth and all the living beings that live on it:

The value of citizenship calls on us to educate people to be capable of creating a nonviolent, just social order on this planet, a global civic order offering equity to all Earth's people offering protection for universal human rights, providing for the resolution of conflict by nonviolent means and assuring respect for the planet that produces the life and the well-being of its people (p. 59).

Based on this description of peace education, leadership characteristics pursued by peace educators can include principles of value, nonviolence, justice, global responsibility, equity, human dignity, conflict resolution skills, respect and well-being for all. Thus, among the various leadership qualities, the types of leaders needed in the reconciliation and peace building process, namely in Asia are citizen leadership, servant-leadership, and transformational leadership, the three types of leadership which I believe reflect the principles mentioned above.

Couto (1992) described citizen leaders as those who "speak in simple terms about the basic dignity of every human being... They are compelled to pass on to the next generation a society less tolerant of human and environmental degradation" (p. 15). Citizen leaders will speak out to authorities when needed and have the power to change the system when necessary. Furthermore, Gerzon (2003) described that becoming a global citizen means "to live according to values not just good for ourselves, not our own tribe or religion, or for our country or region, but good for the world" (p. 9). A global citizenship leader would fulfill the ultimate goal of peace education.

Another type of leader that would have a significant role in peace education is the servant-leader. Greenleaf (1970) used the term "servant-leader" to describe an ethical leader. He explained that "the servant-leader is servant first ... Becoming a servant-leader begins with the natural feeling that one wants to serve, to serve first. Then conscious choice brings one to aspire to lead" (p. 18). A servant-leader prioritizes serving people's needs. Furthermore, Blanchard (1992) described that "Servant-leaders are ones who move among their people in a way that helps them be as responsible as they can in doing their job" (p. 28). A servant-leader can work side by side with others to achieve a common goal in a supportive way. This is a kind of leader pursued in peace education in transforming the present relation between Japan and its neighboring countries in Asia. This is the leader who is servant first because they understand the need to meet the priority needs of others, the answer to the true test of servant-leadership stated by Greenleaf (1970). He explained,

> The best test, and difficult to administer, is: Do those served grow as persons? Do they, while being served, become healthier, wiser, freer, more autonomous, more likely themselves to become servants? And, what is the effect on the least privileged in society; will they benefit, or, at least, not be further deprived? (p. 19)

The third type of leader quality needed in peace education is a transformational leader. This type of leader, such as Mohandas K. Gandhi and Martin Luther King Jr., is often introduced in peace education. Transformational leaders often portray a charismatic or idealized influence that envisions an inspirational motivation for followers and compels them to engage in shared goals (Bass/Steidlmeier 1998, p. 3; Burns 1978, p. 100; Couto 1993, p. 103). Furthermore, Bass/Steidlmeier (1998), described that the intellectual stimulation of a transformational leader "helps followers to question assumptions and to generate more creative solutions to problems. Its individualized consideration treats each follower as an individual and provides coaching, mentoring and growth opportunities" (p. 3). These characteristics of a transformational leader can contribute to peace-building for the common good of all.

It is important to face the challenges of change with new insights and different perspectives. Peace education plays a vital role in educating learners to become global leader citizens, as Gerson (2003) noted:

> For global citizens, however, learning means crossing borders in order to work more effectively with the whole... We might call it 'integral learning' because it is constantly striving to become aware of its own limitations and to expand the boundaries of the known. (p. 20)

Peace education is not complete unless the knowledge and skills acquired, and the attitude and values developed are applied to action for the benefit of all.

17.4 Northeast Asia Regional Peacebuilding Institute (NARPI)

The Northeast Asia Regional Peacebuilding Institute (NARPI) began in 2009 to strengthen and empower people in Northeast Asia through providing peacebuilding training and building cross-cultural networks (NARPI website). Past venues of NARPI were Seoul and Inje, Korea (2011); Hiroshima, Japan (2012); Inje, Korea (2013); Nanjing, China (2014); Ulaanbaatar, Mongolia (2015); Taipei, Taiwan (2016); Okinawa, Japan (2017) and Jeju Island, Korea (2018). Over 300 people from the region have participated in NARPI trainings and have shared a common vision to transform this region to a culture of peace. Participants are NGO workers, university students, professors, teachers, religious workers and community leaders.

The mission of NARPI is to transform the culture and structure of militarism and communities of fear and violence, into just and peaceful ones by providing peacebuilding training, connecting and empowering people to become peace leaders to build a culture of peace in Northeast Asia. Peace education and conflict

Table 17.1 NARPI activity

2012 Hiroshima, Japan	Community-based Restorative Justice for Schools	Historical and Cultural Stories of Peace	Critical Understanding of Conflict & Peace Issues	Peacebuilding Skills
2013 Inje, South Korea	Trauma Awareness & Healing	Restorative Justice: Aiming for Healing and Reconciliation	Gender, Sexuality and Peacebuilding	Nonviolent Communication & Facilitation
2014 Nanjing, China	Restorative Approach to Historical Conflict	Arts and Stories for Peacebuilding	Presenting Our Histories Justly Psychosocial Trauma: Awareness and Response	Peacebuilding Skills: Transformative Mediation
2015 Ulaanbaatar, Mongolia	Peacebuilding and Sustainable Development	Restorative Justice: A New Lens for Justice	Applied Theatre in Peacebuilding	Conflict Transformation in Organizations
2016 Jinshan & Taipei, Taiwan	Restorative Justice: A New Lens for Justice	Trainer's Training	Nonviolent Struggle for Social Change	Optimizing Peace Making by Ending Generational Trauma
2017 Nago, Okinawa	Identity-Based Conflict	Restorative Justice: Rebuilding Identity, Community, and History	Nonviolent Response to Militarization	Optimizing Peace Making by Ending Generational Trauma

Source The author

transformation play a crucial role in preventing armed conflict in the region. NARPI offers a place in Northeast Asia for peace activists and students where they can receive practical education and training. The basic courses offered every year are: Theory and Practice of Peace Education, Critical Understanding of Conflict & Peace Issues, and Conflict & Peace Framework. Table 17.1 with some of the other varied courses that were offered in the past.

17.5   NARPI's Role in Developing Peace Leaders to Build a Culture of Peace

NARPI offers an opportunity to train peace leaders to transform this current situation in Asia from Military based security to human security and the wellbeing of all. Palmer (1990), an author who works on issues of leadership, advised that the peace building people "who wish to serve as agents of nonviolent change need at least four resources in order to survive and persist: a sound rationale for what they intend to do, a sensible strategy for doing it, a continuing community of support, and inner ground on which to stand" (p. 171). These resources should be given attention in the process of establishing good diplomatic relationships. Leadership theory and skills can be applied to create a team of leaders-followers and an action plan to build peace and good diplomatic relations between Japan and the countries in the Pacific. As Northouse (2003) mentioned, "Leadership is a process whereby an individual influences a group of individuals to achieve a common goal" (p. 3). In the Asia-Pacific context, I believe an emerging common goal is for Japan to work together with individuals and countries which they harmed during World War II in order to heal the past and build peace and goodwill.

Past atrocities committed during conflict remain as a scar in the memories of the victims. The harmed have carried a long history of grievances and unless these memories have been identified and understood, the reconciliation process will not be adequately conducted. Therefore, much knowledge and skill is needed to perform the process along with the ethical and moral characteristic of caring. Leaders involved in the reconciliation process require all the traits of a servant-leader and the basic skills of conflict transformation in order to conduct an effective process that promotes healing without causing more anguish to the victims. It is important for the parties in conflict to realize that grievances will not lead them to a positive future and that their well-being will not be improved unless they place a high value on peace. This value is realized through adequate training in conflict resolution, reconciliation and peace-building (Reardon 1997, p. 97).

Healing requires a complex process and studies in this process where Peace Education offers a range of skills and methods in conflict resolution that includes restoration and establishment of positive and mutually beneficial relationships at all levels of education. Thus, NARPI has a role to offer adequate training in conflict resolution, reconciliation and peacebuilding to restore and establish mutually

Table 17.2 Programme of action

Culture of Peace. Program of Action (1999)	NARPI courses
Education for Peace	Theory and Practice of Peace Education
Sustainable Development	Included in all the courses
Respect for Human Rights	"
Equality between Women and Men	"
Democratic Participation	"
Tolerance	"
Free Flow of Information	"

Source The author

beneficial relationships. NARPI provides "educational curricula to promote qualitative values, attitudes and behaviors of a culture of peace, including peaceful
conflict- resolution, dialogue, consensus-building and active non-violence" (Adams
2005). The courses reflect the eight points of the Programme of Action adopted by
the General Assembly as indicated by the Table 17.2.

The program seeks to follow Betty Reardon' s peace education theory, intellectual legacy, and teaching methods. The participants come with a purpose to start
some action for peace learning in their respective country and environment. The
courses offer not only theory but practice, and an opportunity to apply what they
have learned. Thus, participants can plan their own program of action to achieve a
culture of peace.

17.6   A Transformational Experience with Northeast Asia Regional Peacebuilding Institute

The preamble of the United Nations states that one of the purposes of its establishment is 'to save succeeding generations from the scourge of war.' There's a
similar part in the preamble of the Japanese Constitution that says, "We, the
Japanese people, …, determined that we shall secure for ourselves and our posterity
the fruits of peaceful cooperation with all nations …and resolved that never again
shall we be visited with the horrors of war …".

The horrors of war were what the NARPI participants witnessed in 2014 in
Nanjing, China, where they have just experienced the first week of peacebuilding
training program. Peace education has aided the peace building participants process
from this terrible incident and together envisioned a positive way forward by
proposing what they could do to change this cycle of violence and hatred.

The Nanjing Massacre was an incident that happened in 1937 in Nanjing, China
where the Japanese military has committed genocide, according to scholarly
research, the lowest estimate is 50,000 and the highest estimate is 300,000 given by
the Chinese government. This gruesome history was recorded in the museum. After

having taken peacebuilding courses and visited the museum, the participants of the NARPI peacebuilding training, Chinese, Koreans, Mongolians and Japanese, all thought deeply and came up with some questions:

One Mongolian participant explained: "Every horrifying photograph and artifact had an explanation, which said "The Japanese Military did this" or "the Japanese government did that." Can't we change the subject of the sentences to "War did this" or "War brought about this horrifying situation? War changed the normal people into beasts and heartless beings?"

One Korean participant said: "No matter what ethnic background we come from, don't we need to know and predict the possibility that in times of war, we ourselves might build that evil in us and do beastly things that were done in Nanjing?"

One Chinese participant said: "Don't we have to think what we can do from here? What can we do to make this world a better and safer place to live? What can we do to learn from history and prevent any inhumane activities from happening again?

One Japanese participant said: "Such horrifying events still happen to this day. We still hear in the news of one country killing people of another country, of one ethnic group killing another ethnic group."

The Northeast Asian Participants posed such questions and they all responded in solidarity: "What we need to do is to design peace education programs that would enable present and future generations to find nonviolent ways to resolve conflict and change the structure of the world from the culture of war to the culture of peace, just as we have taken the peace building and education sessions." They feel that their attitudes have changed. Some Chinese participants said that they were brought up to hate the Japanese, but through the five-day peace building training they have completely changed their mindset to a more cooperative and accepting attitude. They have eased their ill feelings as they worked together with the Japanese and learned about peace building. They realized that they were all aiming toward a common objective, a peaceful world.

Their change of attitude is a sign of hope, that the participants from various ethnic background and walks of life can learn how to make decisions and find positive ways to go forward.

17.7 Conclusion

Peace educators educate people to build a community for a common good which is beneficial to all living things on this planet. Leadership studies play an important role in peace education. Having explored the role of leadership in peace education, it is crucial that a new strand that addresses development of leadership character- istics be added in the peace education curriculum, particularly in the educational settings of Northeast Asia.

It is hoped that peace education with an additional conceptual content of lead- ership would educate the present and future generation to serve the world as citizen leaders, servant-leaders, and transformational leaders in overcoming historical trauma and peacebuilding for the benefit and wellbeing of all. As Eleanor Roosevelt once said: It isn't enough to talk about peace, one must believe in it and it isn't enough to believe in it, one must work at it.

References

Adams, D. (2005, 2017). *Definition of culture of peace*. Retrieved January 5, 2019, from http://www.culture-of-peace.info/copoj/definition.html.

Allan, A., Allan, M. M., Kaminer, D., & Stein, D. J. (2006). Research report: Exploration of the Association between apology and forgiveness amongst victims of human rights violations. *Behavioral Sciences and the Law, 24*, 87–102.

Barr, C. W. (1998). Politics of apology in the orient. *Christian Science Monitor, 91*(3).

Bass, B. M. & Steidlmeier, P. (1998). *Ethics, character and authentic transformational leadership*.

Blanchard, K. (1992). Servant-leadership revisited. In L. C. Spears (Ed.), *Insights on leadership: Service, stewardship, spirit, and servant-leadership* (pp. 21–28). New York: Wiley.

Burns, J. M. (1978). Transactional and transforming leadership. In J. T. Wren (1995) *The leadership companion: Insights on leadership through the ages* (pp. 100–101). New York: The Free Press.

Couto, R. A. (1992). Defining a citizen leader. In J. T. Wren (1995) *The leadership companion: Insights on leadership through the ages* (pp. 11–17). New York: The Free Press.

Er, L. P. (2002). The apology issue: Japan's differing approaches toward China and South Korea. *American Asian Review, 20*(3), 31–54.

Field, N. (1997). War and apology: Japan, Asia, the fiftieth, and after. *Positions, 5*(1), 1–49.

Freire, P. (1970). *Pedagogy of the oppressed*. New York: The Continuum International Publishing.

Gerzon, M. (2003). *Becoming global citizen: Finding common grounds in a world of differences*.

Greenleaf, R. K. (1970). Servant–leadership. In L. C. Spears (Ed.), *Insights on leadership: Service, stewardship, spirit, and servant-leadership* (pp. 15–20). New York: Wiley.

Heifetz, R. A. (1994). *Leadership without easy answers*. Cambridge, MA: Harvard University Press.

Honda, M. M. (2003). Japan's war crimes: Has justice been served? *East Asia*, Fall 2000, 27–35.

Koschmann, J. V. (2001). National subjectivity and the uses of atonement in the age of recession. *The South Atlantic Quarterly, 99*(4), 741–767.

Northouse, P. G. (2003). *Leadership, theory and practice* (3rd ed.). London: Sage Publications.

Ogawa, S. (2000). The difficulty of apology: Japan's struggle with memory and guilt. *Harvard International Review*, Fall 2000, 42–46.

Palmer, P. J. (1990). Leading from within. In L. C. Spears (Ed.), *Insights on leadership: Service, stewardship, spirit, and servant-leadership* (pp. 197–208). New York: Wiley.

Prince, H. T. II. (1988). Moral development in individuals. In J. T. Wren (1995) *The leadership companion: Insights on leadership through the ages* (pp. 484–491). New York: The Free Press.

Reardon, B. A. (1988). *Comprehensive peace education: Educating for global responsibility*. New York: Teachers College.

Reardon, B. A. (1997). *Tolerance—The threshold of peace: Teacher—Training resource unit 1*. Paris: UNESCO Publishing.

Reardon, B. A. (2001). *Education for a culture of peace in a gender perspective*. Paris: UNESCO Publishing.

Reardon, B. A. (2010). Women and human security: A feminist framework and critique of the prevailing patriarchal security system. In B.A. Reardon & A. Hans (Eds.), *The gender imperative: Human security vs state security* (pp. 7–37). Oxford: Routledge.

The Hague Appeal for Peace Global Campaign for Peace Education. (2004). *Campaign statement.*
UN Documents. (1999). *53/243 B. Programme of action on a culture of peace.* Retrieved January
    5, 2019, from http://www.un-documents.net/a53r243b.htm.
Wren, J. T. (1995). *The leadership companion: Insights on leadership through the ages.* New
    York: The Free Press.

Chapter 18
Health Promotion for Peace Promotion: Applying Reardon's Holistic Model to Health

Albie Sharpe

Betty Reardon's work as a peace scholar and teacher has had a profound influence on my own path as a public health researcher and peace educator. In the early 2000s, I was fortunate to participate in the Teachers College Peace Education program in Tokyo with an outstanding and very international group of educators under Betty's facilitation. At the time, I was teaching in an inter-faculty international studies program at a university in Kyoto. At weekends, I would travel to Tokyo to join my new friends, other aspiring peace educators, as we unpacked the connections between gender, social injustice, and militarism while gradually incorporating our learnings into our own pedagogical practice. Just as rewarding, our out-of-class conversations extended deep into the night, as we dissected the world's problems and reassessed our roles in them.

Around the same time, I was asked to establish a course at my university in Kyoto called "Health and Society." I began by teaching it from a top-down, medicalized perspective, using the transmission, diagnosis, and treatment of disease in the healthcare system as a way of exploring health policy and social inequalities. In seeking to integrate the work I was doing on the weekends in Tokyo with Betty into my own teaching practice, I began to look at the ways that health could be linked to peace.

At the surface level, there are clear connections between health and peace. By its very design, war is a system that purposefully damages health – either through direct violence or through indirect effects, such as destruction of infrastructure and economic systems used to maintain and promote health, including hospitals, water and food systems, and transport networks (Sharpe 2010). While war has clear effects on health, the inverse – how health might affect war – was less clear. The Preamble to the Constitution of the World Health Organization states that "The health of all peoples is fundamental to the attainment of peace" (WHO 1946). What would this mean in practice? In what ways could the provision of health services

Albie Sharpe, Lecturer in Public Health at the University of Technology, Sydney, Australia; Email: albiesharpe@gmail.com.

© Springer Nature Switzerland AG 2019
D. T. Snauwaert (ed.), *Exploring Betty A. Reardon's Perspective on Peace Education*, Pioneers in Arts, Humanities, Science, Engineering, Practice 20, https://doi.org/10.1007/978-3-030-18387-5_18

help to address a pervasive culture of violence? How could bottom-up, community-centered approaches to health help to mitigate – or even prevent – violent conflict? How would we collect meaningful evidence on the interrelationships between health, peace and other social domains? Fifteen years later, now working full-time in public health education and research, I can reflect on the painstaking process of discovery, built very much around the fundamental values and learning processes developed in those early peace education sessions.

In this chapter, I review some of the ways that health is conceptualized and implicated in Reardon's overall holistic framework. Reardon does not often discuss health explicitly, however its importance is very apparent throughout her work, particularly in the use of an ecological approach to examine the interconnections between peace and other social and environmental conditions. It is also evident in Reardon's discussions on the fundamental importance of human rights, the problem of violence, as well as the deleterious effects of the war system and the environment required to support health. These are all encapsulated in an overarching feminist human security framework. This chapter will consider each of these in turn before briefly discussing some broader implications in practice.

18.1 Defining Health in Holistic Terms

Before embarking on this discussion, it is important to understand what is meant by health and how the way that it is defined profoundly affects how it is practiced. The World Health Organization refers to health as a state of "complete physical, mental and social wellbeing and not merely the absence of disease or infirmity" (WHO 1946). Under this definition, with its three broad dimensions,[1] health is something that can never be realized – or even measured. Instead, it becomes a highly aspirational goal. The transformative aspect of this framing of health is that it shifts our understanding away from health being solely a product of the medical system to one that is holistically integrated into our physical and social environments. Health is more than simply the personal experience of feeling healthy or not being sick but a resource that can be used for everyday living and for achieving personal and communal goals, thereby contributing to the overall welfare of our whole society. Such an approach makes health the responsibility of everyone – not just the concern of health workers (WHO 1978). This shift in our understanding of health has powerful implications that encompass and reinforce Reardon's own explorations of feminist security and ecological frameworks.

---

[1]Debate around the utility and comprehensiveness of the WHO definition of health has continued since 1948. Some health scholars have called for the addition of 'spirituality' to the definition (Chirico 2016). A panel of representatives of autochthonous peoples, anthropologists and physicians concluded that the WHO should integrate 'human equilibrium in nature', 'accepted spirituality' and 'adaptation' into its health definition (Charlier et al. 2017).

18.2 Ecological Understandings

Reardon situates health as a component within her 'ecological' framework, an approach that extends beyond the traditional realm of environmental studies to the "broad study of organisms in their environments" (Reardon/Snauwaert 2015a, p. 130). The ecological approach incorporates an awareness that all planetary and human systems, including health and welfare, are fully interdependent and need to be examined holistically rather than in isolation. At the individual, community and global level, health is dependent on access to education, good food, potable water, income and shelter. Populations also depend on a secure and peaceful environment, a stable ecosystem, and good governance, among other things, to maintain health. Conversely, actions that damage each of these components through destruction of our natural environment, violence, economic and social exclusion will likely lead to poorer health, particularly for more vulnerable groups. As a precondition for most aspects of human life, health contributes reciprocally to the realization of these same components, with lack of access to adequate health services potentially leading to further deprivation and in some cases violence. In order to achieve Reardon's goal of sustainable harmonization between these various components (Reardon/Snauwaert 2015a, p. 130), we need to develop an awareness of the interconnections – and map the interlinkages – between the many aspects of human and planetary wellbeing.

The ecological approach described by Reardon has been deeply embedded in the public health sphere for decades (see Milio 1976, 1988), particularly in terms of our understanding of the social determinants of health. The WHO defines the social determinants of health as "the conditions in which people are born, grow, live, work and age" (World Conference on Social Determinants of Health 2011). The Commission on the Social Determinants of Health (WHO 2008) noted that poor health, particularly for poor and marginalized communities, can be attributed to

> the unequal distribution of power, income, goods, and services, globally and nationally, the consequent unfairness in the immediate, visible circumstances of people's lives – their access to health care, schools, and education, their conditions of work and leisure, their homes, communities, towns, or cities – and their chances of leading a flourishing life (p. 1).

Such inequalities, according to the commission, are "killing people on a grand scale" with multiple intersections "across class, education, gender, age, ethnicity, disability, and geography" (p. 18). In Reardon's conceptualization, these same inequalities might be described as forms of structural violence, or "avoidable, intentional harm" (Reardon 2001, p. 35). This provides a clear link between violence – particularly structural violence – and the denial of the fundamental conditions necessary to support health. Thus, it can be argued that a holistic peace cannot be realized without addressing the social determinants of health – as these are also determinants of violence.

Disaggregated health data showing health outcomes for different ethnic, gender, and socioeconomic groups provides a powerful indicator of inequities within and beyond the health system. Using a life course, approach, two infants born into wealth or poverty – or genders or ethnic groups – will have very different chances throughout life. Educational attainment, for example, has profound implications for life pathways that shapes family stability, social standing, working conditions and salary, sense of control over one's life and access to health insurance (see Braveman et al. 2011). When educational opportunities are inadequate or interrupted, this is likely to lead to "subsequent risk of obesity, malnutrition, mental health problems, heart disease, and criminality," and ultimately to increased risk of premature mortality and morbidity (WHO 2008, p. 3). Following life pathways backwards from inequitable health outcomes can therefore provide a means of understanding the consequences of structural violence on different populations, as well as evidence on the effectiveness of actions designed to address them (see Matteucci 2015).

Recognizing this, the Commission on the Social Determinants of Health (WHO 2008) calls on governments and communities to work towards improving the conditions of daily life, tackling the inequitable distribution of power, money, and resources, developing a workforce trained in the social determinants, and knowledge for evidence-based action (p. 2). A focus on health does not mean prioritizing health over other components but recognizing that improvements in wellbeing may derive from actions to address the social and environmental determinants of health; and likewise, improvements in health may lead to better education, employment, and opportunities for more vulnerable communities. It also means that health workers, peace educators, and indeed the whole community, need to play a significant role in addressing the underlying structural causes of violence (Lee/Young 2018). This will be discussed further below.

18.3 Importance and Applications of Rights

Building on this ecological framing, health is considered to be one of a number of rights that all human beings are entitled to. The preamble to the WHO Constitution states that "The enjoyment of the highest attainable standard of health is one of the fundamental rights of every human being without distinction of race, religion, political belief, economic or social condition" (WHO 1946). It is worth noting that the right to health extends far beyond the right of access to health care. A right to health holistically incorporates all aspects of the determinants of health (CESCR 2000). Thus, the determinants listed in the previous section – education, employment, access to clean water and nutritious food, a safe environment and so forth – are also rights that contribute to the realization of a right to health.

Reardon draws particular attention to women's health rights in relation to their roles as both carers and health workers. Women's health, Reardon (1993) notes, is a precondition for such roles, yet women are less likely to receive adequate nutrition, education or care appropriate for their specific health needs – in particular, sexual and reproductive health. Reardon (1993) rightly lauds the role of oral rehydration therapy (ORT) as a treatment for diarrhea, a basic grassroots intervention that costs just a few cents yet has saved the lives of millions of children since it was first developed in Bangladesh in the 1970s (see Glass/Stoll 2018).

While not using the term directly, Reardon here points to the importance of primary health care (PHC) in realizing affordable, accessible and appropriate care. PHC is a global approach to health first clearly articulated in the Declaration of Alma Ata (WHO 1978). It attempts to move away from a vertical model of disease control centered around an expensive, specialized medical system to one aimed at providing accessible, equitable and needs-based care at the local level. In many parts of the world, PHC has led to the training of a workforce of effective community health workers – often women who work as volunteers or for little salary – such as the Lady Health Workers of Pakistan and the Village Health Worker Program of Zimbabwe (Perry et al. 2014). These programs have contributed markedly to ensuring that poorer communities in such areas have access to basic health care and community-centered actions to improve social conditions, thus taking a major step towards the realization of health as a human right.

Moving towards this broader conceptualization of a right to health, Reardon then links health to the right to education: mothers with higher levels of education are more likely to have the skills to respond appropriately to child health issues as they arise. Evidence affirms that mothers, and to a lesser extent fathers, with better education levels are more likely to ensure children receive adequate nutrition, have better knowledge of child development, invest more in child health and education, and experience less stress, although some of these outcomes may also be linked to factors such as household income and access to health services (see Bicego/Ties Boerma 1993; Black et al. 2013; Jeong et al. 2018).

A health system that treats diarrhea as a medical problem without addressing the social and environmental causes is likely to lead to repeated need to visit health clinics, with nutritional loss leading to stunted growth and impaired mental development for affected children (Black et al. 2013). Dirt floors in poor-quality housing, for example, are a significant risk factor for incidence of diarrhea (Sinmegn Mihrete et al. 2014), thus linking the right to health with a right to adequate housing. To this, we could add the rights to clean water and sanitation, as well as a healthy nutritious diet – thus opening up linkages across the whole spectrum of rights.

18.4 Causes and Effects of a Culture of Violence

The third interconnected aspect of Reardon's work with deep connections to health is related to the causes and effects of a culture of violence. Violence was identified as a specific concern for public health in the early 2000s, with the WHO World Report on Violence and Health (Krug et al. 2002). The report focuses on violence in its direct forms, with specific attention to the causes and effects of violence on children, youth, partners, the elderly, as well as sexual, self-directed, and communal violence. Most significantly, the report emphasizes that a public health approach means that violence can and should be preventable, noting that societal factors "help create a climate in which violence is encouraged or inhibited" (p. 10). These include the policy structures that support economic or social inequalities between groups in society (p. 11). However, the report does not cover other, arguably more significant, forms of violence, such as military and structural violence, which could also benefit greatly from integration with this public health approach. This would allow us to apply a social determinants analysis to the very systems that lead to militarism and war.

One way that Reardon links health with militarism is by pointing out how military spending leads to the hollowing out of essential public services. Resources that could be used to promote health and other social services are diverted into building and sustaining military capacity. As Reardon argues, "war and preparation for war have so endangered the health and safety of the human family; they undermine the very purpose they purport to serve" (p. 88). Demilitarization, on the other hand, could transform the economy and promote the development of a peace economy, "by allocating resources for programs that ensure the well being of the world's citizens" (Hague Agenda, Article 43). These were also the concerns of Middleton (1987) who, back in 1987, wrote that health promoters need to be aware of the health and social consequences of nuclear proliferation. However, redistribution of resources to a hierarchically and centrally controlled health system would not necessarily result in any benefit to the poor or socially excluded. The resources would have to be allocated in a bottom-up manner to provide real, sustainable benefits to the world's poor, as PHC seeks to do (see Sharpe 2010).

18.5   Sustainable Environments

The final interconnected aspect of Reardon's approach with relevance to health concerns the unsustainable impacts of human activities on our natural environment. Degradation of the natural environment, overuse of resources, and climate change remain enormous challenges in terms of health. Throughout her work, Reardon makes repeated reference to the enormous importance of maintaining a healthy planet as central to the realization and practice of peace, arguing that just as we are dependent on a healthy environment, the health of the environment depends upon the human species (Reardon/Snauwaert 2015a, p. 138).

Climate change may undo many key health gains – for example, warmer temperatures undermining food and water security, the migration of malaria, dengue and other diseases into new areas, and progress on diarrhea prevention and treatment (Watts et al. 2017). One Lancet Commission report has recently drawn explicit attention to the syndemic (or synergy of pandemics) between climate change, malnutrition and obesity (Swinburn et al. 2019). Beginning its work as a special commission on obesity, the commission expanded beyond its initial remit to argue that climate change itself should be viewed as a pandemic due to the effects it is likely to have on our health and the natural systems necessary to support it. At the same time, economic and social inequalities are undermining improvements in undernutrition rates. Action to address all three problems remains sluggish, with political inertia and continued dominance of corporations over the debate. Regulations are needed to promote the switch to a more sustainable and nutritious food system – such as a plant-based diet – leading to a more sustainable environment. The approach employed demonstrates how an ecological analysis can be used to develop a framework for action that adds value beyond its component parts.

Another concern for Reardon is the immense damage done to human health as a result of militarization (Reardon/Snauwaert 2015b, pp. 66–67). One important aspect of this is the long-term effects of weapons testing – particularly nuclear weapons – on our ecosystem. The Hague Agenda (Article 49) declares that "The nuclear weapons states, in particular, must acknowledge their responsibility for the health and environmental impacts of nuclear testing, production and use." It also specifically calls for greater transparency and accountability of all military activities and their impact on the environment and on health. The People's Health Charter, developed at the People's Health Assembly in 2000, likewise recognizes the importance of peace as a means of realizing a just health and a sustainable world. Among numerous action statements, the Charter calls on the world's people to campaign against "the research, production, testing and use of weapons of mass destruction and other arms, including all types of landmines" (PHM 2000).

18.6 Applying the Framework: Feminist Human Security and Health

These four key aspects of Reardon's work, which provide critical answers to my early questions on links between peace and health, are together incorporated into Reardon's (2001) holistic feminist human security framework. Human security is a framework that places the individual human being and the communities in which they live – rather than the state – at the center of security analysis. As a framework, it is comprised of multiple, interrelated components, such as those described in the above sections. Reardon's approach sees comprehensive, authentic security as deriving from a healthy sustainable planet and environment, meeting the physical needs necessary for human wellbeing and development, human rights and dignity, and the renunciation of violence and promotion of non-violent methods of resolving conflict (p. 127). These need to be addressed not as discrete parallel issues but as integrated concerns (Reardon/Snauwaert 2015b, p. 62). Incorporating the specific use of the term 'feminist' into human security shows both its development as a conceptual approach and the importance of contrasting with and mitigating more historically 'masculine' forms of national security and analytical perspectives (Reardon/Snauwaert 2015b, p. 67). A secure society, Reardon argues, "is a healthy society, physically and psychologically," with health providing a valuable means of assessing well-being (Reardon/Snauwaert 2015a, p. 138). This points to an important role for health as a means of documenting gender, poverty and other forms of inequality – with maternal mortality rates, suicides, and substance abuse, for example, all clearly linked to gender, ethnicity and socio-economic status.

In terms of how the health system might contribute to addressing a culture of violence while promoting a culture of peace, much depends on the underlying values by which health services are provided. Conventional understandings of security can be seen to mirror the conventional medical system: hierarchical, gendered decision-making, business- rather than people-oriented, treatment emphasized over prevention, discrimination against social and economic minorities, and exclusion of those unable to pay for services or the financial ruin of those without insurance. Loss of dignity as well as physical and psychological violence is clearly evident in situations where, for example, women are unable to receive healthcare without the consent of a man, members of the LGBTQI community are subjected to forced medical or psychiatric treatment, rape or physical harm, and people with HIV are denied access to lifesaving treatment. On the other hand, the human security approach is consistent with what has been termed the 'New Public Health' (see Baum 2008), which embraces broad understandings of the origins and causes of disease, emphasizes preventative actions, and places importance on the development of healthy public policy. The basic principles of PHC as defined at Alma Ata – equity, accessibility, intersectoral actions, community participation in decision-making and appropriateness of care – are values that themselves embody and promote a culture of peace (WHO 1978).

The Peace Through Health movement (Arya/Santa Barbara 2008) has made a significant contribution to our understanding of the practice of health and peace. This movement calls for medical practitioners to use their status as health workers to promote trust in conflict settings, work for peace, and promote human rights. The provision and restoration of health services during and after conflict also provides a means by which governments can restore trust amongst former combatants and is essential in preventing a return to fighting. Examples of this include days of peace, where combatants agree on a ceasefire so that health workers can conduct vaccinations of children in combat areas. Such activities can increase levels of trust between combatants and contribute to peace talks. However, these actions focus primarily on the health sector and largely deal with the direct effects of war and violence.

18.7   Health Promotion

Engagement in health-related action by broader society – not just health workers – is an important way to empower communities to address the social determinants of health and reduce structural violence. Health promotion, as set out in the Ottawa Charter for Health Promotion (WHO 1986), provides a means of helping individuals and communities take greater control over their own health. The Ottawa Charter incorporates specific community-based actions to promote healthier lifestyles: building healthy public policy, creating supportive environments, strengthening community actions, developing personal skills and reorienting health services. However, many of these could be retooled to promote other actions, with just such an approach taken in South Africa to the problem of youth violence (Graham et al. 2011). Applying the model to other aspects of human security and situations of structural violence could include actions such as cleaning up communal environments, forcing governments to strengthen environmental regulations, establishing gender equitable collaboration, reducing workplace accidents and stress, increasing decision-making for Indigenous peoples for culturally appropriate services, or promoting equitable access to higher education for marginalized populations. Such actions may help to bring communities together in common purpose to improve the social determinants of health and increase social capital and human security in the community.

School health promotion is one area that should be of particular interest to peace educators, particularly in its potential to improve the health of whole communities. Like peace education, health promotion advocates a Freirean pedagogical approach that eschews the 'banking' and biomedical models in seeking to address poor health and its determinants (Minkler/Cox 1980). Children are taught about the process of identifying barriers to health within the school and community, such as hazards in the classroom and playground, unhealthy food sales in the canteen, and other barriers to health. They then work with teachers and community members to address these problems (St. Leger et al. 2007). Research has shown that learnings from the school are transferred to their homes, where the students have put pressure on parents to reduce smoking and alcohol consumption. They have also become advocates for dietary change, handwashing and sanitation (Yuasa et al. 2015). In this manner, it can help to increase students' sense of efficacy and control over the physical and social environments in which they live. If properly facilitated, with students taking a central role in the decision-making and awareness-raising process, it provides a powerful means of implementing Freire's conscientization process.

Another key concern in both Reardon's work and the People's Health Charter is the impact of gender-based violence, particularly for women. In addressing this, Reardon (1993) argues for the development of healthy relationships designed to promote "social and emotional learning intended to provide education for greater life satisfaction through the development of emotional health and social responsibility" (p. 126). A comprehensive approach to sex and reproductive health education would incorporate much more than the biomedical aspects of reproductive health by including, for example, student-centered discussions on healthy, respectful relationships, regardless of gender or sexual orientation, as well as how to manage negotiations for safe and consensual sex (AAAH 2018). This may contribute to reducing the incidence of bullying and gender-based violence both at school and later in life (see Hammarström/Gådin 2000).

18.8 Mapping the Links

Finally, in building on these ideas in my own research, I have sought to develop evidence-based approaches to 'map' the interlinkages between the various human security components and the processes of health promotion. This has meant developing community-based human security evaluation tools utilizing story-telling, sharing of narratives, participatory observations, and interviews with health workers. The approach also recognizes that security concerns are likely to be localized, and thus many of the methods used to assess human security based on static, national indicators are likely to be inadequate (Sharpe 2018).

For several years, I worked in Sri Lanka with an international organization on a project designed to reduce the burden of non-communicable diseases (NCDs). One of the components of this program was based around the principles of community health promotion, with group participants jointly deciding how to address NCDs in their communities through exercise, dietary change, community gardening and lifestyle modification. I was interested in looking at the broader social outcomes of their activities – effects on gender relationships, post-conflict peacebuilding, relations with other religious groups, and community decision-making. Using a series of wordcards to promote diversity in the stories, I collected almost 200 stories of change in the communities. Community members described outcomes that extended far beyond health, transforming gender relationships in the community as women campaigned against social constraints on physical exercise, and ensuring safe spaces and resources to do so. They also became powerful advocates for health both in their communities and beyond.

In Jaffna, a district deeply affected by the civil war, the evaluation showed how a broad-ranging public health program was able to address many of the crucial nutritional, water, livelihood, and other needs in the community, and to provide support for a massive resettlement project following the war. Enormous challenges remain for the communities involved: the continued military presence and occupation of land in the name of security, along with unemployment and low wages, gender-based violence and untreated war-related trauma. However, by broadening the evaluation away from a focus on direct health-related outcomes, it is possible to show that a simple exercise and lifestyle program can impact on the broader components of human security.

In these ways, while the focus may be slightly different, health promotion may be seen to utilize many of the same practices and goals of peace education. It does so in ways that build communities, challenge adverse policies, reduce inequalities, and promote equitable decision-making. It can do so in post-conflict situations or in communities where there are gender and power imbalances.

18.9 Conclusions

This chapter shows that there are multiple shared and reciprocal links and processes between the broader concept of health and Reardon's vision of a feminist human security. Each seeks to understand and address inequality, violence and poor health through a holistic analysis. In developing and applying this, Reardon argues for educational approaches that emphasize the need to see the planet as a single living system and recognize our place in it:

> The most urgent security need of all is that all human beings see themselves as part of the ecosystem, elements of the biosphere, as well as creators of the socio-sphere. Helping learners to grasp that urgency and the nature of that relationship is a paramount task for ecological and cooperative education, one that can only be properly conceived and implemented within a global framework (Reardon/Snauwaert 2015a, p. 138).

A key challenge is that, too often, health workers, social workers, peace workers and educators have few opportunities for genuine collaboration. Peace educators, for example, may avoid integrating health into their approaches on the grounds that they lack technical expertise in health. Health workers may miss opportunities to act outside of their own professional boundaries in medical services. However, health promoters and peace educators are natural allies, with similar goals and strategies. All health promotion is peace promotion, as Middleton (1987) argued.

Creating equitable and accessible health and social systems requires knowledge and action from empowered communities who are committed to addressing the determinants of poor health and structural violence. Reardon's conceptualization of a feminist human security that draws together core values of a culture of peace – ecological frameworks, human rights, the need to address a culture of violence, and the importance of a sustainable environment – should provide a basis for a greater cross-sectoral integration and development of such values.

References

AAAH. (2018). *Comprehensive sexuality education: Position paper.* Australian Association for Adolescent Health. Retrieved from http://www.aaah.org.au/data/Position_Papers/AAAH_Ltd_ -_CSE_Position_Paper_Final_31Oct2018.pdf.

Arya, N., & Santa Barbara, J. (Eds.). (2008). *Peace through health: How health professionals can work for a less violent world.* Sterling, VA: Kumarian Press.

Baum, F. (2008). *The new public health* (3rd ed.). South Melbourne, VIC: Oxford University Press.

Bicego, G. T., & Ties Boerma, J. (1993). Maternal education and child survival: A comparative study of survey data from 17 countries. *Social Science & Medicine, 36*(9), 1207–1227. https://doi.org/10.1016/0277-9536(93)90241-U.

Black, R. E., Victora, C. G., Walker, S. P., Bhutta, Z. A., Christian, P., de Onis, M., ... Uauy, R. (2013). Maternal and child undernutrition and overweight in low-income and middle-income countries. *The Lancet, 382*(9890), 427–451. https://doi.org/10.1016/S0140-6736(13)60937-X.

Braveman, P., Egerter, S., & Williams, D. R. (2011). The social determinants of health: Coming of age. *Annual Review of Public Health, 32*, 381–398.

CESCR. (2000). *General Comment No.14: The Right to the highest attainable standard of health (Article 12 of the International Covenant on Economic, Social and Cultural Rights).*

Charlier, P., Coppens, Y., Malaurie, J., Brun, L., Kepanga, M., Hoang-Opermann, V., ... Hervé, C. (2017). A new definition of health? An open letter of autochthonous peoples and medical anthropologists to the WHO. *European Journal of Internal Medicine, 37*, 33–37. https://doi.org/10.1016/j.ejim.2016.06.027.

Chirico, F. (2016). Spiritual well-being in the 21st century: It's time to review the current WHO's health definition? *Journal of Health and Social Sciences, 1*(1), 11–16.

Glass, R. I., & Stoll, B. J. (2018). Oral rehydration therapy for diarrheal diseases: A 50-year perspective. *Jama, 320*(9), 865–866. https://doi.org/10.1001/jama.2018.10963.

Graham, L., Bruce, D., & Perold, H. (2011). *Ending the age of marginal majority: An exploration of strategies to overcome youth exclusion, vulnerability and violence in southern Africa.* Midrand, South Africa: Southern African Trust.

Hammarström, A., & Gådin, K. G. (2000). 'We won't let them keep us quiet …' Gendered strategies in the negotiation of power—implications for pupils' health and school health promotion. *Health Promotion International, 15*(4), 303–311. https://doi.org/10.1093/heapro/15.4.303.

Jeong, J., Kim, R., & Subramanian, S. (2018). How consistent are associations between maternal and paternal education and child growth and development outcomes across 39 low-income and middle-income countries? *Journal of Epidemiological and Community Health, 72*, 434–441.

Krug, E., Dahlberg, L., Mercy, J., Zwi, A., & Lozano, R. E. (2002). *World report on violence and health.* Retrieved from Geneva.

Lee, B. X., & Young, J. L. (2018). Clinicians' need for an ecological approach to violence reduction. *AMA Journal of Ethics, 20*(1), 91–98.

Matteucci, I. (2015). Social determinants of health inequalities: Moving toward a socio-constructivist model supported by information and communication technologies. *Global Bioethics, 26*(3–4), 206–217. https://doi.org/10.1080/11287462.2015.1101213.

Middleton, J. D. (1987). Health promotion is peace promotion. *Health Promotion, 2*(4), 341–345.

Milio, N. (1976). A framework for prevention: Changing health-damaging to health-generating life patterns. *American Journal of Public Health, 66*(5), 435–439.

Milio, N. (1988). Making healthy public policy; developing the science by learning the art: An ecological framework for policy studies. *Health Promotion, 2*(3), 263–274.

Minkler, M., & Cox, K. (1980). Creating critical consciousness in health: Applications of Freire's philosophy and methods to the health care setting. *International Journal of Health Services, 10*(2), 311–322. https://doi.org/10.2190/023k-58e7-6tm8-3rrm.

Perry, H., Zulliger, R., Scott, K., Javadi, D., Gergen, J., & Shelley, K. (2014). *Case studies of large-scale community health worker programs: Examples from Afghanistan, Bangladesh, Brazil, Ethiopia, India, Indonesia, Iran, Nepal, Pakistan, Rwanda, Zambia and Zimbabwe.* Developing and strengthening community health worker programs at scale: A reference guide and case studies for program managers and policymakers. Washington, DC: MCHIP.

PHM. (2000). The People's Charter for Health. Retrieved from http://www.phmovement.org/.

Reardon, B. A. (1993). *Women and peace: Feminist visions of global security.* Albany, NY: State University of New York Press.

Reardon, B. A. (2001). *Education for a culture of peace in gender perspective.* Paris: UNESCO.

Reardon, B. A., & Snauwaert, D. T. (2015a). *Betty A. Reardon: A pioneer in education for peace and human rights.* New York: Springer.

Reardon, B. A., & Snauwaert, D. T. (2015b). *Betty A. Reardon: Key texts in gender and peace.* New York: Springer.

Sharpe, A. (2010). Public health and patriarchy: Militarism and gender as determinants of health insecurity. In B. Reardon & A. Hans (Eds.), *The gender imperative: Human security or state security?* (pp. 351–383). New Delhi: Routledge.

Sharpe, A. (2018). *Pathways of change: A human security evaluation of a non-communicable disease prevention project in Sri Lanka* (PhD thesis), University of NSW, Sydney.

Sinmegn Mihrete, T., Asres Alemie, G., & Shimeka Teferra, A. (2014). Determinants of childhood diarrhea among underfive children in Benishangul Gumuz Regional State, North West Ethiopia. *BMC Pediatrics, 14*, 102. https://doi.org/10.1186/1471-2431-14-102.

St. Leger, L., Kolbe, L., Lee, A., McCall, D. S., & Young, I. M. (2007). School health promotion—Achievements and challenges. In D. McQueen & C. Jones (Eds.), *Global perspectives on health promotion effectiveness* (pp. 107–124). Atlanta, GA: Springer.

Swinburn, B. A., Kraak, V. I., Allender, S., Atkins, V. J., Baker, P. I., Bogard, J. R., … Devarajan, R. (2019). The global syndemic of obesity, undernutrition, and climate change: The Lancet Commission report. *The Lancet*. https://doi.org/10.1016/s0140-6736(18)32822-8.

Watts, N., Adger, W., & Ayeb-Karlsson, S. (2017). The Lancet countdown: Tracking progress on health and climate change. *The Lancet, 389*, 1151–1164.

WHO. (1946). Preamble to the Constitution of the World Health Organization as adopted by the International Health Conference, New York, 19–22 June 1946; signed on 22 July 1946 by the representatives of 61 States (Official Records of the World Health Organization, no. 2, p. 100) and entered into force on 7 April 1948.

WHO. (1978). *Declaration of Alma Ata*. International Conference on Primary Health Care, Alma-Ata, USSR, September 6–12. WHO.

WHO. (1986). *Ottawa Charter for Health Promotion*. International Conference on Health Promotion, Nov 21. Ottawa: The World Health Organization.

WHO. (2008). *Closing the gap in a generation: Health equity through action on the social determinants of health*. Final Report of the Commission on Social Determinants of Health. Geneva: World Health Organization.

World Conference on Social Determinants of Health. (2011). *Rio political declaration on social determinants of health*. Rio: World Health Organization.

Yuasa, M., Shirayama, Y., Kigawa, M., Chaturanga, I., Mizoue, T., & Kobayashi, H. (2015). A health promoting schools (HPS) program among primary and secondary school children in Southern Province, Sri Lanka: A qualitative study on the program's effects on the school children, parents, and teachers. *Kokusai Hoken Iryo (Journal of International Health), 30*(2), 93–101.

Chapter 19
"Walking the Talk" on Peace Education with Betty Reardon: Reflection and Action Towards a Transformative Pedagogy

Anita Yudkin

I first met Betty Reardon in 2005, at the International Institute on Peace Education held in Costa Rica. I was familiar with some of her written work and aware I was engaging in a learning opportunity with a giant whose shoulders we stand on. Yet there she was, an accessible educator who shared her knowledge and evoked ours as we explored ideas on the topics, pedagogy, and fields of action of peace education. This encounter moved me to delve into her contributions to peace education. As I studied her works, I came upon profound ideas and key connections that provided a clearer understanding of the obstacles to peace, the road ahead towards achieving peace, and the central role of education in this endeavor. Since then, I have continued sharing learning experiences with Betty that reflect her consistent and coherent way of being in this world, as she "walks the talk", acting on her ideas toward countering the culture of war and forging a culture of peace, based upon human rights, equality, and justice.

In this chapter, I reflect upon Betty Reardon's contributions to peace education, by studying her written works in relation to her practice as a peace scholar and activist. I will focus on two of her publications: *Learning to Abolish War*: *Teaching Toward a Culture of Peace* (Reardon/Cabezudo 2002) and *Human Rights Learning: Pedagogies and Politics of Peace* (Reardon 2010), as they provide key themes on her thoughts on peace, education, and pedagogy. I will also reflect upon Reardon's pedagogy and agency based on several of these learning exchanges, beginning with the International Institute on Peace Education (IIPE). I will address two other events that showcase the connection between knowledge and action towards peace in Reardon's work, the *Vieques Okinawan Women Solidarity Encounter*, and the symposium *Calling the Phoenix: Learning Toward Transcending Political and Natural Disasters*.

Anita Yudkin, Professor in the Educational Foundations Department, and Coordinator of the UNESCO Chair on Education for Peace at the University of Puerto Rico, San Juan, Puerto Rico; Email: anita.yudkin@upr.edu.

© Springer Nature Switzerland AG 2019
D. T. Snauwaert (ed.), *Exploring Betty A. Reardon's Perspective on Peace Education*, Pioneers in Arts, Humanities, Science, Engineering, Practice 20, https://doi.org/10.1007/978-3-030-18387-5_19

19.1 Learning to Abolish War: Critical Understanding for Peace

In *Learning to Abolish War*, Reardon/Cabezudo (2002) provide a conceptual and practical framework for peace education based on the Hague Agenda for Peace and Justice for the 21st Century. They develop a comprehensive approach to worldwide peace education; their core concept being abolition of war, and their overarching objective being achieving a culture of peace. Four conceptual strands guide this tool in educating and learning the knowledge, skills, and values to achieve these ends: root causes of war and culture of peace; international humanitarian and human rights law and institutions; prevention, resolution and transformation of violent conflict; and disarmament and human security.

I will focus on a series of principles that underlie the peace education approach developed throughout this framework. First, is the recognition that peace education should be included in curriculums of schools worldwide, in culturally relevant and age appropriate contents and methods. Reardon/Cabezudo (2002) propose that the solution to social problems like violence, discrimination, and destruction of the earth's resources, requires intentional public education. Such an education would provide learners with information about these problems and possible solutions, as well as skill building for action needed to address and rectify the problems, This education would engage citizens involved in the design and pursuit of solutions to local and global problems. This approach to a comprehensive, public peace education, is based upon a critical understanding of the root causes of the culture of war and violence, and envisions a different world order, toward a culture of peace.

Second, is the affirmation of the social purposes of peace education. Reardon/Cabezudo (2002) set forth that these main purposes are the elimination of injustice, the renunciation of violence, and the abolition of war. They emphasize the importance of understanding war as an institution, a systemic problem interrelated with multiple forms of violence. As such, it requires education programs geared towards addressing this system in its connection to other forms of structural violence that also emphasize possible alternatives for systemic change geared toward sustainable global peace. In pursuing these social goals, peace education seeks to engender a sense of human identity, based upon the promotion of human rights and recognition of our common humanity. It also aims to enable learners to see possibilities for transformation and the mechanisms involved in the development of alternative security systems, aimed at demilitarization, disarmament and human security. Reardon and Cabezudo assert "both a visionary and a practical belief in the possibility of a culture of peace are necessary to the task of abolition" (p. 19). A culture of peace in which justice, equity, and respect for human rights are maximized and violence is minimized in both structural and physical expressions.

A third interrelated principle of this comprehensive peace education approach is that schools should prepare learners to take active roles in civil society, that peace education must be action-oriented. It should develop awareness of social and political responsibilities, as it guides in developing points of view on the problems of peace and justice, while also encouraging the exploration of possible contributions to a culture of peace. Reardon/Cabezudo (2002) emphasize the critical dimension of these thought processes and capacities in educating students for active, responsible global citizenship. They also identify core values, which guide this approach to peace education, such as cultural diversity, gender equality, social responsibility, environmental sustainability, and human solidarity. Furthermore, they point to key capacities to be attained through skill development, including ecological awareness, cultural proficiency, gender sensitivity, conflict competency, and global agency.

A fourth principle that permeates throughout *Learning to Abolish War* is the conviction that pedagogy and methods of peace education must be consistent with its goals and purposes. Reardon/Cabezudo (2002) propose a process-oriented methodology and a participatory teaching and learning approach, that provides clear guidelines for implementing a pedagogy of engagement in peace education. Within a developmental framework, which is related to the central themes set forth for peace education, they suggest key values and capacities to be fostered by this active pedagogy of engagement. They insist on the need to develop critical inquiry and problem-solving skills, as well as nurturing the creative imagination of learners as they envision alternative futures. Reardon and Cabezudo point to human rights learning as a key example of this integrated way of understanding core peace education knowledge, values and capacities. Learning about human rights should engender respect for human dignity. Inquiry based human rights learning should provide a critical understanding of local and global problems. It should also guide students in making connections between rights and social responsibilities, which provide for involvement and action in pursuit of these rights.

19.2 Human Rights Learning: Constitutive to Pedagogies and Politics of Peace

In 2009, Betty Reardon delivered the UNESCO Chair for Peace Education Master Lecture *Human Rights Learning: Pedagogies and Politics of Peace* (Reardon 2010) at the University of Puerto Rico. Here she elaborated her thoughts and proposals on the interconnections between peace education and human rights learning. She advanced seven propositions in her claim that human rights learning is essential to effective pedagogies and politics of peace.

One of Reardon's (2010) propositions is that "human rights are integral and essential to peace and peace education" (p. 47), since they provide an ethical and political framework that allows us to visualize a "transformed peaceful and just global order" (p. 47). Human rights are the core and essential substance of peace education, providing for lived examples of human dignity or violations to this fundamental principle of human existence, thus making the abstraction of peace more tangible and constitutive of the organic functioning of a person in society. As such, she advances the idea that human rights learning is a process inspired toward social justice, mediated through active and reflective involvement of the learner with the substance of human rights. Human rights learning seeks to establish links with the lives of learners and human rights problems, providing for learners to engage with these problems and pursue alternatives in striving toward universal human dignity. Human rights learning follows a holistic approach that also promotes identifying connections among human rights issues and problems by looking at the global social system that perpetuates violence and injustice.

A second key proposition set forth by Reardon (2010) is "the violence and vulnerabilities of the global system frame ethical issues for human rights learning and a politics of peace" (p. 53). Reardon emphasizes the role of ethical reflection and analysis as integral components of peace learning and peace politics; reflection and analysis centered on understanding systemic violence and assuming social responsibility for the vulnerable. She contends that both capacities, those of ethical reflection and social responsibility, are essential to the development of "transformative thinking". They are central to citizen action to overcome various forms of structural violence and thus necessary for a politics of peace. She asserts that violence – defined as intentional, avoidable harm – is the central problematic of peace education, and proposes human dignity and human responsibility as key values to be nurtured in understanding and minimizing the problems of violence. In arguing this proposition, Reardon uses the metaphor of a "zoom lens" to illustrate the need to mentally shift from a wide angle view of the problematic of violence to a narrow focus in studying the specific details or particular forms and problems of violence. She proposes to awaken learners to all forms of violence and vulnerability as goals of peace education, and that political action to claim human dignity and human rights is the politics of justice and transformative politics of learning.

Several propositions advanced by Reardon (2010) make explicit the convergence between human rights learning, peace education, the ideas of Paulo Freire, and the guiding principles and methods of critical pedagogy. Reardon argues that "human rights learning is a contemporary form of Freirian political pedagogy" (p. 50), and that "critical pedagogy is the methodology most consistent with the transformative goals of peace education and human rights learning" (p. 66). Reardon embraces key concepts of Freirean thought, such as conscientization and the political nature of education. She explains her understanding of conscientization as an awakening or becoming aware of the realities of our lives and societies, and the interrelationships between these realms of experience. She also underlines the political nature of peace education as it aims for learners to deliberate on the goals and purposes of society, while engaging in a politics of nonviolence and peace committed to the general public good, social and economic wellbeing, and environmental justice. She suggests that engaging in such a politics of peace would entail "practicing politics as learning and learning as political engagement" (p. 46). Reardon asserts that peace education is committed to transformative change toward reducing violence and vulnerability by means of a pedagogy that enables learners to engage in a critical analysis of political and social structures of power while developing capacities to envision and affect such change.

Reardon (2010) further elaborates on the pedagogy and methods required for this transformative approach to peace education and human rights learning. In this regard, she states the proposition: "inquiry is the teaching mode most consistent with the principles and purposes of critical learning" (p. 67). She proposes that the central learning mechanism is a question; a question that engages the learner with the substance of that which is to be changed. The core learning goal is critical reflection. By inquiry she refers to a series of questions and queries that address core problematics and their sub-problems. Systematically constructed queries are the basis of communal learning process of critical reflection and dialogue. This process should provide for description and understanding of these problems, the questioning of world-views, as well as the consideration of multiple, complex possibilities. It is open, risky, and courageous in seeking such possibilities while inspiring hope that current limits can be surpassed. Reardon insists that human rights learning and peace education require active, participatory and reflective pedagogies, which lead to evaluation, analysis, and envisioning of alternative futures. Reardon asserts, "critical learning has the potential to capacitate learners to live so as to move the world toward what it might become, toward a holistic vision of a social order based on human dignity" (p. 69).

19.3 Walking the Talk: Education, Reflection, and Action for Peace

Reardon's ideas highlighted above are present in her educational and political work for peace. As I have shared learning opportunities with Betty, I have seen her *walk the talk* as she brings these principles, propositions, and pedagogies to life. As previously mentioned, our first encounter took place in 2005, at the International Institute for Peace Education (IIPE) held at the University for Peace in Costa Rica. I later attended other institutes celebrated in Hungary, Colombia, and Japan. The 2013 IIPE was convened at the University of Puerto Rico hosted by the UNESCO Chair for Peace Education. In the past years I have become more involved as both a participant and organizer of this shared learning encounter.

The IIPE was created by Betty Reardon in order to bring together educators, academics, and activists for peace from around the world to exchange knowledge and experiences. It is based on a participatory, cooperative, exploratory pedagogy that leads to deep inquiry into key issues of peace and seeks to advance the theory and practice of peace education (https://www.i-i-p-e.org). Even though Betty is no longer involved directly in the planning and logistics of the institutes, her vision of peace education is always present. She also continues to be an active participant-learner in many sessions providing thought provoking questions and engaging workshops.

Every IIPE centers on a different theme that brings forth crucial issues in educating towards a culture of peace. Over the past decade, these have included: a planetary ethic of individual and shared responsibility; human rights and democracy in times of crisis; educating for justice and peace; learning to read the world from multiple perspectives; toward a possible world free from violence; educating for human security, as well as urban revitalization and peace education in an era of globalization. Although global in nature, they reflect key local matters important to the place and time where IIPEs are held. Reardon's proposal that peace education should foster understanding of the links between global problems and local issues is at the heart of the conceptual planning of the institutes. These connections are also explored in plenary and individual sessions in an emergent web of study, awareness, and understanding.

Essential to the nature of the IIPE, is that all participants contribute to the institutes' subjects of study and pedagogy, promoting involvement and the cultivation of diverse ideas and possible actions toward peace. At the core of the IIPE's learning, are the reflection groups that provide for profound thinking and camaraderie. The IIPE methodology is active and participatory, and often fun, yet it is serious in its commitment to critical reflection and deep understanding of violence in its many forms and the role of education in overcoming them. The IIPE provides a lived learning experience that exemplifies many of the principles and propositions espoused by Reardon's pedagogy for peace. They are learner and learning centered, provide for transformative thinking, cultivate solidarity and a sense of human identity.

Two other events highlight Reardon's commitment to transcend the culture of war and violence by means of educational and political action towards peace. Her concern for the impact of militarism on women and the lives of those communities most directly affected by its destructive power led her to propose an encounter between women from Okinawa and Vieques – two islands that have suffered from United States military practices and munition testing. The *Vieques Okinawa Women Solidarity Encounter*, was held in Vieques in 2010. Betty suggested a public forum where women from both islands spoke about the impact of the training for war on their communities and family's wellbeing. The forum was meant to raise awareness of the larger problematics of militarism, colonialism, and war while engendering understanding of the effects on the lands, lives, and human rights of those most vulnerable. In addition, and faithful to her commitment toward empowerment and action, Betty proposed a working session to plan for future collaborations between the women. This session was also to provide the basis for an education guide on the topic of militarism, women, and peace, seeking to broaden the political-educational impact of the meeting. A *Vieques – Okinawa Women United Solidarity Statement* (2010) was issued as a result of the encounter calling for the governments of the

United States, Japan, and Puerto Rico to assume legal obligations and ethical responsibilities to end the exploitation of these lands and people, safely removing military contaminants, allocating resources for communal development, based on human security and the full respect for human rights and dignity of our peoples.

Since her visit to the University of Puerto Rico in 2009 to deliver the Master Lecture previously referred to, Betty has continued to be attentive to events taking place in the island and concerned over developments that threaten public education, democratic civic engagement, human rights and peace. Coherent with the goals, principles, and pedagogy she proposes for holistic education for peace, she poses questions, studies issues and problems carefully, and proposes mechanisms for action toward transcending the limits of present realities. On September 20th of 2017, Puerto Rico was devastated by a category 5 hurricane, which brought physical, environmental, economic, and social destruction across the island. As communications and power failed for months, some messages from very dear and caring IIPE colleagues managed to come through. One of these was an email from Betty inviting me to come to New York in the spring for a forum on peace education. The farthest thing on my mind at the time was approaching this tragedy as a "teachable moment" for peace, since we were still amidst basic recovery efforts and attempting to reinitiate academic activities at the university. But, Betty insisted this was an important opportunity for educating and learning about the multiple layers of the situation in Puerto Rico, the ongoing economic and political crisis,[1] aggravated by the devastation caused by the hurricane.

In April 2018, I joined admired peace educators, Amada Benavides, Janet Gerson, and Betty Reardon at the forum *"Calling the Phoenix": Learning Toward Transcending Political and Natural Disasters.* The forum addressed the role of peace education in the Colombia peace process, the post-hurricane situation in Puerto Rico, and current implications of post-conflict and post-natural disaster peace education efforts. It brought together educators and activists in a participatory event, for awareness raising and solidarity-based actions. Betty insisted that participants should become aware that people in Puerto Rico were suffering unnecessarily because of inadequate policies, and thus political actions were required. The forum was consistent with Reardon's claim that peace education should provide for an understanding of the links between multiple problems of violence and exclusion in fostering human rights learning and action for peace.

Furthermore, during my visit to New York, Betty arranged for a meeting with Adriano Espaillat, her district representative to the United States Congress. As his constituent, Betty demanded to be heard on the status of public education in the

---

[1]Addressing the political and economic crisis in Puerto Rico is beyond the scope of this chapter. However, a brief note is in order. It is rooted in the colonial relationship between Puerto Rico and the United States. In recent years, the political crisis has become manifest in United States judicial decisions and public policies that reaffirm that "Puerto Rico belongs to but is not a part of the United States". The response to economic recession, and increased debt has been the appointment by the United States Congress of the Financial Management and Oversight Board, with powers over public budget and thus public policy, pushing for reduction of public services.

United States, in New York, and in Puerto Rico. Also on the effects of the Congress imposed Financial Oversight and Management Board for Puerto Rico, as its economic policies gave way to the closing of public schools by the government of Puerto Rico just when they were most needed for recovery and human security. As we met with the Congressman's assistant, Betty's voice became stronger (not louder, stronger) as she explained why these issues were central to his responsibilities and questioned him on the necessary action toward justice. Here I walked along her side with trepidation. I knew she was absolutely right in her claim for responsibility and justice, yet arguing for the United States to take responsibility over its actions for citizens in Puerto Rico requires an ideological turn that made it a complex personal undertaking.

In all three peace education initiatives addressed above, Reardon's thoughts come to fruition through a carefully planned pedagogy that is meant to involve all participants in reflective inquiry that leads to social and political action. Questioning military domination, colonial relationships, and injustice, Reardon guides us in ways of learning and understanding global violence while empowering for action towards justice and peace.

19.4   Denouncing with Indignation and Announcing with Hope: Freirean Politics Toward Transformative Pedagogies for Peace

In closing, I consider ideas advanced by Paulo Freire in his book *Pedagogy of Indignation* (Freire 2004), published after his untimely death, as these shed light on the relevance of Reardon's thoughts and pedagogy to the current problematics of violence and peace. In this book, Freire manifests a growing concern with the world's situation in relation to neoliberal political and economic policies, as well as the impact of globalization on people's lives in general and on education policy and practice in particular. He builds on his previous ideas on the political nature of education and addresses the role and tasks of education in facing such realities.

In the essay *On the Right and the Duty to Change the World*, Freire (2004) underlines the importance of dreams, visions, and utopias in engaging in learning and action to transform the world. He points to an ethic of caring and respect for the dignity of others to surpass the increasingly influential "market ethics" of the neoliberal order. He professes "the future does not make us. We make ourselves in the struggle to make it" (p. 34). A struggle, undertaken in the name of the "universal ethic of human beings", to transform society in overcoming dehumanizing injustice. He reasserts his defense for a radical educational practice that encourages critical curiosity to intervene in the world. In *Education and Hope* (Freire 2004), Freire furthers his proposals by affirming that education is a process of hope-filled search that is needed more than ever; a search and a struggle founded in effective political-ethical action.

In *Denouncing, Announcing, Prophecy, Utopia and Dreams*, Freire (2004) urges that the transgressions on the universal ethic of human beings must be denounced. He affirms we must emerge from today fully aware of reality as a starting point, and based on a critical analysis of the present, denounce how we are living. At the same time, prophetically announce how we could live, in a permanent search for insertion into the world, intervening and reinventing the world through critical curiosity and creative capacities. This can only happen if we see the future as problematic, as a possibility we dare dream of, a dream we must incessantly strive to build. Furthermore, Freire identifies "the issue of violence" - including direct, symbolic, and social-structural violence - as one of the main challenges facing humanity at the end of the 20th century. In this regard, and faithful to his imperative that we must denounce with indignation all forms of injustice and announce with hope a vision of a world we struggle to build, he states "the struggle for peace ... is an imperative requirement of our times" (p. 118). A struggle in favor of justice, undertaken with hope and fearlessness, against all forms of violence.

19.5 Conclusion

Reardon's thoughts and proposals for transcending violence and educating towards peace provide an.ethical and practical framework for action to claim human dignity. Her pedagogy and political actions are exemplary of the trans-formative power of education. In facing the many challenges we encounter at the present time, like the problematics of violence, militarism, neoliberal economic policies, and global sustainability, Reardon's ideas and actions towards peace provide much needed insight and guidance toward building a possible future characterized by justice, equity, human rights and peace. In this regard, her defense of an intentional peace education that provides for understanding of these challenges and the structures of power which sustain them, as well as the development of skills and capacities for action to overcome them is fundamental. Her proposal for a sustained educational effort towards global peace is based on the development of awareness of our social and political responsibilities for achieving it. She thus affirms, in a Freirean perspective, that learning is an act of political engagement toward an active global citizenship. Furthermore, she pro-poses that education towards a culture of peace is to develop the key capacities of ethical reflection in understanding and questioning multiple forms of global violence as well as the social responsibility for the most vulnerable, based upon the recognition of human dignity and the defense of human rights. Critical reflection, inquiry, analysis and dialogue are proposed as central to this type of transformative learning, fostering a pedagogy of engagement and creative imagination. Certainly, Reardon has walked the way towards peace by means of her ideas and actions, leading us to continue this walk equipped with pedagogical knowledge, clarity, hope, and courage.

References

Freire, P. (2004). *Pedagogy of indignation*. Boulder, CO: Paradigm Publishers.

Reardon, B. (2010). *Human rights learning: Pedagogies and politics of peace/Aprendizaje en derechos humanos: Pedagogías y políticas de paz*. 2008–2009 Keynote Address UNESCO Chair in Education for Peace. San Juan, Puerto Rico: University of Puerto Rico. http://unescopaz.uprrp.edu/act/Lecciones/2009reardon/HRLearningBettyReardon.pdf.

Reardon, B., & Cabezudo, A. (2002). *Learning to abolish war: Teaching toward a culture of peace*. New York: Hague Appeal for Peace. http://www.peace-ed-campaign.org/learning-to-abolish-war-teaching-toward-a-culture-of-peace/.

Vieques-Okinawa Women United Solidarity Statement. (2010, September 11). http://unescopaz.uprrp.edu/act/Vieques-Okinawa/VIEQUES-OKINAWA%20STATEMENT.pdf.

Concluding Reflections

Perspectives on the Gifts of Peacelearning: Looking Back, Looking Forward

Betty Reardon

Looking Back: Opportunities and Connections

All that I have done in peace education has been taken from a cornucopia of the gifts from those I encountered in the field. The work unfolded through opportunities often as unexpected as they were welcome. The gifts of peace education are those learnings offered in exchanges with others venturing into the same territory of adapting education to the goals of achieving peace. The opportunities are the situations and events which offer positive possibilities for striving toward that goal. Such exchanges are the medium of what Tony Jenkins has termed "peacelearning," a holistic, organic process of internalizing the insights and honing the skills of agents.

Such are the gifts offered by the chapters of this book that each re-awakened the sense of connection that is the essence of peacelearning, and each recalled some of the multiple shared learning opportunities with the authors (I have shared such opportunities with all but two of the authors in the collection) that have contributed to my own peacelearning over the last few decades of my long life in peace education. I am deeply grateful for these gifts.

I am grateful, as well to Hans Günter Brauch who initiated the project. My special gratitude goes to Dale Snauwaert, who orchestrated and conducted the process of producing this book. His introduction highlights elements of my work reflected in each chapter, a gift in itself as he puts the work in the holistic perspective to which I had aspired. A gratifying complement to Dale's observations was Ursula Oswald Spring's preface contextualizing the forms and stages of the perspectives on gender that as Dale notes, infuse so much of my peace education work. I sincerely and humbly thank all the authors. Each of their chapters was a unique gift, drawing up personal recollections of particular learning moments

Prof. Dr. Betty Reardon, Emerita, Teachers College, Columbia University, New York;
Email: bar19@columbia.edu.

© Springer Nature Switzerland AG 2019
D. T. Snauwaert (ed.), *Exploring Betty A. Reardon's Perspective
on Peace Education*, Pioneers in Arts, Humanities, Science,
Engineering, Practice 20, https://doi.org/10.1007/978-3-030-18387-5

shared with these much valued and respected colleagues, a few with whom common peacelearning began in their days as graduate students. The duration and the vitality of these connections speak volumes of the human qualities of tenacity and ever eager curiosity that are characteristic of peacelearners. The chapters also reveal the depth and breadth of peace education, a rich field that produces rich relationships of reciprocal giving. It is our habit to give to each other the fruits of our respective learnings.

The most valuable gifts of peacelearning are exchanged in the special learning opportunities in our encounters with the multiple perspectives of our fellow peacelearners. The perspectives of all with whom I have shared learning opportunities have profoundly influenced my own personal and professional perspectives. Not that I can claim to fully comprehend the perspectives of others, but the efforts to perceive and appreciate how others see the world, at a minimum, makes it evident that our own view of the world is but one of many, an understanding of which cultivates an appreciation for diversity. The consideration and appreciation of diverse, alternative views is integral to peacelearning. Indeed, all peace edulearners (those who achieve much of their learning in facilitating the learning of others) approach the peace problematic from the perspectives that form their own respective world views, experiences and locations, providing our field with the diversity we prize. This diversity has enriched and strengthened the field, and helped us to develop self-awareness. In becoming self-aware learners, we come to understand the complexity, the multidimensionality of how we look at the world. Cultivating awareness of self, our own perspectives as well as those of others whom we encounter in the contexts of our practice is necessary to comprehending the complexity and multidimensionality of the problems we seek to address. It is a process that leads to the holism many of us acknowledge as our common perspective. Such holism comes from reflection on and integration of the complementarities of the various perspectives of those with whom we interact in the peacelearning process. All contributors to this book have experienced such processes. Their chapters reveal the reflection through which they have integrated their experience into their practice.

The primary task of peace edulearners is to practice and facilitate reflection. Peacelearning is the sum of reflections on all learning experiences – intellectual, social and political, ethical, aesthetic, emotional even physical. Our reflections lead us toward human wholeness and draws us into efforts to restore wholeness to the world. The most authentic and effective medium for facilitation is in actual human encounters, conversations in shared spaces where we see each other in our respective multidimensionalities, as we have in the courses and projects referenced in these chapters. The conversation can be continued through the marvel of electronic media that help us to maintain our connections. But it cannot be fully initiated without the multidimensional, direct encounters with actual persons, our interlocutors in the conversations of peacelearning. The internet can help sustain our web of human relationships, but it does not constitute the web.

We who have lived the contents of this book are gratefully aware of this web of relationships, of experiencing learning as caring, caring for each other as we care for all that makes for peace and for the Earth on which we hope to share it. We hope that the readers of this book may perceive enough of that web to understand the rewards integral to that form of peace education we call peacelearning, taking that perception as validation of the concerns and purposes that lead to this book. Even those who are not sequential, beginning-to-end readers will have read enough before reading this epilogue to have become sufficiently aware of that learning web of peace to understand how those whose practice has interwoven them into it are sustained and validated by it. I hope that in this book readers will catch a glimpse of themselves within the web and so weave their own learning lives into it.

It is this web of relationships that has sustained me throughout my own peacelearning life. Beginning with the seeding years of learning the craft of teaching with young teens, continuing through the first years of the Peace Education Commission of the International Peace Research Association, to the founding and evolution of the International Institute on Peace Education, and on to these days of harvest, the weaving has been constant. Being tethered to this web of human connections became one significant perspective from which the work that was my peacelearning evolved, contributing to the perspectives of wholeness and living systems I came to identify as ecological thinking, centered in the world's living, evolving realities, so constrained by the very structures challenged by all areas peace knowledge. Through colleagues, many becoming friends, I saw multiple views of the world and a variety of approaches to educate to change the structures. From this learning came the perspective of striving, even struggling, as we inquired into the means to overcome or transform the constraints, to design and build alternative structures and the pedagogies that could prepare learners to achieve them.

Through all of this, I never doubted the possibility of peace. However, it took time and squarely facing the obstacles of the institutional and attitudinal realities that confront peace and peace education, to appreciate more fully how great was the challenge to make it probable. There was constant uncertainty in the social/political structures that were the context of all peacelearning, in the institutions in which we conducted the practice and in the efficacy of the practice itself. Inquiry became the preferred learning mode out of the limits to our substantive knowledge, as culti-vation of reflection became the preferred pedagogy out lack of ready answers and of the limitless possibilities of inquiring minds. From the perspective of reflective inquiry the possibilities for peacelearning and the multiple modes of peacemaking and peace building as opportunities to make the possible probable are also unlimited, offering myriad opportunities to learn and act, as so vividly described in this book. I see the task of the peacelearner-builder as one of discerning and acting upon the opportunities that are presented to us.

All who have contributed to this volume have been significant discerners of opportunity. Their discernment has led to the significant contributions each has made to wider peacelearning opportunities for all. As I wrote to them in my initial message of thanks,

> Each of your chapters offers something of significance [to peace education] beyond your
> very kind and relevant references to my perspectives...

Every author reveals learning-provoking elements of their own perspectives, illuminating the significance of the book's title. As they "explore" my perspectives each presents individual and unique recollections of opportunities for peacelearning and peace building. It is the perspectives from which the work is done, the viewpoints that guide the learning inquiry that distinguishes peacelearning from other forms of social and political education. Peace edulearners view all learning within an acknowledged and explicit frame of values at the center of which is human dignity and wholeness. Values are the common bond that ties together the multiple and particular views that comprise our efforts to bring about a world that sustains human wholeness and the wholeness of our Earth.

The perspective from which I look back on my own peacelearning is from this web of human connections woven through encounters with those who made this book and others I have learned with and befriended, the perspective of the familiar. Other than this human web, there is no sustaining familiarity as a perspective from which to look forward. The perspective of uncertainty, of unknown contexts and un-encountered persons is my view forward.

Looking Forward: Aspirations and Initiatives

Looking forward in uncertainty is common to the human family as it is to most peace educators. Practitioners of peace studies and peace education are certainly familiar with not knowing if they will have the resources to carry their work forward. The fields may be more "established" now, yet, we never know when some institutional priority shift might "disestablish" our programs. In recent years in many countries such has occurred. None-the-less, present practitioners carry on, inspiring more young educators to commit to our values, weaving themselves into our ever widening web. Much of this weaving is through the long and vibrant threads of the International Institute on Peace Education and other initiatives such as some described in these chapters. The flourishing of our field is depicted daily on the website of the Global Campaign for Peace Education. The peace education movement continues to grow, to become stronger and to mature in these most uncertain and unsettling times.

Even in these days in which we struggle to "keep hope alive," I have such faith in this generation of peace edulearners that I dare to look forward to continued opportunities for our field. We all know too well that this is a time when everything is "up for grabs." Those of views antithetical to ours have a longer reach and stronger grasp than ours. The greatest challenge will be reaching out to them, to find some ground on which at least a beginning exchange can take place. The future may well depend upon how we take up this challenge. May we be emboldened to do so by the strength of our values, our commitment to strive for them, and the courage to enter into this unknown territory.

We will need such courage and every bit of strength and wisdom we have acquired to withstand much less overcome what we now face. On all sides, in most parts of the world our purposes are intentionally undermined by ways of thinking, policies and actions, by both institutional and individual forces that deny our core values and seek to severe the most fragile fibers of our web. Yet these are the forces with which we must engage. We know not where the next challenges will come from, nor what their natures will be. But we know they will come. We also know the issues producing the conflicts and controversies that are likely to give rise to them: The ecological crisis, the crises of war system and its most lethal component, nuclear weapons and the human rights crises of the patriarchal global order that has produced the whole range of crises by holding the vast majority of the human family in the imposed vulnerability of subordinate status. This severely unjust order denies to the world untold sources of human ingenuity and energy that might be brought to bear in meeting these challenges and the multiple quotidian and local problems they spawn. The unfettering of this ingenuity and energy should be high among the goals of the coming phase of peace education. It is a challenge already taken up by many non-formal, activist peace educators.

Though we all exist in the same web of planetary life, we cannot have the intense learning encounters we value so dearly with any but a tiny portion of the millions of the vulnerable and subordinated. But the peacelearning that has bound us together can become the means through which we edulearners and all committed peace-learners can act upon our responsibility to undertake any and all opportunities to contribute to overcoming the structures that oppress them. The peace education movement, in becoming a vibrant part of global civil society can be a significant force in confronting the forces that hold these oppressive structures in place. We have long done so locally and in recent years nationally and regionally. Now is the time to intentionally interweave our web with those of other global civil society movements, the environmental movement, the movements to abolish war and nuclear weapons and the human rights movements with special attention to those that strive toward gender equity and equality so as the dismantle the global patriarchy.

More than this, with a weaving of the movements together in a common struggle, the holism of our perspectives and our practices can facilitate not only cooperative links, we can illuminate the interrelationships among all the issues we contend with, demonstrate how they not only "intersect" but "*interfunction*," operating together to perform the violence and oppression that sustains the current global system. We can help mobilize learning communities to design strategies that weave these multiple movements into a common endeavor to transform that system to one of nonviolent wholeness in which human dignity is the norm. What we have learned in weaving our own web of multiple perspectives on peace learning, we can use in cultivating a new web, tying it to ours, offering learning opportunities that will affirm and strengthen each distinct movement as it synergizes them into a collaborative global transformation force. To this force we can bring the holistic perspective to these systemically interrelated problems that is so sorely needed for their lasting resolution.

We in the peace education movement will need these new strands of a global web to continue to sustain us, and to continue to learn from the perspectives and strategies of other movements. This learning needs to be more systematic and intentional, even more so than our learning gleaned in study of the issues the various movements address. Should we succeed in forming multi-movement learning communities, we can seek out the types of conversations from which we learned such much in IIPEs and other diverse gatherings of edulearners. We can strive for fresh learnings from those whose more experienced in continuous, direct activism, to learn how to sustain the risks of a strong commitment to the trans-formation of the suffering and outright evil that plagues us. Learning from more regular and intensive direct interaction with these movements will offer a new dimension to our own practice. We will continue to need abstract concepts to understand the problematic, but we need always to keep in mind, especially if we are among those who do not endure the worst, that those entrapped in the prob-lematic are individual human persons, their bodies, minds and souls are the direct recipients of the evils we decry. We are bound not to look away, not to respond only with the ready actions of petitions and demonstrations, but to stand in the authentic solidarity that is not riskless. Perhaps learning how to do so, might be the main inquiry of this present phase of our development. Might not this, our capacity for solidarity be the true test of our maturity? Easy enough for me, who will have so much less time in this land of new uncertainties, to write of risk and sustained solidarity, readers may well think. And I certainly agree. How easy it is to theorize and prescribe, comparatively riskless. However, I am led to state these aspirations by my knowledge of and faith in those who have contributed these chapters. No strangers to professional risks and myriad uncertainties, they have both the capacities and the inclination for active engagement with these unprecedented adversities. All positive possibilities foreseen here are already glimmering in a number of the darker places where peacelearning seeks to shed light. The foreseen can be because it already is. I have every reason to hope that peace education as a movement is adequately equipped to step forward into uncertain contexts with known antagonist and unknown allies, fully able to live the mantra of "peace in the struggle."

Conclusion

I conclude with a bit more of my initial thanks to the contributors,
There is nothing that means more to me than... the further
development of peace education, ever revealing possibilities for
the learning [that] we need to hold fast to our living Earth.
[Let us] continue to do our best to learn with our students
[and others encountered in all our learning experiences]
how we might move our societies toward the world we
know is possible.

To those who have made this book and to all those who have been agents of my peacelearning, I say humbly and sincerely, *thank you.*

Thanks to the "contributors" those in this book and multiplicities of others.

Betty A. Reardon Publications

Reardon, Betty A. (1967). The World Law Fund: World Approach to International Education. *Teachers College Record, 68*(6), 453–465.

Reardon, Betty A., & Mendlovitz, Saul. (1968). World Law and Models of World Order. In J. Becker & H. Mehlinger (Eds.), *International Dimensions in the Social Studies* (Vol. 38th Yearbook). New York: National Council for the Social Studies.

Griffith, Priscilla, & Reardon, Betty A. (Eds.). (1968). *Let Us Examine Our Attitude Toward Peace: An Inquiry Into Some of the Political and Psychological Barriers to World Peace*. New York: World Law Fund.

Reardon, Betty A. (1968). World Order Education. *World Law Fund Progress Report, 1*(2).

Reardon, Betty A. (1969). Prologue, A Unit on Peace and World Order. *Media and Methods, 10* (10), 33–36.

Reardon, Betty A. (1969). War is …? *Ways and Means of Teaching About World Order, 1*(Fall).

Reardon, Betty A. (1969). The World Law Fund. *News and Views, Pennsylvania Council for Social Studies, 16*(1).

Reardon, Betty A., & Thorpe, Gerald. (1970). Peace Games. *AAUW Journal, May*, 192–195.

Reardon, Betty A. (1970). Teaching About Arms Poiicy. *Ways and Means of Teaching About World Order, 2*(Winter).

Reardon, Betty A. (1970). Who Speaks for Man? *Ways and Means of Teaching About World Order, 3*(Spring), 1–2.

Reardon, Betty A. (1970). Who Speaks for Man? The 25th Anniversary of the United Nations. *Ways and Means of Teaching About World Order, 4*(Fall).

Thorpe, Gerald, & Reardon, Betty A. (1971). World Order and Simulation. *The High School Journal, 55*(2), 53–62.

Reardon, Betty A. (1971). A Case for Futurism in the Social Studies. *Social Science Record, April*.

Reardon, Betty A. (1971). Futurism. *Ways and Means of Teaching About World Order, 7*(Fall), 1–2.

Reardon, Betty A. (1971). Introduction, The Human Person and the War System. *Intercom, 13*(1), 21–28.

Reardon, Betty A. (1971). Michael Scott: An Individual and the International System. *Intercom, 13*(1), 66–72.

Reardon, Betty A. (1971). The World Law Fund. *Intercom, 13*(2).

Reardon, Betty A. (1971). World Law: What Does it Mean? What Could It Do For the World? *Vital Issues, 20*(10).

Reardon, Betty A., & Thorpe, Gerald. (1972). Futurism in the Classroom. *California Council for the Social Studies Review, 11*(4), 3–6.

© Springer Nature Switzerland AG 2019
D. T. Snauwaert (ed.), *Exploring Betty A. Reardon's Perspective
on Peace Education*, Pioneers in Arts, Humanities, Science,
Engineering, Practice 20, https://doi.org/10.1007/978-3-030-18387-5

Fraenkel, Jack R, Carter, Margaret, & Reardon, Betty A. (1973). *Peacekeeping*. New York: Random House.

Reardon, Betty A., Fraenkel, Jack R, & Carter, Margaret. (1973). *Struggle for Human Rights*. New York: Random House.

Reardon, Betty A., & Carter, Margaret. (1973). Procedures for Analyzing and Clarifying Values Related to Human Rights. *Pennsylvania Council for Social Studies, 1*(2), 7–12.

Reardon, Betty A. (1973). Legal Education from the Global Perspective. *Law in American Society, 2*(3).

Reardon, Betty A. (1973). Model Building and Systems Inquiry. *Ways and Means of Teaching About World Order, 12*(June), 1–2.

Reardon, Betty A. (1973). Peace is Possible ... Who Can Make It Probable. *Today's Catholic Teacher, 6*(7).

Reardon, Betty A. (1973). Transformations into Peace and Survival: Programs for the 1970s. In G. Henderson (Ed.), *Education for Peace: Focus on Mankind* (pp. 127–151). Alexandria, VA: Association for Supervision and Curriculum Development.

Reardon, Betty A., & Colby, Curtis. (1974). *Beyond the Cold War*. New York: Random House.

Reardon, Betty A., & Colby, Curtis. (1974). *War Criminals, War Victims*. New York: Random House.

Reardon, Betty A. (1974). The Aims of Education for Peace. *Peace and the Sciences*, 74–76.

Reardon, Betty A. (1974). Beyond Nationalism: Education and Survival. In D. W. Allen (Ed.), *Controversies in Education* (pp. 57–64). Philadelphia: W. B. Saunders Company.

Reardon, Betty A. (1974). Beyond Nationalism: Education and Survival. *The New Era, 54*(7), 168–174.

Reardon, Betty A. (1974). Education for Peace and Social Justice. *Geographical Perspective, 34* (Fall).

Reardon, Betty A. (1974). Report of the WCCI Transnational Committee for Constitutional Review. In M. Haavelsrud (Ed.), *Education for Peace: Reflection and Action*. Norway: IDC, Science and Technology Press.

Reardon, Betty A. (1974). The Role of Women in Future Studies. *Earthrise, 2*(5), 181, 188–189.

Fraenkel, Jack R, Carter, Margaret, & Reardon, Betty A. (1975). *The Struggle for Human Rights*. New York: Random House.

Reardon, Betty A. (1975). International Women's Year. *Earthrise, 3*(4).

Reardon, Betty A. (1975). Women's Movements and Human Futures. *Convergence, 8*(3), 41–52.

Reardon, Betty A. (1975). Comments on State of the Globe Report. *Alternatives: A Journal of World Policy, 1*(4), 561–565.

Reardon, Betty A. (1975). A Social Education for Human Survival: A Synthesis of Practices in International Education and Peace Studies. *Social Studies Review, 15*(1), 42–48.

Reardon, Betty A. (1975). Women and Structural Violence: A Crucial Issue for Peace Education. *Journal of Peace Education, India*.

Reardon, Betty A. (1975). Women's Movements and Human Futures. *Convergence, 8*(3), 41–52.

Reardon, Betty A. (1976). Designing a New World Order. In B. Stanford (Ed.), *Peacemaking: A Guide to Conflict Resolution for Individuals, Groups, and Nations*. New York: Bantam Books.

Reardon, Betty A. (1976). Disarmament: A Key Concept for Peace Education. *Journal of World Education, 7*(4), 1, 10.

Reardon, Betty A. (1976). Woman and Food: Personal Perspectives on a Global Problem. *Ways and Means of Teaching About World Order, 20*(January), 1–4.

Reardon, Betty A. (1976). World Law and International Institutions. In T. W. A. C. o. Philadelphia (Ed.), *The INTERdependence Curriculum Aid* (pp. 101–111). Philadelphia: The World Affairs Council of Philadelphia in Cooperation with the School District of Philadelphia.

Reardon, Betty A. (1977). *Discrimination: The Cycle of Injustice*. Sydney, Australia: Holt-Saunders.

Reardon, Betty A. (1977). Human Rights and Education Reform. *Bulletin on Peace Proposals, 8* (3), 247–250.

Reardon, Betty A. (1977). A Teacher's Guide to *World Military and Social Expenditures*. New York: Rockefeller Foundation Educational Publishing Program.

Reardon, Betty A. (1977). Teaching About Arms and Security. *Ways and Means of Teaching About World Order, 23*(May), 1–4.

Reardon, Betty A. (1977). Using World Order Models to Teach Global Law. *Law in American Society, 6*(4).

Reardon, Betty A. (1978). Disarmament and Peace Education. *Prospects: Quarterly Review of Education, 8*(4), 395–408.

Reardon, Betty A. (1978). The Human Person and the War System. In I. W. Charny (Ed.), *Strategies Against Violence: Design for Non-Violent Change*. Boulder, CO: Westview Press.

Reardon, Betty A. (1978). Human Rights. Philadelphia: School District of Philadelphia, World Affairs Council of Philadelphia.

Reardon, Betty A. (1978). Peace as an Educational End and Process. In B. Weston, S. Schwenninger & D. Shamis (Eds.), *Peace and World Order studies*. New York: Transnational Academic Program, Institute of World Order.

Reardon, Betty A. (1978). A Preliminary Study of the Obstacles to, the Status of, and Potential for Education for the Promotion of Disarmament (SS/78) Conf. 603/13. Paris: UNESCO.

Reardon, Betty A. (1978). *Reflections on a Task: Increasing the Volume and Effectiveness of Women's Political Participation*. Background paper for COPRED/UNESCO, International Colloquium on Women's Political Participation.

Reardon, Betty A. (1978). Teaching About Disarmament: The Process, Conversion and Citizen Action. *Ways and Means of Teaching About World Order, 25*(May), 1–4.

Reardon, Betty A. (1978). Teaching About the Arms Race: Its Dynamic, The Costs, and the Consequences. *Ways and Means of Teaching About World Order, 24*(February), 1–4.

Reardon, Betty A. (1979). The Child and World Order. *The Whole Earth Papers, Global Education Associates* (11), 1–10.

Reardon, Betty A. (1979). Obstacles to Disarmament Education. *Bulletin on Peace Proposals, 10* (4), 356–367.

Reardon, Betty A. (1979). Organizer's Report on COPRED International Symposium on Women's Political Participation: COPRED.

Reardon, Betty A. (1980). Commitments to Principles: A Review of Professional and Political Statements on Education for International Understanding, Cooperation and Peace. *World Studies Journal, 1*(4), 12–20.

Reardon, Betty A. (1980). Debating the Future. *Network, 8*(3), 17–20.

Reardon, Betty A. (1980). Disarmament Education in American Universities. *Peace and the Sciences*, 33–41.

Reardon, Betty A. (1980). Equivalents for Equity: New Dimensions of Security. *Planet Earth, Fall*, 18–19.

Reardon, Betty A. (1980). Moving to the Future. *Network, 8*(1), 14–21.

Reardon, Betty A. (1980). Report on a Study of the Plan for the University for Peace, Costa Rica: UNESCO Sector/Bureau Ref. 3139-HRS/31 BOC Ref. 270457.

Reardon, Betty A. (1980). A Report on UNESCO's World Congress on Disarmament Education. *The Peace Chroncile, Fall*.

Reardon, Betty A. (1980). Secondary School and Teacher Training Curricula for Disarmament Education: Problems, Needs, and Priorities (SS/80), Conf. 603 (pp. 1–21). Paris: UNESCO.

Reardon, Betty A. (1980). The Status of Disarmament Education and Recommendations for Its Further Development (SS/80) Conf. 603. Paris: UNESCO.

Reardon, Betty A. (1980). UNESCO's Focuses on Disarmament Education: Educators Gathering in Paris. *Disarmament Times, 3*(3).

Reardon, Betty A. (1980). Women and Disarmament: Traditional Values in a Transnational World. In S. McClean (Ed.), *Women's Contribution to Peace*. Paris: UNESCO.

Reardon, Betty A. (1980). Women Show Skills Despite Limited Roles in Peace. *The Church Woman, December*, 13–14.

Reardon, Betty A. (1980). World Disarmament Education Congress: A Report. *COPRED Proceedings, August,* 7–10.

Reardon, Betty A. (1981). The Challenge of Disarmament Education *Educators Supplement Institute for Global Education* (p. 1).

Reardon, Betty A. (1981). Education for Peace and Disarmament: A Suggested Seqwuence of Learning Objectives. In M. Haavelsrud (Ed.), *Approaching Disarmament Education* (pp. 238–252). England: Westbury House.

Reardon, Betty A. (1981). Militarism and Sexism: Influences on Eduction for War. *Connexion, 9* (3), 6–10.

Reardon, Betty A. (1981). *Militarization, Security, and Peace Education: A Study of Action Prgramme for Concerned Citizens.* Valley Forge: United Ministries in Education.

Reardon, Betty A. (1981). The New Myth: Educating for Global Transformation. *Planet Earth, Fall, 1981* (Fall).

Reardon, Betty A. (1981). The Status of and Recommendations for Disarmament Education. In M. Haavelsrud (Ed.), *Approaching Disarmament Education* (pp. 114–128). England: Westbury House.

Reardon, Betty A. (1982). Disarmament Education as World Order Inquiry, vol 84, no. 1, 1982, 137–149. *Teachers College Record, 84*(1), 137–149.

Reardon, Betty A. (1982). The First Day of Hope. *Teachers College Record, 84*(1), 255–265.

Reardon, Betty A. (1982). *Militarism, Security, and Peace Education.* Valley Forge, PA: United Ministries in Education.

Reardon, Betty A. (1982). Presentation to the Preparatory Committee for UN Second Special Session on Disarmament. *International Peace Research Newsletter, 20*(3).

Reardon, Betty A. (1982). Response: Needs in Peace Education Development Identified by Glass. *Teachers College Record, 84*(1), 237–239.

Reardon, Betty A. (1982). Teaching Unit: UN Special Session on Disarmament. *Macroscope, 11* (Spring), 7–10.

Jacobson, Willard, Reardon, Betty A., & Sloan, Douglas. (1983). A Conceptual Framework for Teaching About Nuclear Weapons. *Social Education, 47*(7), 476–479.

Reardon, Betty A., Scott, John Anthony, & Totten, Sam (1983). Nuclear Weapons: Concepts, Issues, and Controversies Introduction. *Social Education, November/December,* 474–479.

Reardon, Betty A. (1983). A Gender Analysis of Militarism and Sexist Repression: A Suggested Research Agenda. *International Peace Research Newsletter, 21*(2).

Reardon, Betty A. (1983). International Colloquium on Disarmament Education in Institutions of Higher Learning. *International Peace Research Newsletter, 21*(2).

Reardon, Betty A. (1983). Review of *In a Different Voice. Teachers College Record, 84*(4), 966–969.

Reardon, Betty A. (1984). Adult Education for Disarmament and Peace in a North American Christian Context. *Gandhi Marg, July/August,* 344–356.

Reardon, Betty A. (1984). International Education and Teacher Preparation. *Higher Education in Europe, UNESCO, Fall.*

Reardon, Betty A. (1984). Principles and Standards for Curriculum Development and Teacher Preparation. In M. Haavelsrud (Ed.), *Handbook on Disarmament.* Paris: UNESCO.

Reardon, Betty A. (1985). Civic Responsibility for a World Community. In D. Conrad & T. M. Thomas (Eds.), *Images of an Emerging World: From a War System to a Peace System.* Katyam, India: Prakasam Publications.

Reardon, Betty A. (1985). Recent Developments in Peace Education in the United States. In D. Ray (Ed.), *Peace Education: Canadian and World Perspectives* (pp. 203–215). London, Ontario: Third Eye.

Reardon, Betty A. (1986). An Experiment in Education for World Peace. *Education in Asia, 6*(2).

Reardon, Betty A. (1987). Excellence in Education Through Peace-Making. *Breakthrough, Spring/Summer,* 18–21.

Reardon, Betty A. (1988). *Address on Behalf of the International Jury for the UNESCO Prize for Peace Education.* Paris.

Reardon, Betty A. (1988). *Comprehensive Peace Education: Educating for Global Responsibility*. New York: Teachers College Press.

Reardon, Betty A. (1988). *Educating for global responsibility: Teacher-designed curricula for peace education, K-12*. New York: Teachers College Press.

Reardon, Betty A. (1988). Introduction *UNESCO Yearbook on Peace and Conflict Studies*. Paris: UNESCO.

Reardon, Betty A. (1988). *The Teacher's Responsibility for Our Common Future*. Paper presented at the Second Meeting of International Teachers for Peace, Bonn, West Germany.

Reardon, Betty A. (1988). Women, Peace and Development, Development Education Kit 4. Geneva: United Nations.

Reardon, Betty A. (1989). Feminist Concepts of Peace and Security. In P. Smoker (Ed.), *Global Studies Handbook for A Level Examinations*.

Reardon, Betty A. (1989). A Feminist Perspective on World Constitutional Order. *WCCI Forum: Journal of the World Council for Curriculum and Instruction, 3*(2), 16–28.

Reardon, Betty A. (1989). Getting from Here to There: An Educator's Response to Thomas Berry's "The American College in the Ecological Age". *Religion and Intellectual Life, Winter*.

Reardon, Betty A. (1989). Pedagogical Approaches to Peace Studies. In M. T. Klare & D. C. Thomas (Eds.), *Peace and World Order Studies Guide* (5th ed., pp. 20–27). Boulder, CO: Westview Press.

Reardon, Betty A. (1989). Toward a Paradigm of Peace. In L. R. Farcey (Ed.), *Peace: Meanings, Politics, Strategies*. New York: Praeger.

Reardon, Betty A. (1989). Women and Peace: Development Education Kit #4. Geneva: JUNIC/NGO, United Nations.

Reardon, Betty A., & Tierney, James F. (1990). Teaching Peace: A Study Guide to *The Conquest of War*. Scarsdale, NY: Alternative Defense Project.

Reardon, Betty A. (1990). Feminist Concepts of Peace and Security. In P. Smoker, R. Davies & B. Munske (Eds.), *A Reader in Peace Studies*. New York: Pergamon Press.

Reardon, Betty A. (1990). A Memorial Tribute to Lawrence E. Metcalf. *Social Education, 54*, 107–108.

Aziz, Unku Abdul, & Reardon, Betty A. (1991). The UNESCO Prize for Peace Education: The Ten Years of Learning for Peace. *Peace Education Miniprints* (Vol. 19, pp. 1–12). Malmo, Sweden.

Reardon, Betty A. (1991). Challenges for Peace Studies in a Dramatically Changing World. *Peace Studies Bulletin, 1*(1).

Reardon, Betty A. (1991). Feminism and Authentic Globalism: Toward an Inclusive Constitutional Order. *CSWS Review*, 28–31.

Reardon, Betty A. (1991). Feminist Pedagogy and Peace Studies. *Benedictines, XLV*(I), 11–26.

Reardon, Betty A. (1991). Forward. In T. Swee-hin (Ed.), *Journeys of Peace Education*. Sydney: Earth.

Reardon, Betty A. (1991). Ou est la vraie Securite? Pour une Securite Globale. *Journal de la Movement de la Paix, 383*(June).

Reardon, Betty A. (1991). Review of Societies of Peace: Anthropological Perspectives. *New Ideas in Psychology, 9*(3), 409–410.

Reardon, Betty A. (1991). Review of Societies of Peace: Anthropological Perspectives. *Peace & Change, January*, 116–118.

Reardon, Betty A. (1993). Challenges and Opportunities of Disarmament Education. In M. Haavelsrud (Ed.), *Disarming: Discourse on Violence and Peace*. Tromso, Norway: Arena.

Reardon, Betty A. (1993). A Feminist Perspective on World Constitutional Order. In R. A. Falk, R. C. Johansen & S. S. Kim (Eds.), *The Constitutional Foundations of World Order* (pp. 227–243). Albany, NY: State University of New York Press.

Reardon, Betty A. (1993). Foward. D. T. Snauwaert, *Democracy, Education, and Governance: A Developmental Conception*. Albany, NY: State University of New York Press.

Reardon, Betty A. (1993). Pedagogy as Purpose: Peace Education in the Context of Violence. In P. Cremin (Ed.), *Education for Peace*. Limerick, Ireland: Educational Studies Association of Ireland.

Reardon, Betty A. (1993). *Women and Peace: Feminist Visions of Global Security*. Albany, NY: State University of New York Press.

Reardon, Betty A., & Nordland, Eva (Eds.). (1994). *Learning Peace: The Promise of Ecological and Cooperative Education*. Albany, NY: State University of New York Press.

Reardon, Betty A. (1994). A Feminist Critique of "An Agenda for Peace": United Nations, Division of the Advancement of Women GAP/1994/WP.2.

Reardon, Betty A. (1994). Human Rights and Values Education: Using the International Standards. *Social Education, 58*(7), 427–429.

Reardon, Betty A. (1994). Learning Our Way to a Human Future. In B. A. Reardon & E. Nordland (Eds.), *Learning Peace: The Promise of Ecological and Cooperative Education*. Albany, NY: State University of New York Press.

Reardon, Betty A. (1995). *Educating for human dignity: Learning about rights and responsibilities*. Philadelphia: University of Pennsylvania Press.

Reardon, Betty A. (1996). Responding to a Major Problem of Adolescent Intolerance: Bullying *Peace Education Miniprints* (Vol. 82). Malmo, Sweden: Peace Education Miniprints.

Reardon, Betty A. (1996). Review of *Teaching About International Conflict and Peace*. *Teachers College Record, 97*.

Reardon, Betty A. (1996). Women or Weapons? *Peace Review, 8*(3), 315–321.

Reardon, Betty A. (1996). Women's Vision of Peace: Images of Global Security. In J. Turpin & L. A. Lorentaen (Eds.), *The Gendered World Order: Militarism, Development, and the Environment*. New York: Routledge.

Reardon, Betty A. (1996 [1985]). *Sexism and the War System*. Syracuse, NY: Syracuse University Press.

Reardon, Betty A. (1996 [1985]). *Sexism and the War System* (1st Syracuse University Press ed.). Syracuse, N.Y.: Syracuse University Press.

Reardon, Betty A. (1997). Human Rights as Education for Peace. In G. J. Andreopoulos & R. P. Claude (Eds.), *Human Rights Education for the 21st Century*. Philadelphia: University of Pennsylannia Press.

Reardon, Betty A. (1997). The Role of Women in the Struggle for World Peace. *Journal of Hokusei Jr. College, 33*, 1–8.

Reardon, Betty A. (1997). *Tolerance: The Threshold of Peace*. Paris: UNESCO.

Osseiran, Sanaaa, & Reardon, Betty A. (1998). The United Nations' Role in Peace Education. In C. Alger, F (Ed.), *The Future of the United Nations Systems: Potential for the Twenty-first Century*. Tokyo: The United Nations University Press.

Reardon, Betty A. (1998). Gender and Global Security: A Feminist Challenge to the United Nations and Peace Research. *Journal of International Cooperation Studies, 6*(1), 1–28.

Reardon, Betty A. (1998). The Pedagogical Challenges of Peace Education: The Good News and the Bad News. *Peace Studies Newsletter, Peace Studies Association of Japan, 17*.

Reardon, Betty A. (1998). Women or Weapons. In L. A. Lorentaen & J. Turpin (Eds.), *The Women and War Reader*. New York: New York University Press.

Breines, Ingeborg, Gierycz, Dorota, & Reardon, Betty A. (Eds.). (1999). *Toward's a Women's Agenda for a Culture of Peace*. Paris: UNESCO Publishing.

Reardon, Betty A. (1999). Educating the Educators: The Preparation of Teachers for a Culture of Peace (Vol. 99). Malmo, Sweden: Peace Education Miniprints.

Reardon, Betty A. (1999). Women or Weapons: The Militarist Sexist Symbios. In I. Breines, D. Gierycz & B. A. Reardon (Eds.), *Towards a Women's Agenda for a Culture of Peace*. Paris: UNESCO Publishing.

Reardon, Betty A. (2000). The Role of Teachers in the Global Campaign for Peace Education. *Education International, 4*(4).

Reardon, Betty A. (2000). Peace Education: A Review and Projection. In R. Moon, M. Ben-Peretz & S. Brown (Eds.), *Routledge International Companion to Education*. London: Routledge.

Reardon, Betty A. (2001). *Education for a culture of peace in a gender perspective*. Paris: UNESCO.

Reardon, Betty A., & Speigler, Mado. (2001). *Passport to Dignity*. New York: People's Movement for Human Rights Education.

Reardon, Betty A., & Cabezudo, Alicia. (2001). *Learning to Abolish War*. New York: Hague Appeal for Peace.

Reardon, Betty A. (2002). Human Rights and the Global Campaign for Peace Education. *International Review of Education, 48*(3–4), 283–284.

Reardon, Betty A. (2003). Toward Human Security: A Gender Approach to Demilitarization. *Women in Asia, 33*.

Reardon, Betty A. (2003). Women's Organizations Working for Human Rights and Peace. *Social Education, 67*(1), 58–61.

Reardon, Betty A. (2006). Peace Education, An Invaluable Tool for Progress. In I. Breines & H. d'Orville (Eds.), *60 Women Contributing to the 60 Years of UNESCO: Constructing the Foundations of Peace*. Paris: UNESCO.

Jenkins, Anthony & Reardon, Betty A. (2007). Gender and Peace: Towards a Gender Inclusive, Holistic Perspective. In J. Galtung & C. Webel (Eds.), *Handbook of Peace and Conflict Studies* (pp. 209–231). New York: Routledge.

Reardon, Betty A. (2007). Review of *Educating for a Culture of Social and Ecological Peace*. *Journal of Peace Education, 4*(1), 115–117.

Reardon, Betty A. (2008). The Eradication of Torture: The Imperatives of Gender and Education. *New York City Law Review, 11*(2), 265–279.

Reardon, Betty A. (2008). It Doesn't Have to Be That Way: An Interview with Betty Reardon. *SGI Quarterly, 52*(April), 12–13.

Reardon, Betty A. (2008). Peace Education: Current Challenges and Opportunities. *The Ritsumeikan Journal of Peace Studies, 9*(March).

Reardon, Betty A. (2009). *Human Rights Learning: Pedagogies and Politics of Peace*. Paper presented at the UNESCO Chair for Peace Education Master Conference, University of Puerto Rico.

Reardon, Betty A., & Hans, Asha (Eds.). (2010). *The Gender Imperative: Human Security vs. State Security*. New Delhi, India: Routledge.

Reardon, Betty A. (2010). Women and Human Security: A Feminist Framework and Critique of the Prevailing Patriarchal Security System. In B. A. Reardon & A. Hans (Eds.), *The Gender Imperative: Human Security vs. State Security*. New Delhi, India: Routledge.

Reardon, Betty A. (2010). *Human Rights Learning: Pedagogies and Politics of Peace*. San Juan, Puerto Rico: UNESCO Chair for Peace Education, University of Puerto Rico.

Reardon, Betty A. (2010). The Patriarchy Problematic. In M. D. J. Elena & M. S. Romero (Eds.), *Genero y Paz*. Barcelona: Icaria.

Reardon, Betty A. (2011). Introduction to Sexism and the War System. In S. Christine (Ed.), *Feminist International Relations: Critical Concepts in International Relations* (Vol. 1). New York: Routledge.

Reardon, Betty A., & Snauwaert, Dale T. (2011). Reflective Pedagogy, Cosmopolitanism, and Critical Peace Education for Political Efficacy: A Discussion of Betty A. Reardon's Assessment of the Field. *In Factis Pax: Journal of Peace Education and Social Justice, 5* (1), 1–14.

Reardon, Betty A. (2012). Education for Sustainable Peace: Practices, Problems and Possibilities. In P. T. Coleman & M. Deutsch (Eds.), *Psychological Components of Sustainable Peace*. New York: Springer.

Reardon, Betty A. (2012). Human Rights and the Renewal of the University. In C. Brunner & J. Scherling (Eds.), *Bildung, Menschenrecht, Universitat*. Klagenfurt, Austria: Drava Verla.

Reardon, Betty A. (2013). Criminalizing War and Those Who Make It. *Global Campaign for Peace Education Newsletter* (105).

Reardon, Betty A. (2013). Meditating on the Barricades: Concerns, Cautions, and Possibilities for Peace Education for Political Efficacy. In P. P. Trifonas & B. L. Wright (Eds.), *Critical Peace Education: Difficult Dialogues*. New York: Springer.

Reardon, Betty A. and Dale T. Snauwaert (2015). *Betty A. Reardon: A Pioneer in Education for Peace and Human Rights*. Springer Briefs on Pioneers in Science and Practice (PSP Vols. 26). Cham: Springer International Publishing.

Reardon, Betty A. and Dale T. Snauwaert (2015). *Betty A. Reardon: Key Texts in Gender and Peace*. Springer Briefs on Pioneers in Science and Practice (PSP Vols. 27). Cham: Springer International Publishing.

Reardon, Betty A. (2016) People's Action Plans: Pursuing Human Security with Local Civil Society Action to Implement UNSCR 1325. In A. Hans & S. Rajagopalan (Eds.), *Openings for peace*. Sage, New Delhi.

Reardon, Betty A. (2018). On Frameworks and Purposes: A Response to Dale Snauwaert's Review of Jeffrey Sachs' "The Age of Sustainable Development"—Patriarchy is the Problem. Global Campaign for Peace Education, https://www.peace-ed-campaign.org/patriarchy-is-the-problem/.

Reardon, Betty, A. (2018). Learning to Disarm: Educating to Realize the IPB Action Agenda. *In* Disarmament, Peace and Development. Published online: 04 Dec 2018; 135–145. https://doi.org/10.1108/S1572-832320180000027020.

About the University of Toledo

The University of Toledo (UT) is a public research university located in Toledo, Ohio, United States that was established in 1872 and became a member of the state university system in 1967. The University of Toledo and the Medical University of Ohio merged July 2006 to form the third-largest public university operating budget in the state. The University is accredited by The Higher Learning Commission. Toledo has a current enrolment of over 20,000 students.

Peace Education and Peace Studies at The University of Toledo

The *Judith Herb College of Education* at The University of Toledo offers an undergraduate interdisciplinary Minor in Peace Studies and an online Graduate Certificate Program in the Foundations of Peace Education. These academic programs are complemented by an array of research, international and community-based initiatives and supported by a university-wide network of Peace Studies Faculty Fellows.

Peace Studies is concerned with inquiry, scholarship, and action regarding the reduction and elimination of violence and the establishment of the conditions for the possibility of peace and justice to flourish at all levels of human organization. Complementing these perspectives, *Peace Education* at The University of Toledo explores the philosophical, sociological and psychological dimensions of learning

© Springer Nature Switzerland AG 2019
D. T. Snauwaert (ed.), *Exploring Betty A. Reardon's Perspective on Peace Education*, Pioneers in Arts, Humanities, Science, Engineering, Practice 20, https://doi.org/10.1007/978-3-030-18387-5

and education essential for global citizens to critically understand and transform all forms of violence and the patterns of thought that justify and support them.

See at: http://www.utoledo.edu/education/peace/.

Betty A. Reardon Collected Papers at the Canaday Center The University of Toledo

The Collective Papers of Betty A. Reardon were donated to the Canaday Center, October 2007. They include published and unpublished manuscripts, correspondence, curricula, policy documents, reports, presentations, projects, and notes. The Papers are organized by Topic and Type of Document, and are chronologically organized. The Topics include gender, environmentalism, disarmament, peace studies and foundations of peace education, human rights, faith, and peace education. Each of these areas has a very specific and distinct focus, but serves as a component and or building blocks for peace education.

Publications and unpublished manuscripts include articles, book chapters, books, and editorials. Correspondence includes mainly professional correspondence, which in many cases contains substantive scholarly and educational commentary. Curricula include specific peace and human rights curriculum, curricular units and lesson plans, and articulations of pedagogical approaches and methods. Policy documents include specific policy documents for various organizations, including the United Nations. Reports include a variety of reports concerning institutional and grant activity and initiatives. Presentations include papers delivered at scholarly and professional associations as well as those delivered to various institutions and organizations. Projects include various peace, human rights, gender, ecology, and peace education initiatives. Notes include informal written recordings of ideas, insights, thoughts, manuscript preparation, curricula, projects, reports, and presentations. The contents range in date from the 1960s to the present.

See at: http://www.utoledo.edu/library/canaday/guidepages/education.html.

The International Institute on Peace Education

The International Institute on Peace Education is a weeklong residential experience for educators hosted in a different country every other summer. The Institute facilitates exchanges of theory and practical experiences in teaching peace education and serves to grow the field. In serving the field, the IIPE operates as an applied peace education laboratory that provides a space for pedagogical experimentation; cooperative, deep inquiry into shared issues; and advancing theoretical, practical and pedagogical applications.

In 1982 the first IIPE was held at Teachers College, Columbia University. It was organized by Professors Betty A. Reardon, Willard Jacobson and Douglas Sloan in cooperation with the United Ministries in Education. Each of these professors, working in different fields and disciplines, came together to apply their collective knowledge, wisdom and experience toward a problem that threatened the extinction of the human race and all life on the planet – nuclear proliferation. The first IIPE experience examined the practical and theoretical contributions of education to world order and nuclear and general and complete disarmament. In doing so it addressed the political and personal dimensions of the task of disarmament,

© Springer Nature Switzerland AG 2019
D. T. Snauwaert (ed.), *Exploring Betty A. Reardon's Perspective on Peace Education*, Pioneers in Arts, Humanities, Science, Engineering, Practice 20, https://doi.org/10.1007/978-3-030-18387-5

inquiring into worldviews, beliefs and attitudes that sustain and make possible a highly militarized system of global security.

From 1982 the Institute evolved in parallel to other developments in the peace research and peace studies fields and the work of the IIPE founder, Dr. Reardon. Rather than an exclusive focus on disarmament education, the IIPE began to examine peace and violence more holistically. Complementing this systemic and holistic view, the Institute organically developed into an annual, international program that is hosted, cooperatively planned and co-coordinated by a partner academic or non-governmental institution. This internationalization of the IIPE enables it to be inclusive of the multiple, socio-cultural perspectives and concerns of peace and violence and exposes participants to a multitude of educational approaches and transformative pedagogies of peace that are practiced in different socio-cultural contexts. Furthermore, it has enabled the Institute to be adaptive and flexible in its form and in the content chosen that frames each year's program.

From 1982 to 2007 the IIPE secretariat was housed at the Peace Education Center at Teachers College, Columbia University. The IIPE secretariat has since been housed at Global Education Associates (2007–08) and the National Peace Academy (2009–2014). The Judith Herb College of Education at The University of Toledo became the new home of the IIPE secretariat in 2014.

Since its inauguration at Teachers College Columbia University in 1982, the IIPE has brought together experienced and aspiring educators, academics, professional workers, and activists in the field of peace education from around the world to exchange knowledge and experiences and learn with and from each other in its intensive residentially based learning community. The IIPE is held annually at various universities and peace centers throughout the world.

Also an opportunity for networking and community building, the IIPE has spawned a variety of collaborative research projects and peace education initiatives at the local, regional, and international levels.

The International Peace Bureau, in nominating IIPE for the 2005 UNESCO Peace Education Prize described it as "probably the most effective agent for the introduction of peace education to more educators than any other single non-governmental agency."

The objectives of each particular institute are rooted in the needs and transformational concerns of the co-sponsoring host partner, their local community, and the surrounding region. More widely, the educational purposes of the IIPE are directed toward the development of the field of peace education in theory, practice and advocacy. In addition to the important learning of contextually relevant issues and pedagogical approaches, the purposes of the IIPE are threefold:

(1) To aid in the development of the substance of peace education through exploration of new and challenging themes to contribute to the on-going development of the field.

(2) To build strategic international institutional alliances among NGOs, universities and agencies involved in peace education thereby increasing the benefits

of shared expertise on substance and practice as well as advancing educational reform initiatives.

(3) To encourage regional cooperation toward the maximization of resources, cooperation in pedagogical and substantive developments and increasing regional perspectives on the global issues that comprise the content of peace education. This is accomplished through significant involvement of regional organizations and participants with an annual goal of 50% of the participants from the region.

See at: https://www.i-i-p-e.org/about/ and https://www.i-i-p-e.org/about/history/.

About the Editor

Dale T. Snauwaert, Ph.D. is Professor of Philosophy of Education and Peace Studies, Co-Director of the Graduate Certificate Program in the Foundations of Peace Education and the Undergraduate Minor in Peace Studies in the Department of Educational Foundations and Leadership, Judith Herb College of Education, The University of Toledo, USA. He is the Founding Editor of *In Factis Pax: Online Journal of Peace Education and Social Justice*. He is widely published in such academic journals as the *Journal of Peace Education*, *Educational Theory*, *Educational Studies*, *Peace Studies Journal*, and *Philosophical Studies in Education* on such topics as democratic theory, theories of social justice, the ethics of war and peace, and the philosophy of peace education. He is the author of *Democracy, Education, and Governance: A Developmental Conception* (SUNY Press, 1993), the editor of two volumes of Betty Reardon's work: *Betty A. Reardon: A Pioneer in Education for Peace and Human Rights* and *Betty A. Reardon: Key Texts in Gender and Peace* (Springer Briefs on Pioneers in Science and Practice (PSP Vols. 26 and 27, 2015 and 2015), and with Fuad Al-Daraweesh, the co-author of *Human Rights Education Beyond Universalism and Relativism: A Relational Hermeneutic for Global Justice* (Palgrave McMillan, 2015). His core interests and expertise lie within the following topics: peace education, democratic education, human rights education, democratic theory, theories of justice, human rights theory, the philosophy of nonviolence, teaching through reflective inquiry.

Address: Dale T. Snauwaert, Ph.D., Professor of Philosophy of Education and Peace Studies, Gillham Hall Room 5000C, The University of Toledo, Main Campus, Mail Stop 921, Toledo, Ohio 43606, USA.
Email: dale.snauwaert@utoledo.edu.
Website: http://www.utoledo.edu/education/depts/efl/faculty/snauwaert/.

© Springer Nature Switzerland AG 2019
D. T. Snauwaert (ed.), *Exploring Betty A. Reardon's Perspective on Peace Education*, Pioneers in Arts, Humanities, Science, Engineering, Practice 20, https://doi.org/10.1007/978-3-030-18387-5

About Betty A. Reardon

Betty A. Reardon is a feminist peace and human rights educator – activist with six decades in the development and dissemination of the field. The founder of the International Institute on Peace Education (IIPE) and the original peace education graduate specialization at Teachers College Columbia University, and one of the civil society originators of UN Security Council Resolution 1325 on Women, Peace and Security, she has worked in all world regions toward international cooperation among peace educators. Widely published in peace education and gender issues, including *Comprehensive Peace Education*, Teachers College Press (1985), *Educating for Human Dignity*, University of Pennsylvania Press (1995), *Tolerance: The Threshold of Peace*, UNESCO (1997), and *Education for a Culture of Peace in a Gender Perspective*, UNESCO (2001). Most recently she coedited with Dale T. Snauwaert: *Betty A. Reardon: A Pioneer in Education for Peace and Human Rights* and *Betty A. Reardon: Key Texts in Gender and Peace* (Springer Briefs on Pioneers in Science and Practice (PSP Vols. 26 and 27, 2015 and 2015). Her publications are archived in the Ward Canaday Special Collections at the University of Toledo Library.

Address: Prof. Dr. Betty A. Reardon, Teachers College, Columbia University, New York, N.Y., USA.
Email: bar19@columbia.edu.
Website: https://en.wikipedia.org/wiki/Betty_Reardon;
http://www.elhibrifoundation.org/people/betty-reardon;
http://www.afes-press-books.de/html/SpringerBriefs_PSP_Reardon.htm.

© Springer Nature Switzerland AG 2019
D. T. Snauwaert (ed.), *Exploring Betty A. Reardon's Perspective on Peace Education*, Pioneers in Arts, Humanities, Science, Engineering, Practice 20, https://doi.org/10.1007/978-3-030-18387-5

About the Contributors

Fuad Al-Daraweesh, Ph.D. is a staff member of the Center for International Studies and Programs at the University of Toledo. He is the Associate Editor of *In Factis Pax: Online Journal of Peace Education and Social Justice*. He is published in *many journals including Educational Theory*. He is the co-author of *Human Rights Education Beyond Universalism and Relativism: A Relational Hermeneutic for Global Justice* (Palgrave McMillan, 2015). He is interested in democratic education, human rights education, democratic theory, theories of justice, and human rights theory.

Address: Fuad Al-Daraweesh, Ph.D., a staff member of the Center for International Studies and Programs at the University of Toledo, Toledo, OH.
Email: fuad.al-daraweesh@utoledo.edu.

Ronni Alexander is a peace researcher, peace educator and peace activist. She is currently a professor in the Graduate School of International Cooperation Studies, Kobe University. Ronni serves as the Executive Adviser to the Present for Diversity and as the Director of the Kobe University Gender Equality Office. She is also the Chair-holder of the Kobe University UNESCO Chair on Gender and Vulnerability in Disaster Risk Reduction Support. She holds degrees from Yale University (BA, psychology), International Christian University (MA, public administration) and Sophia University (Ph.D., international relations). Ronni's work focuses on how living things can both be, and feel, safe. This interest is reflected in her scholarship on intersections of militarization and gender and security, as well as in her narrative and story-telling work. Current projects include militarization on Guam, and the role of art and expression in disaster support work. Ronni began the Popoki Peace Project in 2006 as a grass roots project to encourage participants of all ages to actively engage in critical imagination, expression and action for peace. The Project uses Ronni's *Popoki's Peace Book* picture book series. This work also includes continuing activities using art and stories in the areas affected by the 2011 Northeastern Japan disaster. Ronni has lived in Japan since 1977, first living and

© Springer Nature Switzerland AG 2019
D. T. Snauwaert (ed.), *Exploring Betty A. Reardon's Perspective on Peace Education*, Pioneers in Arts, Humanities, Science, Engineering, Practice 20, https://doi.org/10.1007/978-3-030-18387-5

279

working in Hiroshima and then moving to Tokyo for graduate school. She has been at Kobe University since 1989.

Address: Kobe University, Kobe, Japan.
Email: ronnialexander@yahoo.co.jp.

Tim Archer, final year Ph.D. candidate, is a Hughes Hall scholar at the University of Cambridge. He is a peace worker and educator, working in both international and domestic peacebuilding settings. Tim's main areas of focus include philosophical and practical approaches to peace and education that include alternative episte-mologies, transrationality, affective pedagogies, and diffraction. Tim works with young men on notions of masculinities and peace, as well as training potential frontline workers, such as teachers or peaceworkers, to work in and on conflict. Central to these approaches are aspects of self-awareness and conflict sensitivity created through holistic self-exploration, second-order reflexivity, and concepts of encountering, resonance and affect. He has co-authored chapters and articles including Transrational Education: Exploring Possibilities for Learning About Peace, Harmony, Justice and Truth in the Twenty First Century with Dr. Hilary Cremin (Springer, 2018), and Transrational Diffractions for Peace Education Theory and Praxis with Dr. Kevin Kester and Dr. Shawn Bryant (*Journal of Peace Education*, 2019).

Address: University of Cambridge, Cambridge, UK.
Email: dta30@cam.ac.uk.

Ingeborg Breines has a humanistic background in philosophy, French literature, history of ideas and history of arts with a MA from the University of Nantes and Master (Cand.Philol.) from the University of Oslo. She has background from teaching and from the Norwegian National Council for Innovation in Education. She served as Secretary-General of the Norwegian National Commission for UNESCO before joining UNESCO Headquarters, where she first held the position as Special Adviser to the Director-General on Women and Gender, then as Director of the Women and the Culture of Peace Program. Subsequently she was appointed Director of the UNESCO Office in Islamabad and then the UNESCO Liaison Office in Geneva. After retirement from UNESCO she was for some three years Director of Nordland Academy for Arts and Sciences, Northern Norway. She has authored, co-authored or edited publications notably on gender issues, education, conflict resolution and a culture of peace, e.g. for UNESCO: *"Towards a Women's Agenda for a culture of Peace"*, *"Male roles, Masculinities and Violence. A culture of Peace Perspective"* and *"Building the foundations of peace. 60 women for the 60 years of UNESCO"*. She was from 2006 to 2016 on the board of the International Peace Bureau, IPB, Geneva, the last seven years as co-president. She has close relations with international and Norwegian peace organizations e.g. from the board of the UN Association, WILPF, the Forum on Development and Environment and the

Peace Alliance. She is also senior advisor to the Secretariat of the Nobel Summits and on the board of the Academic University for Nonviolence, Beirut.
Address: Oslo, Norway.
Email: i.breines@gmail.com.

Janet Gerson (Ed.D.) took Betty Reardon's 1996 *Human and Social Dimensions of Peace* course, Dale Snauwaert presented, and the collaboration continues, with Tony Jenkins, through International Institute on Peace Education (IIPE) Secretariat. Gerson is IIPE Education Director; former Co-Director, Peace Education Center, Teachers College, Columbia University; and long-time collaborator with the Morton Deutsch International Center on Cooperation and Conflict Resolution (MD-ICCCR). In 2018, she received the Lifetime Achievement Award from the Human Dignity and Humiliation Studies Association, and in 2014, the Peace and Justice Studies Association (PJSA) Award for her dissertation *Public Deliberation on Global Justice: The World Tribunal on Iraq*. Other publications include contributions to *In Factis Pax: Journal of Peace Education and Social Justice*; *The Handbook of Conflict Resolution* (Eds., Coleman, Deutsch, & Marcus; *GCPE Newsletter*; *Learning to Abolish War: Teaching toward a Culture of Peace* (Reardon & Cabezudo); *Theory into Practice*; *Analysis of Social Issues and Public Policy*; *Holistic Education*; and Co-Editor with Anita Yudkin of *In Factis Pax*, "Peace Building in Post-Conflict Contexts" English & Spanish 2017 Special Edition. A political theorist and peace educator, her research focuses are democratizing justice, tribunals, rethinking political institutions, public deliberation, conflict processes, and peace pedagogy.

Address: New York, N.Y.
Email: gerson@i-i-p-e.org.

Ian Gibson teaches (and practices) peace education and civic engagement. He is an Associate Professor at Kyoto University of Foreign Studies and is currently the Director of the Kyoto University of Foreign Studies JUEMUN (Japan University English Model United Nations) program. He has published work on peace education and gender inclusion within human security (with Betty Reardon).

Address: Kyoto University of Foreign Studies, Kyoto, Japan.
Email: irgibson12@yahoo.com.

Asha Hans is a former Professor of Political Science and Founder Director School of Women's Studies Utkal University India. Writes on issues of gender, conflict and peace. Her recent writings focus on UNSCR 1325 and also Human Security from a gendered perspective. She has also written on issues of disability. Her latest books include The Gender Imperative: Human Security vs State Security co ed. Betty A. Reardon and co-ed with Swarna Rajagopalan Openings for Peace: UNSCR 1325: Women and Security in India. She is Co-Chair Pakistan India Peoples Forum for Peace and Security. Member editorial Journal of Peace Education and member board Women's Peace and Humanitarian Fund.

Address: Utkal University, India.

Email: ashahans10@gmail.com.

Magnus Haavelsrud is Emeritus Professor at the Norwegian University of Science and Technology since 2010 and was Distinguished Fellow of the South African Research Chair in Development Education, University of South Africa (2008–2017). His work deals with the critique of the reproductive role of education and the possibilities for transcendence of this reproduction in light of the traditions of educational sociology and peace research. He took part in the creation of the Peace Education Commission of the International Peace Research Association and served as its 2nd Executive Secretary 1975–79. He worked at the School Program of the Institute for World Order in New York and served as the Carl-von-Ossietzky Guest Professor of the German Council for Peace and Conflict Research. He co-chaired (with Reardon) the panel for the launching of the Global Campaign on Peace Education, Hague Appeal for Peace in 1999. Since 2001 he has worked with education for human rights, participative democracy and peace in Latin America and since 1980 with Nomura Centre for Lifelong Integrated Education in Tokyo. He is a Patron of the International Centre of Nonviolence Australia since 2013. Member of (1) Transcend International since 1993, (2) editorial board of Journal of Peace Education since 2004, (3) Global Advisory Group of Human Dignity and Humiliation Studies since 2008 (4) Arigatou Foundation's Interfaith Council on Ethics Education for Children (2005–2009) and (5) International Peace Research Association since 1972. For writings see www.cristin.no/english/.

Address: Norwegian University of Science and Technology, Norway.
Email: magnush@alumni.ntnu.no.

Colins Imoh is a doctoral candidate in the Department of Educational Foundations & Leadership at the University of Toledo. His areas of interest are multicultural movements, development, diversity, and peacebuilding. Professionally, he holds an MA in Conflict Transformation from Eastern Mennonite University and MPhil from the University of Cape Town in Environmental Management. He was the pioneer coordinator of the Africa Network of Young Peace Builders, working from their International Secretariat in the Netherlands. He was also the Partners for Peace Project Manager, a network whose mission is to build social capital around peacebuilding. He has consulted for various organization globally on peacebuilding, development, and governance. He is the author of the following articles: Reconciliation the Missing Link in the Niger Delta Amnesty. In Peace & Conflict Resolution in Africa: A Reader (Cambridge Scholars Publishing, 2018); Integrated Approach to Human Right in the Niger Delta. (In Factis Pax Journal of Peace Education and Social Justice, 2017); Peace Education in Marginalised Communities in Nigeria: The 'Protect Our Future' Project (Infactispax – Journal of Peace Education and Social Justice. Volume 2 Number 2, 2008). He is a member of the Mediators Beyond Borders - International Consultancy Panel; International Institute for Peace Education (IIPE) Advisory Board Member, Children of the Earth Board

Member and International Steering Committee Member of the African Fellows – California State University, Sacramento.

Address: The University of Toledo, Toledo, OH, USA.
Email: Colins.Imoh@rockets.utoledo.edu.

Tony Jenkins, Ph.D. has 15+ years of experience directing and designing peace-building and international educational programs and projects and leadership in the international development of peace studies and peace education. Tony is currently an adjunct professor of justice and peace studies at Georgetown University and George Washington University. Since 2001 he has served as the Managing Director of the International Institute on Peace Education (IIPE) and since 2007 as the Coordinator of the Global Campaign for Peace Education (GCPE). Tony's applied research is focused on examining the impacts and effectiveness of peace education methods and pedagogies in nurturing personal, social and political change and transformation. He is also interested in formal and non-formal educational design and development with special interest in teacher training, alternative approaches to global security, systems design, disarmament, and gender.

Address: Georgetown University, Washington, DC.
Email: jenkins@i-i-p-e.org.

Kevin Kester, Ph.D. is Tenure-Track Assistant Professor of International Education and Global Affairs at Keimyung University in Daegu, Korea, where he holds a joint appointment in the Graduate School of Education and School of Global Affairs. His research interests lie in the sociology and politics of education with a focus on comparative and international education; education, conflict, and peacebuilding; the global governance of education in conflict-affected societies; peace and conflict studies; and social theory (de/postcolonial and postmodern thought, and critical pedagogy). Among his recent authored or co-authored books is *The United Nations and Higher Education: Reproduction, Peace and Epistemic Justice in the 21st Century* (Information Age Publishing, forthcoming), and with Vandana Shiva and Shreya Jani, *The Young Ecologist Initiative Water Manual: Lesson Plans for Building Earth Democracy* (Navdanya Press, 2007). He has published over 50 articles, book chapters and reports in such journals as *Education as Change; Educational Philosophy and Theory; Globalisation, Societies and Education; Journal of Peace Education; Peace Review;* and *Teaching in Higher Education*. Kevin was introduced to the field of peace education by Betty Reardon in Tokyo, Japan, in 2004.

Address: Department of International Education and Global Affairs, Keimyung University, Daegu, South Korea.
Email: kevinajkester@gmail.com.

Kathy Matsui, Ph.D. is Professor at the Department of Global Citizenship Studies, Seisen University (Tokyo, Japan) and teaches courses on conflict resolution and peace related subjects. Her research concerns the development of capacities for conflict resolution and reconciliation. She works with peace researchers and educators internationally in the International Institute on Peace Education and Global Partnership for Prevention of Armed Conflict. As a peace educator, she focuses her activities on Northeast Asia Regional Peacebuilding Institute (NARPI), Global Campaign for Peace Education and Peace Education Task Force of World Conference of Religions for Peace (WCRP), Japan.

Address: Department of Global Citizenship Studies, Seisen University, Tokyo, Japan.
Email: matsuikathy@hotmail.com.

Sally McLaren is currently teaching media law and ethics at Western Sydney University. She has a Ph.D. from Ritsumeikan University (Kyoto) in media studies. Sally's professional media experience includes working on the foreign desk of *The Independent* in London, writing about Japan as a Kyoto-based freelance journalist, and documentary filmmaking in Sri Lanka. In 2006, she was editor of *Unbound: Gender in Asia*, a special issue of Kyoto Journal that explored gender and sexuality in the Asian region. Sally's research takes an interdisciplinary approach, focusing on gender, media and power in the Asia-Pacific region. Her current research projects are concerned with militarization, media and gender in Japan and audience research on media representations of gender inequality in Japan and Sri Lanka. Sally is co-convenor of the Asian Network of Women in Communication (ANWIC), a network of media educators, professionals and activists. In 2017 the group conducted media literacy and journalism workshops at the Third Asia Pacific Feminist Forum in Chiang Mai, Thailand.

Address: Western Sydney University, Sydney, Australia.
Email: sallyjmclaren@gmail.com.

Michele W. Milner, Ph.D. and Principal Fellow of the Higher Education Academy, PFHEA, is the Director of Learning and Wellbeing at the Royal Veterinary College Royal Veterinary College (RVC), University of London, London, UK where she leads a department that provides academic enhancement and student support services to the College community. The department aims to create opportunities, spaces and learning experiences that are inclusive and accessible and which build a sense of community across RVC. It seeks to support academic staff to develop approaches to their teaching that promote intellectual and emotional flexibility, and to help students to develop skills to manage stress in order to thrive during their studies. Prior to joining RVC, Michele established the Centre for Excellence in Learning and Teaching at the University of East London where she led on strategic projects on competency based learning and a one-device Mobile Learning project that distributed tablet devices to all students as a learning tool. She is a lifelong educationalist with interests and expertise in critical discourse analysis, media studies, language and gender, peace studies, technology enhanced learning, student-centred and active learning pedagogies and proactive approaches to student support. She has worked in Asia as a linguist, teacher trainer, curriculum developer and course director. While in Asia she also developed and implemented key strategic initiatives for transnational educational collaborations for UK and US universities.

Address: Royal Veterinary College (RVC), London, UK.
Email: milnermw@yahoo.com.

Úrsula Oswald Spring is a full time Professor/Researcher at the National Autonomous University of Mexico (UNAM) in the Regional Center for Multidisciplinary Research (CRIM) and is member of IPCC and RIOCC. She was national coordinator of water research for the National Council of Science and Technology, first Chair on Social Vulnerability at the United National University Institute for Environment and Human Security; founding member of the Latin American Peace Research Association (CLAIP), founder of El Colegio de Tlaxcala; General Attorney of Ecology in the State of Morelos (1992–1994), Minister of Ecological Development in the State of Morelos (1994–1998). She was also President of the International Peace Research Association (IPRA, 1998–2000), its Secretary General (2016–2018), and General Secretary of the Latin-American Council for Peace Research (2002–2006). She has studied medicine, clinical psychology, anthropology, ecology, classical and modern languages and obtained her Ph.D. from University of Zürich (1978). For her scientific work she received multiple prices. She published together with Hans Günter Brauch the handbooks on reconceptualising security and on the transition to sustainability with peace. Her core interests are on nonviolence, engendered-sustainable peace, equality, justice, sustainable transition, and sustainable agriculture with groups of peasants and women. She has written alone and in collaboration 56 books and more than 348 scientific articles and book chapters on sustainability, water, gender, development, poverty, drug consumption, brain damage due to under-nourishment, peasantry, social vulnerability, genetic modified organisms, bioethics, and human, gender, and environmental security, peace and conflict resolution, democracy, and conflict negotiation.

Address: Cuernavaca, National Autonomous University of Mexico (UNAM).
Email: uoswald@gmail.com.

Tina Ottman, M.A. Oxon Ph.D. is associate professor at Doshisha University's Faculty of Global and Regional Studies, in Kyoto, Japan. She was educated at the University of Oxford, Teachers College (Columbia University), where she studied a Peace Education Professional Development Certification under Dr. Betty Reardon, and received her Ph.D. from the Department of Peace Studies and International Development at the University of Bradford, UK. Her background is broadly in the field of Middle East studies (particularly the Israel-Palestine issue) and she has also lived and worked in Israel/Palestine, in addition to teaching at Japanese universities, largely in environments that emphasize educating students for a global citizenship. She is co-editor of *Peace and Welfare in the Local and Global Community* (Peace as a Global Language series) and programme chair, Peace as a Global Language conference series, in 2004, 2005, 2006 and 2013.

Address: Faculty of Global and Regional Studies, Doshisha University's, Kyoto, Japan.
Email: etottman@yahoo.com.

Anaida Pascual Morán is professor at the Graduate Studies Department of the School of Education at the Río Piedras Campus of the University of Puerto Rico. She obtained a Ph.D. in Curriculum and Teaching at Fordham University, a Masters in Education at the University of New Mexico, and did her undergraduate studies in Art and Humanities at UPR. She has been founder and coordinator of the *Teaching for Freedom Project*, sponsored by Amnesty International and the *UNESCO Chair for Peace Education at the University of Puerto Rico*. She has worked as pedagogical consultant with various pedagogical ecumenical organizations, such as the *Hispanic Theological Initiative*, the *Hispanic Summer Program*, and *Servicios Pedagógicos Teológicos* in Bolivia. She is the author of the book *Acción civil no-violenta: Fuerza de espíritu, fuerza de paz* (2003). And with Anita Yudkin Suliveres, co-edited *Educando por la paz en y desde la Universidad: Antología conmemorativa de una década* (2008). In her teaching, research and publications she intertwines the following topics: peace and human rights education, nonviolence, liberation pedagogies, differentiated education, personalized learning, talent development, curriculum enrichment, project-based methodology, and construction of investigative/creative projects. Recently, she has published in academic journals such as *Revista Pedagogía* (University of Puerto Rico), *In Factis Pax: Online Journal of Peace Education and Social Justice* (Toledo University), and *Revista Ra Ximhai* (Universidad Autónoma Indígena y Consorcio de Universidades Cátedra UNESCO, México). And contributed chapters in four books published in Argentina (2017), Brazil (2014), Chile (2010), and by the Baptist World Alliance (2015).

Address: Graduate Studies Department of the School of Education at the Río Piedras Campus of the University of Puerto Rico.
Email: rivepas@gmail.com.

Swarna Rajagopalan is a political scientist by training and a peace educator at heart. She has sought and found opportunities to innovate peace education activities and platforms right from her student days. She has been a part of regional initiatives designed to promote interaction and confidence, and is a founding member of the Women's Regional Network. The Education for Peace Initiative at Prajnya, an organisation Swarna founded in Chennai, India, has in a small but persistent way reached out to students, teachers and the larger community through training, play and creative activities. Swarna writes both as an independent scholar and for the general public. She most recently co-edited "Openings for Peace: UNSCR 1325, Women and Security in India" (Sage 2016) with Asha Hans. Swarna's full portfolio is online at swarnar.com/portfolio and she is active on Twitter @swarraj.

Address: Chennai, India.
Email: swarnar@gmail.com.

Albie Sharpe is a lecturer in Public Health at the University of Technology Sydney, where he teaches in areas related to primary health care and non-communicable disease. In 2017, he was awarded a Ph.D. from the School of Public Health and Community Medicine at the University of New South Wales. He also has a Masters in Health and International Development from Flinders University. His research focuses on exploring the complex interlinkages between human security and public health, social and environmental justice, and evaluation methods. His current work includes several ongoing health evaluation projects in Sri Lanka and Australia. Before returning to Australia, he was formerly an associate professor in the International Institute for Interfaculty Studies, Ritsumeikan University in Kyoto, where he taught international health, development and peace studies. Albie has been involved in the organization of several peace education activities in Japan, including the Peace as a Global Language Conferences, Youth at the Millennium, and PEACEworks, a group of photographers involved in a visual exploration of the concept of peace photography.

Address: Public Health, the University of Technology, Sydney, Australia.
Email: albiesharpe@gmail.com.

Dale T. Snauwaert, Ph.D. is Professor of Philosophy of Education and Peace Studies, Co-Director of the Graduate Certificate Program in the Foundations of Peace Education and the Undergraduate Minor in Peace Studies in the Department of Educational Foundations and Leadership, Judith Herb College of Education, The University of Toledo, USA (see as editor).

Address: Department of Educational Foundations and Leaders, The University of Toledo, Toledo, OH.
Email: dale.snauwaert@utoledo.edu.

Toshiyasu Tsuruhara, Ph.D. is a postdoctoral research associate and undergraduate supervisor at the University of Cambridge. He is also an accredited community mediator. Toshiyasu's research interests lie in conflict mediation and restorative justice, with a focus on personal and relational transformation through dialogue, and the role of active listening, empathy, and silence in conflict transformation. His doctoral dissertation, titled Relational Transformation through Dialogue: Conflict Mediation in a Secondary School in the UK, used Martin Buber's philosophy of dialogue and Carl Rogers' humanistic psychology to examine teacher-mediator facilitated dialogues amongst students. Toshiyasu has published in such journals as *The Journal of the Academy of Experts*, and co-authored a book chapter titled Understanding Conflict Transformation Dialogue through Conversation Analysis with Dr. Hilary Cremin (Routledge, 2019).

Address: Postdoctoral research associate, University of Cambridge.

Werner Wintersteiner, Ph.D., is a retired Professor for German Didactics of Klagenfurt University, Austria. From 2005 to 2016, he was the founding director of the Centre for Peace Research and Peace Education. He is still the director of the University Master Programme (further education) "Global Citizenship Education". His overall research interest is the development of a complex transdisciplinary peace research with a strong focus on cultural dimensions, including comprehensive peace education, linking citizenship education, conflict resolution, and a culture of remembrance. His main fields of research and teaching are peace education and global citizenship education; peace movements; culture and peace; globalization, post-colonialism, transculturality and literature education. He is member of the editorial board of *Wissenschaft & Frieden, Zeitschrift für Friedens- und Konfliktforschung, Jahrbuch Demokratiepädagogik, Journal of Peace Education* and *Europea*. His books include, among others, *Pädagogik des Anderen* (Pedagogy of the Other. Building blocks for a peace education in the age of postmodernism, 1999) and *Poetik der Verschiedenheit. Literatur, Bildung, Globalisierung* (Poetics of the Diverse. Literature, Education, and Globalisation, 2006). Some of his edited volumes: with Viktorija Ratković: *Culture of Peace. A Concept and a Campaign Revisited* (Drava 2010); with Bettina Gruber: *Learning Peace – an Integrative Part of Peacebuilding. Experiences from the Alps-Adriatic Region* (Drava 2014); with Cordula Wohlmuther: *International Handbook on Tourism and Peace* (Drava 2014); with Lisa Wolf: *Friedensforschung in Österreich* (Peace Research in Austria, Drava 2016); with Wilfried Graf: *Herbert C. Kelman: Resolving deep-rooted conflicts. Essays on the Theory and Practice of Interactive Problem-Solving* (Routledge 2017).

Address: Klagenfurt University, Austria.
Email: Werner.Wintersteiner@aau.at.

Anita Yudkin, Ph.D. is Professor in the Educational Foundations Department, and Coordinator of the UNESCO Chair on Education for Peace at the University of Puerto Rico, where she teaches Education for Peace in the Undergraduate Minor on Human Rights. She is an experienced educator with interests in research and action initiatives in education for peace and human rights, children's rights, learning to live together in schools, critical and transformative pedagogies, and critical qualitative research. She serves on the International Institute on Peace Education Transnational Advisory Board, and the Editorial Board of *In Factis Pax: Online Journal of Peace Education and Social Justice*. She is active in key regional initiatives, Red de Cátedras UNESCO en Derechos Humanos (REDCUDH-CIPDH), and Red Latinoamericana y Caribeña de Educación y Derechos Humanos. Author of numerous publications in international journals and edited books, including: *Educar en y para los derechos humanos y la paz: Principios emergentes de la práctica universitaria* (2017), *Life as an educator for human rights and peace: A history of conjunctions and possibilities* (2016), *Educar para la convivencia escolar y la paz: Principios y prácticas de esperanza y acción compartida* (2014), *The United Nations Convention on the Rights of the Child: An overview of the first twenty five years of the movement in Puerto Rico* (2012), *Action ideas in educating for human rights and towards a culture of peace in Puerto Rico* (2009). She is co-editor with Anaida Pascual Morán of the anthology *Educando para la paz en y desde la Universidad: Antología conmemorativa de una década* (2009).

Address: Educational Foundations Department, the University of Puerto Rico, San Juan, Puerto Rico.
Email: anita.yudkin@upr.edu.

Index

CPSIA information can be obtained
at www.ICGtesting.com
Printed in the USA
LVHW010503210519
618494LV00002B/36/P